MASTERING U.S. HISTORY

Second Edition

James Killoran

Stuart Zimmer

Mark Jarrett

JARRETT PUBLISHING COMPANY

THE GOLD STANDARD IN TEST PREPARATION

East Coast Office:
P. O. Box 1460
Ronkonkoma, NY 11779
631-981-4248

West Coast Office:
10 Folin Lane
Lafayette, CA 94549
925-906-9742

1-800-859-7679   Fax: 631-588-4722
www.jarrettpub.com

Layout and typesetting by Maple Hill Press, Huntington, N.Y.
Maps and graphics by Computerized Cartography

This book is dedicated

to my wife Donna, and my children Christian, Carrie and Jesse,
    and to my grandchildren Aiden and Christian

—*James Killoran*

to my wife Joan, my children Todd and Ronald, and to my
    grandchildren Jared and Katie

—*Stuart Zimmer*

to my wife Goska, and my children Alexander and Julia

—*Mark Jarrett*

ISBN 1-882422-50-3
Printed in the United States of America
Second Edition
10 9 8 7 6 5 4 3 2   08 07

ABOUT THE AUTHORS

James Killoran is a retired Assistant Principal. He has written *Government and You* and *Economics and You*. Mr. Killoran has extensive experience in test writing for the N.Y. State Board of Regents in social studies and has served on the Committee for Testing of the National Council of Social Studies. His article on social studies testing has been published in *Social Education*, the country's leading social studies journal. Mr. Killoran has won many awards for outstanding teaching and curriculum development, including "Outstanding Social Studies Teacher" and "Outstanding Social Studies Supervisor" in New York City. In 1993, he was awarded an Advanced Certificate for Teachers of Social Studies by the N.C.S.S. In 1997, he served as Chairman of the N.C.S.S. Committee on Awarding Advanced Certificates for Teachers of Social Studies.

Stuart Zimmer is a retired social studies teacher. He has written *Government and You* and *Economics and You*. Mr. Zimmer served as a test writer for the N.Y. State Board of Regents in Social Studies, and has written for the National Merit Scholarship Examination. He has published numerous articles on teaching and testing in social studies journals. He has also presented many demonstrations and educational workshops at state and national teachers' conferences. In 1989, Mr. Zimmer's achievements were recognized by the New York State Legislature with a Special Legislative Resolution in his honor.

Mark Jarrett is a former social studies teacher and an attorney. Mr. Jarrett has served as a test writer for the New York State Board of Regents, and has taught at Hofstra University. He was educated at Columbia University, the London School of Economics, the Law School of the University of California at Berkeley, and Stanford University, where he is a doctoral candidate in history. Mr. Jarrett has received several academic awards including the Order of the Coif at Berkeley and the David and Christina Phelps Harris Fellowship at Stanford.

ALSO BY KILLORAN, ZIMMER AND JARRETT

The Key to Understanding U.S. History and Government
The Key to Understanding Global History
Mastering Global History
A Quick Review of Global History
A Quick Review of U.S. History and Government
Ohio: The Buckeye State
Mastering the Ohio Graduation Test in Social Studies
Michigan: Its Land and Its People
Mastering Michigan's High School Test in Social Studies
New York: Its Land and Its People
Mastering New York's Grade 8 Intermediate Social Studies Test
North Carolina: The Tar Heel State
Texas: Its Land and Its People
Mastering the Grade 8 TAKS Social Studies Assessment
Mastering the Grade 10 TAKS Social Studies Assessment
Mastering the Grade 11 TAKS Social Studies Assessment
Los Estados Unidos: Su historia, su gobierno
Claves para la comprensión de historia universal
Principios de economía

TABLE OF CONTENTS

CHAPTER 1

STUDYING FOR SUCCESS

The United States is a democracy, and all its citizens are given an opportunity to participate in important decisions once they reach the age of 18. To prepare for the responsibilities of citizenship and to better understand the society in which they live, American students are asked to take and pass a high school course in U.S. history, geography and government. You will be expected to master many important terms, concepts, and people in American history. This chapter will show you techniques to help you learn and remember this information.

REMEMBERING IMPORTANT INFORMATION

TERMS

Terms are the basic units of history. They are words or phrases that refer to specific things that have happened (*World War II*) or existed (*the League of Nations*). These terms are of several different basic types. The following chart is one way of classifying them. Complete the chart by filling in the right-hand column.

TYPE	EXAMPLE	ANOTHER EXAMPLE
Place	Washington, D.C.	_____
Document	U.S. Constitution	_____
Event	Bombing of Pearl Harbor	_____
Group	Carpetbaggers	_____
Movement	Civil Rights Movement	_____
Policy	Open Door Policy	_____
Organization	League of Nations	_____
Time Period	Roaring Twenties	_____
Court Case	*Roe v. Wade* (1973)	_____
Law	Social Security Act (1935)	_____

■ **What to Focus on When Learning a New Term**. Although each test question usually asks that you know **what** the term is, test questions may also ask for different kinds of things depending on the type of term. It is therefore important to understand different things about each type of term. For example:

TYPE OF TERM	WHAT TO FOCUS ON
Place	its location or significance
Document	its purpose or effect
Event	its causes / effects
Group	its goal / purpose
Movement	its characteristics
Policy	its goal / purpose
Organization	its goal / purpose
Time Period	its characteristics
Court Case	its decision / significance
Law	its goal / purpose

ANALYSIS

Please complete:

Term: **What you should focus on:**

- Great Depression   • _____

- World War II   • _____

- U. S. Constitution   • _____

- *Roe v. Wade* Decision   • _____

■ **Using Index Cards**. One reason many students find history to be such a difficult subject is that they do not know how to study properly. Simply reading and re-reading the pages of a book will not help you to learn and remember the many facts, dates and events that you encounter. You have to take a more active approach, deciding what is important, thinking about it, and learning it. One of the best ways to learn a new term is to use an index card. In each content chapter of this book, you will be asked to prepare index cards at the end of each section on the most important terms in the chapter.

- You will be directed to write some specific information about the term on the front of the card. You will be asked to identify the term and its special focus points.

- You should then turn over the index card and draw a picture of what you think the term should look like. Turning written information into a **picture** helps clarify the meaning of the term. To change a person's ideas about a term from one medium (**words**) to another (**pictures**) is only possible if that person truly understands the term. By "seeing" the key points of a term, you create an impression in your brain. This process of turning words into pictures will help you remember the term. Look at the following example:

DECLARATION OF INDEPENDENCE

What is it?
A document written mainly by Thomas Jefferson in 1776. It declared America's independence from England.

Major Cause: The colonists wanted to announce to the world their reasons for declaring independence and to explain their beliefs about how governments should behave.

Major Effect: The document established the basic principle upon which the U. S. government is based — that the government is created to protect people's rights.

Note: Your drawing can appear on the front of the card as shown above, or on the back of the card. If the pictures are on the back of the cards, you can study by looking at the pictures and trying to recall what the other side of the card says about the term.

CONCEPTS

In most history courses, there are important concepts for you to learn and remember. **Concepts** are the building blocks of knowledge — they are ways of grouping individual things, rather than the things themselves. Concepts give a name to things that may be ideas, systems or patterns. Some examples of concepts are: democracy, racism, and federalism. Most questions about concepts ask you to give:

- the meaning or definition of the concept; and
- an example.

For example, the definition of a "third party" is any political party other than the two mainstream political parties — the Democratic and Republican Parties. Most third parties usually concern themselves with a single issue. An example of a third party is the "Right to Life" Party. Its main purpose is to outlaw abortions. When you learn a new concept, it will help you to know both the *definition* of the concept and an *example* that illustrates the concept.

Your memory will again be helped if you translate this information about the concept into picture form. Each time you read about an important concept, you should therefore fill out an index card similar to the following example:

DEMOCRACY

Definition: Citizens participate in the decisions of government by voting directly or by electing people to represent them.

Example: The system of representative government found in the United States.

PEOPLE

There are many individuals in U.S. history who you need to learn about and remember. Most questions will ask you why that person is famous. Therefore, when you learn about a new person, it will be helpful if you remember:

- when the person lived
- the person's major beliefs or actions
- the person's impact (*how the person affected other people, ideas or events*)

Again, one of the best ways to remember this information is to translate it into picture form, as shown in this example:

FRANKLIN D. ROOSEVELT

Time period: 1930s and 1940s

What he did: Introduced New Deal legislation that helped end the Great Depression; led the U.S. during World War II.

Impact: 1. Many of the laws proposed by F.D.R., such as the Social Security Act, are still in effect. 2. He advanced the idea that government should help protect individuals from economic risks they cannot deal with on their own.

Once you know the key terms, concepts and people, think about how they relate to each other. Which terms illustrate the concepts you have learned? Which people were involved in which events?

CHAPTER 2

GEOGRAPHY AND AMERICAN HISTORY

American history is the study of human activity in the area now known as the United States. The United States consists of several distinct geographical regions. Because the diversity of America's geography has been of great significance to its history, it is important to be familiar with the nation's physical setting.

LOCATION, TOPOGRAPHY, AND CLIMATE

The United States is located in the middle of the continent of North America, and extends from the Atlantic Ocean to the Pacific Ocean. In addition to the continental United States, the United States includes Alaska and Hawaii.

Cut off from many parts of the world by two large oceans, America's location separated Native American Indians from the cultures of Africa and Eurasia. Later in history, Americans felt protected from the world's problems and wars by these vast oceans.

The continental United States has been described as a giant saucer, with a lower central plain in the middle, flanked by higher mountain ranges on each side. The two mountain ranges are the Appalachians and the Rocky Mountains.

Between these two mountain ranges are the Central Lowlands, while a

wide coastal plain extends along the Atlantic coast. The lowlands and the coastal plain, as well as the Central Valley in California, have very fertile soil.

The United States also has the **Great Lakes** — some of the largest fresh water lakes in the world. In addition, the U.S. contains several major rivers systems. The largest is the Mississippi River system, with the Missouri and Ohio Rivers and other tributaries draining almost half the continental United States. Other major river systems are the Rio Grande, Colorado River, and Hudson River. Major mineral resources include iron ore, coal, and oil.

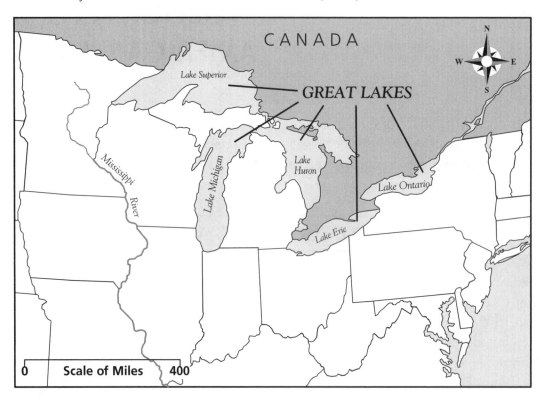

The United States benefits from plentiful rainfall in the East and Midwest, with generally moderate temperatures. The West is drier, and areas of the Southwest, including parts of Texas, New Mexico, Arizona, Nevada, Utah, and California, are desert.

THE PHYSICAL REGIONS OF THE UNITED STATES

A **region** is an area that shares certain features and has greater contact with places within the region than outside it. Because of its diverse **topography** (*surface features*) and climate, the continental United States can be thought of as one nation consisting of several geographic regions. Indeed, there are many ways to divide the United States into regions. One way is as follows:

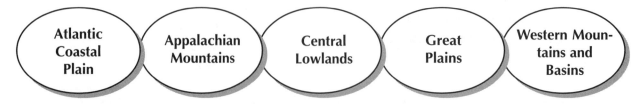

The locations of these five regions are indicated on the following map:

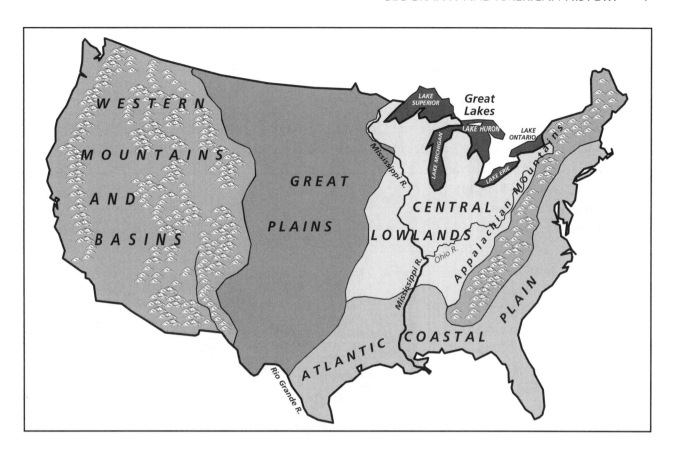

THE ATLANTIC COASTAL PLAIN

The **Atlantic Coastal Plain** is one of the world's largest coastal plains. It stretches southward from New England to Georgia. From Georgia it widens out to Texas while continuing southward. This was the region first settled by colonists from Europe in the 1600s. Much of the area was forest before settlers cleared the land and turned it into farmland. Today it is the region with the highest concentration of people in the United States. The Atlantic Coastal Plain rises up to a hilly area as it approaches the Appalachian Mountains.

THE APPALACHIAN MOUNTAINS

The **Appalachian Mountains** are located in the eastern part of the United States. They extend from Maine in the north to Alabama in the south, where they are cut off by the coastal plain. The Adirondack Mountains, the Allegheny Mountains, the Blue Ridge Mountains and the Great Smoky Mountains are all part of the Appalachians. The Appalachian Mountains were originally formed by the folding and wrinkling of the Earth's crust.

The Great Smoky Mountains

Thousands of years ago, the Appalachians were higher than they are today. Over time, their peaks eroded and became rounded. They were difficult for the first settlers to pass through because they presented an almost unbroken chain of mountains with few gaps.

THE CENTRAL LOWLANDS

To the west of the Appalachians are the **Central Lowlands**. The northern part of this region was once scraped by **glaciers** *(huge moving sheets of ice)* and is a continuation of a sheet of ancient rocks extending down from Canada. The Superior Uplands in Minnesota and northern Michigan and the Adirondack Mountains in northern New York are part of this northern system.

Glaciers created rich farmland in the Central Lowlands.

Farther south, where the elevation is lower, glaciers and winds deposited soil and silt, making the land well suited for farming. Windblown topsoil, known as *loess*, makes parts of the Central Lowlands among the most fertile regions of the United States. The eastern part of the Central Lowlands consists of grasslands known as **prairies**. The Mississippi, Missouri, and Ohio Rivers drain this vast region.

THE GREAT PLAINS

West of the Mississippi, the grasslands become much drier and more hilly. This region is called the **Great Plains**. Before the settlers arrived, these plains were covered with sod and thick grasses.

Early settlers often used the thick sod of the plains as roofing material for their houses.

Today, the Central Lowlands and the Great Plains provide some of the world's best farmland — producing vast amounts of corn, wheat and soybeans, and large amounts of cattle, hogs, and other livestock.

If you were flying over this area in a plane, its many farms would look like a giant checkerboard quilt spread out below and stretching as far as your eye could see.

THE WESTERN MOUNTAINS AND BASINS

To the west of the Great Plains the land rises sharply, forming the Rocky Mountains. These mountains extend from western Canada as far south as New Mexico. Still further west are the Cascade and Sierra Nevada Ranges, and the Pacific Coastal Ranges. Some of these mountains were formed by volcanoes, but most of them, like the Appalachian Mountains in the east, were formed by the shifting and folding of the Earth's crust. These western areas generally receive little rainfall.

The Great Basin, separating the Rocky Mountains and the Sierra Nevada Range, is dry and desert-like. California's Central Valley, located between the Sierra Nevada and the Coastal Range, has excellent soils, almost continuous sunshine, and a long growing season. Although the Central Valley gets little rainfall in summer, irrigation has been made it into very productive farmland.

Many mountains in the West were formed by the shifting and folding of the Earth's crust.

To help familiarize you with the important role that geography has played in the unfolding of our nation's history, you will find special sections throughout this book entitled *The Impact of Geography on American History.* In addition, the *Test Helper* section in Chapter 5 is further devoted to exploring the impact of geography on our nation's history.

CHAPTER 3

FROM EARLIEST TIMES TO INDEPENDENCE

Native American Cultures
  A. The First Americans
  B. Native American Empires
  C. Native Americans In the U.S.

The Europeans Come to the Americas
  A. The Spanish and Portuguese
  B. The First English Colonies
  C. Why Settlers Came
  D. The English Colonies Expand

From Colonies to an Independent Nation
  A. The American Revolution
  B. The Articles of Confederation
  C. The Constitutional Convention
  D. The States Debate Ratification

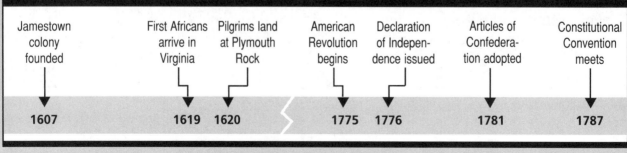

Jamestown colony founded	First Africans arrive in Virginia	Pilgrims land at Plymouth Rock	American Revolution begins	Declaration of Independence issued	Articles of Confederation adopted	Constitutional Convention meets
1607	1619	1620	1775	1776	1781	1787

WHAT YOU SHOULD FOCUS ON

In this chapter, you will learn about the people who first settled the lands that came to be called the Americas. By the 1500s, Europeans began exploring and colonizing the Americas. Eventually, the British emerged as the leading power in North America. In the 1770s, a conflict developed between the American colonies and Great Britain, leading the colonies to declare their independence from Britain. The American Revolutionary War began, and the colonists eventually defeated the British.

The United States achieved its independence, but faced new problems in trying to form a government. As you read this chapter, you will learn about:

The Declaration of Independence being read in public for the first time

Settlement of the Americas	American Revolution	The Critical Period	The Constitutional Convention
The first people to settle in North and South America came from Asia thousands of years ago. They developed a variety of lifestyles. In the 1500s Europeans began to arrive — at first a small number, and then a flood of settlers. In North America, Europeans founded colonies along the Atlantic coast.	North American colonists objected to the British imposing taxes on them without their consent. Their protests started a conflict that led to independence from Great Britain. In the Declaration of Independence, Americans asserted that the purpose of government was to meet the needs of the governed.	Under our first system of national government, called the Articles of Confederation, most governmental powers were held by the states. Under this system, the national government proved to be too weak to deal with the problems facing the new nation.	A Constitutional Convention met in Philadelphia to create the framework for a new national government. After a series of difficult compromises, they wrote the U.S. Constitution, which has remained the basis for our national goverment for more than 200 years.

In studying this period, you should focus on the following questions:

❖ What factors motivated Europeans to come to the Americas?
❖ What problems did the American colonists face?
❖ What basic ideas are found in the Declaration of Independence?
❖ What problems did the new nation face under the Articles of Confederation?

SECTION 1

ROOTS: NATIVE AMERICAN INDIAN CULTURES

In this section you will read how the land that was to become the United States was first settled by people who came from Asia and made their way south from Alaska.

THINK ABOUT IT

What do you know about the people who first settled in the lands we now call North and

South America? _____

_____

Important Terms and Concepts: As you read this section, look for the following:

✦ Native American Indians   ✦ Maya / Aztecs / Incas

To help you find these terms, this symbol ✦ appears in the margin where each term is first explained.

THE FIRST AMERICANS

More than twenty thousand years ago, the first settlers came to North America from Asia, crossing the narrow plain that once connected Siberia and Alaska. From Alaska, these peoples spread southwards into North and South America. They developed different life-styles depending upon the resources and climates that they found. Since these peoples were in lands geographers call the
✦ Americas, they are now referred to as **Native American Indians**.

The new arrivals were hunters and gatherers, moving from place to place in search of food. As they settled, some groups (*sometimes known as tribes*) began to grow their own food. By 1492, when Europeans first came into contact with the peoples of the Americas, about one million Native American Indians lived in what is now Canada and the United States. Another five million lived in Mexico and Central America. As many as twenty million people lived in South America. Several million more Native American Indians lived on the islands in the Caribbean Sea.

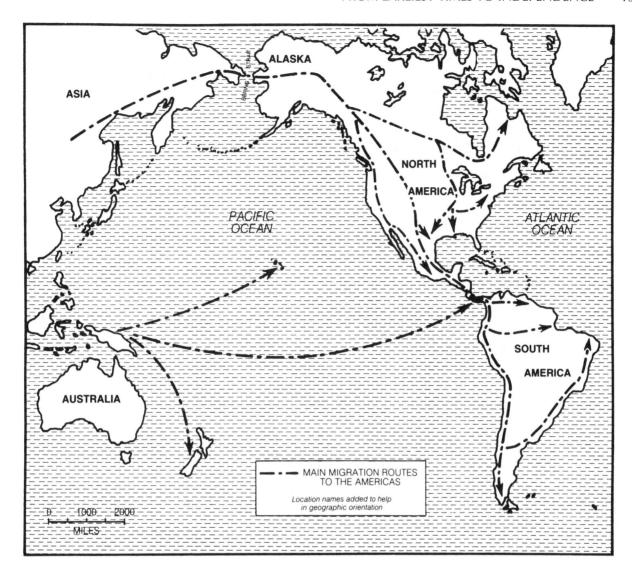

THE NATIVE AMERICAN INDIAN EMPIRES OF MEXICO AND SOUTH AMERICA

In Mexico, Central America and South America, several Native American Indian peoples had created highly developed societies. The **Maya** were the earliest Native American Indian civilization. They were located in southern Mexico and Guatemala. The Maya made discoveries in science, astronomy (*the study of stars and planets*), and mathematics. They developed the use of zero, calculated the solar year, and could accurately predict eclipses. They also created unique forms of sculpture and painting. Some of their pyramids and temples still stand today. The **Aztecs** were a powerful people who created an empire in central Mexico about 700 years ago. They built stoneworks, pyramids and temples. They developed picture writing and a calendar. Along the Andes Mountains in South America, the **Incas** formed a large empire. They built bridges and extensive roads to connect their territories. Like the Aztecs, they built canals and terraces to improve farming. Although the Incas had no system of writing, they kept records by a system of tying knots on strings.

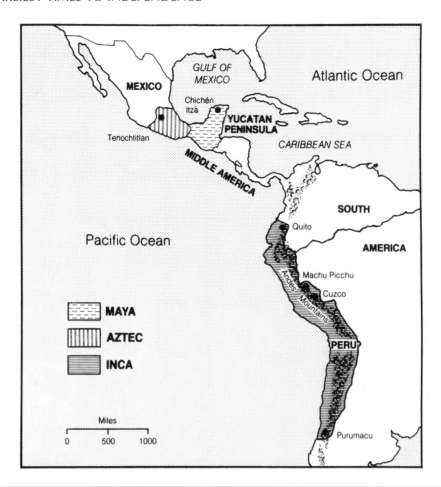

NATIVE AMERICAN INDIAN CULTURES IN THE UNITED STATES

A great variety of Native American Indian cultures existed in the lands that would later become the United States. These Native American Indians spoke over 500 different languages. They grew plants like corn, potatoes and tobacco. Each group developed its own music, art and rituals.

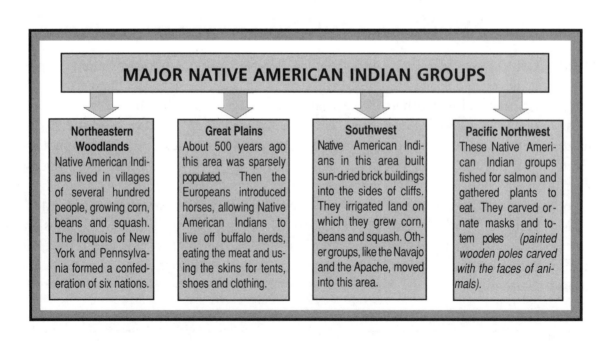

MAJOR NATIVE AMERICAN INDIAN GROUPS

Northeastern Woodlands	Great Plains	Southwest	Pacific Northwest
Native American Indians lived in villages of several hundred people, growing corn, beans and squash. The Iroquois of New York and Pennsylvania formed a confederation of six nations.	About 500 years ago this area was sparsely populated. Then the Europeans introduced horses, allowing Native American Indians to live off buffalo herds, eating the meat and using the skins for tents, shoes and clothing.	Native American Indians in this area built sun-dried brick buildings into the sides of cliffs. They irrigated land on which they grew corn, beans and squash. Other groups, like the Navajo and the Apache, moved into this area.	These Native American Indian groups fished for salmon and gathered plants to eat. They carved ornate masks and totem poles (painted wooden poles carved with the faces of animals).

MAJOR NATIVE AMERICAN INDIAN TRIBES

SUMMING UP: NATIVE AMERICAN INDIAN CULTURES

The first people to settle in North and South America came from Asia by crossing the land bridge that once joined Alaska and Asia. Known as Native American Indians, they developed a variety of lifestyles based on the resources and climates they found.

THINKING IT OVER

What new information can you now add about the people who first came to the Americas?

_____

_____

CHECKING YOUR UNDERSTANDING

Directions: Complete the following cards. Then answer the multiple-choice questions.

NATIVE AMERICAN INDIANS
Define this term: _____
Name two groups of Native American Indians:
1. _____   2. _____

MAYA / AZTECS / INCAS
Who were they? _____
Name their major accomplishments: _____
_____

NOTE: _Throughout this book you will find multiple-choice questions similar to those on comprehensive school and state examinations. Always answer **every** question. Even if you have to guess, there is a chance that you may choose the correct answer. Since there is no penalty for guessing, you should **never** omit an answer to a multiple-choice question on any examination. Blank answers are always counted as wrong._

1   The Iroquois, Navajo and Apache would most likely be topics discussed in an essay dealing with
    1   economic conditions in America
    2   European explorers
    3   Native American Indian tribes
    4   European religions

2   The first people to settle in the Americas were
    1   hunters and gatherers of food
    2   enslaved peoples
    3   industrialists and businesspeople
    4   miners and plantation owners

3   The Maya, Aztecs, and Incas are names of
    1   Native American Indian gods
    2   European explorers
    3   Native American Indian civilizations
    4   North American rivers

4   Which statement is most accurate?
    1   There were no Native American Indian settlements in California.
    2   The Apaches lived in New York State.
    3   The Iroquois often settled in the Pacific northwest.
    4   Native American Indians on the Great Plains hunted buffalo herds.

SECTION 2

THE EUROPEANS COME TO THE AMERICAS

In this section you will read about the reasons for European interest in exploring and colonizing the lands that are now called the Americas.

THINK ABOUT IT

What do you think motivated Europeans to come to the Americas? _____

_____

Important Terms and Concepts: As you read this section, look for the following:

- ✦ Mayflower Compact
- ✦ Indentured Servants
- ✦ Trans-Atlantic Slave Trade
- ✦ Democracy

THE SPANISH AND PORTUGUESE REACH AMERICA

About 600 years ago, life in Europe underwent great changes. Better navigational skills and technological advances made it possible to sail farther than ever before. Gunpowder made it possible for Europeans to build strong armies. The travels of European missionaries and traders such as **Marco Polo** stimulated an interest in goods from East Asia. Spices from Asia and gold from Africa brought high prices in Europe. These factors led Europeans to find and explore other lands. Two European countries, Portugal and Spain, sought to control trade with these new lands. They began by sending out explorers to seek new routes to Asia and Africa.

■ **Prince Henry of Portugal** (1394-1460) established a school of navigation for sailors and mapmakers. He collected information about stars, tides, and ocean currents. Under his direction, the Portuguese began sailing southward, exploring the west coast of Africa.

■ **Christopher Columbus** (1451-1506), an Italian navigator sailing for Spain, believed that he could reach the Far East by going westward. In 1492, Columbus set sail. No one knew if he would find land or how far he would have to sail to find it. When Columbus sighted land in the Caribbean he believed he had arrived in the East Indies, and he called the inhabitants "Indians." Columbus made several later voyages to the Americas, establishing the first Spanish settlements there.

■ **Ferdinand Magellan** (1480-1521), a Portugese sailor, led the first expedition of ships around the world in 1519. He took his crew of 265 sailors across the Atlantic, around South America, and across the Pacific. Only 18 sailors lived to complete the three-year voyage. Magellan's voyages finally proved that the world was round.

Spanish and Portuguese conquerors, missionaries and colonists followed the explorers. They came to the Americas (*which the Europeans named the "New World"*) for a variety of reasons. Many were in search of gold and silver. Others hoped to convert the Native American Indianss to Christianity. Spanish soldiers quickly conquered the great Aztec and Inca empires and seized their land. The Spaniards set up plantations and used the Native American Indians for forced labor. How was it possible for so few Europeans to conquer so many Native American Indians — especially fierce warriors like the Aztecs and Incas?

HOW EUROPEANS CONQUERED THE NATIVE AMERICAN INDIANS

European Technology	Divisions within Indian Societies	Spread of Disease
The Europeans had superior weapons: crossbows, steel swords, and iron-tipped lances. Most important, they had horses, cannons and gunpowder, which were unknown to Native American Indians.	The Aztecs were bitterly hated by other Native American Indian groups, who were forced to send them gifts and humans for sacrifice. These groups helped the Spaniards to overthrow the Aztecs.	Europeans brought diseases such as smallpox and measles with them. Since the Native American Indians had no resistance to these new diseases, millions of them died.

Both Spain and Portugal wanted control over what they called the "New World." To prevent a conflict between these two countries, the **Pope** (*the religious leader of all Roman Catholics*) divided the New World between Spain and Portugal. As a result, Brazil was settled by the Portuguese, while the rest of South America, Central America, and Mexico were settled by the Spanish.

THE FIRST ENGLISH COLONIES

Spain's vast empire in the New World increased the interest of Spain's rivals, England and France. England thought it necessary to develop its own **colonies** (*lands ruled by another country*) to avoid being overwhelmed by Spanish power. As a result, English colonies were founded.

JAMESTOWN (1607)

The first permanent English settlement was established at Jamestown, Virginia in 1607. The first colonists at Jamestown hoped to make money by finding gold and were not interested in growing crops. About two-thirds of the original settlers died in the first year. Others wanted to return to England. However, with the help of Native American Indians, the settlers survived, learning to grow corn and to fish. Jamestown soon grew rich by growing tobacco for sale in England.

THE PILGRIMS (1620)

In England, religious disagreements led a small group called the **Pilgrims** to decide to sail to the Americas, where they could worship God in their own way. They chose to leave England rather than to face persecution by the king for their religious beliefs. After a ten-week voyage, 102 men, women and children arrived at Plymouth Rock in Massachusetts in 1620. Before going ashore,

they signed an agreement known as the **Mayflower Compact**. In it they pledged themselves to self-government — all laws would need common approval and consent. The first year they faced many hardships. The Pilgrims survived because of the help they received from Native American Indians, who taught them how to hunt animals, fish, and grow crops.

The Pilgrims sign the Mayflower Compact

THE PURITANS (1630)

The **Puritans** were another, much larger religious group in England. They arrived in Massachusetts in 1630 and established the Massachusetts Bay Colony. Within a few years, over 10,000 more Puritans sailed to America. The Puritans believed they were establishing God's kingdom on earth, and did not tolerate other views or opinions. Attendance at church was required. They sought to "purify" the Puritan religion by making services and life as simple and plain as possible; dancing and other amusements were forbidden.

WHY SETTLERS CAME

ESCAPE FROM RELIGIOUS PERSECUTION

People went to Massachusetts, Pennsylvania and Maryland to practice their religion without interference. At first, the Massachusetts colony allowed only Puritanism to be practiced. As a result, in 1636, **Roger Williams** founded Rhode Island, the first American colony to allow freedom for most religions. Maryland became a haven for Catholics, while Quakers went to Pennsylvania.

DESIRE FOR LAND

People also went to the colonies so that they could eventually own their own land. Many of them came as **indentured servants**. A colonial landowner paid for their passage, and the new arrival promised to work on the landowner's plantation or farm, usually for seven years. Once the debt was paid off, these "servants" obtained their freedom and began saving to buy land of their own.

A BETTER LIFE

Life in Europe was hard for most people. Frequent wars between European powers destroyed many farms and damaged trade. Also, many people who had been imprisoned for nonpayment of debts saw the colonies as a place to start over. The promise of a better life in the Americas attracted people to move to the English colonies.

THE TRANS-ATLANTIC SLAVE TRADE

Africans were brought to the Americas by force. Starting in the 1500s, ship captains went to the coast of West Africa to buy captured Africans and transport them to the Americas as slaves. Slaves were used to work the mines and plantations of the Spanish colonies, and the practice was imitated in Virginia and the other Southern colonies. The first Africans arrived in Jamestown in 1619. Despite the hardships of slavery, these Africans managed to preserve elements of their heritage and developed a unique culture with a strong sense of community.

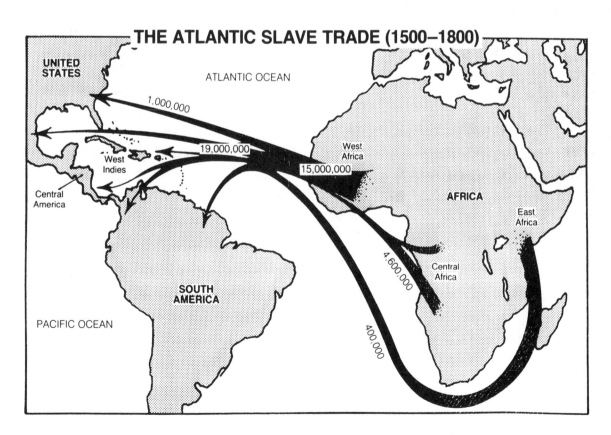

THE ATLANTIC SLAVE TRADE (1500–1800)

FOCUS ON THE ARTS

Phillis Wheatley, Poet

Born in Africa, Phillis Wheatley was brought to the United States as a slave at age 7. She distinguished herself as the first female African-American poet in the United States. While working as a housemaid, she was taught to read and write by her master's wife.   At age 13 she was already writing poetry. Her poems told of the American Revolutionary War. Her best known works were "His Excellency George Washington" and "On The Death of Reverend George Whitefield."

LIFE IN THE ENGLISH COLONIES

English settlements quickly extended up and down the Atlantic coast. By the 1730s, all of the coast between present-day Florida and present-day Canada was divided into English colonies. Geographic, religious and social differences soon created differing patterns of life in the colonies.

NEW ENGLAND

The population of New England grew quickly, even though it had less fertile land and was colder than the other colonies. People usually lived in towns and villages. The New England colonists had small farms where they primarily grew crops for their own use. Others became sailors, ship-builders and fishermen. New England also developed into a center for making finished goods.

MIDDLE COLONIES

Fertile soil and uncleared forest drew settlers to the "Middle Colonies" — Delaware, Pennsylvania, New York, New Jersey and Maryland. Farming was the major occupation of the area. Small and large farms grew wheat, oats, corn and other grains that were sold to the other colonies. The Middle Colonies also benefited from trade between New England and the Southern colonies. The Middle Colonies had several groups with differing religious beliefs. For example, the **Quakers**, who settled in Pennsylvania, believed everyone was equal before God. Catholics started a colony in Maryland. This religious diversity (*existence of differences*) led the Middle Colonies to follow policies of religious toleration.

SOUTHERN COLONIES

Virginia was the oldest English colony in the New World. The Carolinas were settled by a chartered company formed by English nobles in the 1660s. Georgia was originally founded as a place for imprisoned debtors and other convicts sent from England. The plantations of the Southern Colonies — Virginia, North Carolina, South Carolina and Georgia — produced tobacco, rice and indigo (*blue dye*) for shipment to England, in exchange for manufactured goods. On the larger plantations, the labor force consisted of indentured servants and enslaved peoples from Africa.

THE THIRTEEN ENGLISH COLONIES (1750)

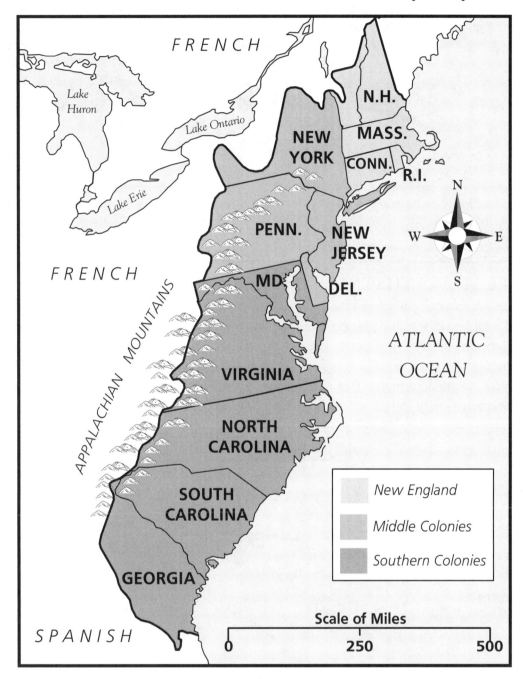

LIMITED DEMOCRACY IN THE ENGLISH COLONIES

The word **democracy** comes from the Greek language and means "government by the people." ✦
In ancient Greece, democracy referred to a government in which all citizens took part in the
making of the laws. In more modern times, democracy has come to mean a government in which
the people do not actually make the laws, but choose **representatives** who do. Democratic governments recognize the rights of each person to be treated fairly and equally. The English colonists who settled in North America brought with them strong traditions of individual rights and
limited self-government.

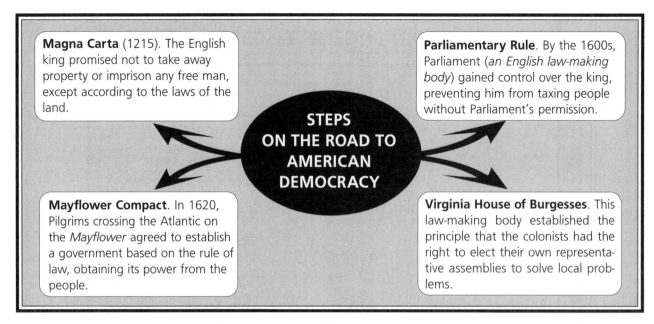

Magna Carta (1215). The English king promised not to take away property or imprison any free man, except according to the laws of the land.

Parliamentary Rule. By the 1600s, Parliament (*an English law-making body*) gained control over the king, preventing him from taxing people without Parliament's permission.

STEPS ON THE ROAD TO AMERICAN DEMOCRACY

Mayflower Compact. In 1620, Pilgrims crossing the Atlantic on the *Mayflower* agreed to establish a government based on the rule of law, obtaining its power from the people.

Virginia House of Burgesses. This law-making body established the principle that the colonists had the right to elect their own representative assemblies to solve local problems.

ECONOMIC LIFE IN THE ENGLISH COLONIES

The economy of the colonies was largely based on Europe's demand for colonial products. The colonists sold tobacco, rice, indigo and fish to earn money to buy English and European imports. Much of colonial America's prosperity came from trade. The colonies were involved with many trading partners. The most frequent exchanges came to be known as the **Triangular Trades** — since the routes formed triangles *(see map below)*. As the North American colonies grew, their trade became increasingly important to England's own economic well-being.

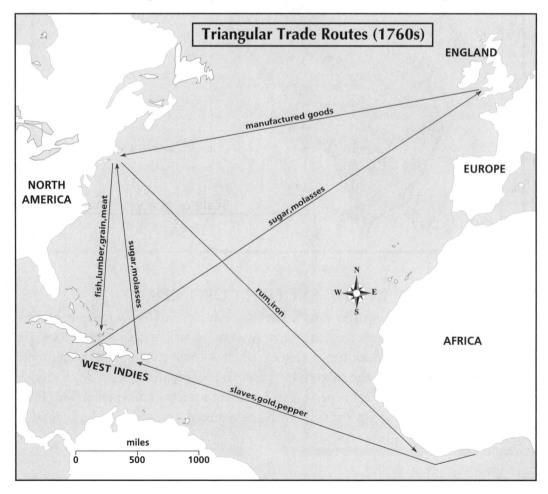

Triangular Trade Routes (1760s)

ANALYSIS

Trace the lines of one of the trade route triangles, and describe how it worked.

_____

_____

_____

THINKING IT OVER

Now can you name two reasons why Europeans were interested in Colonial America?

1._____   2._____

SUMMING UP: THE EUROPEANS COME TO AMERICA

In the 1500s, Europeans began arriving in North and South America. They found thriving Native American Indian civilizations located throughout what they called the "New World." Soon the Europeans conquered the Native American Indians. England established colonies along the Atlantic coast from New England to Georgia. At first a small number, and then a flood of settlers came seeking personal freedoms and a better way of life. As different groups arrived, a variety of lifestyles developed in the English colonies.

CHECKING YOUR UNDERSTANDING

Directions: Complete the following cards. Then answer the multiple-choice questions.

MAYFLOWER COMPACT

What was it? _____

Its importance: _____

_____

TRANS-ATLANTIC SLAVE TRADE

What was it? _____

Major effect: _____

_____

1   The Mayflower Compact is important because it established the principle that
    1   all slaves shall be freed
    2   there would be freedom of religion
    3   government gets its powers from the people
    4   there should be one leader

2   People living in colonial America adopted most of their principles of government from
    1   Europe   3   sub-Saharan Africa
    2   Latin America   4   East Asia

3   Which feature of government was most fully developed during the Colonial Era?
    1   voting rights for women
    2   representative assemblies
    3   equal rights for minorities
    4   direct election of senators

4   The Trans-Atlantic Slave Trade refers to
    1   the forced transfer of Africans
    2   African workers in slave ships
    3   Africans buying slaves
    4   Muslims trading spices for slaves

SECTION 3

FROM COLONIES TO AN INDEPENDENT NATION

In this section you will read about the conflict that developed between the colonists and the British government. Eventually this conflict led the thirteen colonies to form their own country.

THINK ABOUT IT

What problems do you think people might have in creating a new government? _____

_____

Important Terms and Concepts: As you read this section, look for the following:

- ✦ Mercantilism
- ✦ Declaration of Independence
- ✦ American Revolution
- ✦ Articles of Confederation
- ✦ Great Compromise
- ✦ Constitutional Convention

THE AMERICAN REVOLUTION: 1775-1783

✦ Members of the British government believed in **mercantilism** — the idea that colonies existed for the benefit of the country that ruled them. Mercantilism helps explain why differences began to grow between the colonists and Great Britain. The American colonies were expected to sell crops like tobacco to the British at a low price. In exchange, the colonists were expected to buy expensive British-made goods, such as manufactured products.

THE CONFLICT BEGINS

During the 1750s and 1760s, Britain and France were struggling over territories in the "New World." When the British finally won in 1763, they imposed new taxes on the colonists, to repay Britain for the cost of protecting the colonies. The colonists protested against laws in which they had no voice or representation. They particularly objected to the **Stamp Act** (1765) which taxed newspapers, books and official documents. In response to these protests, the British soon canceled all the new taxes, except for the tax on tea. In 1773, the colonists protested against this tax by dumping a shipment of British tea into Boston harbor. This action became known as the **Boston Tea Party**. It brought about a strong reaction from the British king, who wanted to teach the colonists a lesson. The British closed the harbor and limited the freedom of citizens in Massachusetts until the tea was paid for. This event greatly increased tensions between the colonists and Great Britain.

Thomas Paine, Writer

FOCUS ON THE ARTS

Writers of pamphlets have often played a key role in influencing public opinion. In 1776, Thomas Paine wrote a pamphlet, *Common Sense*, in which he attacked the English king. Paine argued that it was foolish for a great continent such as America to be ruled by a tiny, far-off island like Great Britain. Paine's writings encouraged American colonists to declare their independence from Great Britain.

THE IDEA OF INDEPENDENCE GROWS

Representatives from the colonies met in Philadelphia to discuss their common problems. At the meeting, known as the **First Continental Congress**, they decided to continue their protest against British taxes. The dispute soon grew worse. In 1775, shots were fired between British soldiers and colonists at Concord, Massachusetts. The fighting quickly spread to the other colonies. This fighting set in motion the chain of events known as the **American Revolutionary War**. The colonists met again in Philadelphia and began to discuss the possibility of independence. After much debate, they decided to declare their independence from Great Britain.

"We hold these truths to be self-evident, that all men are created equal, that they are endowed by their Creator with certain Unalienable Rights, that among these are Life, Liberty and the pursuit of Happiness. That to secure these rights, Governments are instituted among Men, deriving their just powers from the consent of the governed; That whenever any Form of Government becomes destructive of these ends, it is the right of the People to alter or abolish it, and to institute new Government..."

A DECLARATION OF INDEPENDENCE IS ISSUED

Thomas Jefferson was named to head a committee to write a "Declaration of Independence." This document, issued on **July 4, 1776**, explained the reasons why the colonists had decided to seek independence from Great Britain. The second paragraph of the Declaration is shown at the left.

Sometimes words written more than 200 years ago are hard to understand. See how well you understand the Declaration of Independence by answering the following questions.

ANALYSIS

I. Words have different meanings for different people. What do you think the writers meant by the following words or phrases?

- All men are created equal: _____
- Life: _____
- Liberty: _____
- Unalienable Rights: _____
- Pursuit of Happiness: _____

II. The second paragraph sets out the writer's belief about why governments are needed.

- Explain the writer's argument in your own words. _____

_____

- Do you agree with this argument? _____ Explain. _____

_____

III. Some people have pointed to the last sentence of the second paragraph as the most revolutionary statement in the whole Declaration. It states that if a government takes away the basic rights and freedoms of its people, then the people have the right to get rid of the existing government and to form a new one. Do you agree that people should be able to overthrow their governments in some situations?_____ Explain._____

_____

_____

IMPORTANCE OF THE DECLARATION OF INDEPENDENCE

In 1776, the Declaration of Independence made the colonies independent from Great Britain. It laid the foundation for the United States to become the first democratic republic in modern times, and has served as an inspiration for later generations.

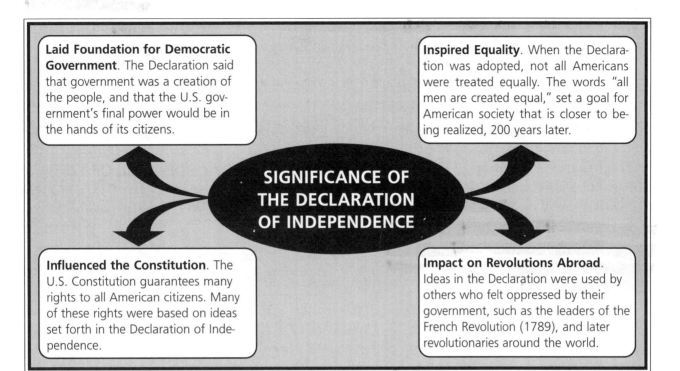

Laid Foundation for Democratic Government. The Declaration said that government was a creation of the people, and that the U.S. government's final power would be in the hands of its citizens.

Inspired Equality. When the Declaration was adopted, not all Americans were treated equally. The words "all men are created equal," set a goal for American society that is closer to being realized, 200 years later.

SIGNIFICANCE OF THE DECLARATION OF INDEPENDENCE

Influenced the Constitution. The U.S. Constitution guarantees many rights to all American citizens. Many of these rights were based on ideas set forth in the Declaration of Independence.

Impact on Revolutions Abroad. Ideas in the Declaration were used by others who felt oppressed by their government, such as the leaders of the French Revolution (1789), and later revolutionaries around the world.

THE AMERICAN REVOLUTION (1775-1783)

In the early stages of the fighting, the colonial army barely managed to escape from one disaster after another. However, under the leadership of General **George Washington**, the colonists won battles at Trenton, New Jersey (1776) and Saratoga, New York (1777). These victories helped convince France to supply military assistance to the Americans. With the help of the French, Washington managed to force the British to surrender at Yorktown in 1781. Under the terms of the **Treaty of Paris** (1783), the British recognized American independence and surrendered all the land between the Mississippi River and the Atlantic coast, from the Great Lakes to Florida.

British commander surrendering after the battle of Saratoga

THE ARTICLES OF CONFEDERATION: THE NATION'S FIRST GOVERNMENT

After winning independence, each of the former colonies became an independent state. They soon realized the need for some form of national (*central*) government. At the same time, they were afraid of creating a central government that would be too powerful. They had already had a bad experience with the strong central government of Great Britain. In 1781, the thirteen states adopted the **Articles of Confederation**, which provided for a weak central government. The state governments, not the central government, held most of the power. Most actions by the central government required the cooperation of the states. For example, the central government could not collect taxes, settle disputes among states, control trade or enforce laws. It was left to each state to carry out the acts of the Confederation Congress.

THE ARTICLES OF CONFEDERATION: SOME ACCOMPLISHMENTS

The Articles of Confederation helped keep the new nation together and created a method for admitting new states to the nation. After winning independence from Great Britain, the United States found itself in possession of lands north of the Ohio River and east of the Mississippi. The new Confederation Congress passed the **Northwest Ordinance of 1787**, a law that divided this territory into smaller areas, and set up procedures for their admission into the union as new states.

THE ARTICLES OF CONFEDERATION: SOME PROBLEMS

Many Americans felt that the new central government had too little power to do its job properly. For example, the central government did not have the power to tax or borrow directly. It had to request money from the states. Each state printed its own money, making trade between states difficult. The central government also had no national army. To make matters worse, some former Revolutionary War soldiers were losing their farms because they were unable to pay their state taxes or their debts to wealthy merchants. When a small uprising — known as **Shays' Rebellion** — broke out in Massachusetts in 1786, there was no national army to be called upon to restore order. Many people, especially merchants and landowners, began demanding a stronger national government.

NOTE: *Some class tests, as well as state examinations, contain several kinds of data-based questions. Knowing the different types of data and learning how to interpret them will be a regular feature found in every content chapter of this book. The following section deals with interpreting one type of data — a political cartoon. Since political cartoons may appear on your class test or on state examinations, it will be helpful to know how to interpret them.*

SKILL BUILDER: INTERPRETING CARTOONS

What is a Political Cartoon?

A political cartoon is a drawing that expresses an opinion about a topic or issue. Many political cartoons are humorous, but the point they make is usually serious.

Keys to Understanding a Cartoon

First take a look at its major parts:

Medium. Cartoonists want to draw your attention to a particular issue, or want you to believe what they believe about a problem or issue. They use the size and type of objects, facial expressions, exaggerations, or words spoken by characters to persuade you.

Symbols. Cartoonists often use symbols. A symbol can be any object that stands for, or represents, something else. Animals are often used as symbols — a bear to represent Russia, or an elephant to represent the Republican Party.

Russia	United States	Republican Party
Democratic Party	Liberty	Congress

Can you name any other symbols? _____

_____

People. Cartoonists sometimes show certain individuals because they are closely associated with a particular issue. For example,

U.S. Presidents often appear in cartoon form. It is helpful to recognize them, as well as other key people.

G. Washington	T. Roosevelt	F. D. Roosevelt
Nixon	Reagan	Bush

The ship symbolizes the central government under the Articles of Confederation.

■ What situation is shown in the cartoon? The ship is sailing in rough waters, and appears to be sinking.

■ Which items in the cartoon are exaggerated or highlighted? The problems produced by the Articles of Confederation are highlighted.

■ What is the main idea of the cartoon? The government under the Articles of Confederation is overwhelmed by problems.

✦ THE CONSTITUTIONAL CONVENTION

In 1787, representatives from the states met in Philadelphia to revise (*change*) the Articles of Confederation. Fifty-five of the nation's leaders attended — including George Washington, Benjamin Franklin, James Madison and Alexander Hamilton. The representatives quickly decided that a new national **constitution** (*a plan for government*) was needed to replace the existing Articles of Confederation. It was agreed that a stronger central government was necessary. This government would be led by a chief executive and would have a national legislature and a national court system. They also thought the new central government should have the power to raise taxes and form an army. However, there were some disagreements, requiring the delegates to compromise. Two of the main compromises reached at the Convention involved representation in the national government, and slavery.

MAJOR CONSTITUTIONAL COMPROMISES

ISSUE: *How should states be represented in the national legislature?*

✦ **GREAT COMPROMISE.** The thirteen states had different size populations. The larger states, such as Virginia, felt they should have a greater say in the national government. Smaller states, such as Georgia, felt each state should have an equal voice. In the end a compromise was reached. Two "houses" were created in the legislature. In the **House of Representatives**, each state would be represented according to the size of its population. This allowed states with a larger population to have a greater number of representatives. In the **Senate**, each state, no matter how large or small, would be equal — represented by two Senators. This satisfied the states with smaller populations. Approval by both houses of Congress would be needed to pass a law.

ISSUE: *How should slaves be counted?*

THREE-FIFTHS COMPROMISE. Southern states wanted slaves counted as part of their population, to increase their membership in the House of Representatives, but not for purposes of taxation. Northern states wanted slaves counted for taxation but not for representation. The states compromised by agreeing to count every 5 slaves as 3 free persons for the purposes of both taxation and representation.

THE STATES DEBATE RATIFICATION

It was decided that, before the Constitution could become the law of the country, nine states would have to **ratify** (*approve*) it. People in each state had strong opinions as to whether to accept or reject the new system of government proposed in the U.S. Constitution.

REASONS FOR ACCEPTANCE

Some of the reasons given by supporters for accepting the Constitution were these:

■ A stronger central government was needed to replace the Articles of Confederation. Such a government needed a national leader (*like a President*) and greater powers to better protect the nation from internal unrest or an attack by foreign enemies. A national court system was also needed to settle disputes between states.

■ There was no reason to fear that a strong central government would use its powers against the people. The Constitution provided that powers would be separated among the different **branches** (*parts*) of the central government and divided between the states and the central government. No single branch would be too strong.

REASONS FOR REJECTION

Some of the reasons given by opponents for rejecting the Constitution were these:

■ A strong central government might take away people's freedom. For example, the new government could build a strong army and then use it to collect unpopular taxes.

■ There was no **Bill of Rights** in the proposed Constitution to protect important individual liberties, such as the right to a fair trial and freedom of speech.

By the end of 1788, eleven states voted to accept the Constitution. Support was won in many states by promising that a Bill of Rights would soon be added to the Constitution. In 1789, George Washington was inaugurated as the first President of the United States.

SUMMING UP: FROM COLONIES TO AN INDEPENDENT NATION

The colonists in the British colonies established many important democratic traditions. Unhappy with British taxation, the American colonists declared their independence from England. The Declaration of Independence was issued to justify the colonists' actions. Although the American Revolution was successful, the new government created under the Articles of Confederation faced many problems. To correct the problems, the Articles of Confederation were replaced with the U.S. Constitution in 1787.

THINKING IT OVER

What difficulties do you **now** think people might have in creating a new government?

_____

_____

CHECKING YOUR UNDERSTANDING

Directions: Complete the following cards. Then answer the multiple-choice questions.

DECLARATION OF INDEPENDENCE

What was it? _____

Key ideas: _____

Importance: _____

ARTICLES OF CONFEDERATION

What was it? provided for a weak central government.

Strengths: Northwest ordiance

Weaknesses: shays rebellion

AMERICAN REVOLUTION

What was it? _____

Major cause: _____

Major result: _____

THE GREAT COMPROMISE

compromse of representives

What was it? house of represenatie

Significance: the house beniffed large states + the senate benifited small states.

all states have a say.

---

1 The major problem facing the thirteen newly independent states was how to
   1 attract foreign nations to build factories in America
   2 lower taxes
   3 create some form of central government
   4 establish a Supreme Court

2 The Articles of Confederaion created a
   1 republic with a chief executive
   2 strong central government
   3 national government with legislative and judicial branches
   4 loose association of free and independent states

3 The right of the people to overthrow a government that abuses its power is a main theme of the
   1 Mayflower Compact
   2 Articles of Confederation
   3 Declaration of Independence
   4 U.S. Constitution

4 One of the major arguments for independence in the Declaration of Independence was that
   1 the British refused to buy goods from the colonies
   2 a government run by a king was evil
   3 the colonists were superior to the British
   4 people have natural rights as human beings

5 Which document contains the phrase "all men are created equal"?
   1 Magna Carta
   2 Mayflower Compact
   3 Stamp Act
   4 Declaration of Independence

6 Which belief is expressed by the quotation: "we ... will not hold ourselves bound by any laws in which we have no voice or representation"?
   1 the necessity of a separation of powers
   2 government by the consent of the governed
   3 freedom of the press and of assembly
   4 the right to a writ of habeas corpus

7 Which document has been accused of giving too little power to the central government?
(1) Articles of Confederation
2 United States Constitution
3 Declaration of Independence
4 Bill of Rights

8 At the Constitutional Convention of 1787, the agreement known as the "Great Compromise" was concerned mainly with
(1) a state's representation in Congress
2 the question of slavery
3 the powers of the President
4 control of foreign trade

PROFILES IN HISTORY

PRINCESS POCAHONTAS

In 1607, John Smith of Great Britain arrived in Virginia to establish a settlement at Jamestown. He was soon taken captive by Native American Indians and was brought before Chief Powhatan. The chief's young daughter Pocahontas helped to win his release. She went on to help other settlers by bringing them food and supplies. In 1614,

Pocahontas in European dress

she married John Rolfe, a Jamestown settler. Pocahontas died of smallpox at age 21, while on a visit to London.

FATHER JUNIPERO SERRA

In 1769, Father Serra, a Franciscan priest living in Mexico, joined a group on a trip north to present-day California. He helped found a mission at San Diego — the first European settlement in present-day California. After a few years, Father Serra established similar missions throughout California to convert the Native American Indians to Christianity and to teach them to raise new crops, tend livestock, and build roads and bridges.

ANNE HUTCHINSON

Anne Hutchinson lived in Massachusetts. She was a strong-minded religious woman. She believed a person could directly communicate with God. She also believed that churches and ministers were unnecessary. Such opinions got her in trouble with Puritan leaders, who viewed her beliefs as an attempt to destroy the Puritan Church. She was put on trial and found guilty. She was banished from the colony of Massachusetts, and fled to Rhode Island. Hutchinson is credited with being an

Statue of Anne Hutchinson

important leader in developing religious freedom in the American colonies.

CRISPUS ATTUCKS

Crispus Attucks was killed in 1770 by a band of British soldiers while he was participating in a demonstration against British rule in the colo-

Crispus Attucks

nies. A former slave, Attucks was the first American to lose his life in the coming struggle for independence. He became a symbol of American opposition to the harsh rule imposed by the British in the colonies. A memorial monument was erected in Boston to Attucks and the other four patriots killed that day.

SUMMARIZING YOUR UNDERSTANDING

Directions: Confirm your understanding of the following terms and concepts by checking those you can explain. For those you are unfamiliar with, find the ✦ symbol in the margin next to the term and review the information.

CHECKLIST

- ❑ Native American Indians
- ❑ Maya, Aztecs, Incas
- ❑ Mayflower Compact
- ❑ Indentured Servants
- ❑ Trans-Atlantic Slave Trade
- ❑ Mercantilism
- ❑ Declaration of Independence
- ❑ American Revolution
- ❑ Democracy
- ❑ Articles of Confederation
- ❑ Constitutional Convention
- ❑ Great Compromise

Directions: Fill in the information called for in the following organizers.

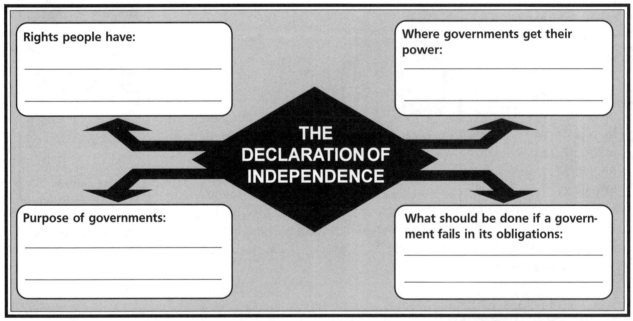

Rights people have:
_____
_____

Where governments get their power:
_____
_____

THE DECLARATION OF INDEPENDENCE

Purpose of governments:
_____
_____

What should be done if a government fails in its obligations:
_____
_____

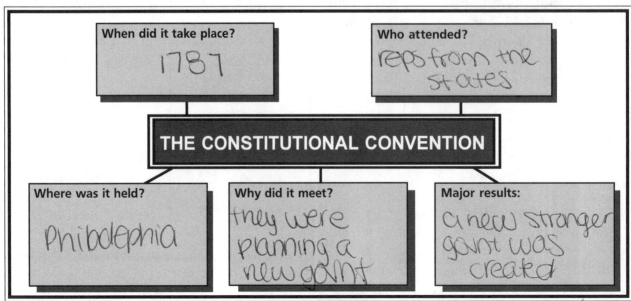

When did it take place?
1787

Who attended?
reps from the states

THE CONSTITUTIONAL CONVENTION

Where was it held?
Philadelphia

Why did it meet?
they were planning a new govnt

Major results:
a new stronger govnt was created

popular soverty- people rule

Each chapter of this book ends with a test. Before each test there is a special "Test Helper" section that will help you to find new ways to think about the materials found in the chapter. Each section explores a major theme that runs through the chapter. This section looks at the study of history.

TEST HELPER   LOOKING AT HISTORY

WHAT IS HISTORY?

The word *history* refers to what happened in the past. Historians want to understand and explain particular events, and want to know about people's ideas, plans, actions and their effects.

THE IMPORTANCE OF HISTORY

Just as your own life would be confusing if you had no memory of who you were or what you had done, each society looks to its history for a sense of identity. History helps a society remember what it is and where it has been going. Knowledge of history can also give us insights into what may happen, or act as a guide on which to base our future actions.

THE FIELDS OF HISTORY

There are many types of historians. Some of them study politics, diplomacy and wars; others study past economies; still others study the history of the arts, culture, family life, or ideas. Some historians recount a series of events; others attempt to establish a series of hypotheses (*educated guesses*) about a period in history; some study one country; others a whole civilization.

THE EMERGENCE OF MULTICULTURAL HISTORY

In the past, most records were kept by a relatively small group of people — rulers, government officials and religious leaders — and most historical writing was devoted to their concerns. In the United States, much of this historical writing also centered on European history, since European immigrants made up the largest group of Americans. Today, many historians recognize that focusing on the most powerful part of society provides too narrow and limited a historical view. They have therefore begun to investigate what it was like to be a poor farmer, a factory worker, or a slave. Historians have also become just as concerned with studying the experiences of women as well as men, and children as well as adults. In addition, historians today try to understand events from different perspectives. For example, we no longer look at the voyages of Columbus only from the European viewpoint, but also try to learn what his arrival meant to the Native American Indians. This attempt to understand events from several perspectives is sometimes referred to as **multicultural history.**

THE HISTORICAL METHOD

Like literature, history must be well-written to communicate ideas. Like science, history should be accurate.

HISTORICAL SOURCES AND THEIR INTERPRETATION

Usually, a historian begins by framing a question. For example: How were women treated during the American Revolution? What were the lives of slaves like in the South? Once the historian has framed a historical question, he or she next gathers materials that help to answer it. These sources are of two kinds:

PRIMARY SOURCES

These are original records of the event under investigation. They include eyewitness reports, official records made at the time of the event, the texts of speeches and reports, letters sent by people involved in the event, diaries, photographs, audio and video tapes, and so forth. Most of the facts used to reconstruct historical events come from primary sources.

SECONDARY SOURCES

These are the writings and interpretations of historians and other writers. Secondary sources such as textbooks and articles often provide convenient summaries of the information contained in primary sources. Historians also read these writings to learn more about other historians' ideas.

Using historical sources presents many problems. Primary sources are sometimes incomplete and the historian can never know exactly what happened before. History, therefore, relies on the interpretation of surviving sources. This can be a very tricky matter. Being a historian is like being a detective. When a historian discovers a particular record, he or she must interpret it. For example: Is the document authentic or a forgery? Is the document really what it seems to be? Because historians often disagree about the interpretation of sources, there are many conflicting viewpoints about what actually happened.

SELECTING AND INTERPRETING SIGNIFICANT FACTS

Of the thousands of facts, which are important in telling the story of a past event? In selecting some facts to include, and in discarding others, historians make judgments about what they think is important. Others might not agree with these judgments. History therefore poses problems both in interpreting specific documents and records, and in deciding which facts are important and which are not. These problems give rise to historical controversies (disputes). What you find in your textbook is often only a summary of key points about which some historians have agreed.

SHARPENING YOUR TEST-TAKING SKILLS

Like most activities, test-taking requires certain skills to do well. At the end of each content chapter you will find a special section to help you sharpen your test-taking skills. These sections will show you how to answer each type of question that may appear on classroom or state tests. These sections will examine multiple-choice questions, thematic essay questions, and document-based essay questions. This first section deals with multiple-choice questions. These questions require you to select the best answer to a question from a number of choices.

TYPES OF MULTIPLE-CHOICE QUESTIONS

The majority of multiple-choice questions can be grouped into a few basic types. They test your knowledge of the following information:

RECOGNITION OF KEY TERMS, CONCEPTS, AND PEOPLE

Many multiple-choice questions test your knowledge of important terms, concepts, and people. The examples below illustrate some of the ways these questions may be phrased:

- The concept of [democracy] is best illustrated by ...
- Which statement about the [American Revolution] is most accurate?

> To help you recognize major terms, concepts, and people, these will be highlighted in **bold print** in each content chapter. Key terms, concepts, and people are also listed as Vocabulary Cards and are found in questions at the end of each content section.

COMPREHENSION OF DATA

Comprehension questions test whether you understand data presented as part of a data-based question. Comprehension questions may be worded in several different ways. Here are two examples of typical comprehension questions:

- Which reform movement is represented by the following [quotation]?
- According to the table, how many [slaves were imported in 1805]?

> The crucial factor in answering comprehension data questions is your ability to understand the various types of data. You will learn how to analyze each type of data in the *Skill Builder* sections. Data-based questions will also appear throughout the book, providing you with many opportunities to practice interpreting different kinds of data.

MAKING A GENERALIZATION

Some questions will test your ability to make or understand a generalization. The following are typical examples of generalization questions:

- Which is the most accurate statement about the [*American Revolution*]?
- In this outline, one of the items is the main topic, and the other three are sub-topics. Which is the main topic?

> To help you answer this type of question, generalizations are identified throughout this book. In addition, generalization questions are found in each content chapter.

COMPARING AND CONTRASTING

The act of comparing and contrasting allows us to highlight and separate particular events, ideas, and concepts, placing them in sharper focus. Compare-and-contrast questions might appear as follows:

- The [*Articles of Confederation*] and the [*Constitution*] were similar in that both ...
- A major difference between the [*Southern Colonies*] and [*New England*] was that ...

> As you read through each content chapter, test yourself by comparing and contrasting **new** terms, concepts, and people with those you already know. It is important to understand both how these things are **similar** and how they **differ**.

IDENTIFYING CAUSE AND EFFECT

Cause-and-effect questions test your understanding of the relationship between an action or event and its effects. In answering these questions, be careful to understand what answer is being asked for: the *cause* or the *effect*. Such questions might appear as follows:

- Which was a significant cause of [*defeat of the Aztecs*]? (asks for a *cause*)
- Which was a direct result of the [*European exploration*]? (asks for an *effect*)

> To help you answer these types of questions, important cause-and-effect relationships are identified in each content chapter. In addition, many cause-and-effect relationships are found in graphic organizers in each content chapter.

DETERMINING CHRONOLOGY

A list of events in **chronological order** starts from the earliest event and progresses to the latest one. This arrangement allows us to see patterns and sequences in a series of events. Chronological questions might appear as follows:

- Which events occurred last?
- Which group of events is in correct chronological order?

> To help you answer these types of questions and to make you aware of the sequence of events, timelines are presented at the beginning of each chapter.

DISTINGUISHING FACT FROM OPINION

Certain questions require you to understand the difference between facts and opinions.

❖   A **fact** is a statement that can be verified. For example, the following is a factual statement: "The Declaration of Independence was written in 1776." We frequently check the accuracy of factual statements by looking at several sources.

❖   An **opinion** is an expression of someone's belief, and cannot be verified. An example of an opinion would be: "Washington was the wisest man of the Revolutionary War period."

Questions asking you to distinguish fact from opinion are phrased as follows:

- Which statement about the *[English colonies]* expresses an opinion rather than a fact?
- Which statement about *[Benjamin Franklin]* would be impossible to prove? *(An opinion statement would be the correct answer.)*

> The crucial factor is to know the difference between facts and opinions. To help you answer this type of question, several content chapters will have a multiple-choice question asking you to distinguish facts from opinions.

USING REFERENCE BOOKS

Historians and social scientists consult a variety of reference books. One standard reference book is an atlas. An **atlas** contains a collection of maps. It may also have information about topography, natural resources, population, and other topics. Other reference books include **encyclopedias** and **almanacs**. Some test questions may ask you to identify one of these specialized books of information.

- To find information about the topography of *[the United States]*, which source would you most likely consult?

> The crucial factor is to know what types of information are contained in various kinds of reference books. To help you answer questions dealing with reference books, some multiple-choice questions regarding sources of information are provided in this book.

TESTING YOUR UNDERSTANDING

Directions: Circle the number next to the phrase or sentence that correctly answers the question or statement.

Base your answer to question 1 on this cartoon and on your knowledge of social studies.

1 What is the main idea of the cartoon?
  1 The Articles of Confederation gave too much power to the President.
  2 The government under the Articles of Confederation could not be changed.
  3 State governments had the real power under the Articles of Confederation.
  4 The central government had the power to make the states obey.

2 According to the Declaration of Independence, the purpose of government is to
  1 protect the rights of individuals
  2 provide a strong military force
  3 maintain the leader's authority
  4 establish a court system

3 The "unalienable rights" mentioned in the Declaration of Independence refer to
  1 the rights of accused persons
  2 the right to vote in all elections
  3 rights that cannot be taken away
  4 right-to-work laws

4 The Constitutional Convention of 1787 was called primarily to
  1 settle the issue of western lands
  2 create a procedure for admitting new states
  3 give the central government additional power
  4 provide help to solve urban problems

5 The Constitution of the United States is best described as a
  1 set of rules and procedures for governing
  2 summary of governmental customs and traditions
  3 guarantee of prosperity for all citizens
  4 justification for rebellion against Great Britain

6 The authors of the Articles of Confederation wanted to
  1 create a powerful central government
  2 provide a system of checks and balances within the central government
  3 limit the power of the central government
  4 model the American central government after the British government

7 At the Constitutional Convention, the agreement known as the "Three-fifths Compromise" dealt with
  1 amendments to the Constitution
  2 representation in the House of Representatives
  3 rights of the accused
  4 powers of the President

8 At the Constitutional Convention, differences about representation were settled by creating a
  1 judicial system
  2 single President
  3 two-house legislature
  4 government with three branches

9 In the late 1780s, some states were persuaded to ratify the Constitution by the promise of
  1 low taxes
  2 a national court system
  3 a Bill of Rights
  4 a woman's right to vote

CHAPTER 4

OUR CONSTITUTIONAL SYSTEM OF GOVERNMENT

Principles of the U.S. Constitution
   A. Problems of Creating a National Government
   B. Organization of the U.S. Constitution
   C. Constitutional Principles

The Federal Government
   A. Congress: The Legislative Branch
   B. The Presidency: The Executive Branch
   C. The Federal Courts: The Judicial Branch
   D. The Unwritten Constitution

Constitutional Protection of Individual Rights
   A. The Bill of Rights
   B. The Fourteenth Amendment
   C. Other Important Rights

WHAT YOU SHOULD FOCUS ON

In this chapter, you will learn about the basic ideas of the U.S. Constitution and how the American government is organized and operates.

With George Washington presiding, delegates sign the new U. S. Constitution.

The main challenge of the "Framers" (*writers*) of the new Constitution was to strike a balance between the powers of the federal and state governments without threatening the rights of individual citizens. To meet this challenge, the authors of the Constitution created a document that would help to delicately balance these two important goals.

As you read this chapter, you will learn about:

The Principles of the U.S. Constitution

The new U.S. Constitution provided a strong government. This government was to be based on certain principles. Federalism, the separation of powers, and a system of checks and balances would assure that no one branch of government overpowered the others.

The Federal Government

The federal (*national*) government created under the Constitution was divided into three branches: a legislature (*Congress*), an executive (*the Presidency*), and a judiciary (*the Federal courts*). Each was organized and operated differently.

Constitutional Protection of Individual Rights

To protect the rights of individual citizens, the first Congress added ten amendments, which became known as the Bill of Rights. Later, other important protections of individual rights were added.

In studying this chapter, you should focus on the following questions:

❖ How did the Constitution create a strong central government without threatening individual liberties?

❖ How does our federal system of government work?

❖ How are individual rights protected by the Constitution and Bill of Rights?

PRINCIPLES OF THE U. S. CONSTITUTION

In this section you will read about the basic ideas
found in the U.S. Constitution.

THINK ABOUT IT

Describe one way you have been affected by each level of government:

National Government: _____

State Government: _____

Local Government: _____

Important Terms and Concepts: As you read this section, look for the following:

- ✦ Popular Sovereignty
- ✦ Preamble
- ✦ Federalism
- ✦ Delegated Powers
- ✦ Reserved Powers

- ✦ Concurrent Powers
- ✦ Separation of Powers
- ✦ Checks and Balances
- ✦ Elastic Clause
- ✦ Amendments

To help you find these terms, this symbol ✦ appears in the margin where the term is first explained.

To correct the problems of the Articles of Confederation, the writers of the U. S. Constitution had to rethink the whole idea of what a government is supposed to be.

THE PROBLEMS OF CREATING A NATIONAL GOVERNMENT

WHAT IS A GOVERNMENT?

Human beings are social; they need to live with others in groups or communities. As a result, communities must make rules to settle disagreements among members, and to protect the community from those who violate the rules. The organization set up for these purposes is called a **government**. Just as a captain guides a ship, a government guides the members of a community in their dealings with each other and outsiders. All governments are given powers to carry out their authority over the members of society. These powers include:

a legislative power
to make the laws

an executive power
to carry out the laws

a judicial power
to interpret the laws

WHAT KIND OF GOVERNMENT SHOULD BE CREATED?

Creating a government is a matter of great concern to each of us. How much power can we give to a government without it threatening our liberties? This question helps you to appreciate the difficulty facing the people who established our system of government. The members of the Constitutional Convention in 1787 had several different types of government from which to choose:

One Person	**Monarchy** (*rule by a king or queen*)
A Select Few	**Oligarchy** (*rule by a few wealthy and powerful citizens*)
All Citizens	**Democracy** (*rule by representatives chosen by the people*)

The delegates to the Constitutional Convention were committed to **democracy** — power would remain in the hands of the people, who would choose their own representatives. After making this decision, the delegates next had to concern themselves with how power was going to be shared between a national government and the state governments. Finally, the authors of the Constitution had to decide what the goals of the new national government would be, how the representatives would be chosen, and what their particular powers would be.

THE GOALS OF THE UNITED STATES GOVERNMENT

The goals of our national government were made clear in two documents: the Declaration of Independence and the Constitution. The Declaration stated that the main goal of government should be to protect the rights of the members of the community, especially the rights to "life, liberty and the pursuit of happiness." The **Preamble** of the Constitution spelled out the specific goals of our national government — to ensure internal peace, to promote the general welfare, to provide for the nation's defense, and to establish justice.

BALANCING GOVERNMENTAL POWER AND INDIVIDUAL LIBERTY

Once they had arrived at the goals of the government, the authors of the Constitution had to create a government that could fulfill those aims. They sought to strike a balance between the powers of government and the rights of the individual. The central problem in forming our government was:

> *How much power should be given to government officials — so that they can carry out their duties — without taking away the people's liberties?*

THE ORGANIZATION OF THE U.S. CONSTITUTION

The final plan of government reached by the delegates at the Constitutional Convention is contained in a document called the U. S. Constitution. It opens with a Preamble which lists the major goals of the government. The rest of the Constitution is divided into seven Articles: think of them as chapters in a book. In addition, 27 amendments (*additions*) have been ratified since the

Constitution was adopted. The **Twenty-seventh Amendment**, dealing with raising the salaries of members of Congress, was proposed nearly 200 years ago and was only recently ratified by the states.

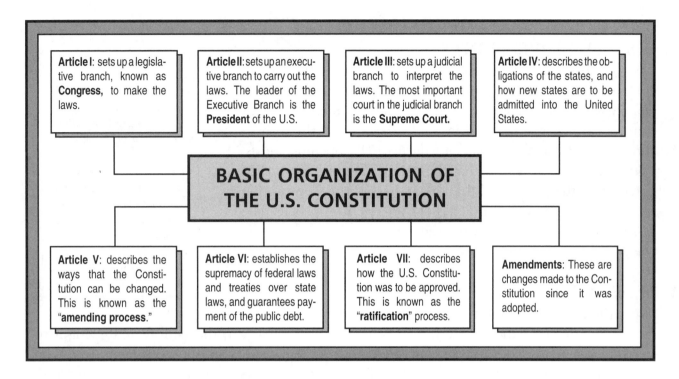

It would be hard to exaggerate the significance that the Constitution has had on American life.

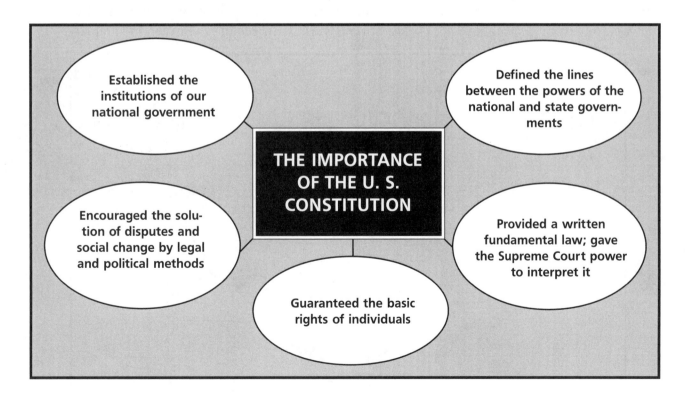

CONSTITUTIONAL PRINCIPLES

The system of government set up by the U.S. Constitution rests on a number of important principles.

POPULAR SOVEREIGNTY

The Constitution is considered the supreme law of the nation. It is based on the idea of **popular sovereignty** (*the will of the people*) in which the people decide, by majority rule, what they want. This principle is stated in the first section of the Constitution, called the **Preamble** (*introduction*). Its opening words, "We the People ..." tell us that the right to form a government comes from the people and that the authors of the Constitution were acting as the representatives of the American people. The rest of the Preamble states what the authors believed should be the goals of the new government.

We, the people of the United States, in order to form a more perfect Union,
- *establish justice,*
- *insure domestic tranquillity,*
- *provide for the common defense,*
- *promote the general welfare,*
- *and secure the blessings of liberty to ourselves and our posterity,*

do ordain and establish this Constitution for the United States of America.

✦ FEDERALISM

The writers of the Constitution knew that under the Articles of Confederation the national government was too weak. However, they still feared giving it too much power because of their bitter experience with the powerful British government, which had taxed them without their consent. They decided to create a system where power was *shared* between the national government and the state governments. This division of powers is called **federalism**. The national government deals with matters that affect the whole country, as well as relations among the states. The terms "national," "federal," and "central" government all refer to the government in Washington, D. C. The state governments handle their own local affairs.

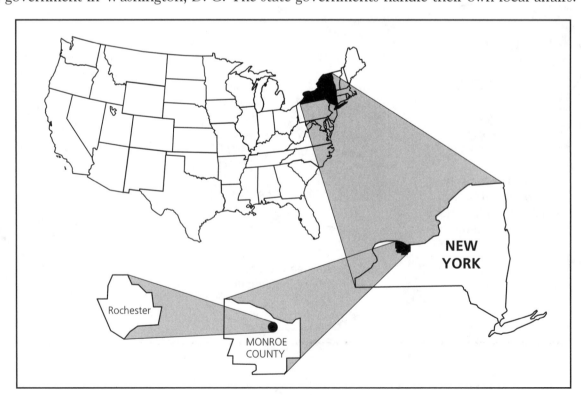

The powers to govern are shared as follows:

Delegated Powers: powers which the Constitution gives exclusively (*only*) to the national government. ◆

Reserved Powers: powers which were reserved (*kept*) by the states and belong exclusively to the state governments. ◆

Concurrent Powers: powers shared by both the state governments and the national government. ◆

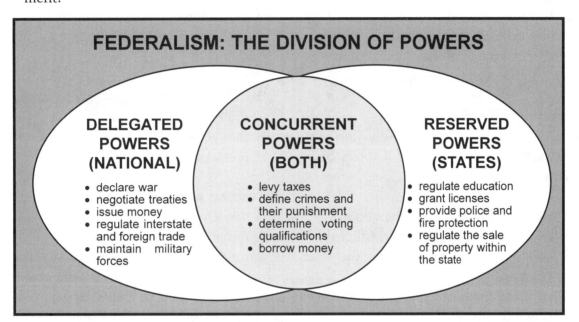

FEDERALISM: THE DIVISION OF POWERS

DELEGATED POWERS (NATIONAL)
- declare war
- negotiate treaties
- issue money
- regulate interstate and foreign trade
- maintain military forces

CONCURRENT POWERS (BOTH)
- levy taxes
- define crimes and their punishment
- determine voting qualifications
- borrow money

RESERVED POWERS (STATES)
- regulate education
- grant licenses
- provide police and fire protection
- regulate the sale of property within the state

The Framers of the U.S. Constitution realized that in creating a new government, there were bound to be conflicts between the national government and the various state governments. Anticipating such conflicts, they added Article VI, known as the **Supremacy Clause**. This article states that the Constitution is the law of the nation. It was on the basis of this clause that the Supreme Court declared that national laws were supreme over state laws.

The Shrine at the National Archives contains the Declaration of Independence, the Constitution, and the Bill of Rights.

**SKILL BUILDER:
UNDERSTANDING
A READING**

Since reading selections often appear on state examinations, it will be helpful if you know how to interpret them.

What Is a Reading Selection?
A reading selection consists of one or more statements about a particular subject. It may be a short quotation or paragraph.

Interpreting a Reading Selection
The main purpose of a reading selection is to present someone's ideas about a topic. Start by asking yourself the following questions:

- What do you know about the writer?
- What term or situation is being discussed?
- What is the writer saying about the term or situation?
- What is the main idea of the reading?
- Why was it written?

Questions about reading selections often ask about the main idea of the passage. Usually, the opening sentence will contain the main idea. Therefore, pay particular attention to it. However, sometimes the main idea is expressed in another sentence, or is implied.

Practice your understanding by reading the following selection and answering the questions that follow:

... Our country is too large to have all its affairs directed by a single government. I truly believe that if the central government took over all the powers of the state governments, eliminating the need for states, the central government would be the most corrupt government on earth ...
— Thomas Jefferson

1 The main idea of the reading is that
   1 the powers of government should be shared
   2 all governments are corrupt
   3 state and national governments should unite into a single government
   4 the government's power comes from the people

The correct answer is choice #1. In the first sentence Jefferson states, "Our country is too large to have all its affairs directed by a single government." He implies that since the nation is too large for one government, the powers of government should be shared among the national government and the states.

2 Which type of government would the author most favor?
   1 communism
   2 federalism
   3 monarchy
   4 imperialism

The answer is choice #2. Jefferson warns that if only one government were to exist, it would become corrupt. Of the four choices, there is only one type that implies the existence of more than one government sharing power — federalism. We know from the reading that Jefferson favored federalism. Communism, monarchy and imperialism all require a single, central government. Therefore, they are the wrong answers.

SEPARATION OF POWERS

Because the authors of the Constitution feared leaving too much power in the hands of one government, they also **separated** the three main powers of the national government into different branches — the **legislative** (*the power to make laws*), the **executive** (*the power to carry out laws*), and the **judicial** (*the power to interpret laws*). This separation made it difficult for any one person or branch of government to become too powerful. State governments, like New York State, also follow the same model of separating powers among three branches.

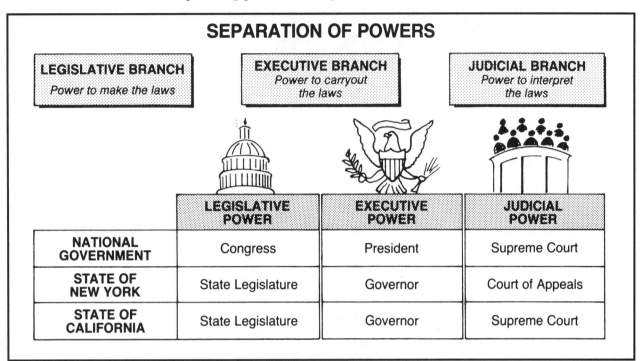

SEPARATION OF POWERS

LEGISLATIVE BRANCH
Power to make the laws

EXECUTIVE BRANCH
Power to carryout the laws

JUDICIAL BRANCH
Power to interpret the laws

	LEGISLATIVE POWER	EXECUTIVE POWER	JUDICIAL POWER
NATIONAL GOVERNMENT	Congress	President	Supreme Court
STATE OF NEW YORK	State Legislature	Governor	Court of Appeals
STATE OF CALIFORNIA	State Legislature	Governor	Supreme Court

The courtroom in which the nine Supreme Court Justices hear cases

CHECKS AND BALANCES

In order to prevent any one of the three branches from becoming too powerful, the Constitution gave each branch ways to stop or "check" the other branches. For example, the Senate must approve most Presidential appointments, while the President may veto bills passed by Congress. In this way, power is kept in "balance" among the branches.

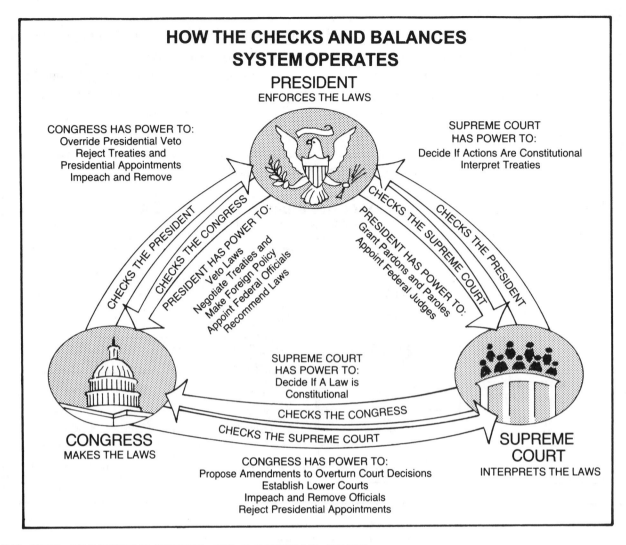

LIMITS ON THE POWER OF GOVERNMENT

The authors of the Constitution took great care to spell out the specific powers of the federal government.

■ The federal government can only use those powers that are **delegated** (*specifically given to it by the Constitution*). For example, some of the major powers of the legislative branch (*Congress*) are as follows:

Congress Has the Power to:	This Means That:
Regulate interstate commerce	Congress can control trade among the states
Impose and collect taxes	Congress can create and collect taxes.
Coin money	Congress can print money and issue coins.

The Constitution allows the federal government to "stretch" its delegated powers to some degree. The government may take additional unlisted actions that are "necessary and proper" for Congress to carry out its delegated powers. This "necessary and proper" clause is sometimes called the **Elastic Clause** because it "stretches" the powers of Congress. For example, the Constitution does not specifically give Congress the power to set up a national bank. But the Constitution does give Congress the power to collect taxes and to regulate interstate commerce (*trade*). In order to exercise these powers, Congress might decide that it is "necessary and proper" to establish a national bank, even though the power to establish a national bank is not specifically mentioned in the Constitution.

ANALYSIS

What other powers can you name that Congress uses that are "necessary and proper" to

carry out its delegated powers in the Constitution? _____

_____

_____

■ The Constitution also says that both the national and state governments are prevented from taking certain actions. These are called the **Denied Powers**

Powers Denied to the Federal Government	Powers Denied to Both the Federal & State Governments	Powers Denied to the State Governments
• To suspend the *writ of habeas corpus* • To spend money without Congressional approval • To give preference to one state over another	• To pass *ex post facto* laws • To pass *bills of attainder* • To grant titles of nobility • To tax exports • To deny people due process of law	• To print money • To enter into treaties • To tax imports • To tax the federal government • To declare war

FLEXIBILITY

Although it was written over 200 years ago, the Constitution has been able to keep up with the changing needs of the country. Changing interpretations of the Constitution, especially by the U.S. Supreme Court, have helped adapt the Constitution to new conditions. For example, the delegated power to regulate interstate commerce has been interpreted to mean that Congress can pass a minimum wage law, since products made by workers in one state can be sold in another state. Another way the Constitution keeps pace is through the process of **amendment** (*an addition to or change in the text of the Constitution*). To prevent changes for unimportant reasons, the amending process was made far more difficult than passing an ordinary law. It is only when there is a general demand for fundamental change that amendments get ratified. One example was the widespread public demand in the 1970s for 18-year-olds to have the right to vote.

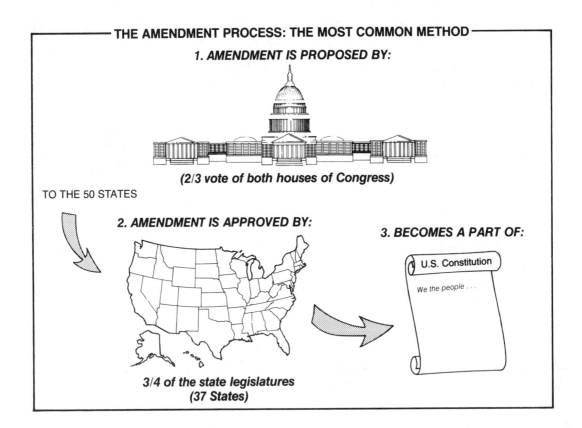

THE AMENDMENT PROCESS: THE MOST COMMON METHOD

1. AMENDMENT IS PROPOSED BY:

(2/3 vote of both houses of Congress)

TO THE 50 STATES

2. AMENDMENT IS APPROVED BY:

3/4 of the state legislatures
(37 States)

3. BECOMES A PART OF:

U.S. Constitution

We the people . . .

SUMMING UP: PRINCIPLES OF THE CONSTITUTION

The U.S. Constitution contains a number of important principles. These principles include popular sovereignty, federalism, separation of powers, checks and balances, limiting the powers of government, and having the flexibility to adapt to new conditions.

THINKING IT OVER

Now that you have read this section, are there any additional jobs you think each level of government should have?

National Government: _____

State Government: _____

Local Government: _____

CHECKING YOUR UNDERSTANDING

Directions: Complete the following cards. Then answer the multiple-choice questions.

FEDERALISM

Definition: _____

Give an example: _____

_____

SEPARATION OF POWERS

Definition: _____

Give an example: _____

_____

CONCURRENT POWERS

Definition: _____

Give an example: _____

_____

CHECKS AND BALANCES

Definition: _____

Give an example: _____

_____

---

1 According to the principle of "popular sovereignty," political power rests with the
  1 Supreme Court   3 President
  2 Congress   4 people

2 Which is an example of a "delegated power" of the national government?
  1 setting speed limits on state roads
  2 building schools
  3 regulating interstate commerce
  4 determining the price of goods

3 An example of a "reserved power" held by the state governments is the power to
  1 establish post offices   3 coin money
  2 set marriage qualifications   4 raise an army

4 An example of a "concurrent power" of both the state and national governments is to
  1 collect taxes   3 establish foreign policy
  2 declare war   4 print money

5 The "elastic clause" of the U.S. Constitution refers to powers of
  1 the states   3 Congress
  2 the President   4 the Supreme Court

6 The basic purpose of constitutional checks and balances is to
  1 protect the states from invasion by foreign governments
  2 prevent any one branch of the federal government from becoming too strong
  3 enable the federal government's power to grow
  4 provide a written guarantee of the rights of each citizen

7 State laws that govern teenage driving in different parts of the United States provide an example of
  1 checks and balances
  2 popular sovereignty
  3 a reserved power
  4 a delegated power

8 A basic feature of a "federal" system of government is that it
  1 punishes citizens who break the law
  2 divides power between the national and state governments
  3 has an elected national court system
  4 makes sure all minorities receive equal pay

THE FEDERAL GOVERNMENT

In this section you will read about the three branches
of the U.S. government and how they are organized.

THINK ABOUT IT

The Constitution divides the power of government into separate parts or branches: the legislative, executive, and judicial. What do you think is the major job of each?

Legislative: _____   **Executive:** _____ **Judicial:** _____

Important Terms and Concepts: As you read this section, look for the following:

- ✦ Branches of Government
- ✦ Electoral College
- ✦ Judicial Review
- ✦ Unwritten Constitution

✦ The federal government is divided into three **branches** (*parts*):

Let's take a closer look at each of these three branches of government.

CONGRESS: THE LEGISLATIVE BRANCH

The legislative branch of the federal government is called **Congress**. Congress consists of two parts, called "houses" — the **Senate** and the **House of Representatives**.

	HOUSE OF REPRESENTATIVES	SENATE
Total Members	435 members	100 members
Determined by	Population: the more people living in the state, the more Representatives the state has	Two from each state, no matter what the size of the state's population
Length of Term	2 years	6 years
Special Powers	• introduces spending bills • selects a President if the Electoral College fails to do so	• conducts impeachment trials • approves Presidential appointments • ratifies (approves) treaties

POWERS OF CONGRESS

Congress has the power to make laws. All laws start out as **bills** (*proposed laws*).

HOW A BILL BECOMES A LAW

Introduction of a Bill. Bills can start in either house of Congress. All *spending* bills must start in the House of Representatives. Once proposed, the bill is sent to a committee (*group of legislators dealing with specific issues such as foreign affairs*).

Committee Stage. Committee members investigate the bill and debate whether to approve, amend, or "kill" it. If approved, the bill is sent to the floor for debate.

Consideration of the Bill. On the floor of the house, the bill is debated. Then it is either approved or "killed." If approved, the bill is sent to the other legislative body, where it is sent to a committee. If approved by the committee, the bill is sent to the other house.

Consideration by the Other House. On the floor of the second house, the bill is again debated. Then it is either approved or "killed." If the same version of the bill is approved by both houses, it is then sent to the President.

OR

The President. If the President signs the bill, it then becomes the law of the land. If the bill is **vetoed** (*rejected*) by the President, the veto can be overridden.

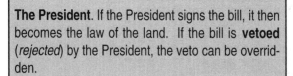

Conference Committee. If differences exist between the Senate and House versions, a Conference Committee, made up of members of both houses, "irons out" differences between the versions. Then they send the bill to the President.

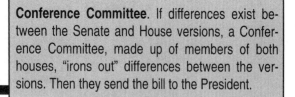

Overriding A Veto. Congress can override a Presidential veto; it requires two-thirds of the members of each house to vote again in favor of the bill. The bill then becomes law even though the President opposed it.

The law-making process was deliberately made complicated, so that only well-supported bills would become laws. Once a bill is passed and is signed by the President, it becomes part of the law of the land. All citizens must obey it. Those who do not may face fines and even imprisonment.

THE PRESIDENCY: THE EXECUTIVE BRANCH

The **executive power** — the power to carry out laws — is given to the President.

QUALIFICATIONS AND TERM OF OFFICE
The President must either be born in the United States or have parents who are U.S. citizens, and must be at least 35 years old. The President is elected for a four-year term. As a result of the **Twenty-second Amendment**, adopted in 1951, the President is limited to two terms in office.

CHOOSING PRESIDENTIAL CANDIDATES
The road to the Presidency is long and difficult. Usually a person must first win the nomination of one of the two major political parties — the Democrats or Republicans. To do this, candidates enter **primaries** (*state-wide elections between rivals from the same political party*). The more primaries a candidate wins, the more delegates will vote for him or her at the party's **national convention**. To be nominated, a candidate must win a majority of delegates at the national convention.

THE PRESIDENTIAL CAMPAIGN
The candidates give speeches and get exposure on television, radio and newspapers in a wide-ranging **campaign**. The campaign ends on Election Day, the first Tuesday in November, when citizens go into voting booths throughout the country to elect the next President.

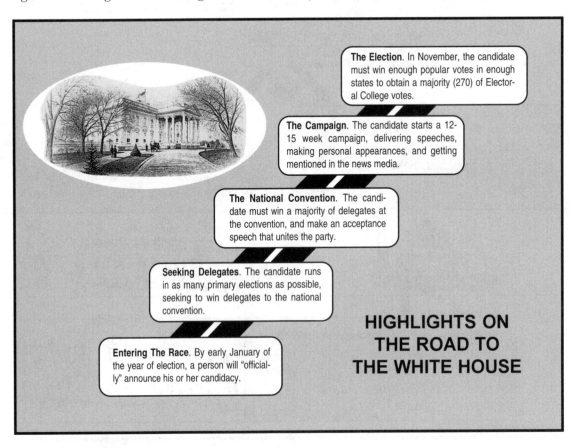

The Election. In November, the candidate must win enough popular votes in enough states to obtain a majority (270) of Electoral College votes.

The Campaign. The candidate starts a 12-15 week campaign, delivering speeches, making personal appearances, and getting mentioned in the news media.

The National Convention. The candidate must win a majority of delegates at the convention, and make an acceptance speech that unites the party.

Seeking Delegates. The candidate runs in as many primary elections as possible, seeking to win delegates to the national convention.

Entering The Race. By early January of the year of election, a person will "officially" announce his or her candidacy.

HIGHLIGHTS ON THE ROAD TO THE WHITE HOUSE

THE ELECTORAL COLLEGE ELECTS THE PRESIDENT

In 1787, the Framers of the Constitution did not trust the common people enough to let them elect the President directly. Instead, they turned the selection of the President over to a group known as **electors**. Electors chosen from each state make up the **Electoral College**. On Election Day, when citizens vote for a President, they are really voting for electors. The candidate who gets the most votes in each state gets all of that state's electors — a "winner take all" arrangement.

- The number of electors from each state is equal to the numbers of its Representatives in the House combined with the number of its Senators. To become President, a candidate must win a majority (270 votes) of the votes in the Electoral College.

- If no candidate receives a majority of electoral votes, the election is then decided in the House of Representatives, where the winner must receive a majority of state votes (26). Each state has only one vote.

THE PRESIDENT'S ROLES

Today, the President has many responsibilities. **Political scientists** (*people who study government*) say that the President "wears many hats, one for each job."

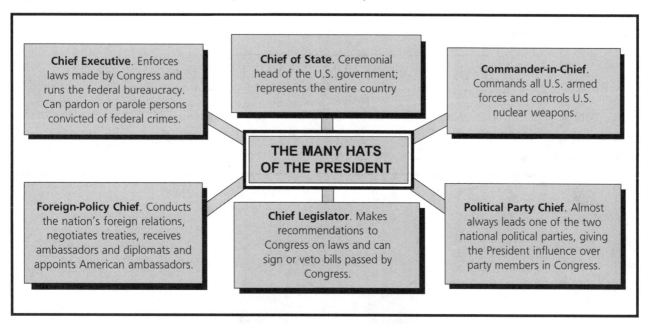

Chief Executive. Enforces laws made by Congress and runs the federal bureaucracy. Can pardon or parole persons convicted of federal crimes.

Chief of State. Ceremonial head of the U.S. government; represents the entire country

Commander-in-Chief. Commands all U.S. armed forces and controls U.S. nuclear weapons.

THE MANY HATS OF THE PRESIDENT

Foreign-Policy Chief. Conducts the nation's foreign relations, negotiates treaties, receives ambassadors and diplomats and appoints American ambassadors.

Chief Legislator. Makes recommendations to Congress on laws and can sign or veto bills passed by Congress.

Political Party Chief. Almost always leads one of the two national political parties, giving the President influence over party members in Congress.

THE FEDERAL COURTS: THE JUDICIAL BRANCH

The **Supreme Court** and the other federal courts make up the judicial branch. It is their responsibility to interpret the laws. They try cases involving federal laws. The President nominates all federal judges, but they must be approved by the Senate. The highest court in the nation, the Supreme Court, has nine members. Like all federal judges, Supreme Court Justices hold office for life, to protect their decisions from political interference. The Supreme Court's most important power is known as **Judicial Review**, which allows the Court to decide whether laws or government actions go against what is written in the Constitution. If the Supreme Court decides that a law is not constitutional, the law becomes void and can no longer be enforced.

THE ORGANIZATION OF THE FEDERAL AND STATE COURTS

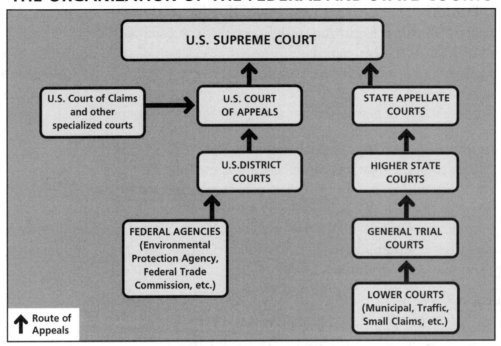

Appeals to the U.S. Supreme Court from state courts can only be made on federal issues, such as a denial of constitutional rights.

THE UNWRITTEN CONSTITUTION

The operation of the U.S. government today is based on many customs, traditions and practices that were not written into the Constitution. These are called the **unwritten constitution**, and make up an important part of our present-day system of government.

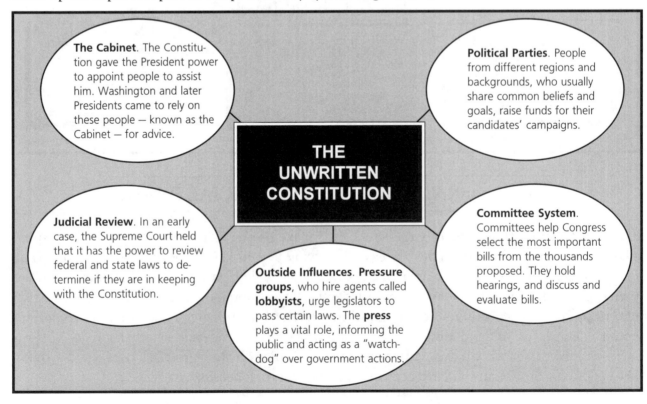

SUMMING UP: THE FEDERAL GOVERNMENT

The government of the United States is made up of three branches. The legislative branch, **Congress**, makes the laws. The executive branch, headed by the **President**, carries out the laws. The judicial branch, headed by the **Supreme Court**, interprets the laws.

THINKING IT OVER

Were you correct in identifying the jobs of each branch of government? _____ If not, make your corrections on the lines below.

Legislative: _____

Executive: _____

Judicial: _____

CHECKING YOUR UNDERSTANDING

Directions: Complete the following cards. Then answer the multiple-choice questions.

BRANCHES OF GOVERNMENT

How many are there? _____

What is the job of each? _____

_____

JUDICIAL REVIEW

What is it? _____

Why is it important? _____

_____

ELECTORAL COLLEGE

What is its main job? _____

What happens if no candidate gets a majority

vote in the Electoral College? _____

_____

UNWRITTEN CONSTITUTION

What is it? _____

List 3 examples: 1. _____

2. _____

3. _____

1   The U.S. Senate has the power to
   1 interpret federal laws
   2 approve Presidential appointments
   3 veto legislation
   4 declare laws to be unconstitutional

2   Laws can best be defined as
   1 rules that only criminals must obey
   2 fines for committing crimes
   3 duties the Congress must live up to
   4 rules that regulate people in society

3   Making foreign policy for the nation is a primary responsibility of the
   1 President   3 electoral college
   2 states   4 Supreme Court

4   The Commander-in-Chief of all U.S. military forces is the
   1 Vice-President
   2 Chief Justice of the Supreme Court
   3 President of the United States
   4 Secretary of State

5   Who nominates persons to serve on the Supreme Court?
   1 the President   3 the Congress
   2 political parties 4 the states

6   The main responsibility of the executive branch of government is to
   1 interpret laws   3 make laws
   2 carry out laws   4 defeat laws

7   A treaty cannot take effect until it has been ratified by two-thirds of the
   1 House of Representatives
   2 President
   3 Senate
   4 Supreme Court

8   Much of the Supreme Court's authority is based on its power to
   1 propose laws to Congress
   2 impose military rule
   3 interpret the U.S. Constitution
   4 suggest Constitutional amendments

9   The major role of a political party is to
   1 represent minorities in a political election
   2 nominate candidates and conduct political campaigns
   3 manage the government during an election
   4 ensure that candidates are honest and obey the law

10 Which feature of the American Presidency resulted from a constitutional amendment?
   1 a two-term limit in office
   2 the power to appoint U.S. ambassadors to foreign countries
   3 the responsibility to act as Commander-in-Chief of the armed forces
   4 the ability to nominate Justices to the U.S. Supreme Court

SECTION 3

CONSTITUTIONAL PROTECTION OF INDIVIDUAL RIGHTS

In this section you will learn how the Constitution protects our individual rights and liberties.

THINK ABOUT IT

What do you think are your major rights protected by the U.S. Constitution? _____

_____

Important Terms and Concepts: As you read this section, look for the following:

   ✦ Ex Post Facto Laws   ✦ Fourteenth Amendment
   ✦ Writ of Habeas Corpus   ✦ Due Process Rights
   ✦ Bill of Rights   ✦ Equal Protection Rights

THE BILL OF RIGHTS

One of the most important features of the Constitution is the protection it provides to individuals. Individual liberties are specifically spelled out and guaranteed in the Constitution.

RIGHTS PROTECTED IN THE ORIGINAL CONSTITUTION

Some rights were protected by the original Constitution. For example, the federal and state governments were prohibited from passing certain laws:

■ **No Ex Post Facto laws**. Neither the federal nor the state governments may punish an individual for doing something that was not already a crime at the time it was committed. ◆

■ **No suspension of the Writ of Habeas Corpus except during invasion or rebellion**. A writ of habeas corpus is a court order to release a prisoner who is being held without being properly charged with a crime. The government cannot stop such releases in ordinary times. ◆

■ **No Bills of Attainder**. The Constitution prohibits Congress from passing laws convicting individual citizens of particular crimes.

THE NEED FOR A BILL OF RIGHTS (1791)

When the Constitution was sent to the states for approval, many citizens feared the new national government would use its powers against the people. They demanded the addition of a "Bill of Rights" guaranteeing individual liberties. The Constitution was ratified without it, but shortly thereafter ten amendments were ratified and became part of the Constitution. Because many of our basic freedoms are protected by these amendments, they are called the **Bill of Rights**. ◆

The Bill of Rights

1st Amendment	Guarantees freedoms of religion, speech, and the press, and rights to peacefully assemble and petition
2nd Amendment	Guarantees the right to keep and bear arms
3rd Amendment	Prohibits the quartering of soldiers in one's home
4th Amendment	Prohibits "unreasonable" searches and seizures
5th Amendment	Contains guarantees and prohibitions: • no citizen may be deprived of life, liberty or property without **due process of law** (*legal procedures carried out according to established rules, such as a fair trial*) • requires **grand jury** indictments (*formal charge for committing a serious crime*) • prohibits **double jeopardy** (*being tried twice for the same crime*) • prohibits **self-incrimination** (*individuals may not be forced to give evidence against themselves*)
6th Amendment	Guarantees that those accused of a crime have the right to: • a speedy trial by jury • confront accusers • be represented by a lawyer
7th Amendment	Guarantees a jury trial in many civil cases
8th Amendment	Prohibits excessive bail and cruel and unusual punishment
9th Amendment	The listing of some Constitutional rights does not mean that people do not have other rights
10th Amendment	Reserves to the states and the people all rights not delegated to the federal government

THE FOURTEENTH AMENDMENT

The Bill of Rights originally protected individuals only from the actions of the federal government. It had no effect on the state governments and provided no protection against their actions. After the Civil War, Congress proposed the **Fourteenth Amendment** (1868) to grant citizenship to former slaves, and also to protect all citizens from abuses by state governments. It has accomplished this in two ways:

■ **Due Process Rights**. The state governments must follow the same procedures as the federal government when arresting, searching, and convicting persons accused of a crime. States cannot take away freedom of expression except for the same narrow reasons that the federal government can. Due process rights also include the "right to privacy."

■ **Equal Protection Rights**. The Fourteenth Amendment also guarantees "equal protection" of the laws. This means governments cannot treat some groups differently unless there is an overriding reason. For example, governments can refuse to give three-year-olds the right to vote because they are not mature enough, but cannot deny women the right to vote.

OTHER IMPORTANT RIGHTS

Besides the Bill of Rights and the Fourteenth Amendment, several other amendments help to protect important individual rights. For example, the Thirteenth Amendment outlawed slavery in 1865. Other amendments that protect individual rights include the following:

Other Amendments Protecting Individual Rights

15th Amendment	Guaranteed freed slaves the right to vote (1870)
17th Amendment	Changed the election of Senators from selection by state legislatures to direct election by voters (1913)
19th Amendment	Gave women the right to vote (1920)
23rd Amendment	Gave residents of Washington DC the right to vote for President (1961)
24th Amendment	Prohibited poll taxes in federal elections (1964)
26th Amendment	Gave individuals the right to vote upon reaching the age of 18 (1972)

SUMMING UP: CONSTITUTIONAL PROTECTION OF INDIVIDUAL RIGHTS

The U.S. Constitution increased its protection of individual rights by adding a Bill of Rights. Over time, other amendments guaranteed additional rights to American citizens.

THINKING IT OVER

What do you think is your most important right? _____

Why? _____

_____

CHECKING YOUR UNDERSTANDING

Directions: Complete the following cards. Then answer the multiple-choice questions.

BILL OF RIGHTS

What is it? _____

Some rights it protects: 1. _____

2. _____   3. _____

FOURTEENTH AMENDMENT

What is it? _____

How does it protect people? _____

_____

1 The purpose of the first ten amendments to the U.S. Constitution was to
  1 provide a strong judicial branch
  2 protect the rights of individuals
  3 assure citizens of fair elections
  4 maintain a powerful army

2 The Bill of Rights was added to the U.S. Constitution in order to protect
  1 corporations   3 states
  2 individuals   4 foreign governments

3 Which right is guaranteed by the Bill of Rights of the U.S. Constitution?
  1 voting in elections   3 attending school
  2 working at a job   4 speaking freely

4 The expression "due process of law" refers to
  1 the right of the Supreme Court to declare laws to be unconstitutional
  2 the power of the police to arrest suspicious individuals
  3 protections given citizens against unfair government actions
  4 bills which have been passed by Congress

5 The Fourteenth Amendment was important because, in addition to granting citizenship to formerly enslaved peoples, it specifically
  1 guaranteed women the right to vote
  2 abolished the poll tax
  3 guaranteed equal protection under the law
  4 provided protection against illegal searches

6 After the Civil War, the adoption of the Fourteenth Amendment led to
  1 the protection of citizens against unfair actions by state governments
  2 the loss of equal rights for minorities
  3 an expansion of the power of the states to tax
  4 a narrowing of the role of the federal government

7 An important effect of the Fourteenth Amendment was that it
  1 extended Bill of Rights protections to include actions by state governments
  2 permitted states to define United States citizenship in their own state
  3 made state governments less democratic
  4 reduced the control of the federal government over the states

SUMMARIZING YOUR UNDERSTANDING

Directions: Confirm your understanding of the important terms and concepts in this chapter. Check those you can explain. For those you are not sure of, find the ✦ symbol in the margin next to the term and review it.

CHECKLIST

- ❏ Constitution
- ❏ Government
- ❏ Legislative Power
- ❏ Executive Power
- ❏ Judicial Power
- ❏ Popular Sovereignty
- ❏ Federalism
- ❏ Delegated Powers
- ❏ Reserved Powers

- ❏ Concurrent Powers
- ❏ Supremacy Clause
- ❏ Separation of Powers
- ❏ Checks and Balances
- ❏ Elastic Clause
- ❏ Amendment
- ❏ National Convention
- ❏ Electoral College
- ❏ Judicial Review

- ❏ Unwritten Constitution
- ❏ Cabinet
- ❏ Political Parties
- ❏ Ex Post Facto Laws
- ❏ Writ of Habeas Corpus
- ❏ Bill of Rights
- ❏ Fourteenth Amendment
- ❏ Due Process Rights
- ❏ Equal Protection Rights

Directions: Fill in the information called for in the following organizers.

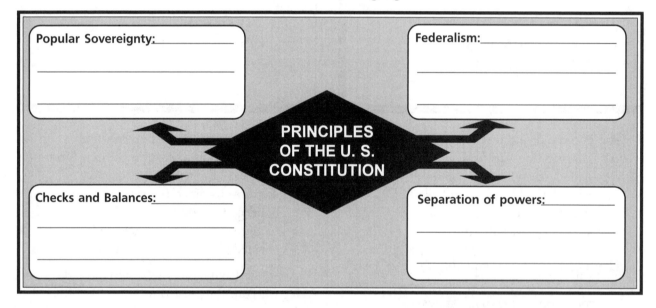

Popular Sovereignty: _____

Federalism: _____

PRINCIPLES OF THE U. S. CONSTITUTION

Checks and Balances: _____

Separation of powers: _____

LIBERTIES PROTECTED BY THE BILL OF RIGHTS

TEST HELPER
LOOKING AT GOVERNMENT

State examinations frequently ask you to write essays in answer to questions about American government. To prepare you for these questions, this section reviews the principles of government that you read about in this chapter.

We have seen that it was difficult to design a system of national government. The central problem for the members of the Constitutional Convention was: *How much power should be given to the national government — so that it can meet its goals — without taking away the people's liberties?*

To meet this challenge, the delegates to the Convention developed the principles of the U.S. Constitution. They created branches that they thought would make the new government strong enough to meet national goals, but not so powerful that it would endanger individual freedoms. They also adopted the following devices:

- **Federalism**: power is shared among the federal and state governments.

- **Separation of Powers**: the powers of the federal government are divided among the legislative, executive and judicial branches.

- **Checks and Balances**: each branch of the federal government has special powers to check or stop the other branches.

- **Limited Government**: the federal government can only exercise the powers specifically given to it by the Constitution.

- **Individual Rights**: the Bill of Rights was not part of the original Constitution, but was added in 1791. These rights protect citizens from unfair actions by the federal government.

Our national system of government has changed over time. Constitutional amendments, decisions of the Supreme Court, and informal political practices have played key roles in adapting our system of government to changes in society. Often, essay questions about government focus on these changes, as well as on the following issues and themes:

- What are the main principles of our Constitution?

- How has our Constitution managed to adapt to the needs of our society?

- What has been the role of the Supreme Court in interpreting individual rights and the powers of our national government?

- How has the power of the Presidency grown in recent times?

- How do the different branches of our federal government check each other?

SHARPENING YOUR TEST-TAKING SKILLS

THE "ACTION WORDS" OF ESSAY QUESTIONS

Essay questions require you to understand certain key words. The instructions for what you are to do in writing your answer are contained in the "action words." The most common action words are:

Describe or Discuss

Explain or Show How

Explain or Show Why

In this section we will examine each of these "action words" to see specifically what they require you to do in answering an essay question.

DESCRIBE OR DISCUSS

Describe or *discuss* means to "tell about it." "Describe" or "discuss" are used when you are asked for the **who, what, when,** and **where** of something. Not every "describe" or "discuss" question requires all four of these elements. However, your answer must go beyond just a single word or sentence. The following are examples of "describe" and "discuss" questions:

- *Describe* a compromise at the Constitutional Convention.
- *Discuss* the major differences between the Articles of Confederation and the U.S. Constitution.

Here is what your answer might look like to the "describe" question above:

Sample Answer: *When representatives meeting in Philadelphia in 1787 decided to write a new Constitution, there was an important disagreement. Larger states wanted states to be represented in the new legislature based on the size of their population. Smaller states wanted each state to have an equal number of members. This was resolved by the "Great Compromise." Congress would have two houses, one based on population (the House of Representatives), and one in which each state would have an equal number of members (the Senate).*

Notice how the answer **describes** one of the compromises at the Constitutional Convention. The description creates a verbal picture of **who** (*representatives of large and small states*), **when** (*in 1787*), **where** (*in Philadelphia*) and **what** (*a legislature with two houses, to satisfy both sides*). **A *helpful hint:*** Go through your own mental checklist of *who, what, when* and *where* whenever you are asked to *describe* or *discuss* something.

EXPLAIN AND SHOW

Explain and *show* are often linked to the additional word *how* or *why*. The key in approaching any question with these words is to determine whether the question requires you to give an answer for *how* something happened or *why* it happened.

❖ **HOW QUESTIONS.** This type of question asks you to explain "how" something works or "how" it relates to something else. It usually focuses on events or effects, not causes. Let's look at two examples:

- *Show how* the passage of the Bill of Rights had a lasting impact on the nation.
- *Explain how* improvements in technology can affect a country's development.

In each case you must provide facts and examples that show that the generalization is true. Let's look at the first sample question about the Bill of Rights. Following is an example of how this question might be answered:

Sample Answer: *The Bill of Rights had a lasting impact on the nation by guaranteeing individual liberties. Because of the Bill of Rights, Americans are able to worship freely and are not forced to follow a particular religion. Americans are also guaranteed free speech and a free press. This means they can criticize their government. Government leaders cannot put their opponents in prison, or close down newspapers that disagree with their policies. Finally, even people accused of a crime have certain rights: the right to a trial by jury, to have a lawyer, and to hear witnesses who accuse them of the crime. By guaranteeing these rights, the Bill of Rights has kept government in check and protected individuals' "life, liberty and the pursuit of happiness," which has had a lasting impact on the nation.*

Notice that the answer provides specific information to *show how* the statement is true. These facts include: (1) that the Bill of Rights guarantees our freedom of religion; (2) it allows people to criticize government freely; and (3) even people accused of a crime have protected rights. **A helpful hint:** Think of a *show how* answer as several columns supporting the generalization you are explaining.

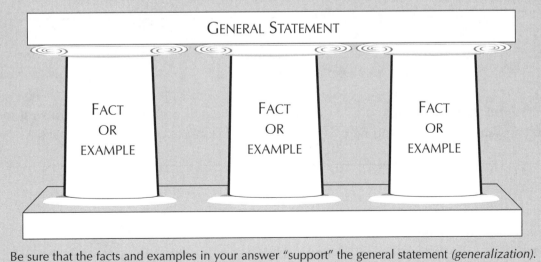

GENERAL STATEMENT

FACT OR EXAMPLE

FACT OR EXAMPLE

FACT OR EXAMPLE

Be sure that the facts and examples in your answer "support" the general statement *(generalization)*.

❖   **WHY QUESTIONS.** To explain *why* means to give reasons why an event took place or why a relationship identified in the question occurred. *Explain why* questions focus on causes. Your answer should identify the reasons why the event or relationship took place and briefly describe each reason. Two examples of such questions are:

• *Explain why* the American colonists rebelled against British rule.
• *Show why* representatives met to change the Articles of Confederation in 1787.

In each case, you must present reasons or causes to explain why the event occurred. Let's look at a sample answer to the first question above.

Sample Answer: *After the French and Indian War, the British government imposed a series of new taxes on the American colonists to help pay off British debts from the war. The colonists objected to these taxes, since the British Parliament had not consulted them. When protesters against the new tax on tea dumped tea from British ships into Boston Harbor, the British government closed the harbor. Many colonists objected to this use of force by the British. Soon afterwards, shots were fired between British troops and colonists. Colonists were also influenced by the writings of Thomas Paine, who wrote that it was ridiculous for the colonists to be governed by a tiny, far-off island. All these factors help to explain why fighting broke out between the colonists and the British, leading the colonists to declare independence from Britain in 1776.*

Notice how the answer provides reasons that *explain why* the American colonists rebelled against British rule:

    (reason 1) the British taxed them without their consent
+
    (reason 2) the British used force to close Boston Harbor
+
    (reason 3) the writings of Thomas Paine

_____

=   (conclusion) These factors explain why the American colonists rebelled against British rule.

A helpful hint: When asked to explain *why*, go through a checklist of various reasons or causes. Be sure they add up to a satisfactory explanation.

TESTING YOUR UNDERSTANDING

Directions: Circle the number preceding the word or expression that correctly answers the statement or question.

Base your answer to questions 1 and 2 on the following reading and on your knowledge of social studies.

> *The President has a great many powers given to him in the Constitution. But the principal power that the President has is to bring people in and try to persuade them. That's what I spend most of my time doing. That's what the power of the President amounts to.* —Harry Truman

1 The main idea of the reading selection is that
  1 the President is more powerful than anyone else
  2 Presidential power is found only in the Constitution
  3 the President's chief power is that of persuasion
  4 the President relies on no one

2 Which statement best describes Truman's view of Presidential power?
  1 The President needs less power than Congress.
  2 More power must be given to the Supreme Court.
  3 The President is not as powerful as some people might think.
  4 Federal leaders must refuse to share power.

3 Presidential vetoes, overriding vetoes by Congress, and judicial review are examples of
  1 laws that limit free speech
  2 election procedures
  3 state powers
  4 checks and balances

4 Which aspect of the U.S. Constitution allows the nation to deal with changes that may occur?
  1 creating freedom of religion
  2 conducting local elections
  3 providing for the nation's defense
  4 allowing for the passage of amendments

5 The authors of the Constitution believed that
  1 the President should impeach corrupt government officials
  2 a government should have limited powers
  3 the President should control the Congress
  4 slaves and women should vote

6 The relationship between the national and state governments in the U.S. system of government is frequently referred to as
  1 democracy   3 federalism
  2 the electoral process   4 checks and balances

7 Which statement is true about amendments to the U.S. Constitution?
  1 Amendments often involve foreign relations.
  2 Most amendments are unnecessary.
  3 Fewer than 30 amendments have been passed.
  4 Amending the Constitution is an easy process.

8 The Preamble to the U.S. Constitution lists the
  1 powers of the federal government
  2 civil liberties of each citizen
  3 goals of the federal government
  4 powers of the state governments

9 Which is a concurrent power shared by the federal and state governments?
  1 approving treaties   3 declaring war
  2 collecting taxes   4 printing money

10 The fact that New York State controls its public schools is an example of
  1 federalism   3 unconstitutional action
  2 judicial review   4 checks and balances

11 The supreme law of the United States is the
1 constitution of each state
2 Declaration of Independence
3 United States Constitution
4 President of the United States

12 The purpose of a primary election is to
1 decide on party nominees
2 establish the amount needed for a poll tax
3 ratify treaties passed by Congress
4 approve Supreme Court decisions

13 The Bill of Rights refers to the
1 Declaration of Independence
2 first ten amendments to the Constitution
3 separation of powers in the federal government
4 emancipation of the slaves

14 In the United States, who may declare a federal law to be unconstitutional?
1 the President
2 the Supreme Court
3 any state governor
4 the Electoral College

15 The purpose of most of the early amendments to the U.S. Constitution was to
1 guarantee individual civil and political rights
2 ensure the proper functioning of the checks and balances system
3 strengthen the authority of state governments
4 expand the power of the Presidency

16 The main reason only a small number of amendments have been added to the Constitution is because
1 the executive branch fears a loss of power
2 the amending process is extremely difficult
3 of the public outcry against its use
4 the Constitution is clear and seldom needs to be amended

17 Federal judges are appointed for life in order to
1 prevent their being influenced by popular opinion or politics
2 allow them to gain legal experience
3 eliminate the need for useless elections
4 reward lawyers who are loyal to the President

18 According to the Constitution, when the President nominates someone for a government position, the nominee must be approved by the Senate. This illustrates the principle of
1 judicial review
2 executive privilege
3 checks and balances
4 minority rights

19 Which is an example of a part of the "unwritten constitution"?
1 political parties
2 Electoral College
3 delegated powers
4 amending process

20 The Bill of Rights of the Constitution includes a guarantee of the right to
1 vote in elections
2 peacefully assemble and petition for change
3 have a job
4 strike against a employer

21 The partial outline below concerns the U.S. Constitution.

I. _____
   A. Checks and Balances
   B. Federalism
   C. Limited Government

Which entry is most appropriate for line I?
1 Powers of the Federal Government
2 Constitutional Flexibility
3 Basic Constitutional Principles
4 Powers of the Chief Executive

22 Which Constitutional principle includes the concepts of reserved powers, delegated powers, and concurrent powers?
1 the amending process
2 federalism
3 judicial review
4 the unwritten constitution

23 The Supreme Court's power of judicial review is a result of
1 an order by the President
2 the Court's own interpretation of the Constitution
3 a provision in the Bill of Rights
4 the Court's decision to hear appeals regarding taxation

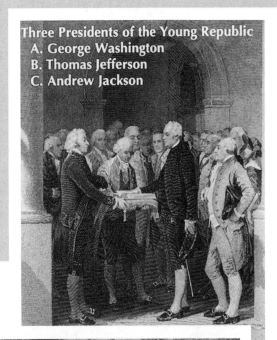

CHAPTER 5

THE CONSTITUTION TESTED

Three Presidents of the Young Republic
A. George Washington
B. Thomas Jefferson
C. Andrew Jackson

The Civil War
A. Causes
B. Highlights

Reconstruction
A. Reconstruction Plans
B. Effects on the South
C. African American Leaders

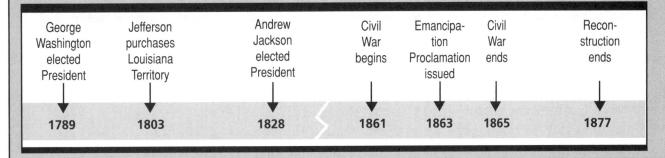

George Washington elected President	Jefferson purchases Louisiana Territory	Andrew Jackson elected President	Civil War begins	Emancipation Proclamation issued	Civil War ends	Reconstruction ends
1789	1803	1828	1861	1863	1865	1877

WHAT YOU SHOULD FOCUS ON

In this chapter, you will read how under its first Presidents, the new American nation developed a government founded on the Constitution and doubled in size because of the Louisiana Purchase.

Different sections of the country developed different lifestyles. Western expansion raised the question of whether slavery would be allowed in new Western states. Within its first 75 years, the nation thus endured its greatest test since independence — the Civil War between the Northern and Southern states. After four years of fierce fighting (1861-1865), the South lost the war. The Union was preserved and slavery came to an end.

During the Reconstruction Era following the war, Southerners struggled with these changes and developed new ways of life. As you read this chapter, you will learn about:

After the Civil War, many cities in the South lay in ruins

Early Presidents of the Young Republic

After independence, early American leaders sought to strengthen the nation by developing a policy of westward expansion. George Washington, the nation's first President, warned Americans against becoming entangled in European wars. The foreign policy of the early American Presidents became one of cautious neutrality towards Europe.

The Civil War

When Abraham Lincoln was elected President in 1860, Southern states seceded from the Union and formed the Confederate States of America. The North's larger population, manufacturing facilities, and greater naval power enabled it to win the long and bloody war that followed. During the conflict, Lincoln issued the Emancipation Proclamation, which freed many enslaved people in the South.

Reconstruction Era

To re-enter the Union, Southern states had to approve the 14th Amendment, enabling the federal government to protect the rights of Americans from the acts of state governments. Congress imposed military rule and Reconstruction governments on the South. After the end of Reconstruction, Southern state governments introduced racial segregation and denied African Americans the right to vote and other rights.

In studying this period, you should focus on the following questions:

❖ What were the goals of the early American Presidents?
❖ What were the causes of the Civil War?
❖ How did the South cope with the problems of the Reconstruction Era?
❖ How did African Americans lose their rights following Reconstruction?

SECTION 1

THREE PRESIDENTS OF THE YOUNG REPUBLIC

In this section you will read about three of our nation's early Presidents. You will learn how, through their leadership, the country grew and developed.

THINK ABOUT IT

Historians have written that George Washington, Thomas Jefferson and Andrew Jackson were three of America's most important Presidents. Which one do you consider the most important? _____ Explain. _____

_____

Important Terms and Concepts: As you read this section, look for the following:

- ✦ Cabinet
- ✦ Hamilton's Financial Plan
- ✦ Political Parties
- ✦ Protective Tariff

- ✦ Neutrality
- ✦ Washington's Farewell Address
- ✦ Louisiana Purchase
- ✦ War of 1812

To help you find these terms, this symbol ✦ appears in the margin where the term is first explained.

PRESIDENT GEORGE WASHINGTON, 1789-1797

After the Constitution was ratified, George Washington was elected the nation's first President. Two major problems facing Washington were the formation of a government and the fact that the nation's treasury was empty.

WASHINGTON'S DOMESTIC POLICY

> **Note:** *Domestic policy* refers to the steps a President takes to deal with problems within the United States. *Foreign policy* concerns relations with other countries. war

economy health taxes

FORMING A GOVERNMENT (1789)

The Constitution allowed the President to appoint people to be in charge of executive departments, but did not state what these departments were. To help carry out the many jobs facing him, Washington created four executive departments. He appointed a Secretary of the Treasury, a Secretary of State, a Secretary of War, and an Attorney General. They began meeting in a

◆ group that has come to be known as the **Cabinet**. Every President since Washington has followed this precedent (*an action that becomes a way of doing things in the future*). Over the years, as the national government assumed new duties, new departments were created.

ANALYSIS

How many of today's Cabinet members can you name? Fill in the ones you know. Use an almanac to help you with the ones you do not know.

THE CURRENT PRESIDENTIAL CABINET

Department	Created by	Year	Who is the current occupant?
State	Washington	1789	_____
Treasury	Washington	1789	_____
Justice	Washington	1789	_____
Interior	Taylor	1849	_____
Agriculture	Harrison	1889	_____
Commerce	T. Roosevelt	1903	_____
Labor	Wilson	1913	_____
Defense	Truman	1947	_____
Housing and Urban Development	Johnson	1965	_____
Transportation	Johnson	1966	_____
Energy	Carter	1977	_____
Health and Human Services	Carter	1977	_____
Education	Carter	1979	_____
Veterans Affairs	G.H.W. Bush	1989	_____
Homeland Security	G.W. Bush	2003	_____

Note: The Vice President is also a member of the Cabinet.

RAISING MONEY

The new nation faced a large debt from the Revolutionary War. The job of finding solutions to the nation's economic problems was given to **Alexander Hamilton**, the new Secretary of the Treasury. Hamilton drew up a four-part financial program.

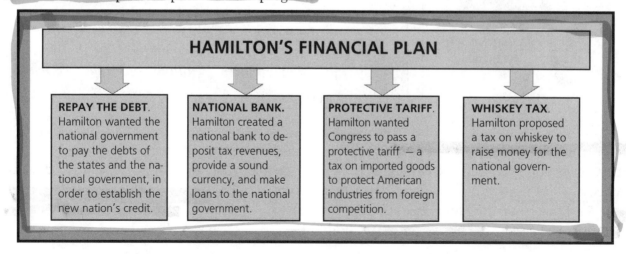

HAMILTON'S FINANCIAL PLAN

REPAY THE DEBT. Hamilton wanted the national government to pay the debts of the states and the national government, in order to establish the new nation's credit.

NATIONAL BANK. Hamilton created a national bank to deposit tax revenues, provide a sound currency, and make loans to the national government.

PROTECTIVE TARIFF. Hamilton wanted Congress to pass a protective tariff — a tax on imported goods to protect American industries from foreign competition.

WHISKEY TAX. Hamilton proposed a tax on whiskey to raise money for the national government.

Thomas Jefferson, the Secretary of State, opposed the plan. Jefferson and his followers believed that the plan favored the wealthy and hurt the majority of Americans, who were farmers.

THE FORMATION OF POLITICAL PARTIES

The differences between the followers of Hamilton and Jefferson grew greater. This split over ideas about how the government should operate led Jefferson and Hamilton to organize their followers into America's first **political parties** (*groups that try to elect their members to government offices so they can pass laws favorable to their ideas*). Hamilton's followers were known as the **Federalists,** and the supporters of Jefferson called themselves **Democratic-Republicans**.

Alexander Hamilton

DEFEAT OF THE PROTECTIVE TARIFF

Although Hamilton was successful in getting most of his plan passed in Congress, he failed in his attempt to pass a strong **protective tariff**. It would have raised duties (*taxes*), increasing the price of foreign goods and helping American producers to sell their products on the home market. The Southern states were opposed to it because they felt it would only benefit the industrial North.

THE WHISKEY REBELLION (1794)

West of the Appalachian Mountains, farmers often converted their grain into whiskey before shipping it to market. It was cheaper to transport whiskey in barrels over the mountain trails than to carry bushels of grain. The Whiskey Tax caused great resentment among these farmers. When farmers on the Pennsylvania frontier refused to pay the tax, Washington called up the militia and Hamilton personally led them in putting down the rebellion.

WASHINGTON'S FOREIGN POLICY

THE PROCLAMATION OF NEUTRALITY (1793)

As a new nation, the United States was militarily weak and feared losing its independence to a strong European nation. When war between France and Britain broke out in 1793 (*as a result of the French Revolution*), many Americans worried that the U.S. might be drawn into the war. To calm fears, President Washington adopted a policy of **neutrality**. This policy stated that the U.S. would avoid taking sides in European disputes and not become involved in foreign wars.

TREATIES WITH EUROPEAN POWERS

Even though the British had signed a peace treaty with their former colonies in 1783, they still regularly seized American ships and searched them for deserters from the British Navy. Washington, fearing war with Great Britain, sent **John Jay** to London to resolve these difficulties. A treaty was signed, but the British made few concessions. The treaty said nothing about seizing American sailors as British deserters. Spain also concluded a treaty with the United States. Spain and the U.S. agreed on the northern boundary of Florida. Spain gave Americans permission to navigate the Mississippi River and to deposit goods on the docks of New Orleans. These rights were essential to Western farmers, who used this route to ship their crops to market.

John Trumbull, Painter

The camera was not yet invented when the American Revolution took place. The American people witnessed the whole series of events by way of scenes painted by John Trumbull. His paintings romanticized and dramatized the battles of the American Revolution. The colonists who fought in the battles for independence always appeared as heroes. In addition, Trumbull was well known for painting inspiring portraits of most of the nation's early leaders.

◆ WASHINGTON'S FAREWELL ADDRESS (1796)

After two terms in office, Washington decided not to run a third time. At the end of his Presidency, Washington advised Congress that the United States should be cautious about entering into permanent alliances with foreign countries. Washington wanted the nation to devote itself to developing its trade and assuming leadership of the Western Hemisphere. This message has become known as **Washington's Farewell Address**.

PRESIDENT THOMAS JEFFERSON, 1801-1809

Jefferson was the leader of the Democratic-Republican Party. As a young man, he had written the Declaration of Independence. From 1784 to 1789, he had witnessed the events leading up to the revolution in France. He was a philosopher, writer, architect and inventor, as well as a politician.

JEFFERSON'S VIEWS ON GOVERNMENT

Jefferson called his election as President the **Revolution of 1800,** because he believed it marked a turning point in the direction the nation was moving. Jefferson believed the best government was a weak government. He opposed giving special privileges to the wealthy. He vowed to make government more democratic by representing the interests of ordinary citizens. Jefferson had strong sympathies for the common farmer, believing in equal justice for all men. When he became President, he set about reducing the size of the army, halting plans for naval expansion, and lowering the costs of government.

◆ THE LOUISIANA PURCHASE (1803)

Jefferson had always dreamed of a large America. He had an opportunity to realize his dreams with the purchase of the Louisiana Territory. Napoleon, the ruler of France, offered to sell it to the United States for $15 million. Although President Jefferson was uncertain whether the Constitution allowed the federal government to buy territory, he went ahead with the purchase. The Louisiana Territory doubled the size of the United States. Jefferson sent **Meriwether Lewis** and **William Clark** to explore the region and report on the Native American Indians they met. The expedition lasted two years. Lewis and Clark pushed westward all the way to the Pacific Ocean.

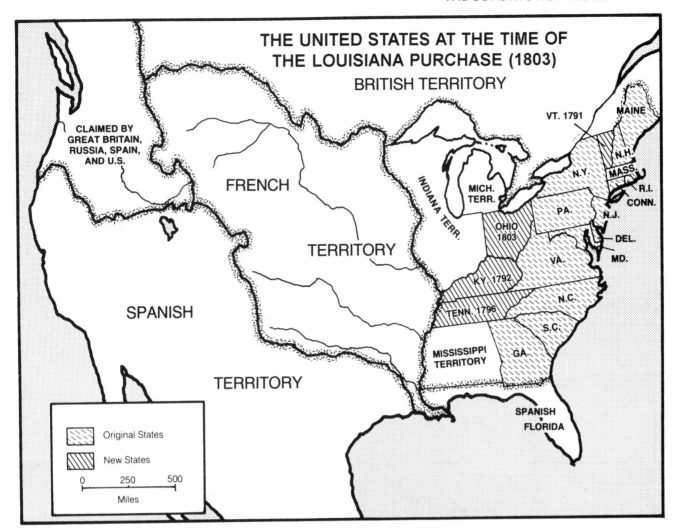

THE UNITED STATES AT THE TIME OF
THE LOUISIANA PURCHASE (1803)

EMBARGO ACT OF 1807

British warships continued to stop American ships to search for deserters from the British Navy. This humiliated Americans and put pressure on Jefferson to act. Trying to avoid war, Jefferson proposed and Congress passed the **Embargo Act**, which stated that American ships would no longer carry food to Europe. Jefferson hoped this act would force Europeans to respect America's rights as a neutral. Jefferson's policies succeeded in keeping the U.S. out of war during his Presidency.

THE WAR OF 1812

Three years after Jefferson's Presidency ended, America was finally drawn into conflict with England in the **War of 1812**. U.S. forces tried unsuccessfully to invade Canada. British troops briefly ✦ occupied Washington, D.C. and burned the White House. In 1814, a peace was signed which left things much as they had been before the war, except that the British stopped seizing American ships to search for British deserters.

PRESIDENT ANDREW JACKSON, 1829-1837

One of the great heroes of the War of 1812 was General **Andrew Jackson**, who helped to defeat British forces at the **Battle of New Orleans** in 1815.

JACKSON BECOMES PRESIDENT

Andrew Jackson's election in 1828 marked a turning point in American history. He was the first President who was not born to wealth. Coming from the state of Tennessee, he was also the first President not from an Eastern state.

THE AGE OF JACKSONIAN DEMOCRACY

Most of the authors of the Constitution feared "mob rule." They believed that only the most educated people should hold public office. They counted on various protections to prevent the new government from becoming controlled by the uninformed or uneducated. For example, most states had special laws which allowed only white male property owners to vote. This changed with Jackson's election, which has been called the **Revolution of 1828** because of the many democratic changes that followed. Jackson believed he was a direct representative of the people.

Andrew Jackson

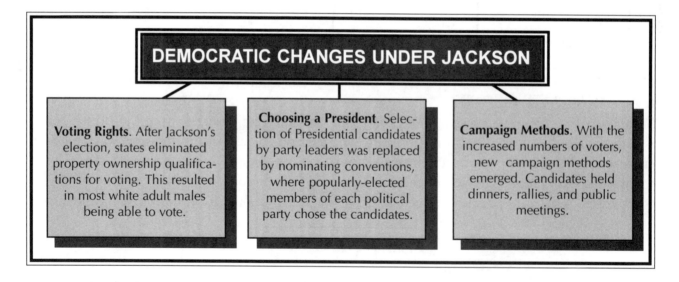

DEMOCRATIC CHANGES UNDER JACKSON

Voting Rights. After Jackson's election, states eliminated property ownership qualifications for voting. This resulted in most white adult males being able to vote.

Choosing a President. Selection of Presidential candidates by party leaders was replaced by nominating conventions, where popularly-elected members of each political party chose the candidates.

Campaign Methods. With the increased numbers of voters, new campaign methods emerged. Candidates held dinners, rallies, and public meetings.

JACKSON CREATES A POWERFUL PRESIDENCY

Jackson believed that the President was the people's most important voice in government. He therefore favored a strong Presidency. When elected, he introduced what became known as the **spoils system**. Under this system, government officials who had served under a previous President were replaced with the people who had worked on the campaign to elect the new President. Jackson argued that the duties of public office were so plain and clear that any intelligent man could fill them. He believed that it was good to change office-holders because more people would then get experience in government. Finally, Jackson thought that a group of permanent government officials was likely to become corrupt.

JACKSON DECLARES WAR ON THE BANK

Washington had introduced a National Bank as part of Hamilton's financial plan. Jackson disliked the National Bank because he thought it gave an unfair monopoly to the rich and powerful. Although the Bank was found to be constitutional by the Supreme Court, Jackson decided to eliminate it. When Jackson was re-elected in 1832, he removed all federal deposits from the National Bank, effectively destroying the Bank. He placed these funds in state banks. He felt that state banks were more willing to lend money to farmers, and less open to corruption.

ANALYSIS

The following cartoon first appeared in the 1830s during the Presidency of Andrew Jackson.

1. How is President Jackson dressed? _____

   _____

2. What object is he holding? _____

   Why? _____

3. What is he standing on? _____

4. What do you think is the main idea of the cartoon? _____

   _____

THE RISE OF LABOR

During Jackson's Presidency, a new industrial society began to emerge in the U.S. There was an increased use of machines and a shift from working at home and in small shops to working in factories. This development, known as the **Industrial Revolution**, led to new industries, expanded transportation and rapidly growing cities. Many workers welcomed the Industrial Revolution because it meant more jobs and higher wages. However, by the 1830s and 1840s, labor conditions began to worsen, as workers became increasingly dependent on factory owners. Often workers were required to put in 16-hour days in crowded, poorly lit and unsafe factories. As worker discontent grew, labor organizations developed in an attempt

Early factories were often built alongside rivers, to make use of the water power

to improve wages and working conditions. Andrew Jackson was popular among these early labor groups because they believed he represented the interests of the common man.

THE IMPACT OF GEOGRAPHY ON AMERICAN HISTORY

The Erie Canal, completed in 1825, followed ancient Native American trails through the Mohawk Valley, connecting the Hudson River to Lake Erie. It was a natural link between the Central Lowlands and the Atlantic Coastal Plain. The canal made it possible to ship goods by water from the Great Lakes all the way down to New York City. The canal made huge profits from the tolls (*fees*) it collected. The cost of shipping a

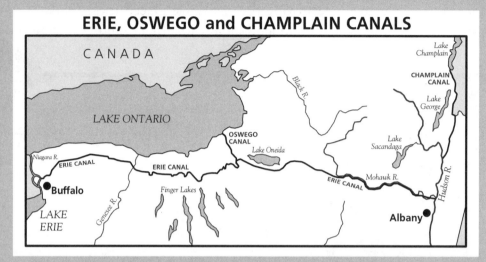

ERIE, OSWEGO and CHAMPLAIN CANALS

ton of wheat fell from $100 to less than $5. Midwestern farmers could ship their goods to Eastern markets. New York City became the fastest-growing city in the nation.

AN AGE OF REFORM

The period of Jacksonian Democracy saw the rise of several reform movements. **Horace Mann** helped develop free, public elementary schools. **Dorothea Dix** fought for prison reforms: she demanded better conditions in jails, an end to whipping and imprisonment for debts, and better treatment of the mentally ill.

SUMMING UP: THREE PRESIDENTS OF THE YOUNG REPUBLIC

When George Washington became the nation's first President, he hoped to unify the nation while avoiding dangerous alliances with foreign countries that might threaten the new nation's independence. Thomas Jefferson helped the nation to prosper, and doubled its size. Under President Andrew Jackson, a number of democratic reforms were introduced.

THINKING IT OVER

Now that you have read the previous section, check who you think was the greatest President among these three, and explain why:

❏ George Washington: _____

❏ Thomas Jefferson: _____

❏ Andrew Jackson: _____

CHECKING YOUR UNDERSTANDING

Directions: Complete each of the following cards. Then answer the multiple-choice questions.

NEUTRALITY

Define it: _not getting involved_

Why did Washington recommend it? _____

he thinks it we make more drama.

LOUISIANA PURCHASE

What was it? _____

What was its effect? _____

_____

---

1 Which statement concerning the President's Cabinet is correct?
   1 Its members are elected by the voters.
   2 Its size has remained unchanged.
   3 The President must follow its decisions.
   4 New departments have been added over the years. *(circled)*

2 Which statement best summarizes a belief of President Thomas Jefferson's?
   1 Only the wealthy should serve in government.
   2 The nation must have a powerful central government.
   3 All men are entitled to equal justice. *(marked)*
   4 The United States should play the role of a world leader.

3 The American Revolution and the War of 1812 were similar in that both
   1 led to the principle of "no taxation without representation"
   2 helped lead to the downfall of the Federalist Party
   3 were fought against the British *(circled)*
   4 represented defeats for the United States

4 A believer in "Jacksonian democracy" would have supported
   1 rule by a royal family
   2 government service open to all
   3 the elimination of all job training
   4 reduced military spending

5 The "spoils system" can best be defined as
   1 replacing officeholders with members of your own political party
   2 stopping one branch of government from becoming too powerful
   3 limiting the term of office of Presidential candidates
   4 allowing people to vote for their representatives in Congress

6 Which best represents the advice George Washington gave in his Farewell Address? The United States must
   1 build a large army
   2 establish a global empire
   3 join many military alliances
   4 avoid involvement in European alliances and wars

SECTION 2

THE CIVIL WAR, 1861-1865

In this section you will read about the Civil War and how it
changed the nation. The primary goals of preserving
national unity and ending slavery were achieved, but
at a tremendous cost in lives and property.

THINK ABOUT IT

What do you think was the main cause of the U.S. Civil War? _____

_____ Explain. _____

Important Terms and Concepts: As you read this section, look for the following:

- ✦ Civil War
- ✦ Sectionalism
- ✦ Abolitionists

- ✦ Dred Scott Decision
- ✦ Emancipation Proclamation
- ✦ Thirteenth Amendment

CAUSES OF THE CIVIL WAR

✦ The **Civil War** was one the bloodiest wars in American history. Great events such as the Civil
War usually have many causes. Here we briefly examine some of them: sectionalism, slavery,
states' rights, and the breakdown of compromise.

SECTIONALISM
During the early 1800s, the Northeast, South, and Northwest sections of the United States each
developed their own different ways of life.

THE NORTHEAST	THE SOUTH	THE NORTHWEST
This section became a center of manufacturing, shipping, fishing and small farms. The Northeast witnessed the first growth of the new class of factory workers. Factories and cities were beginning to change lifestyles dramatically.	The major institution was slavery. Although most Southerners did not own slaves, much of the South's economy was based on profits obtained by using slave labor on large plantations, and growing export crops such as cotton.	This section — now Wisconsin, Illinois, Indiana, Michigan, and Ohio — became the breadbasket of the nation. Its grain was shipped by river and canal to the Northeast and South. Most people in this area were small farmers.

✦ These different ways of living led to **sectionalism** — the greater loyalty many Americans felt toward their own section (*region*) than to the country as a whole. Such differences played an important part in leading to the Civil War.

DISAGREEMENTS OVER STATES' RIGHTS

Many Southerners believed in **states' rights** — the idea that since the states had created the federal government, each state could reject federal laws within its territory or even leave the Union (*the United States*) if it wanted to. Northerners argued instead that the Constitution was the work of the American people, and that states did not have the right to leave the Union.

SLAVERY

One of the major institutions in the South was slavery. It was also the most explosive issue. **Abolitionists** (*people who wanted to end slavery*) played an important role in persuading others of the evils of slavery. Among the most important abolitionists were **Frederick Douglass**, **Sojourner Truth**, **Harriet Tubman**, and **William Lloyd Garrison**.

In the 1840s the United States gained new territories as a result of a war with Mexico. A dilemma rose as to whether slavery should be allowed in these territories. Southerners felt that only by extending slavery could they preserve the balance between slave states and free states in the Senate. Many Northerners were shocked at the possibility of the further expansion of slavery.

FOCUS ON THE ARTS

Harriet Beecher Stowe, Author

In 1852, Harriet Beecher Stowe wrote *Uncle Tom's Cabin*, a novel about a loyal and loving slave named Tom. His master, facing financial problems, is forced to sell Tom to a slave trader. In the end, Tom dies, killed by his new master's cruel and vicious treatment. Although the book has been called overly sentimental, it affected millions of people around the world by pointing out the evils and brutality of slavery. Many began to question the morality of one person "owning" another.

THE BREAKDOWN OF COMPROMISE

To keep the Union together, the states had agreed to a series of compromises about the admission of "slave" and "free" states. The **Missouri Compromise of 1820** and the **Compromise of 1850** had kept the peace. However, in the 1850s, new events destroyed the earlier compromises. This breakdown of compromise made conflict between the North and South inevitable.

- **Kansas-Nebraska Act**. In 1854, Congress introduced a law that allowed settlers in these two new territories to vote on whether they wanted slavery or not. This resulted in killing and bloodshed between those favoring and opposing slavery.

- **Dred Scott Decision**. In 1857, the Supreme Court ruled that Congress could not prohibit slavery in any of the new territories. The Court argued that slaves were property, and that Congress had no right to take away a slaveholder's property.

- **John Brown's Raid**. In 1859, John Brown, an abolitionist, began a slave revolt. His uprising was quickly crushed, but the attempt stirred a sense of alarm among Southerners. Their fears of future slave revolts turned many Southerners away from compromise as a means of settling conflicts.

U.S. During the Civil War: 1861–1865

UNION (FREE) STATES

BORDER STATES
LOYAL TO UNION

CONFEDERATE STATES
OF AMERICA

HIGHLIGHTS OF THE CIVIL WAR

In 1860, **Abraham Lincoln** was elected President. As a member of the new **Republican Party**, he had campaigned against the Dred Scott decision and the extension of slavery to new territories. Although Lincoln said he would allow slavery to continue in those states where it existed, most Southerners did not believe him. Soon after his election, the Southern states declared that they were no longer part of the United States. They formed their own government, calling it the **Confederate States of America**. Lincoln declared that he would take all necessary steps to keep the United States together. In 1861, when Confederate troops attacked Fort Sumter in South Carolina, the fighting began. The Civil War divided many American families — in some cases, family members fought on opposite sides.

The South had the advantage of fighting a defensive war, but the North had great advantages in population, resources, and transportation. Despite this, it took the Union (*as the North was called*) almost four years to defeat the Confederacy.

Abraham Lincoln

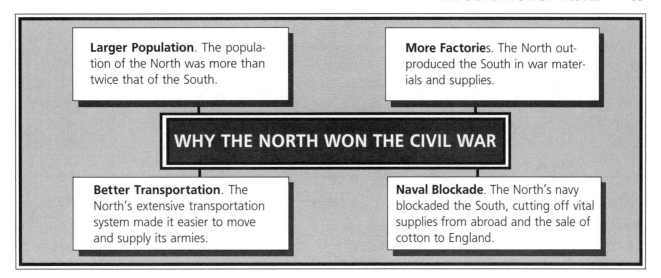

One of the most important events of the Civil War was Lincoln's issuance of the **Emancipation Proclamation** in 1862. According to the Proclamation, all enslaved people living in states fighting against the Union were declared free on January 1, 1863. Slavery remained legal in the border states within the Union — Missouri, Kentucky, West Virginia, Maryland and Delaware.

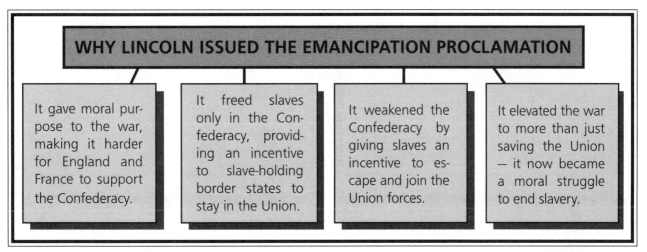

Unsure whether Lincoln had the power — according to the Constitution — to give enslaved people their freedom, Congress proposed the **Thirteenth Amendment**. Its ratification in 1865 ended slavery throughout the United States.

FOCUS ON THE ARTS

Matthew Brady, Photographer

In the mid-1800s, photography was beginning to be used for recording events. When the war began, Matthew Brady was given permission to travel with Union soldiers. He set out to create a photographic history of the Civil War. His remarkable collection of photographs document the people and the events that took place during the "War Between the States." They have allowed future generations to view with their own eyes the suffering, destruction, and devastation of the Civil War.

SUMMING UP: THE CIVIL WAR

The war kept the Union together and ended slavery, but at a significant cost: thousands of people were killed or injured, and the South lay in ruins. The industrialization of the North was pushed forward, but serious disputes arose over how the South should be rebuilt.

THINKING IT OVER

Now that you have completed this section, what do you believe was the main cause of the

Civil War? _____ Explain. _____

_____

CHECKING YOUR UNDERSTANDING

Directions: Complete the following cards. Then answer the multiple-choice questions.

ABOLITIONISTS

What did they believe? _____

Name two abolitionists: 1. _____

_____ 2._____

CIVIL WAR

What was it? _____

List one cause and one result of the Civil War:

Cause: _____ Result: _____

1 The term "abolitionist" described a person who
   1 believed in free trade
   2 opposed foreign alliances
   3 wanted to end slavery
   4 supported obtaining colonies

2 In the term "Civil War," the word "civil" means
   1 a riot in society
   2 among citizens of the same country
   3 polite behavior
   4 a type of government

3 A major cause of the Civil War was the issue of
   1 sending black Americans to Africa
   2 taxes paid on slaves
   3 whether or not the states had a right to secede from the Union
   4 the kidnapping of U.S. sailors

4 The major purpose of the Emancipation Proclamation was to
   1 defeat the British in the Revolutionary War
   2 justify the actions of politicians in the South
   3 free slaves in the Confederacy
   4 provide for the creation of new state governments

5 A major result of the Civil War was that
   1 slavery was prohibited
   2 the U.S. won its independence
   3 states won the right to secede
   4 women gained the right to vote

6 The 13th Amendment is important because it
   1 ended slavery in the United States
   2 granted women the right to vote
   3 abolished the poll tax
   4 guaranteed free speech to all

SECTION 3

RECONSTRUCTION AND ITS AFTERMATH

In this section you will read about the Reconstruction Era, the name given by historians to the period of American history following the Civil War. During this time, the nation devoted much of its energies to rebuilding the South.

THINK ABOUT IT

Section 3 is divided into four main parts. What do you think each of these parts is about? Look at pages 89-92 for the answers. (*To understand outlining, read the Skill Builder below.*)

Part I ——————————————   Part III ——————————————

Part II ——————————————   Part IV ——————————————

Important terms and concepts: As you read this section, look for the following:

- ✦ Reconstruction Plans   ✦ Jim Crow Laws
- ✦ Black Codes   ✦ Plessy v. Ferguson

SKILL BUILDER: UNDERSTANDING OUTLINES

What Is an Outline?
An outline is a summary showing how a topic (*or major idea*) is divided up into smaller units. The main purpose of an outline is to show the relationships between a topic and its subtopics. Outlining also helps to organize and guide a writer's thinking.

Keys to Understanding an Outline
To understand an outline, you must look at its major parts:

Title. The title is like an umbrella or overview covering the main topic.

Format. Outlines follow a specific format so that you can easily understand how the topic is divided up. Usually, the first subtopics are given Roman numerals (I, II, III). When these sub-topics are further divided, they are given capital letters (A, B, C). If the sub-divisions are divided again, they are given Arabic numbers (1, 2, 3). As an example, let's see how Section 2 of this chapter was organized:

THE CIVIL WAR: 1861-1865

We could write many different things about this topic. To narrow down the things we want to cover, an outline uses sub-topics like this one:

I. Causes of the Civil War

The outline now tells us we will be looking at the causes of the Civil War. But what will be written about the causes of the Civil War?

I. Causes of the Civil War
A. Sectionalism
B. Disagreements over States' Rights
C. Slavery
D. Breakdown of Compromise

The outline now shows us that there are at least four causes that brought about the Civil War. To tell more about any of these causes, the outline would need further sub-topics:

I. Causes of the Civil War
A. Sectionalism
1. The Northeast developed factories
2. The South exported cotton grown by slaves
3. Northwestern farmers grew food

Notice how outlining shows you which details support or explain the "big" ideas or major facts.

Interpreting an Outline

Remember that in an outline you start with a large idea and break it down into smaller and smaller units. In our example, each smaller unit helps to develop the larger concept. Understanding outlines helps you to answer data-based questions on state examinations, and is also a useful tool to organize your thoughts when writing an essay.

Outline-type questions may also appear as follows:

In an outline, one of these is the main topic and the others are sub-topics. Which is the main topic?

1 Election of Abraham Lincoln
2 Causes of the Civil War
3 Sectionalism
4 Slavery

Remember that the main topic is the broadest one covering all of the smaller ones. In this question, the main topic is the "Causes of the Civil War" because the other three choices are all items that led to the start of the Civil War. Now that you have learned about outlines, it will be easier to follow how the present section is organized. After you have read this section, fill in the blank outline at the end, on page 93.

THE DEBATE OVER RECONSTRUCTION PLANS

After the Civil War ended, the South was in ruins. One of the main problems facing the national government was to determine the conditions under which the Southern states would be admitted back into the Union. Another problem was how to help the freed slaves.

Photo by Matthew Brady of the ruins of Charleston, South Carolina

THE PRESIDENTIAL PLAN

President Lincoln believed that the Southern states should be given easy treatment to regain their loyalty and to help rebuild national unity. Lincoln did not live long enough to carry out his plan, however, because he was assassinated just when the war ended. The new President, **Andrew Johnson**, sought to continue Lincoln's proposed plan.

Meanwhile, the Southern states were slow to extend voting rights and liberties to the **freedmen** (*former slaves freed by the Thirteenth Amendment*). The federal government set up the **Freedmen's Bureau**, but Southern states passed new **Black Codes** to regulate the lives of former slaves. Their aim was to preserve traditional Southern society despite the end of slavery. For example, the Black Codes made it illegal for freedmen to hold public office, to travel freely, or to serve on juries.

THE CONGRESSIONAL PLAN

Northerners were outraged at the Black Codes. As a result, Congress refused to recognize the new Southern state governments. A group of members of Congress known as the **Radical Republicans** wanted African Americans to be granted full equality. Their plan called for passing a Civil Rights Bill and imposing military rule on the South. President Johnson opposed Congress's plan, believing it was the President's responsibility to decide under what conditions the Southern states should be readmitted. Many in Congress disagreed, stating that the Constitution gave Congress, not the President, the power to admit states into the Union.

THE POLITICS OF RECONSTRUCTION

PASSAGE OF THE FOURTEENTH AMENDMENT

To make sure that the Civil Rights Act would not be held unconstitutional, the Radical Republicans in Congress rewrote the act as the **Fourteenth Amendment**. Besides granting citizenship to the former slaves, this amendment also prohibited state governments from denying any American the "rights and privileges" of citizens, including a fair trial and equal protection of the laws. Southern states were forced to ratify the Fourteenth Amendment before they were re-admitted into the Union.

CONGRESS IMPEACHES THE PRESIDENT

When Congress passed a law prohibiting the President from dismissing members of his Cabinet, Johnson fired his Secretary of War. Congress tried to remove Johnson from office, using a process known as **impeachment** (*the political process of trying to remove a public official*). The House of Representatives voted to impeach Johnson, but not enough members of the Senate agreed to convict and remove him. Johnson finished out his term as President.

RECONSTRUCTION GOVERNMENTS IN THE SOUTH

While the South remained under military occupation, new leaders gained control of the governments in the Southern states. Some of these leaders were Northerners who came south, and were called **carpetbaggers**. Some carpetbaggers hoped to improve conditions for blacks, while others

The first black Senator and Representatives

came to make money for themselves in business. Other leaders were Southern whites who had opposed the Confederacy in the Civil War. They were called **scalawags**. A third group was made up of freedmen, who could vote and hold office during Reconstruction. These new state governments were both praised and criticized. Among the accomplishments of Reconstruction governments were the creation of new schools, rebuilding of roads and railroads, and passage of laws banning racial discrimination. Reconstruction governments were criticized when some dishonest leaders took government funds. Others wasted money on unnecessary programs.

EFFECTS OF RECONSTRUCTION ON THE SOUTHERN STATES

In 1877, Reconstruction officially ended when Northern troops were withdrawn from the South. Once again white Southerners took control of their governments, and moved to prevent African Americans from voting and participating in government.

ECONOMIC EFFECTS

Without the workforce provided by enslaved people, the plantation system fell apart and the economy of the South was forever changed. The failure to give freedmen their own plots of land after the Civil War meant that most African Americans in the South remained dependent on their former masters. Many freedmen became **sharecroppers**. Under this arrangement, plantation owners provided a cabin, a mule, tools and a plot of land to the sharecropper. In return, the sharecropper gave a large share of his crop to the landowner.

Southern agriculture gradually changed and improved. New methods of farming allowed people in the South to raise larger and more varied crops. Northerners invested large sums of money to build railroads and factories in the South. As a result, people began moving from farms to cities, looking for jobs.

SOCIAL EFFECTS

The social system that developed after the period of Reconstruction in the South was one of racial **segregation** (*separating blacks and whites in society*) and white supremacy. Most of the freedmen were uneducated, and this weakened their ability to compete with whites on equal terms. Secret societies like the **Ku Klux Klan** terrorized Southern blacks with threats and acts of violence against those who tried to assert their rights.

The Ku Klux Klan terrorized African Americans after Reconstruction

POLITICAL EFFECTS

Following Reconstruction, Southern state governments systematically stripped African Americans of their basic political and civil rights. They used a variety of methods:

Literacy Tests. Many freedmen, lacking a formal education, could not pass reading and writing tests. As a result, they were barred from voting.

Grandfather Clauses. People who were qualified to vote in 1867 could avoid literacy tests and poll taxes. This helped poor whites but not blacks, since they gained voting rights only in 1870.

METHODS USED IN THE SOUTH TO DENY AFRICAN AMERICANS THEIR RIGHTS

Poll Taxes. African Americans could not afford to pay special voter registration fees, called poll taxes, and therefore were barred from voting.

Jim Crow Laws. Southern legislatures passed laws segregating blacks from whites in restaurants, hotels, and theaters.

♦   In the case of **Plessy v. Ferguson** (1896), the Supreme Court upheld the system of racial segregation established by Jim Crow laws. As a result of this decision, whites and African Americans in Southern states attended different schools, rode in separate railway cars, ate in different restaurants, used separate public toilets and water fountains, and swam at different public beaches.

AFRICAN AMERICAN LEADERS SPEAK OUT

African Americans reacted to these unfair conditions in different ways. Many began to move north. Others relied on their local black communities. Two important African-American leaders who spoke out publicly at this time were Booker T. Washington and W.E.B. Du Bois.

BOOKER T. WASHINGTON

Booker T. Washington was born into slavery just before the Civil War. In 1881, he founded the Tuskegee Institute in Alabama, a school for African Americans that focused on practical, job-related education. In his book *Up From Slavery*, he advised blacks that they should first prepare themselves to earn a decent living before they tried to gain equal rights. African Americans could do this, he said, by receiving training and becoming skilled at specific jobs. He held this view in part because he feared that immigrants coming to the United States would take away available jobs.

Booker T. Washington

W.E.B. Du Bois

W.E.B. DU BOIS

W.E.B. Du Bois received a Ph.D. in history from Harvard University in 1895, and became a prominent scholar. Unlike Booker T. Washington, Du Bois believed that African Americans should immediately begin the struggle for equal rights and not settle for an inferior social and economic position. In 1909, Du Bois helped form the **N.A.A.C.P.** (*National Association for the Advancement of Colored People*). This organization, working through the courts, took a number of steps to fight for the rights of African Americans. Du Bois was a director of the N.A.A.C.P. for twenty years, and edited its official publication, *The Crisis*.

SUMMING UP: RECONSTRUCTION AND ITS AFTERMATH

During the Reconstruction period, the nation devoted its energies to rebuilding the South and settling major political, economic, and social problems left by the Civil War. Although African Americans were freed from slavery, state governments in the South deprived them of their civil and political rights once Reconstruction ended.

THINKING IT OVER

Now that you have read this section, fill in the blanks in the outline below. The outline has already been started for you. If you need to refresh your memory about writing outlines, re-read the Skill Builder on pages 87 and 88.

RECONSTRUCTION AND ITS AFTERMATH

I. THE BATTLE OVER RECONSTRUCTION PLANS

    A. THE PRESIDENTIAL PLAN

    B. _____

II. _____

    A. _____

    B. _____

    C. _____

III. EFFECTS OF RECONSTRUCTION ON THE SOUTHERN STATES

    A. _____

    B. _____

    C. _____

        1. Literacy Tests

        2. _____

        3. _____

        4. _____

IV. AFRICAN AMERICAN LEADERS SPEAK OUT

    A. _____

    B. _____

CHECKING YOUR UNDERSTANDING

Directions: Complete the following cards. Then answer the multiple-choice questions.

```
RECONSTRUCTION PLANS

Name two: 1. _____

2. _____

How did they differ? _____
```

```
JIM CROW LAWS

What were they? _____

How did they try to accomplish their goal?

_____
```

1 A term paper containing the topics "Jim Crow" laws, "carpetbaggers" and the Ku Klux Klan would probably be about the
 1 thirteen colonies
 2 American Revolution
 3 Civil War
 4 Reconstruction Era

2 The Black Codes and Jim Crow laws were similar in that they both sought to
 1 expand the power of the national government
 2 deny African Americans equal treatment with white people
 3 reduce the power of state governments
 4 prevent segregation

3 Following the Civil War, a major concern of the United States government was
 1 passing a Bill of Rights
 2 preserving slavery
 3 rebuilding the South
 4 creating a national government

4 Southern segregation laws sought to
 1 raise educational levels for blacks
 2 give blacks full citizenship
 3 increase the number of black Congressmen
 4 keep blacks separated from whites

5 The Reconstruction Period was a time in United States history when the
 1 U.S. Constitution was written
 2 President was George Washington
 3 North and the South fought a war
 4 South was rebuilt

6 A primary goal of the Ku Klux Klan was to
 1 impeach President Lincoln
 2 maintain segregation in the South
 3 help integrate the South
 4 promote equality among all citizens

7 Which development caused the other three?
 1 The Reconstruction Era began.
 2 The North won the Civil War.
 3 Freedmen gained the right to vote.
 4 African Americans participated in government.

8 Booker T. Washington believed that African Americans should
 1 all be sent to Africa
 2 concentrate on job training to improve their lives
 3 use force to secure their civil rights
 4 refuse all attempts at integration

PROFILES IN HISTORY

BENJAMIN FRANKLIN (STATESMAN)

In addition to helping to write the Declaration of Independence and the Constitution, Franklin was a scientist. He conducted experiments and invented bifocal glasses, a stove, and a lightning rod. An author as well, he wrote *Poor Richard's Almanack*. He served the nation as ambassador to France, and as the first U.S. Postmaster General.

ANTONIO JOSE MARTINEZ (PRIEST)

Antonio Jose Martinez was born in 1793 in New Mexico territory. At age 29, he established the first public school there. The school grew in importance and popularity, and attracted students from throughout the territory. In 1835, Father Martinez brought in the first printing press, using it to publish a newspaper. The paper, like its editor, Father Martinez, supported religious freedom, the separation of church and state, and the need to protect farmers from the abuses of large landowners.

HENRY DAVID THOREAU (ESSAYIST)

Thoreau believed it was his duty to disobey unjust laws. In protest against the nation's war with Mexico, Thoreau refused to pay his taxes, and was sent to jail. Thoreau felt people should follow their conscience when it conflicted with government laws. His ideas on civil disobedience were later adopted by Martin Luther King, Jr. and the Civil Rights Movement for African Americans.

GEORGE WASHINGTON CARVER (BOTANIST)

Carver was an African-American scientist who trained at the Tuskegee Institute. His discoveries helped to revolutionize agriculture by teaching scientific farming. Farmers learned to rotate their crops in order to prevent erosion of the soil. Carver also instructed them about planting peanuts, sweet potatoes, clover and other crops to replace nitrates in the soil. Carver is credited with developing hundreds of new products and helping to end the South's dependence on cotton.

NOTE: *Beginning with this chapter, you will find a section called* **The Constitution at Work** *at the end of each chapter. These sections focus on the most important amendments, laws, and Supreme Court cases of each time period.*

THE CONSTITUTION AT WORK

During this time period three amendments, often called the **Civil War Amendments**, were added to the Constitution:

THIRTEENTH AMENDMENT (1865)
Prohibited slavery.

FOURTEENTH AMENDMENT (1868)
Made United States citizens of those who were formerly enslaved. It also required all states to give their citizens, including formerly enslaved people, "due process of law" and "equal protection of the laws."

FIFTEENTH AMENDMENT (1870)
Gave the right to vote to all African American males, including those who had formerly been enslaved.

KEY AMEND-MENTS

JIM CROW LAWS (1881-1890)
"Jim Crow" laws, passed by many Southern states, forced blacks and whites to use separate public facilities. This separation of the races was called **segregation**. Segregation was accomplished by creating separate schools and separate sections of streetcars, railroads, parks, playgrounds and beaches for African Americans and whites. Jim Crow laws were upheld by the U.S. Supreme Court (see below).

KEY LAWS

John Marshall was Chief Justice of the Supreme Court from 1801 to 1835. He helped to expand the power of the national government over the state governments, and laid the groundwork for establishing the importance of the federal courts. The decisions in the cases below helped create a feeling that the U.S. was a nation, not a group of individual states. Among Marshall's most important decisions were:

MARBURY vs. MADISON (1803)
Here the Court stated for the first time that it had the right to overturn a federal law which it believed was **unconstitutional** *(went against the rules and principles of the Constitution)*. This power, which is known as **judicial review**, greatly strengthened the Supreme Court.

McCULLOCH vs. MARYLAND (1819)
The Court ruled that a state could not tax an organization *(a bank, in this case)* that is part of the federal government. Marshall said the Constitution is the supreme law of the land; whenever state and federal laws conflict, the federal law has to be followed.

The following case was decided after Marshall was no longer Chief Justice:

PLESSY vs. FERGUSON (1896)
Plessy, an African American, was arrested when he refused to leave a "whites only" railroad car. He said that according to the 14th Amendment he had the right to ride in any railway car. The state said that the railroad provided "separate but equal" railway cars for people of different races. The Supreme Court agreed, saying that as long as conditions in the railway cars were equal, the state could separate African Americans and white people. This case allowed Southerners to continue to separate blacks and whites in many areas of life.

THE COURT SPEAKS

CHECKING YOUR UNDERSTANDING

Directions: Confirm your understanding of the important terms and concepts in this chapter. Check those you can explain. For those you are not sure of, find the ♦ symbol in the margin next to the term and review it.

- ❏ Cabinet
- ❏ Hamilton's Financial Plan
- ❏ Political Parties
- ❏ Protective Tariff
- ❏ Neutrality
- ❏ Washington's Farewell Address
- ❏ Louisiana Purchase
- ❏ Sectionalism
- ❏ Civil War
- ❏ Abolitionists
- ❏ Dred Scott Decision
- ❏ 13th Amendment
- ❏ Emancipation Proclamation
- ❏ Reconstruction Plans
- ❏ Black Codes
- ❏ Segregation
- ❏ Jim Crow Laws
- ❏ *Plessy v. Ferguson*

Directions: Fill in the information called for in the following organizers.

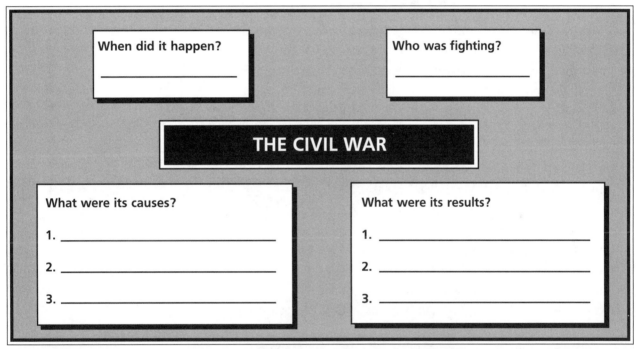

When did it happen?
_____

Who was fighting?
_____

THE CIVIL WAR

What were its causes?

1. _____

2. _____

3. _____

What were its results?

1. _____

2. _____

3. _____

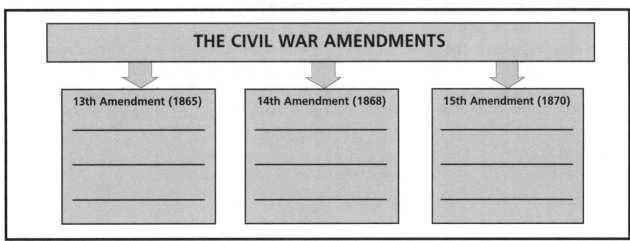

THE CIVIL WAR AMENDMENTS

13th Amendment (1865)
_____
_____
_____

14th Amendment (1868)
_____
_____
_____

15th Amendment (1870)
_____
_____
_____

TEST HELPER   LOOKING AT THE IMPACT OF GEOGRAPHY

Earlier in this book, you learned that the physical geography of the United States has had an important impact on the development of American history and culture. This section further explores the relationship between America's geography and history, to better prepare you to answer questions dealing with this subject.

LOCATION

Geographers often consider the **location** of a place. The importance of location may change over time as a result of changes in transportation and communications.

Native American Indians, for example, both benefited and suffered from a location that separated them from other civilizations. For centuries, Native American Indians were protected from people on other continents, but were also isolated from the technological innovations of Asia, Europe, and Africa. Because of improvements in ocean-going transportation, by 1492 the islands of the Caribbean, the Atlantic coast of North America, and the Native American Indian empires of Mexico and Peru were no longer beyond the reach of European explorers, conquerors, missionaries, and settlers. The larger population of Europe, their superior technology, and a host of new diseases like measles and small pox had a devastating impact on the Native American Indians.

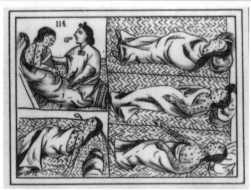

Many Aztecs died of smallpox, against which they had no immunity

PLACE

The characteristics of **place** — topography, climate, and natural resources — had an equally important effect on America's development. Europeans found a continent of largely unexploited natural resources with a much smaller population. These circumstances turned North America into a magnet for European colonization. In time, much of Europe's surplus population was willing to brave trans-Atlantic travel in order to share in the opportunities afforded by North America. These conditions also allowed the settlers to develop a society without a hereditary nobility, and encouraged individualism.

Topography and climate affected patterns of settlement as well. The first areas settled were along the Atlantic Coastal Plain. By the time of the American Revolution, pioneers were crossing the Appalachians and entering the Ohio River Valley. Settlements around the Great Lakes increased after the opening of the Erie Canal in 1825. This event likewise transformed the relative location of New York City, turning it into the "Gateway to the West." Farmers around the Great Lakes region could ship their goods to Buffalo, along the Erie Canal, and down the Hudson River to New York City, where they could be shipped to other states or across the Atlantic to Europe.

REGION

Even in early colonial times, three distinct American **regions** had emerged: the North, the South, and the West. Differences among these three regions led directly to the sectionalism of the early 1800s and eventually to the outbreak of the Civil War.

Because of differences in topography and climate, different ways of life emerged in each of these three regions. This in turn attracted different types of people, reinforcing differences in physical geography. The closest thing to an American hereditary nobility, for example, developed among the Planter class in the South, who owned large plantations worked by armies of slave laborers.

HUMAN-ENVIRONMENT INTERACTION

The location of key natural resources and important transportation routes dictated the location of cities and industries. Cities emerged at the hubs of several transportation routes, especially along the Atlantic seaboard, the Great Lakes, and great inland rivers. The rise of cities further transformed the landscape from forests and rolling plains to farms, towns, and cities.

Settlers interacted with the land by clearing out the trees, building homes and starting to farm.

The laying of railroad tracks in the North, and the greater development of Northern industry, played a crucial role in the North's triumph over the South in the Civil War. Later, Pennsylvania coal and the iron ore of the Mesabi range in Minnesota helped transform the Midwest into America's industrial heartland.

SHARPENING YOUR TEST-TAKING SKILLS

Examinations in U.S. history often include essay questions. An essay question tests your ability to answer a question in depth by organizing and presenting information in written form. The U.S. History and Government Regents Examination in New York State, for example, will contain two essay questions. One of these two essay questions will require you to focus on a particular theme or generalization. This is known as a **thematic essay question**.

Let's look at a typical thematic essay question:

Directions: Write a well-organized essay that includes an introduction, several paragraphs explaining your position, and a conclusion.

Theme: Divisive Issues in American History

> Throughout their history, Americans have been divided over important public issues.

Task:

> Choose **two** issues from your study of U.S. history and government.
>
> For *each* issue:
> - Describe how Americans were divided over it.
> - Explain how the issue was finally resolved.

You may use any examples from your study of U.S. history. Some suggestions you might wish to consider include: independence from Great Britain, ratifying the U.S. Constitution, slavery, secession of the Southern states, and readmission of the Southern states to the Union during Reconstruction.

You are *not* limited to these suggestions.

Notice that a thematic essay question opens with *directions* that tell you the form in which your answer must be written. The directions are followed by a *generalization*. Here, the general statement is about issues over which Americans have been divided. The question then presents a *task* to be completed. The task describes what you have to do to answer the question, and is related to the opening generalization. Finally, a group of *suggestions* provide examples you might use in your essay, although you are not limited to these.

WHAT IS A GENERALIZATION?

To answer a thematic essay question, you must understand what a generalization is and how to support it. **Generalizations** are powerful organizing tools that allow us to summarize large amounts of information in a simple form. To understand what a generalization is, first read the following list of facts:

> ➤ New York City borders the Atlantic Ocean.
> ➤ Albany is located on the Hudson River.
> ➤ Buffalo is next to Lake Erie.
> ➤ Geneva borders Seneca Lake.

These are four separate facts about cities in New York State. However, they have something in common: all of these cities are located next to a body of water. When a general statement identifies a common pattern, it is called a generalization. A generalization shows what several facts have in common. Let's see how this generalization might be presented in a diagram:

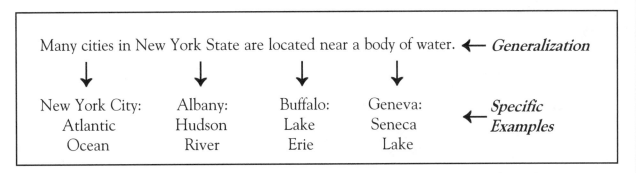

The specific examples support the generalization that many cities in New York State are located near a body of water. Thus, the key is to use specific examples to support the general statement.

WRITING A WELL-ORGANIZED ESSAY

Start by looking at the **Task** on page 100. Be sure you understand what you must do. It will be helpful if you get into the habit of underlining the "action words" in the Task. To refresh your memory about "action words" in essay questions, look back to pages 66-67. It is also useful to circle the *number of examples* that the Task requires you to use in support of your thesis statement or generalization.

NOTES FOR YOUR ESSAY
Making notes first can help you to organize your essay. The sample on the following page is based on the thematic essay question on page 100. Use this sample as your guide for writing notes:

The American people have been divided over important issues throughout U.S. history.

> *Reword the thematic generalization to write your thesis statement*

FIRST PART OF EACH TASK: Choose two issues

> *from Task*

Issues: (1) Slavery; (2) Readmission of Southern states

> *your choice*

Action Words: <u>Describe how</u>

> *from the question*

Specific Information:

> *from your knowledge of American history*

- **Slavery:** By the early 1800s, Southern states allowed slavery while Northern states did not. Abolitionists believed that owning a human being was immoral, and wanted to end slavery. Most Southerners argued that slaves were treated better than workers in Northern factories.

- **Readmission of Southern states**: After the Civil War, Lincoln and then Johnson wanted to make it easy for Southern states to rejoin the Union. Radical Republicans in Congress did not trust Southerners and wanted to guaranteed freedmen's rights before readmitting the Southern States.

SECOND PART OF EACH TASK:

Action Words: <u>Explain how</u>

> *from the question*

Specific Information:

> *from your knowledge of American history*

- The issue of slavery was finally resolved by the Civil War (1861-1865). After Lincoln was elected, Southern states seceded to preserve the slave system. Lincoln fought to preserve the Union. He also freed Southern slaves in the Emancipation Proclamation. Northern victory ensured the end of slavery, guaranteed by the 13th Amendment.

- After Southern states enacted Black Codes, Radical Republicans got the upper hand in Congress and imposed military rule on the South. They banned former Confederates from serving in Reconstruction governments, and forced Southern states to ratify the 14th Amendment before they could be readmitted into the Union.

USING THE "CHEESEBURGER" METHOD

Now let's use your notes to write a thematic essay. It's helpful in organizing your essay to imagine that it resembles a cheeseburger — with a top bun, a slice of cheese, patties of meat, and a bottom bun. The top bun is your **thesis statement** (*generalization*). The cheese slice serves as your **transition sentence**. The patties of meat make up the **body of the essay**. The bottom bun is your **conclusion**.

One characteristic of democracy is that citizens often disagree. The American people have been divided over important public issues throughout U.S. history.

Two important issues that once divided Americans were the existence of slavery and the readmission of the Southern states into the Union in the Reconstruction Era after the Civil War..

By the early 1800s, Southern states allowed slavery while Northern states did not. Abolitionists believed that owning human beings was immoral, and wanted to end slavery. Southerners claimed that slaves were treated better than Northern factory workers. After Lincoln's election in 1860, Southern states seceded and the Civil War began. Lincoln freed slaves in the Emancipation Proclamation. The North won the war, and abolished slavery with the 13th Amendment.

In the Reconstruction Era after the Civil War, Lincoln and then Johnson wanted to make it easy for Southern states to rejoin the Union. Radical Republicans in Congress, mistrusting Southerners, wanted to guarantee freedmen's rights before readmitting Southern states. The issue was resolved after Southern states enacted Black Codes. Radical Republicans convinced Congress to impose military rule on the South. Former Confederates were banned from serving in Reconstruction governments, and Southern states had to ratify the 14th Amendment before being readmitted to the Union.

In conclusion, we can see that Americans have often been divided over important public issues. In the case of slavery, and in the Reconstruction Era, both these disagreements were resolved by force.

Thesis Statement

Transition Sentence

These paragraphs make up the body of the essay

Conclusion

TOP BUN *(THESIS STATEMENT)*

In the first paragraph, start with your thesis statement. This generalization states the main idea of the essay so your reader knows what the theme of your essay is. To write the thesis statement, you can often take the generalization in the *Theme* part of the question and express it as a statement. Include additional background information in your introduction to set the context for your answer.

CHEESE SLICE *(TRANSITION SENTENCE)*

The "cheese slice" sentence is also part of the first paragraph. It connects your thesis statement to the specific information you plan to give in the main part of the essay.

PATTIES OF MEAT *(BODY OF ESSAY)*

This is the main part of your essay and provides your factual support. You should provide specific examples to support your thesis statement. Place each group of facts in its own paragraph or group of paragraphs. Notice how each main paragraph in the example above corresponds to one of the two examples in your notes.

BOTTOM BUN *(CONCLUSION)*

The last part of your essay should be similar to your first sentence *(the thesis statement)*, except that it is now expressed as a conclusion. There are several ways to begin your conclusion: *"Therefore, it is clear that ..."* or *"In conclusion, we can see that ..."* Notice how this closing reminds the reader of your thesis statement. It also adds a generalization based on the examples — that both these issues were resolved by force.

TESTING YOUR UNDERSTANDING

Directions: Circle the number next to the phrase or sentence that correctly answers the question or statement.

Base your answer to question 1 on the following cartoon and on your knowledge of social studies.

1 Which would be the best title for the cartoon?
   1 *The Union can no longer be saved*
   2 *Loyalty will save the Union*
   3 *Lincoln can save the Union*
   4 *Some issues help to unite a nation*

Base your answers to questions 2 through 4 on the following outline and on your knowledge of social studies.

Three items have been omitted from the outline. For each blank space in the outline, select the number of the item from the list below that best completes the blank.

ITEMS

1. Emancipation Proclamation
2. Causes of the Civil War
3. Louisiana Purchase
4. Slavery

THE CIVIL WAR

2   I _____
        A. Sectionalism
3   B. _____
        C. Failure of Compromise
     II Highlights of the Civil War
        A. The Start of the War
        B. Why the North Won
4   C. _____

5 The purpose of the Cabinet, as created by President Washington, was to
   1 protect the rights of citizens
   2 approve treaties and appointments
   3 give advice to the President
   4 settle disputes with foreign nations

6 Booker T. Washington and W.E.B. Du Bois were similar in that they both believed that African-American success depended upon
   1 progress through education
   2 a total restructuring of American society
   3 African Americans being given the land they had worked as slaves
   4 benefits from Southern state governments

7 Laws that promoted the establishment of segregation generally sought to
   1 give African Americans full equality
   2 return African Americans to Africa
   3 separate African Americans and white people
   4 provide African Americans with better jobs

8 Which right is protected by the Fourteenth Amendment?
   1 freedom of speech
   2 equal protection of the law
   3 freedom of religion
   4 no more slavery

9 The decision of *Dred Scott v. Sandford* (1857) was important because it
  1 strengthened the determination of abolitionists to end slavery
  2 was the main cause for the outbreak of the Civil War
  3 ended the importation of slaves into the United States
  4 excluded slavery from territories that were going to become new states

10 Which period in American history included the Freedmen's Bureau, sharecropping, and the rise of the Ku Klux Klan?
  1 Colonial Period   3 Civil War Period
  2 Revolutionary War   4 Reconstruction Era

11 The Supreme Court decision in *Plessy v. Ferguson* primarily involved the issue of
  1 free speech
  2 national supremacy
  3 segregation
  4 freedom of religion

12 A major reason the Radical Republicans opposed Lincoln's Reconstruction plan was that it
  1 demanded payments from the South that would damage its economy
  2 postponed readmission of Southern states into the Union for many years
  3 granted too many rights to the freedmen
  4 did not sufficiently punish the South

13 The practice of racial segregation in the South was based on the belief that
  1 each culture contributed equally to society
  2 some racial groups are superior to others
  3 all races should be treated equally
  4 the freedmen required special assistance

14 Booker T. Washington and W.E.B. Du Bois differed in their approach to equality for African Americans mainly with regard to the
  1 speed with which African Americans should try to gain equality
  2 use of violence to achieve their goals
  3 lack of voting rights for women
  4 necessity for blacks to help themselves

THEMATIC ESSAY QUESTION

Directions: Write a well-organized essay that includes an introduction, several paragraphs explaining your position, and a conclusion.

Theme: Major Events in American History

> Major events have often had an important impact on the lives of Americans.

Task:

> Choose **two** major events from your study of American history.
>
> For **each** event:
>
> • Discuss the historical background leading up to the event.
> • Describe the event.
> • Discuss the impact of the event on the lives of Americans.

You may use any example from your study of U.S. history. Some suggestions you might consider include: the French and Indian War (1755-1763), the American Revolution (1775-1783), the Constitutional Convention (1787), the purchase of the Louisiana Territory (1803), the Civil War (1861-1865), and Reconstruction (1865-1877).

You are *not* limited to these suggestions.

CHAPTER 6

AMERICA INDUSTRIALIZES

The Rise of Industry in the United States
A. The Free Enterprise System
B. Becoming an Industrial Giant
C. Great Business Leaders: Heroes or Villains?
D. Regulating Competition

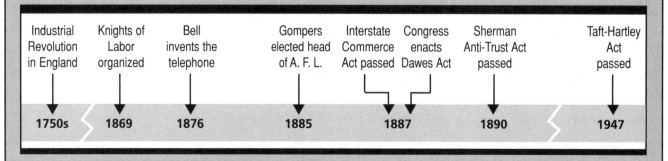

The American Frontier
A. Settlement of the Frontier
B. The Importance of the Frontier
C. The Occupation of the Great Plains
D. Native Americans and the U.S. Government

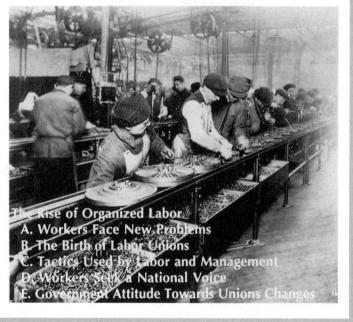

The Rise of Organized Labor
A. Workers Face New Problems
B. The Birth of Labor Unions
C. Tactics Used by Labor and Management
D. Workers Seek a National Voice
E. Government Attitude Towards Unions Changes

Industrial Revolution in England	Knights of Labor organized	Bell invents the telephone	Gompers elected head of A. F. L.	Interstate Commerce Act passed	Congress enacts Dawes Act	Sherman Anti-Trust Act passed	Taft-Hartley Act passed
1750s	1869	1876	1885	1887		1890	1947

WHAT YOU SHOULD FOCUS ON

In this chapter, you will learn how the United States became one of the world's leading industrial powers in the decades following the Civil War.

Industrialization touched almost every aspect of American life: it changed the way people worked and where they lived, as well as having a profound impact on the lives of the Native American Indians and the American frontier.

During this period in American history, several important changes occurred in the following areas:

One of the most important changes in the U.S. was the growth of rail lines into every corner of the nation.

The Rise of Industry in the U.S.

The development of new machines led to the rise of factories and mass production. Population growth, immigration and the expansion of railroads led to the rise of a nationwide market. Entrepreneurs such as Andrew Carnegie and John D. Rockefeller were leaders of these changes.

The Rise of Organized Labor

Often ill-treated and poorly paid, industrial workers eventually organized into unions to obtain better wages and working conditions. At first, public opinion was opposed to unions, but attitudes changed in the early twentieth century.

The American Frontier

The completion of transcontinental railroads allowed settlers to occupy the Great Plains and the Far West. This flood of settlers onto the Great Plains and the Far West had an important impact on Native American Indian tribes, who were forced off their land onto reservations.

In studying this period, you should focus on the following questions:

❖ What factors enabled the United States to emerge as a major industrial power?

❖ What impact did the emergence of transcontinental railroads have on U.S. development?

❖ What measures did government take to regulate competition?

❖ How were workers affected by the rise of industry?

❖ How did the settlement of the frontier affect Native American Indians?

THE RISE OF INDUSTRY IN THE UNITED STATES

In this section you will learn how the United States
changed from an agricultural nation into one of
the world's leading industrial countries.

THINK ABOUT IT

Look at the street on which you live. Carefully note what you see. Now close your eyes and imagine you are looking at the same street 150 years ago. List four things that you see today that would not have been there 150 years ago.

*   _____   *   _____

*   _____   *   _____

What might account for these changes? _____

_____

Important Terms and Concepts: As you read this section, look for the following:

♦ **Industrial Revolution**   ♦ **Laissez-faire Capitalism**
♦ **Capitalism**   ♦ **Monopoly**
♦ **Corporation**   ♦ **Sherman Anti-Trust Act**

To help you find these terms, this symbol ♦ appears in the margin where the term is first explained.

THE FREE ENTERPRISE SYSTEM

♦ The **Industrial Revolution**, which began in England in the 1750s, changed the way people produced goods. Instead of being made at home by hand, goods were now produced in factories with the help of machines. In the period following the Civil War, the United States became one of the world's leading industrialized nations.

One of the factors stimulating the industrialization of the United States was its economic sys-
♦ tem — **capitalism**, sometimes called the **free enterprise system**. Under this system, **capital** (*money*) is controlled by individuals, rather than controlled by the government. Investors risk their money in businesses that they believe will give them **profits** (*the money a business makes after business costs are paid*). Consumers are free to choose what they want to buy. Under the impact of industrialization, the American economy displayed the following characteristics in the decades following the Civil War:

MAIN FEATURES OF THE INDUSTRIAL REVOLUTION

Rise of Cities

Workers moved to cities where they could find factory work. In the 1850s, most Americans lived in rural areas working as farmers. By 1920, half of all Americans lived in cities.

The Factory System

People now worked in factories where they used large, powerful machines driven by water and steam power. Workers put in long hours in unsafe factory conditions, and received little pay.

Mass Production

Production increased tremendously as large-scale production methods were introduced. As production increased, prices for factory items decreased, leading to a greater demand for more goods.

STEPS ON THE ROAD TO BECOMING AN INDUSTRIAL GIANT

Several reasons help to explain the rise of the United States as an industrial giant.

THE GROWTH OF THE RAILROADS

One key to the growth of the United States as an industrial power was the building of railroads. In 1869, the **transcontinental railroad**, connecting the east and west coasts of the United States, was completed. Other connecting lines were soon built. The railroads affected just about every aspect of American life. They brought people from the east to the frontier. They made it possible to move food from farms and goods from factories to far-off cities. Railroad advertisements, describing new opportunities, attracted many immigrants to the United States.

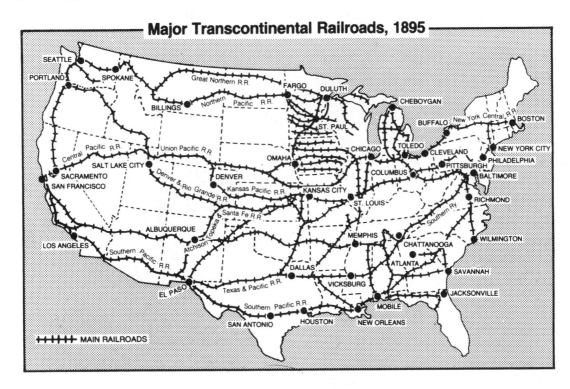

Major Transcontinental Railroads, 1895

THE GROWTH OF POPULATION AND A NATIONAL MARKET

The population of the United States doubled between 1860 and 1900. An increasing population was good for business because there were more people to buy goods and work in factories. The fact that goods made in one part of the country could be sent to other parts of the country led to the creation of a national market. This was important to the owners of large businesses, who could now sell more of their goods. New methods of selling, like the mail order catalogue and the department store, came about as a result of the existence of a national market.

NEW INVENTIONS AND WAYS OF PRODUCING GOODS

New technologies, innovations and inventions helped fuel the economic expansion of the late 1800s. For example, **Alexander Graham Bell** invented the telephone (1876), and **Thomas Edison** developed the electric light bulb (1879). By 1900, electricity was used to power such items as motors, electric streetcars and subways.

NEW WAYS OF ORGANIZING BUSINESSES: THE CORPORATION

Before the Civil War, most businesses were owned by individuals or partners. After the Civil War, the corporation became a very popular form of business. A **corporation** is a company that is treated by state law as though it has all of the legal rights of an individual person. The key advantage of a corporation is that it can raise large sums of money by selling shares of the business to anyone who wishes to buy them. People who purchase these shares are **stockholders**. Each stockholder is a part owner of the corporation, but is not liable (*responsible*) for the corporation's debts beyond his or her own investment.

As a result of all the factors described above, the number and size of businesses in America began to expand rapidly in the years following the Civil War.

THE IMPACT OF GEOGRAPHY ON AMERICAN HISTORY

When gold was discovered in California in 1848, those struck by "gold fever" needed to get to the Far West. They either had to sail around South America, or take a ship to Central America *(which could be crossed by land)* and then sail up the West Coast, or go across the prairies and mountains in a horse-drawn coach or wagon. Even before the Civil War, Americans realized the need for a transcontinental railroad, but were divided about the route. Southerners proposed a route through New Mexico and Arizona; Northerners preferred Utah and Nevada. Americans rightly suspected the train would have an important impact on the geographical environment. After the Civil War, the Northern route was chosen. Completion of the transcontinental railroad made it possible to cross the continent in days instead of months. The railroad opened the Great Plains to settlement, and made it possible for farmers and ranchers to ship their crops and livestock back east.

The transcontinental railroad provided a fast and safer way to reach the West.

SKILL BUILDER: UNDERSTANDING BAR GRAPHS

This Skill Builder will show you how to "read" bar graphs and how to answer questions about this type of data.

What Is a Bar Graph?

A bar graph is a chart that uses parallel bars to show a comparison of two or more items.

Keys to Understanding a Bar Graph

First, look at its main components:

Title. The title states the overall topic. For example, in this bar graph, the title is **"The Growth of Businesses in America: 1870-1900."** Thus, the graph shows how the number of businesses in America grew from 1870 to 1900.

Legend. When more than one kind of bar is used, the legend explains what each bar color or pattern represents. However, since there is only type of bar in our graph (*showing the number of businesses*), no legend is needed.

Vertical and Horizontal Axis. Bar graphs are composed of a **vertical axis** (*which runs from bottom to top*) and a **horizontal axis** (*which runs from left to right*). In the bar graph on this page, the vertical axis shows the years being examined (*1870 to 1900*), and the horizontal axis indicates the number of businesses in America.

Note: Some graphs show the bars running up and down instead of sideways. In an up-and-down bar graph with the same information as given here, the horizontal axis would indicate the years, and the vertical axis would indicate the number of businesses.

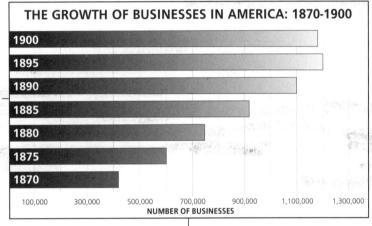

THE GROWTH OF BUSINESSES IN AMERICA: 1870-1900

Interpreting a Bar Graph

First, look at the title to find out what information is in the graph. To find specific information, examine the individual bars. For example, how many businesses were there in America in 1880?

To find the answer, go to the vertical axis and run your finger up the row of bars until you reach the bar representing 1880. Now run your finger straight across to the right, to the end of the bar. If you look at the number scale along the horizontal axis, you will see that the bar ends at about 750,000. Thus, the answer to the question — How many businesses were there in America in 1880? — is about 750,000.

GREAT BUSINESS LEADERS: HEROES OR VILLAINS?

As a result of the growth of American businesses between 1865 and 1900, some people became very wealthy. Their wealth enabled them to have an important influence on the American way of life. Many saw these business people as heroes; others saw them as villains.

ANDREW CARNEGIE (1835-1919)

Andrew Carnegie worked his way up from being a poor Scottish immigrant to becoming one of America's richest men. He dominated the steel industry. He sold steel at very low prices and put other steel companies out of business. Carnegie forced workers to put in long hours at low wages and stopped them from joining unions. Later in life, he gave large sums of money to support education, cultural activities and medical research.

JOHN D. ROCKEFELLER (1839-1937)

John D. Rockefeller formed the Standard Oil Company. Because he controlled most of the oil refinery business, he forced the railroad companies to give him special low rates for shipping oil, while they charged higher rates to his competitors. By 1900, Rockefeller had almost total control over the oil business. Later in life he, too, gave away his money to education and science.

Andrew Carnegie

THE IMPACT OF GEOGRAPHY ON AMERICAN HISTORY

The backbone of American industry was iron and steel, needed for locomotives, railroad tracks, machinery, shipbuilding, and construction. By the late 1850s, the rich coal resources of western Pennsylvania made possible the construction of larger furnaces. The new **Bessemer Process** for making steel by removing impurities in the iron was introduced in the late 1860s. The plentiful iron ore of the Upper Peninsula of Michigan and Minnesota's Mesabi Range was shipped across the Great Lakes to Ohio and Western Pennsylvania, where it was smelted, refined, and rolled in large steel mills. Pennsylvania coal fed the enormous furnace fires.

Pittsburgh, 1886: Making steel using the Bessemer process

Andrew Carnegie constructed his first steel mill just outside of Pittsburgh, at the focal point of these natural resources. For nearly a century, the region from Chicago to Pittsburgh remained America's industrial heartland.

REGULATING COMPETITION

As America industrialized, many people believed that big business should be allowed to grow without government interference. The belief that government should not interfere with business is called **laissez-faire capitalism**. Many government leaders felt that allowing businesses to operate with few rules would lead to the best and cheapest goods being produced. Supporters of laissez-faire capitalism believed that the government had no constitutional right to control business.

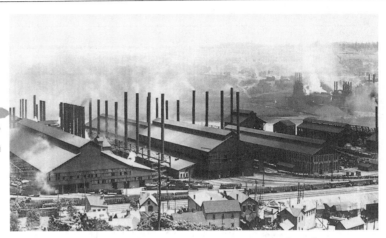

The Carnegie Steel Works in Pennsylvania

As a result, companies owned by Carnegie and Rockefeller, as well as others, grew more powerful by driving smaller companies out of business. In other cases, companies selling similar products made agreements to join together. As a result of these agreements, monopolies were created. A **monopoly** is a company that controls most or all of the business in a particular industry. The aim of a monopoly is to get rid of all competition so that the seller can control the price. Once the monopoly is the only provider of a product, customers who need that particular product must pay whatever price is demanded. By the 1890s, monopolies in the United States had grown to dominate some of the nation's largest industries.

A large number of people believed that the government should do something to control big business. They argued that big businesses, with little or no competition, had no reason to lower their prices. They believed that by putting smaller companies out of business, big companies were forcing the public to pay higher prices. As a result, Congress finally passed two important laws:

- **Interstate Commerce Act (1887).** This law made certain practices of railroad companies illegal, such as entering into agreements with other railroad companies to control rates. An Interstate Commerce Commission was set up to make sure the provisions of the law were followed.

- **Sherman Anti-Trust Act (1890).** This law was created to stop the growth of monopolies. It made illegal many actions that companies had been using to take business away from their competitors. The act showed that Congress believed something had to be done to stop the unfair practices of many big businesses.

SUMMING UP: THE RISE OF INDUSTRY

Over the last 150 years, the United States has become the greatest industrial power in the world. The growth of industry and big business helped this country in many ways, but also led to a number of serious problems, such as unfair competition.

THINKING IT OVER

Close your eyes and imagine that you are looking at your street 150 years into the future. List four things you might see:

- _____
- _____
- _____
- _____

CHECKING YOUR UNDERSTANDING

Directions: Complete the following cards. Then answer the multiple-choice questions.

INDUSTRIAL REVOLUTION

What was it? *change in the way we produce goods.*

Two main features: 1. _____

2. _____

"free enterprise system"

CAPITALISM

Definition: *economic system where individuals not gvnt*

How does it work? _____

_____

---

laizee fair economics. controls the economy.

1 A major result of the Industrial Revolution in the United States was
   1 a decreased number of factories
   2 a decreased population
   ③ an increase in the number of cities
   ④ a sharp increase in all prices of goods

2 The economic system of the United States in the late 1800s can best be described as
   1 communism   3 mercantilism
   2 socialism   ④ capitalism

3 Which type of business organization has the ability to raise the largest amount of capital?
   1 cooperatives   ③ corporations
   2 partnerships   4 communes

4 The major purpose of the Sherman Anti-Trust Act was to
   ① promote greater competition
   2 stop the growth of corporations
   3 increase management's power over labor
   ④ disband large corporations

5 The growth and development of large American cities was a direct result of
   1 the American Revolution
   2 the Civil War
   3 Reconstruction
   ④ industrialization

6 In which economic system do businesses compete for profits?
   ① capitalism   3 communism
   2 socialism   4 imperialism

7 In an outline, one of these is the main topic, and the other three are sub-topics. Which one is the main topic?
   ① The Industrial Revolution
   2 Growth of Population
   3 New Inventions
   4 New Forms of Business Organization

8 The primary aim of a monopoly is to
   ① get rid of all competition
   2 lower prices
   3 stimulate competition
   4 control stock prices

SECTION 2

THE RISE OF ORGANIZED LABOR

In this section you will learn how, as a result of poor working conditions, workers began to organize into labor unions.

THINK ABOUT IT

What rights, if any, do you think workers should have?

● _____   ● _____

Important Terms and Concepts: As you read this section, look for the following:

✦ Labor Unions   ✦ Closed Shop
✦ American Federation of Labor (A.F.L.)   ✦ Collective Bargaining

---

WORKERS FACE NEW PROBLEMS

Although the Industrial Revolution brought increased profits to business people and more and better goods to consumers, workers often suffered.

Poor Working Conditions. Working was often extremely hazardous. There were few safeguards around machinery. Thousands of workers were injured or killed in accidents each year.

Long Hours. Working hours were very long. Employees faced a six-day week with between 10 and 14 hours of work a day.

PROBLEMS FACED BY INDUSTRIAL WORKERS

Low Wages. Employers hired the cheapest possible laborers. Women and children were especially low-paid. Child laborers missed sunshine, fresh air, play, and the chance to better their lives through schooling.

Boring, Repetitive Tasks. As industrialists sought to achieve greater speed and efficiency, the worker became nothing more than a human machine. Work became less skilled, more repetitive, monotonous, and boring.

Lack of Security. The worker could be fired at any time for any reason. There was no unemployment insurance, health insurance, old-age pensions, paid holidays, or paid sickdays.

THE BIRTH OF LABOR UNIONS

Industrial workers in the late 1800s had no power to make big business raise their pay or improve their working conditions. Since most work required little skill, workers could easily be replaced. Eventually, workers realized that by organizing into **labor unions** (*a group of workers organized to achieve common goals*) they would have more power. If an employer refused a union's demands for better working conditions and higher pay, union members could **strike** (*walk off the job*). In addition, unions could use their voting power and resources to persuade the government to pass laws favoring workers.

TACTICS USED BY LABOR AND MANAGEMENT

Attempts to form unions or gain better working conditions often pitted workers and their employers against each other. Both labor and management used a variety of tactics to achieve their goals.

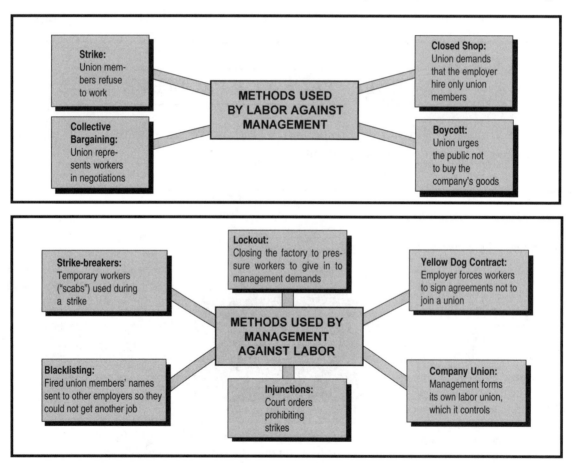

WORKERS SEEK A NATIONAL VOICE

By the end of the 1800s, many workers believed that the only way to overcome their problems was to join together in a national union of all workers.

THE KNIGHTS OF LABOR

The Knights of Labor was organized in 1869. Its founders hoped to form one large union that would include both skilled and unskilled workers, and even women. The Knights demanded an 8-hour work day, higher wages and safety codes for factories. They also proposed laws limiting immigration, since they saw immigrants as competitors for their jobs. After losing several strikes, the Knights of Labor fell apart. One reason for their failure was that many skilled workers refused to be grouped in the same union as unskilled workers.

THE AMERICAN FEDERATION OF LABOR

The **American Federation of Labor (A.F.L.)** was begun in 1881 by **Samuel Gompers**. He hoped

to organize a powerful union by uniting workers with the same economic interests. The A.F.L. brought together several small unions of skilled workers (*such as carpenters, cigar makers, shoemakers*) into a single national union. The goals of the American Federation of Labor included higher pay, an 8-hour work day, and better working conditions. The A.F.L. used strikes as one of its main tactics. Striking workers were paid from a special fund established by the union, making their strikes an effective weapon. The A.F.L. also fought for the **closed shop** (*workplaces that hire only union members*). The American Federation of Labor emerged as the major voice of organized labor. However, the growth of the union was weakened by the fact that, in its early years, it excluded unskilled workers.

Samuel Gompers

WORKERS DEMAND THAT THE GOVERNMENT LISTEN

One problem that early unions faced was that government leaders in those years favored businesses over unions. There were several reasons why this was so:

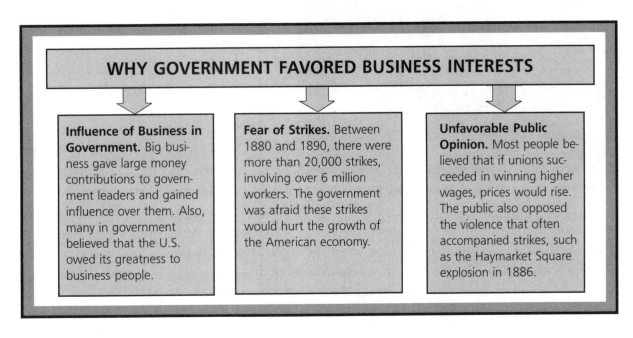

WHY GOVERNMENT FAVORED BUSINESS INTERESTS

Influence of Business in Government. Big business gave large money contributions to government leaders and gained influence over them. Also, many in government believed that the U.S. owed its greatness to business people.

Fear of Strikes. Between 1880 and 1890, there were more than 20,000 strikes, involving over 6 million workers. The government was afraid these strikes would hurt the growth of the American economy.

Unfavorable Public Opinion. Most people believed that if unions succeeded in winning higher wages, prices would rise. The public also opposed the violence that often accompanied strikes, such as the Haymarket Square explosion in 1886.

GOVERNMENT CHANGES ITS ATTITUDE TOWARDS UNIONS

In the early 1900s, government and public attitudes towards unions began to change.

DANGEROUS CONDITIONS FOR WORKERS

In 1911, a fire killed 146 workers, mostly women, at the Triangle Shirtwaist factory in New York.

Investigation showed that the workers could not escape because the doors were locked from the inside, and there was only one fire escape. Because of this tragedy, the public began to demand that the government take action. In 1913, the government created the **Department of Labor** to study the problems of workers and to propose solutions.

Child workers in a Pennsylvania coal mine, 1911

WORKERS AND THE DEPRESSION

The Great Depression and World War II had a major effect on the role of unions in American life. There was tremendous unemployment during the Great Depression, which began in 1929. In 1933, when Franklin D. Roosevelt became President, he sought to help workers. Under his Presidency, the **Wagner Act** was passed, which guaranteed workers the right to unions and to collective bargaining. **Collective bargaining** requires the management of a company to discuss wages, hours and working conditions with a union representing its workers. With the passage of the Wagner Act, membership in unions expanded greatly.

Little girls at work in a New York City "sweatshop"

PASSAGE OF THE TAFT-HARTLEY ACT (1947)

By the time World War II ended, many people believed that unions were growing too strong. It was feared that some strikes could hurt the country. Congress passed the **Taft-Hartley Act**, which made some union actions illegal. Most importantly, this law gave the government the power, under certain conditions, to tell unions to stop a strike for a "cooling-off period." During this period of time, it was hoped that the union and employers would settle their differences.

UNIONS TODAY

Unions have had a tremendous impact on American society. Workers have better pay and better conditions than in the days before unions. Some critics (*people who disagree or disapprove of something*) have argued that unionization has made American labor too expensive and has driven some jobs overseas, where labor is cheaper. Today, only 16% of U.S. workers are unionized. This is because many workers are in **service industries** (*any industry which provides a service instead of producing goods*) or small businesses where people do not usually join unions.

Members of the United Auto Workers at a Ford Motor Company plant in Louisville, Kentucky

FOCUS ON THE ARTS

Thomas Nast, Cartoonist

Nast, an artist, achieved national fame for his political cartoons. He is credited with raising the political cartoon to a serious art form. Nast's illustrations focused on the political situation in America after the Civil War. His cartoons highlighted the corruption in New York politics. His symbol of the Democratic Party as a donkey and the Republican Party as an elephant have come to represent both parties in the public mind.

THINKING IT OVER

If you were a labor leader today, what would be your goals for workers? _____

_____

_____

SUMMING UP: THE RISE OF ORGANIZED LABOR

Workers began to form unions to fight for higher wages and improved working conditions. At first the government favored big business over unions. Eventually, the government took steps that allowed unions to grow. As a result, the power of workers grew stronger and their lives improved. Later on, the government took steps to prevent unions from using their power in ways that might hurt the well-being of the nation.

CHECKING YOUR UNDERSTANDING

Directions: Complete the following cards. Then answer the multiple-choice questions.

LABOR UNION

Definition: _____

What are its goals? _____

_____

COLLECTIVE BARGAINING

Definition: _____

What items might be discussed? _____

_____

1 The collective bargaining process is used to determine
  1 the provisions of a labor-management contract
  2 the level of unemployment in an industry
  3 the growth level of certain industries
  4 which consumer goods to produce

2 Which "tool" of labor is sometimes used in disagreements with management?
  1 strikes   3 lockouts
  2 firings   4 blacklists

3 Workers traditionally join labor unions to
  1 improve the level of production
  2 improve working conditions
  3 lower prices for consumers
  4 stop discrimination

4 The Knights of Labor and the American Federation of Labor both sought
  1 government ownership of industry
  2 higher pay for managers
  3 a shorter workday for workers
  4 reduced medical benefits

5 A major result of the development of labor unions is that
  1 workers have better working conditions today
  2 poverty has been eliminated in the U.S.
  3 the free market economy has been destroyed
  4 there is increased trade with European nations

6 Which event is correctly paired with one of its major effects?
  1 American Revolutionary War — freeing thousands of enslaved peoples
  2 Civil War — giving women the right to vote
  3 Industrial Revolution — growth of labor unions
  4 Reconstruction — achieving American independence

7 Which development was a result of the other three?
  1 poor working conditions in factories
  2 formation of labor unions
  3 12-hour work day
  4 low pay for workers

SECTION
3

THE AMERICAN FRONTIER

In this section you will learn how wilderness areas disappeared as settlers and farmers moved west. One important result was that Native American Indians were removed from lands they had occupied for centuries.

THINK ABOUT IT

When you hear the term "the West," what images come to your mind? _____

_____

Important Terms and Concepts: As you read this section, look for the following:

✦ Frontier
✦ Native American Indians

✦ Homestead Act
✦ Dawes Act

THE SETTLEMENT OF THE FRONTIER, 1860-1890

Just as ways of producing things were affected by the Industrial Revolution, so too did other aspects of American life change. This was especially true of the **frontier**. The frontier marked the ✦ dividing line between the areas occupied by **Native American Indians**, and the areas in which ✦ new settlers lived.

The map on the next page shows how the frontier line has shifted westward since colonial days. It shifted especially rapidly during the late 1800s. The area settled between 1850 and 1875 was known as the **Great Plains**. These vast, grassy lands once provided a home to millions of buffalo and to the Native American Indians who lived off them. Within thirty years *(roughly between 1860 and 1890)*, the herds of buffalo were destroyed by hunters with guns, forcing Native American Indians onto **reservations** *(lands set aside by the government)*. The completion of the transcontinental railroad brought new settlers. The Great Plains were divided up into farms and ranches.

A Native American Indian village on the move

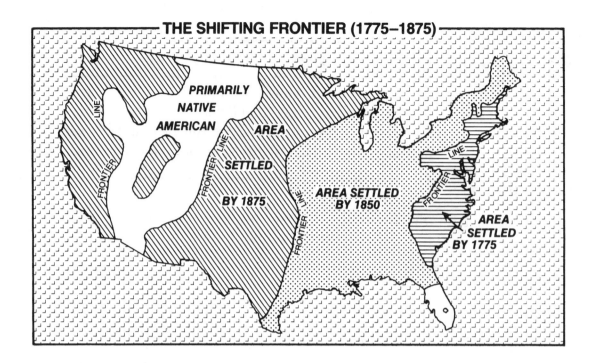

THE SHIFTING FRONTIER (1775–1875)

Several factors led to the settlement of the Great Plains and the disappearance of the frontier:

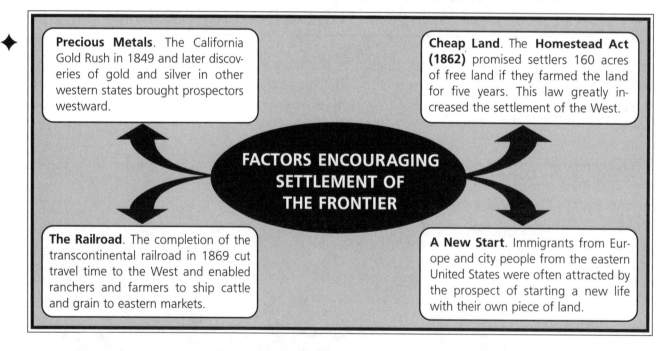

Precious Metals. The California Gold Rush in 1849 and later discoveries of gold and silver in other western states brought prospectors westward.

Cheap Land. The **Homestead Act (1862)** promised settlers 160 acres of free land if they farmed the land for five years. This law greatly increased the settlement of the West.

FACTORS ENCOURAGING SETTLEMENT OF THE FRONTIER

The Railroad. The completion of the transcontinental railroad in 1869 cut travel time to the West and enabled ranchers and farmers to ship cattle and grain to eastern markets.

A New Start. Immigrants from Europe and city people from the eastern United States were often attracted by the prospect of starting a new life with their own piece of land.

THE IMPORTANCE OF THE FRONTIER IN AMERICAN LIFE

Some historians have claimed that the frontier played an important role in shaping the character and values of the American people. For example, they argue that the frontier:

■ **Acted As a Safety Valve.** The frontier allowed people living in crowded conditions in eastern cities to move to the West, where a greater degree of freedom existed.

- **Promoted Self-Reliance.** On the frontier, families had to learn to make it on their own. In this way the frontier promoted self-reliance (*relying on one's own abilities*) and individualism (*pursuing one's own ideas rather than following the crowd*).

- **Promoted the Growth of Democracy.** People on the frontier did not have the same rigid social class divisions as in the East. Facing hardships created a spirit of cooperation. For these reasons, life on the frontier promoted personal freedom and democracy. For example, in the 1820s, Jacksonian democracy was associated with the frontier spirit. Later, Wyoming and Colorado were the first two states to give women full voting rights.

THE OCCUPATION OF THE GREAT PLAINS

The Great Plains went through a series of stages based on different economic activities.

THE MINING TOWNS

The discovery of gold and silver attracted prospectors and mining companies. Towns sprang up overnight when precious metals were discovered; they often disappeared just as quickly when all the metals had been extracted.

COWBOYS AND THE OPEN RANGE

Cattle grazed freely on the southern Great Plains. Cowboys kept the herds together and drove them northwards to the railroad lines in Kansas. The steers were shipped by rail to Chicago, where they were slaughtered. The beef was then shipped in refrigerated railroad cars to eastern cities. American cowboys originally learned many of their special techniques of riding, roping and branding cattle from Mexican cowboys.

THE ARRIVAL OF THE FARMERS

The Homestead Act (1862) allowed settlers to claim 160 acres of land per adult, if they farmed it for five years. The plains were dry, but farmers dug deep water wells and used barbed wire fences to prevent cattle from eating the crops on their lands. The arrival of the farmers put an end to the open range.

Frontier settlers clearing the land

A NOTE ON NAMES: The earliest settlers in the Western Hemisphere (*North and South America*) have been called by different names throughout history. When Columbus landed, he called them **Indians**, since he thought he had landed in India. In the 1960s, the term **Native American** began to be used, since they were the first inhabitants of the Americas. More recently, some have called them **Indigenous Peoples** or **Native American Indians**.

NATIVE AMERICAN INDIANS AND THE U.S. GOVERNMENT, 1790-1990

Native American Indians consisted of many different groups, speaking hundreds of languages and following different ways of life. Various groups of Native American Indians once occupied what is today known as the United States. However, the movement of people from the eastern United States and immigrants from abroad, as well as death from diseases like small pox, pushed the Native American Indians further westward and reduced their numbers.

The clash of cultures on the Great Plains

EARLY GOVERNMENT POLICY

During the 1800s, the American government followed a policy that pushed Native American Indians from their traditional lands onto government lands in the West. Time and time again the government broke its promises and allowed its citizens to move into tribal lands, forcing the Native American Indians still further westward. The final takeover of Native American Indian lands was encouraged by the completion of the transcontinental railroad in 1869, and by a series of battles between Native American Indians and federal troops. The Great Plains tribes could no longer rely on herds of buffalo, which had been destroyed by sharpshooters firing from the trains. Those Indian tribes that went along with U.S. policy were settled on reservations. However, reservation lands were usually small and not very desirable.

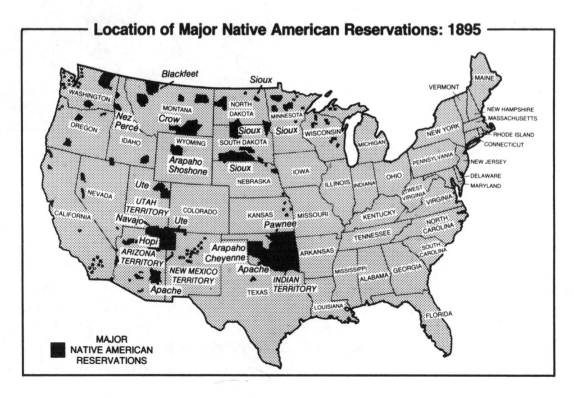

Location of Major Native American Reservations: 1895

George Catlin, Painter

Catlin was a self-taught artist. His paintings focused on the excitement of frontier life. He was the first painter to shape our views of the Native American Indians living in the West. Catlin's paintings often showed them hunting, riding and performing ceremonial rituals. His paintings were so accurate that they now serve as one of our best sources of information on many Indian tribes. In the 1850s, he traveled to South America to record the lives of Indian peoples of that region.

THE DAWES ACT (1887)

Many people believed that the Native American Indians should give up their traditional ways of life and follow lifestyles similar to those of other people in the United States. To accomplish this, the government passed the **Dawes Act**, which officially abolished the authority of the Native American **tribes** and provided farm land to each family. Eventually, this was to lead to Native American Indians being given U.S. citizenship and the right to vote. However, the Dawes Act threatened traditional tribal ways of life. For example, the act encouraged individual farm ownership, which went against the Native American Indian custom of sharing land. Moreover, most Native American Indians had been hunters, not farmers. Lastly, lands given to the tribes often proved unsuitable for growing crops. Reservation schools usually provided a poor education. People on the reservations suffered from poor health, malnutrition, poverty, and despair.

Catlin painting of a Native American Indian girl

U.S. GOVERNMENT POLICY CHANGES

Government policy towards Native American Indians has changed a number of times. In some instances, the government has encouraged Native American Indians to keep up their traditional ways by restoring tribal governments and stopping the breakup of tribal lands. At other times, the government has tried to encourage Native American Indians to become part of mainstream American society, by providing job training and placement programs. During the 1970s, Native American Indians were given federal funds for housing, health care, education and economic improvement. Thus far, government programs have met with little success in improving the lives of most Native American Indians.

NATIVE AMERICAN INDIANS DEMAND THEIR RIGHTS (1960s-Present)

Since the 1970s, Native American Indians have become more forceful in demanding their rights. Some formed a new organization, the **American Indian Movement (A.I.M.)**, which took such actions as the temporary takeovers of public sites like Alcatraz Island in California and the Wounded Knee Monument in South Dakota. In addition, they have suggested programs to restore pride to Native American Indians. For example, A.I.M. protests against textbooks, television shows and movies that promote prejudiced views against Native American Indians.

NATIVE AMERICAN INDIAN PROBLEMS TODAY

Today, the population of Native American Indians is about 1.4 million, more than four times the number of Native American Indians in 1890. Despite their steady growth in numbers, Native American Indians continue to face very serious problems:

CURRENT PROBLEMS OF NATIVE AMERICAN INDIANS

Reservation Life. About 25% of Native American Indians live on reservations. They have among the lowest incomes in the nation, and suffer from high unemployment, alcoholism, and high suicide and infant mortality rates. Some reservations now profit from running gambling casinos.

Cultural Crisis. Native American Indians are divided over whether to follow their traditional culture or that of mainstream America. For example, their culture is group-oriented; American culture is individualistic. Traditional culture preserves land in its natural state, while industries often seek to use it.

Frustration with Government. Various tribes often compete for the same government funds. Unlike other ethnic groups, Native American Indians can cite treaties guaranteeing their rights. As a result, they feel they are owed a better deal for their loss of lands and their suffering.

THINKING IT OVER

Now that you have read this section, has your view of "the West" changed? _____

Explain. _____

_____

SUMMING UP: THE AMERICAN FRONTIER

Some people believe that life on the frontier played a key role in shaping the values of the American people. Industrialization eventually led to the closing of the American frontier. The frontier was occupied in stages, by miners, cattlemen and farmers. The closing of the frontier led to a great deal of suffering on the part of Native American Indians. The policy of the U.S. government toward Native American Indians has undergone many changes over the years, but Native American Indians continue to face serious problems today.

PROFILES IN HISTORY

THOMAS EDISON
(INVENTOR)

Many consider Edison to be one of the greatest inventors in U.S. history. After his first invention at age 22, he set up a laboratory in New Jersey where he and his staff invented over 1,000 devices, includ-

ing the phonograph, the light bulb and the motion picture projector.

ALEXANDER GRAHAM BELL
(INVENTOR)

Alexander Graham Bell, a speech teacher,

invented the telephone in 1876. Bell's invention helped bring together people from widely separated parts of the nation by transmitting the human voice over a telegraph wire. Bell devoted his life to improving and perfecting his invention.

CYRUS MCCORMICK
(INVENTOR)

In 1831 McCormick invented the reaper, a horse-drawn machine used to harvest grain. Before this invention, farmers used to cut grain with a hand-held scythe. Since Western farmers were faced with a labor shortage, McCormick's reapers allowed farmers to har-

vest larger crops with less labor. This invention helped to spur western settlements.

The McCormick reaper

GERONIMO
(APACHE CHIEF)

Geronimo refused to be forced to live on a reservation, far from his people's traditional homeland. Geronimo fought against settlers along the southwest plains who sought to take over his people's land. He was captured in 1886.

A. PHILIP RANDOLPH
(LABOR LEADER)

Randolph was both a union organizer and a leader in the fight for African-American civil rights. In 1925, he founded the Brotherhood of Sleeping Car Porters, which won pay raises and a shorter work week. Later he worked to bring about equality for African Americans in government jobs and in the armed forces. He threatened to bring 100,000 marchers to Washington, D.C. in 1941. As a result, President Franklin D. Roosevelt issued a directive to promote minority hiring and fair employment practices in government offices.

CHECKING YOUR UNDERSTANDING

Directions: Complete the following cards. Then answer the multiple-choice questions.

HOMESTEAD ACT (1862)

What did it do? _____

Its impact: _____

_____

DAWES ACT (1887)

What did it do? _____

Its impact: _____

_____

---

1 A landless settler heading west in the 1870s would most likely have supported passage of the
1 Dawes Act
2 Sherman Anti-Trust Act
3 Homestead Act
4 Taft-Hartley Act

2 Native American Indians are unlike other minorities in the United States in that some of their rights are guaranteed in
1 the Bill of Rights
2 treaties with the federal government
3 the Fourteenth Amendment
4 state constitutions

3 The arrival of which group ended the "open range" on the Great Plains?
1 cowboys
2 miners
3 farmers
4 Native American Indians

4 Which is a trend that occurred in the United States from the 1830s to the 1890s?
1 American industry became less productive.
2 Native American Indians were forced onto government reservations.
3 The government took over most businesses.
4 People moved from cities to suburbs.

THE CONSTITUTION AT WORK

IN RE DEBS (1895)

Background: Eugene Debs, a union official, refused to obey a court ruling that ordered him to halt a strike of railroad workers. He argued that the federal government had no right to prevent strikes.

Decision/Significance: The Court upheld the federal government's right to issue injunctions to halt strikes. The decision permitted businesses to use the federal courts as a tool to prevent strikes by labor unions.

THE COURT SPEAKS

NATIONAL LABOR RELATIONS ACT (1935)

This act, often called the Wagner Act, was largely responsible for helping unions to grow. It protected the right of labor to organize, and guaranteed the right of unions to bargain collectively with employers.

TAFT-HARTLEY ACT (1947)

The major focus of this act was to limit some union practices. The act prohibited unions from engaging in certain types of strikes, charging excessive initiation fees, and taking part in secondary boycotts.

KEY LAWS

SUMMARIZING YOUR UNDERSTANDING

Directions: Confirm your understanding of the important terms and concepts in this chapter. Check those you can explain. For those you are not sure of, find the ✦ symbol in the margin next to the term and review it.

CHECKLIST

- ❑ Industrial Revolution
- ❑ Capitalism
- ❑ Corporation
- ❑ Monopoly
- ❑ Laissez-faire capitalism

- ❑ Sherman Anti-Trust Act
- ❑ Labor Unions
- ❑ American Federation of Labor
- ❑ Closed Shop
- ❑ Collective Bargaining

- ❑ Frontier
- ❑ Native American Indians
- ❑ Homestead Act
- ❑ Dawes Act
- ❑ A. I. M.

Directions: Fill in the information called for in the following organizers.

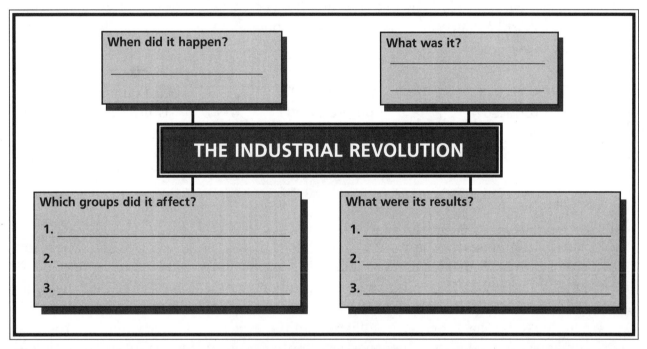

When did it happen?
_____

What was it?
_____
_____

THE INDUSTRIAL REVOLUTION

Which groups did it affect?
1. _____
2. _____
3. _____

What were its results?
1. _____
2. _____
3. _____

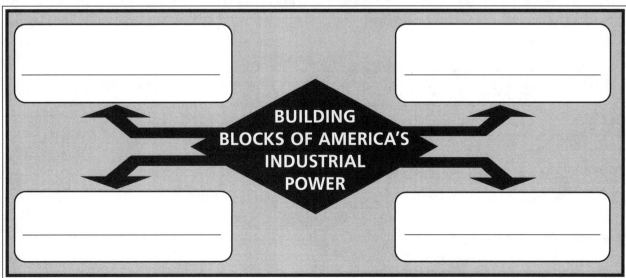

_____

_____

BUILDING BLOCKS OF AMERICA'S INDUSTRIAL POWER

_____

_____

TEST HELPER   LOOKING AT ECONOMIC CHANGE

The Industrial Revolution began a period of great economic growth and change in human history. To better understand the Industrial Revolution and its influence on American life, this section takes a look at economics, how a market economy works, and the main causes and effects of economic change.

WHAT IS ECONOMICS?

Most people's wants are unlimited. We can never be completely satisfied because we have **limited** resources at our disposal to meet **unlimited** wants. For example, everyone in New York City may want a new home, but there is not enough space, materials, or money to build them. Instead, there must be some way to decide how many homes to build and who will own them. Every society makes similar choices in answering the three basic economic questions:

What should
be produced?

How should it
be produced?

Who gets what
is produced?

Economics is the study of how societies use limited resources to try to meet unlimited wants.

HOW THE FREE MARKET WORKS

All societies must seek answers to these basic economic questions. In the United States, we have a **market economy** that answers these questions. People are free to produce whatever they want, and to buy whatever they can afford. The **profit motive** gives people an incentive to produce goods and provide services, while competition and the laws of supply and demand determine how much will be produced and what will be charged. However, even in a free market system, there is some government influence on the economy. The government provides stable conditions and a system of laws under which people can conduct business. The government acts as a "police officer" of the marketplace, making sure that people and businesses treat each other fairly.

WHAT CAUSES AN ECONOMY TO CHANGE AND DEVELOP?

Economists have identified a number of important causes of economic change.

TECHNOLOGICAL INNOVATION

One of the most important factors influencing an economy is **technology** — the use of knowledge, skills, and tools for making things. The Industrial Revolution was one of the great turning points in the development of technology. People learned to use new sources of energy to replace human and animal power. Factories and machines replaced hand labor in the production of goods.

CAPITAL INVESTMENTS AND PRODUCTIVITY

When a society invests labor and resources to build homes, roads, schools, factories, and equipment, its workers and businesses become more productive. As technology improves and investment in the equipment used by each worker increases, each worker can produce more in the same amount of time. This is called **productivity**.

NEW FORMS OF BUSINESS ORGANIZATION

The development of new forms of business organization and finance make it possible to bring together labor and **capital** (*money*) in large amounts, to mass-produce goods that meet business and consumer needs. For example, the rise of corporations in 19th-century America promoted a greater pooling of private capital.

NATURAL RESOURCES

Natural resources provide sources of energy and raw materials for agriculture and manufacturing. The discovery of new resources or the development of new ways to use existing resources can stimulate economic change. For example, during the early stages of the Industrial Revolution, the development of new uses for coal and iron helped speed industrialization.

CONTACTS WITH OTHER SOCIETIES

Contacts with others can help introduce new products, markets, or ways of producing things. However, contacts with other societies may lead to disputes and wars, which can have significant economic consequences.

GOVERNMENT POLICIES

Government policies can also greatly affect a nation's economy. They create the conditions in which businesses operate. Governments spend money, provide jobs, impose taxes, raise tariffs, and create laws and regulations.

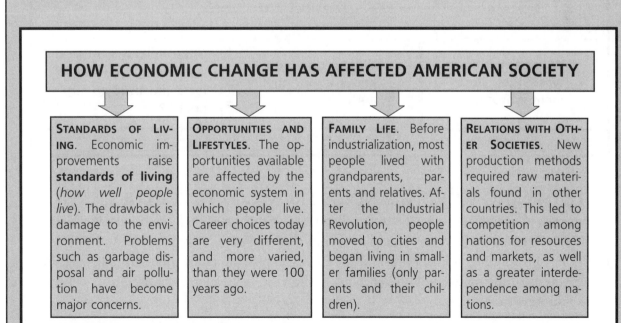

HOW ECONOMIC CHANGE HAS AFFECTED AMERICAN SOCIETY

STANDARDS OF LIVING.	OPPORTUNITIES AND LIFESTYLES.	FAMILY LIFE.	RELATIONS WITH OTHER SOCIETIES.
Economic improvements raise **standards of living** (*how well people live*). The drawback is damage to the environment. Problems such as garbage disposal and air pollution have become major concerns.	The opportunities available are affected by the economic system in which people live. Career choices today are very different, and more varied, than they were 100 years ago.	Before industrialization, most people lived with grandparents, parents and relatives. After the Industrial Revolution, people moved to cities and began living in smaller families (only parents and their children).	New production methods required raw materials found in other countries. This led to competition among nations for resources and markets, as well as a greater interdependence among nations.

SHARPENING YOUR TEST-TAKING SKILLS

INTERPRETING HISTORICAL DOCUMENTS

U.S. history tests will often require you to read and interpret historical documents. This section looks at the process of reading and understanding original historical sources.

THE SEARCH FOR MEANING

Most document-based questions on state-wide tests will present short passages of only a few sentences. These passages will often be excerpts from longer speeches or writings. When reading historical documents, use your imagination to send yourself back in time to understand someone else's point of view. A writer in the past often had very different attitudes and concerns than we have today.

UNDERSTANDING DIFFERENT POINTS OF VIEW

In reading historical documents, you must be a critical reader. It will help if you know something about the writer's position and background, so that you can see how these factors affect the writer's ideas. These are some of the main questions you should ask yourself when reading a historical document or passage:

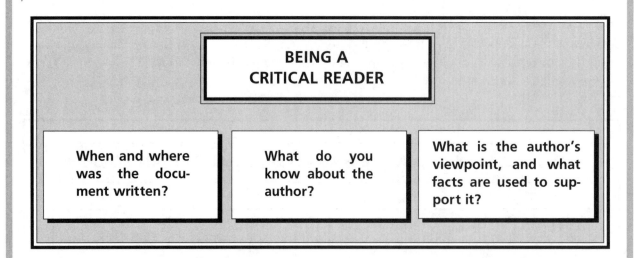

BEING A CRITICAL READER

When and where was the document written?

What do you know about the author?

What is the author's viewpoint, and what facts are used to support it?

DETERMINING WORD MEANINGS FROM CONTEXT CLUES

Sometimes you may come across unfamiliar words or phrases in a historical document. **Context clues** will help you to figure out what they mean. Think of yourself as a detective. The surrounding words, phrases and sentences provide clues that can help you uncover the meaning of the unfamiliar word. Following is a fuller explanation of context clues and how to use them.

USING CONTEXT CLUES TO FIND THE MEANING

Part of Speech	Related Familiar Words	Substitute Words	Bypass the Word
From the words in the sentence, can you guess what part of speech the unfamiliar word is: adjective, noun, verb or adverb?	Is the word similar to other words you know? Does that help you to figure out what the word means? Can you make out what the word is by breaking it up into parts, such as a prefix, word stem, or suffix?	Can you guess the meaning of the word from the context or meaning of the passage? What other words would seem to make sense if you substituted them in place of the unfamiliar word?	Can you understand the main idea of the sentence without knowing the meaning of the unfamiliar word? If so, it may not be important to spend time trying to figure out its meaning.

At the bottom of this page are specific examples that show how to use context clues.

STEPS TO INTERPRETING DOCUMENTS

Let's practice interpreting historical documents by examining two passages about the Industrial Revolution.

DOCUMENT 1:

"A child of eight — one of a dozen — stripped feathers, and had for a year earned three dollars a week. She was dwarfed in growth from confinement in the air of the workshop, from lack of proper food and no play, and thousands of these little feather-strippers are in this job forever."

—Helen Campbell, *Darkness and Daylight,* (New York, 1891)

Suppose you did not understand the word "confinement" in the second sentence. Let's use context clues to figure out the meaning of this word:

What part of speech is the word?	*Confinement* is a noun, because it designates a person, place, or thing.
Do you know any related words?	*Confinement* is made up of the word *confine* with the suffix *ment*. To confine someone is to limit the person's movement, often through imprisonment.
Is the word referred to in the surrounding text?	The young girl's *confinement* keeps her from fresh air, proper food, and play — blocking her growth. *Confinement* in the workshop is almost like a form of imprisonment.

Now let's look at the document as a whole. Consider the background of the author and what the author is saying in this document.

When and where was the document written?	New York in 1891.
What do you know about the author?	The author is a writer, describing the experiences of child laborers.
What is the author's viewpoint?	The author is sympathetic to the child and seems to oppose child labor. She states that the work is hard for the eight-year old, and sees it as a form of confinement. She goes on to say that thousands of other children share the same fate.

Now let's compare this viewpoint with a second reading selection about the Industrial Revolution, written by a woman who worked in a textile mill in Lowell, Massachusetts, from the ages of 11 to 22.

DOCUMENT 2:

"We didn't forget we were working girls, wearing coarse aprons, and that there was some danger of our becoming drudges. Sometimes the confinement of the mill became very wearisome to me. In the sweet June weather, I would lean out of the window, and try to block out the never-ending clash of sounds inside. Looking away to the hills, my whole being would cry out."

— Lucy Larcom, *A New England Girlhood*, (Boston, 1889)

When and where was the document written?	*Your Answer:* _____
What do you know about the author?	*Your Answer:* _____
What is the author's viewpoint?	*Your Answer:* _____

TESTING YOUR UNDERSTANDING

Directions: Circle the number in front of the word or expression that correctly answers the statement or question. Following the multiple-choice questions, answer the essay questions.

Base your answers to questions 1 and 2 on the following bar graph below and on your knowledge of social studies.

LABOR UNION MEMBERSHIP, 1900-1991

% OF WORKERS / Year

Source: U.S. Bureau of Labor Statistics

1 What percentage of U.S. workers were union members in 1980?
 1 15.5%
 2 16.1%
 3 2.8 %
 4 25.1 %

2 Which statement is most accurate?
 1 Union membership has remained the same.
 2 Union membership has continued to rise.
 3 Union members work hard.
 4 Union membership has dropped off recently.

3 During the second half of the 1800s, the U.S. government encouraged westward settlement by
 1 making low-interest loans to settlers
 2 paying western farmers to grow certain crops
 3 giving free land to homesteaders
 4 honoring Native American territorial claims

4 The right to collective bargaining allows
 1 employers to dismiss workers who strike
 2 workers to influence government officials
 3 government officials to set a minimum wage
 4 workers to form unions to negotiate with employers

5 In the nineteenth century, industrialization of the United States became concentrated in the Northeast because
 1 this region had the greatest supply of capital and labor
 2 the climate of the South was not suitable for industrial development
 3 other regions lacked good water transportation
 4 the West and South had few natural resources

6 Strikes, boycotts and picketing are used by
 1 unions against workers
 2 unions against employers
 3 business against unions
 4 corporations against government

7 Decisions in the collective bargaining process primarily involve
 1 labor leaders and Congress
 2 workers and management
 3 producers and consumers
 4 government and unions

8 The main purpose of anti-trust legislation was to
 1 promote mergers in business
 2 restrict foreign trade agreements
 3 preserve business competition
 4 limit the growth of union membership

9 The main benefit of an economy using mass production is that it
 1 makes workers earn their money
 2 raises production levels
 3 makes it easier for workers
 4 raises the price of goods

10 A major cause leading to the industrialization of the United States was the
1 Fourteenth Amendment
2 Sherman Anti-Trust Act
3 development of labor unions
4 expansion of railroads

11 What was the greatest problem facing America's industrial workers in the late 1800s?
1 shortage of farm crops
2 inability to vote in elections
3 decreased rates charged by railroads
4 harsh working conditions

12 Which was a major reason for the failure of 19th century labor unions in the United States?
1 public disapproval of unions
2 Congressional measures outlawing unions
3 an abundance of technical workers
4 workers were satisfied with their conditions

13 After the Civil War, the U.S. government
1 moved Native American Indians from ancestral lands onto reservations
2 encouraged Native American Indians to retain their customs and traditions
3 educated society about the cultural heritage of the Native American Indians
4 shifted responsibility for Native America Indian affairs to state governments

THEMATIC ESSAY QUESTION

Directions: Write a well-organized essay that includes an introduction, several paragraphs explaining your position, and a conclusion.

Theme: The Impact of Economic Change

> Throughout United States history, certain social groups have been profoundly influenced by economic change.

Task:

Choose *two* social groups from your study of United States history.

For *each* group:
- Discuss the major characteristics of that group.
- Describe an economic change in the 19th century that affected that group.
- Discuss an immediate or long-term effect of the economic change you selected on that group..

You may use any example from your study of American history. Some suggestions you might wish to consider include: Native American Indians, factory workers, businessmen, labor union members, farmers, and city-dwellers.

You are *not* limited to these suggestions.

CHAPTER 7

A CHANGING AMERICA

The Women's Rights Movement
  A. The Role of Women Changes
  B. The Struggle for Voting Rights
  C. The Nineteenth Amendment is Passed

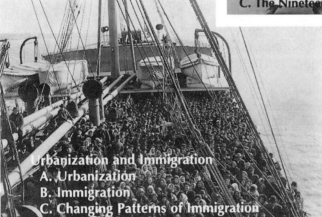

Urbanization and Immigration
  A. Urbanization
  B. Immigration
  C. Changing Patterns of Immigration

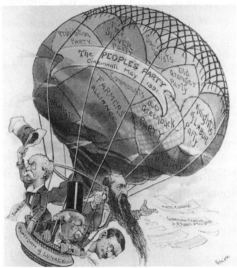

The Grange and Populist Movements
  A. America: A Nation of Farmers
  B. The Grange Movement
  C. The Populist Party

The Progressive Movement
  A. Goals
  B. Accomplishments
  C. The Progressive Presidents

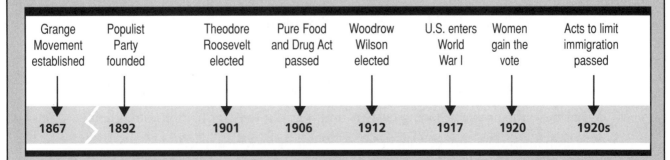

Grange Movement established	Populist Party founded	Theodore Roosevelt elected	Pure Food and Drug Act passed	Woodrow Wilson elected	U.S. enters World War I	Women gain the vote	Acts to limit immigration passed
1867	1892	1901	1906	1912	1917	1920	1920s

WHAT YOU SHOULD FOCUS ON

In this chapter, you will learn how the women's movement, after a long struggle beginning in the 1840s, finally obtained the right to vote for women.

Also during this period, industrial growth brought a vast increase in the number of immigrants coming to the United States, and a growing population in the cities. Meanwhile, farmers organized to protest against lower food prices, which were causing their incomes to fall.

Americans began to adopt important reforms to meet the many new problems posed by industrialization and urbanization. Progressive writers made people more aware of abuses that needed to be corrected, and government leaders pushed for laws that made social and economic conditions more just.

In this chapter you should be aware of the following:

Susan B. Anthony (left) and Elizabeth Cady Stanton began the women's movement.

The Women's Rights Movement	**Urbanization and Immigration**	**The Grange and Populist Movements**	**The Progressive Movement**
American women organized to achieve equal rights with men. Women struggled for the right to own property, to get a higher education, and to vote.	People flooded into cities in search of jobs and a better life. Immigrants were also attracted to city life. The urban population grew so rapidly that cities could not deal with problems of inadequate housing, poor sanitation, and medical care.	In the late 1800s, farmers' incomes were sharply reduced by falling food prices while their expenses remained high. To protect their livelihood and support their families, American farmers organized to demand "cheap money" and the regulation of the railroads.	Progressive reformers sought to end political corruption, to curb big business, and to remedy the social problems caused by industrialization. Presidents Theodore Roosevelt and Woodrow Wilson introduced Progressive reforms at the national level.

In studying this period, you should focus on the following questions:

❖ What changes took place in the lives of American women?

❖ What problems did the nation face as cities grew and immigrants flooded in?

❖ What were the problems facing farmers and how did they try to overcome them?

❖ What changes were brought about by the Progressive Movement?

THE WOMEN'S RIGHTS MOVEMENT

In this section you will learn how women struggled
for equality from the 1840s through the early 1900s.

THINK ABOUT IT

How important do you think is the right to vote? _____

Why? _____

Important Terms and Concepts: As you read this section, look for the following:

- ◆ Seneca Falls Convention
- ◆ Women's Rights Movement
- ◆ Suffrage
- ◆ Nineteenth Amendment

To help you find these terms, this symbol ◆ appears in the margin where the term is first explained.

CHANGES IN THE ROLE OF WOMEN, 1840-1920

HOW WERE WOMEN TREATED IN THE MID-1800'S?

Legally. Women were denied full equality of citizenship. They lacked the right to vote, to serve on juries and to hold public office.	**Economically.** Once a woman was married, her husband took control of her income and property. Women were paid less than men for the same work. Higher-paying jobs were closed to women.	**Socially.** Women were expected to run the home and care for the children. They received little schooling. In fact, no American colleges were willing to accept women, except Oberlin College (1837).

As you can see, in the mid-1800s women had few rights and limited opportunities. Many people believed women to be inferior in intelligence and ability. However, as a result of the Industrial Revolution, several important changes occurred in the status of women.

WOMEN AND EDUCATION

Since the mid-19th century, free public elementary schools had been open to both boys and girls. In the late 19th century, small numbers of women began obtaining a college education. These women were better able to fill the increasing numbers of jobs created by industrialization.

WOMEN AND CITIES

Because of industrialization, many families moved to cities in search of jobs. Women in the cities came across new ideas and products. New thoughts about their role in the family and society led women to work outside the home, to marry later in life, and to have smaller families. By the early 1900s, new products such as the washing machine and vacuum cleaner reduced housework.

FOCUS ON THE ARTS

Mary Cassatt, Painter

Mary Cassatt was an American artist who painted in the late 1800s and early 1900s. She spent much of her time living in France, where she studied with French painters. Cassatt is one of America's best known women artists. Her favorite subjects were mothers and children. Her paintings are admired for their simplicity and pleasing use of pastel colors. Some of her most famous works include "Mother and Child," "Lady at the Table" and "Modern Women."

THE STRUGGLE FOR VOTING RIGHTS, 1840-1870

To improve their lives, women began to organize to bring about change.

WOMEN LEADERS PRESS FOR CHANGE

Among the first leaders in the drive for women's rights were **Lucretia Mott** and **Elizabeth Cady Stanton**. In 1848, Stanton and Mott helped organize a women's rights meeting in Seneca Falls, New York. The **Seneca Falls Convention**, which passed resolutions declaring that women were equal to men, is seen as the starting point of the **Women's Rights Movement** in the United States.

ORGANIZING TO GET VOTING RIGHTS

By the late 1800s, the chief goal of the Women's Rights Movement was to obtain **suffrage** (*the right to vote*). While women were able to obtain suffrage in several western states, supporters of women's rights could not succeed in getting a constitutional amendment passed that would require all states to give women the vote. A number of groups in favor of women's suffrage came together to form

Lucretia Mott

the **National American Woman Suffrage Association**, under the leadership of Elizabeth Cady Stanton and **Susan B. Anthony**.

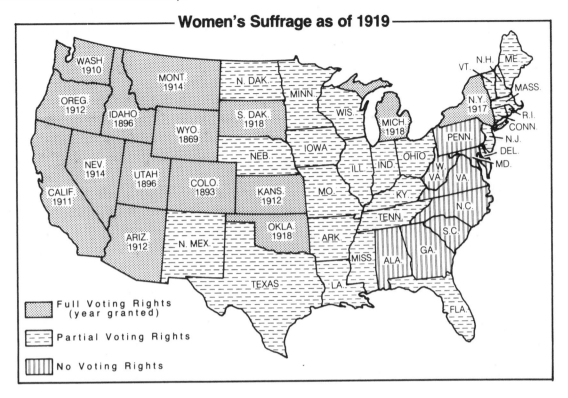

THE NINETEENTH AMENDMENT IS PASSED, 1920

During World War I, when men went off to fight in Europe, millions of women filled their jobs in factories, mills, and mines. After the war, it became hard for opponents of women's suffrage to deny that women were the equals of men. As a result, the **Nineteenth Amendment** to the Constitution was passed. It said that no state could deny a citizen the right to vote on the basis of gender. The amendment was a step forward in making the United States a true democracy of all its people. However, the amendment failed to bring about the economic equality between the sexes that its sponsors had hoped for. Women continued to face discrimination and were usually paid less for the same work than their male counterparts were.

Suffragettes demonstrating at the White House

THINKING IT OVER

Why do you think the Women's Rights Movement succeeded in obtaining suffrage? _____

_____

_____

SUMMING UP: THE WOMEN'S RIGHTS MOVEMENT

For many years, women did not have equal rights with men. During the late 1800s, women's rights groups organized, focusing their attention on gaining suffrage. After a great deal of struggle, women won the right to vote when the 19th Amendment was passed in 1920.

CHECKING YOUR UNDERSTANDING

Directions: Complete the following cards. Then answer the multiple-choice questions.

SENECA FALLS CONVENTION
Why was it held? _____
Name two Women's Rights leaders:
1._____   2._____

NINETEENTH AMENDMENT
What did it do? _____
Effects on American society:
1._____   2._____

1 The primary goal of the Women's Rights Movement in the early 1900s was to obtain
   1 cabinet positions for women
   2 reforms in prisons
   3 civil rights for all minorities
   4 suffrage for women

2 "Suffrage" can best be defined as
   1 the right to vote
   2 freedom of speech
   3 freedom of religion
   4 economic equality

3 The purpose of the Nineteenth Amendment was to
   1 give full civil rights to African Americans
   2 give women the right to vote
   3 provide for freedom of speech
   4 provide women with better jobs

4 Which statement most accurately describes the position of American women during the 1800s?
   1 Women were treated as the equals of men.
   2 Most women worked outside the home.
   3 Women were regarded as inferior to men.
   4 Most women were active in political life.

URBANIZATION AND IMMIGRATION

As America industrialized, increasing numbers of immigrants from other countries arrived,
and its cities began to grow.

THINK ABOUT IT

What do you think would be the hardest adjustment you would have to make if you moved
to another country? _____

Important Terms and Concepts: As you read this section, look for the following:

- ✦ Urbanization
- ✦ Ghettos
- ✦ Assimilation
- ✦ Cultural Pluralism
- ✦ Nativists
- ✦ Ethnocentrism

URBANIZATION

In 1865, most Americans lived in the countryside. By 1920, half the people lived in urban areas
(*cities*) like Chicago and New York. This movement of people to the cities is called **urbanization**. ✦

REASONS FOR URBANIZATION

People flocked to the cities for a number of reasons. New factories were built there, attracting people in search of work. Many people came from farms, where they had lost their jobs because of new machinery. Others moved to the city for excitement — theaters, museums, and libraries. In the late 1800s, immigrants from Europe began moving to American cities in growing numbers. By the 1900s, many African Americans moved to Northern cities in search of a better life.

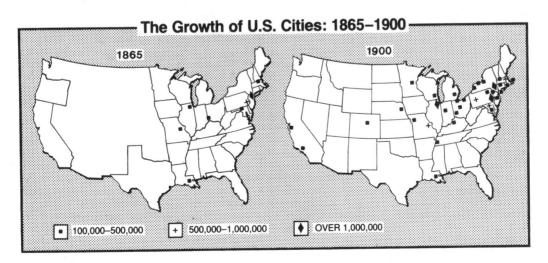

The Growth of U.S. Cities: 1865–1900

1865   1900

■ 100,000–500,000   ＋ 500,000–1,000,000   ◆ OVER 1,000,000

U.S. POPULATION BY RESIDENCE AND MEDIAN AGE: 1840-1910				
Year	Total Population	% Living in Urban Areas	% Living in Rural Areas	Median Age
1840	17 million	11%	89%	18
1850	23 million	15%	85%	19
1860	31 million	20%	80%	19
1870	40 million	26%	74%	20
1880	50 million	28%	72%	21
1890	63 million	35%	65%	22
1900	76 million	40%	60%	23
1910	92 million	46%	54%	24

Source: U.S. Historical Abstract

Sometimes state examinations contain questions on how to interpret information found in a table. This Skill Builder section explains how to answer these types of questions.

What Is a Table?

A table is an arrangement of words or numbers into columns and rows. It is used to organize large amounts of information so that it can be easily located and compared.

Keys to Understanding a Table

To understand a table of information, look at its major parts:

Title. The title tells you the overall topic. For example, the title of the above table is "U. S. Population by Residence and Median Age: 1840 -1910." It compares the total population of the U.S. living in urban and rural areas during the years 1840 through 1910.

Categories. Tables are composed of categories of information listed in different columns. The categories are named in the headings across the top. In the table above, the categories listed are the *year*, the *total population* of Americans, the percentage of people living in *urban areas* and *rural areas*, and the *median age*.

Interpreting a Table

First look at the title: it tells you the overall meaning of the information presented. For specific information, you must find where the columns and rows of categories intersect. For example, if you want to find the percentage of Americans living in rural areas in 1880, start from the top of the column marked *% Living in Rural Areas* and slide your finger down the column until you reach the year *1880*. The point at which they intersect shows that in 1880, 72% of the population lived in rural areas.

Sometimes a question about tables may ask you to identify a **trend** (*a general direction or tendency*). You can figure out a trend by looking at the information in the table. For example, one trend indicated by our table is that the number of Americans living in urban areas was increasing each year. Identify two other trends based on this table:

1. The median age of Americans _____

2. _____

THE CITIES FACE NEW PROBLEMS

As cities grew, new problems began to develop. These problems often proved difficult to solve.

PROBLEMS FACED BY GROWING CITIES

Public Services. Cities could not deliver proper public services — hospitals, police and firemen, schools, or garbage collection. Families were crowded into **tenements** (*single room apartments*), often without heat or light.

Social Tensions. The rich enjoyed lives of luxury. Seeing the wealth of the rich made it harder for the poor to bear their terrible conditions, and increased the tensions of city life.

Political corruption. Many cities were run by corrupt political bosses who provided jobs and services to immigrants in exchange for their votes.

A crowded Chicago street in 1915, typical of city life in the early 20th century

IMMIGRATION

One reason cities grew so fast was because of the flood of immigration. The majority of immigrants came to the United States for the following reasons:

WHY PEOPLE EMIGRATED TO AMERICA

To Escape. Some came to escape horrible conditions of poverty. For example, the potato famine in Ireland in the 1840s led large numbers of Irish immigrants to come to America.

To Seek Freedom. Some came to escape religious and political persecution. For example, Russian Jews came in the 1880s to escape from government-sponsored violence against them.

A Better Life. Many came because they had heard about better living conditions and the availability of jobs in America. For example, many Poles, Hungarians, Austrians, Swedes and Chinese came looking for better-paying jobs.

PROBLEMS OF EARNING A LIVING

Most of the immigrants arriving after 1880 were poor, and usually settled in cities. Besides having to overcome poverty, the immigrants had to adjust to a new language and new customs. Most had to work as unskilled laborers for long hours and very low pay. In addition, immigrants usually lived in overcrowded apartments and suffered from unhealthy living conditions.

ADJUSTING TO A NEW WAY OF LIFE

Since many immigrants could not speak English and had ways of life different from those of the people already living here, they faced discrimination. In order to feel more comfortable in their new surroundings, immigrants often settled in **ghettos** (*communities made up of people of the same nationality*). However, living in ghettos made it more difficult for immigrants to become "Americanized" — to learn the English language and the American way of life. In the public schools, however, their children learned English and adopted American ways.

Do immigrants assimilate into American culture or continue to identify with their former national cultures?	
POINT: ASSIMILATION	COUNTERPOINT: CULTURAL PLURALISM
Under the "melting pot" theory, by adopting American customs and the English language, immigrants "melt" into the American culture. As part of the process, many foreign customs become part of American life, as seen in some of the foods we eat, our music, and some of the expressions in our language.	Under the "salad bowl" theory, America has no uniform culture. Each immigrant group proudly retains its own unique identity, while possessing some values in common with the other groups that make up America. With cultural pluralism, many diverse peoples live side by side rather than "melting together."

CHANGING PATTERNS OF IMMIGRATION

"OLD" AND "NEW" IMMIGRANTS

In the first hundred years after independence, the United States had no laws limiting immigration. Most immigrants came from northern Europe, especially Great Britain, Ireland and Germany. In general they were Protestant, except for the Irish, who were Catholic. Most spoke English. They became known as the **"Old Immigrants."** The pattern of immigration changed in the 1880s. Immigrants now came from southern and eastern Europe, especially, Italy, Greece, Poland, Austria-Hungary, and Russia. They were Catholic or Jewish, rather than Protestant. They often were extremely poor, spoke little or no English, and dressed differently from most Americans. For these reasons, they were called the **"New Immigrants."**

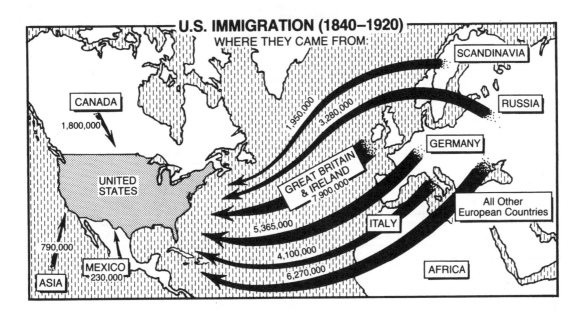

U.S. IMMIGRATION (1840-1920)
WHERE THEY CAME FROM:

SCANDINAVIA
RUSSIA
GERMANY
All Other European Countries
GREAT BRITAIN & IRELAND 7,900,000
ITALY
AFRICA
ASIA
MEXICO 230,000
790,000
UNITED STATES
CANADA 1,800,000
1,950,000
3,280,000
5,365,000
4,100,000
6,270,000

ATTEMPTS TO LIMIT IMMIGRATION (1880-1965)

At the end of the 1800s, as the number of immigrants increased, some Americans spoke out against further immigration. Those opposing immigration were known as **nativists**. They were often accused of **ethnocentrism** — the belief that one's own race and culture are superior to others. Nativists wanted immigration slowed or stopped. They feared the "new immigrants," with their foreign customs and languages, would never adjust to American society. In addition, nativists felt that immigrants would take jobs from other Americans because they were willing to work for less. As nativist feeling spread, Congress passed laws to limit immigration. The earliest laws were directed against Asians. In the 1920s, laws were also

U.S. officials inspect immigrants arriving at Ellis Island.

passed to limit immigration from southern and eastern Europe.

■ The **Chinese Exclusion Act (1882)** and the **Gentlemen's Agreement (1907)** were measures limiting immigration from China and Japan.

■ **Immigration Acts of 1921, 1924, and 1929.** These acts established quotas limiting immigration from eastern and southern Europe. In large part, these acts were passed as a result of ethnic prejudice against the so-called New Immigrants.

IMMIGRATION SINCE 1965

Immigration laws were greatly changed in 1965. Since then, people who already have relatives in the United States, who have specific job skills, or who are political **refugees** (*people escaping from persecution in their native lands*) are permitted to enter the United States before other groups.

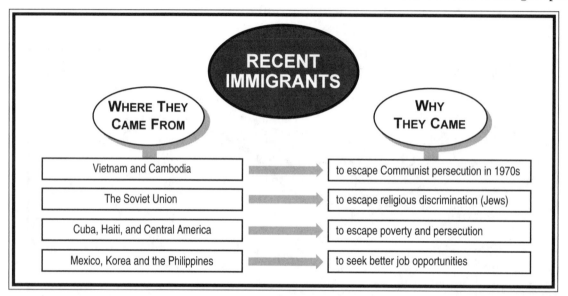

In recent years there has been a rise in illegal immigration. Perhaps a million so-called **undocumented aliens** illegally enter the country each year. Since 1965, the largest number have come from Latin America and Asia, and very few from Europe. The fact that so many people still want to come to the U. S. has created a problem.

ANALYSIS

The tremendous increase in immigration has raised some important questions. How do you feel about each question?

• Should the United States put some limits on immigration? _____

• How many people should we admit each year?_____

• Which groups should we allow in? _____

• How strictly should we enforce laws against illegal immigrants?_____

THINKING IT OVER

Now that you have read this section, what do you think is the hardest adjustment faced

by most immigrants? _____

Explain. _____

SUMMING UP: URBANIZATION AND IMMIGRATION

Cities grew with the rise of industry, attracting people in search of jobs. In the late 1800s and early 1900s, immigrants came to U.S. cities in large numbers — escaping political and economic conditions in their countries, and hoping for a better life. The immigrants faced many problems. The United States has since limited the number of legal immigrants. America continues to attract people from other nations, and shaping immigration policy is difficult.

CHECKING YOUR UNDERSTANDING

Directions: Complete the following cards. Then answer the multiple-choice questions.

URBANIZATION

Definition: _____

List two reasons why it happened:

1._____
2._____

NATIVISTS

Definition: _____

List two reasons why they oppose more immigration:

1._____
2._____

1 Which statement accurately describes an experience shared by most immigrants to the U.S. in the 1890s?
 1 They frequently met with hostility and resentment.
 2 They mainly settled in farming areas.
 3 They immediately adopted the American lifestyle.
 4 They soon enrolled in colleges to get an advanced education.

2 Which development in the late 1800s was a cause of the other three?
 1 Hard times were experienced by many people living in Europe.
 2 Immigration to the United States increased.
 3 Immigrants settled in American cities.
 4 Many immigrants had difficulty adjusting to life in the United States.

3 The movement of people from rural areas to cities is called
   1 nativism   3 urbanization
   2 imperialism   4 communism

4 Which is the most accurate statement about immigration to the United States?
   1 Immigrants have always adopted "American" customs and traditions.
   2 The nations from which immigrants have come have changed over time.
   3 Today, the United States admits all people who wish to come here.
   4 Immigrants rarely face any problems when coming to America.

5 Which best explains why immigration laws were passed in the 1920s?
   1 Industrialization reduced the demand for immigrant labor.
   2 Many nativist groups opposed continued immigration.
   3 Labor unions favored unlimited immigration.
   4 Urbanization was on the decline.

6 The Chinese Exclusion Act and the Gentleman's Agreement both sought to
   1 increase European immigration
   2 set up an Asian cultural exchange
   3 restrict Asian immigration
   4 attract skilled Asian workers

SECTION 3

THE GRANGE AND POPULIST MOVEMENTS

In this section you will read about how new political parties were formed in an effort to get the government to help farmers and other groups.

THINK ABOUT IT

Let's suppose the local utility company — the only one in town — doubles its price for electricity. What are some things you could do in response to this action? _____

_____

Important Terms and Concepts: As you read this section, look for the following:

◆ **Grange Movement**   ◆ **Populist Party**
◆ **Interstate Commerce Act** ◆ **Third Parties**

AMERICA: A NATION OF FARMERS

Today, less than 2% of the United States population lives on farms. However, life was quite different in the 1870s, when the majority of Americans were farmers.

THE PROBLEMS OF FARMERS: 1870-1900

In the late 1800s, farmers experienced great difficulties as food prices dropped lower and lower, while their own expenses remained high. This situation resulted from a number of causes.

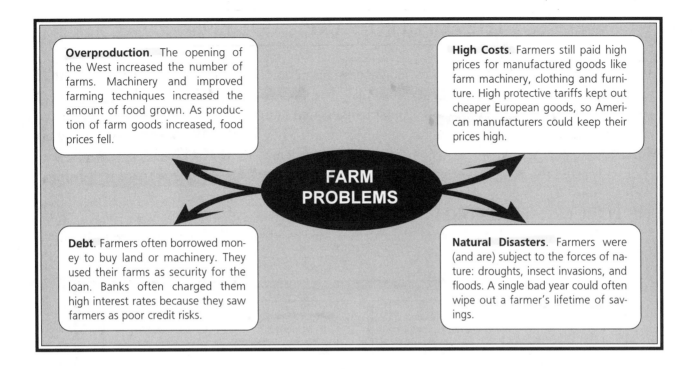

Overproduction. The opening of the West increased the number of farms. Machinery and improved farming techniques increased the amount of food grown. As production of farm goods increased, food prices fell.

High Costs. Farmers still paid high prices for manufactured goods like farm machinery, clothing and furniture. High protective tariffs kept out cheaper European goods, so American manufacturers could keep their prices high.

FARM PROBLEMS

Debt. Farmers often borrowed money to buy land or machinery. They used their farms as security for the loan. Banks often charged them high interest rates because they saw farmers as poor credit risks.

Natural Disasters. Farmers were (and are) subject to the forces of nature: droughts, insect invasions, and floods. A single bad year could often wipe out a farmer's lifetime of savings.

THE GRANGE MOVEMENT

Many farmers began to organize into groups to deal with their problems. In 1867, the **Grange ✦ Movement** was established. The Grange (*the word mean barns or farmhouses*) was a national association of farmers' clubs. At first it was primarily a social group focusing on activities like picnics, lectures and dances. As the problems of farmers grew, the Grangers became a group whose goal was to influence the government to improve farmers' standards of living.

Most farmers saw the railroads as the main cause of their difficulties, since the railroads charged them high prices for shipping crops to market. In several Midwestern states, Grangers elected candidates who passed **Granger laws** (*laws favoring farmers*) which controlled the rates that railroads could charge farmers. Eventually, the Supreme Court declared many of the Granger laws unconstitutional because they interfered with interstate commerce (*trade between states*). The Grangers then turned to Congress for help. In 1887, Congress passed the **Interstate Commerce Act**. This ✦ act created a government agency to regulate the railroads and interstate commerce.

Farming on the Great Plains was often a hard and lonely existence.

THE POPULIST PARTY, 1891-1896

Although the Grange Movement had some success, farmers continued to have difficulties. In 1892 they joined forces with a new political party called the **Populist Party**. The Populists represented farmers, laborers, and factory workers against bankers and railroads. The Populists were convinced that big business had too much influence on government. They felt that they could no longer count on the two major parties — the Democrats and Republicans — to make needed changes. The Populists wanted the federal government to take more responsibility for the people's well-being.

THE POPULIST PLATFORM

In 1892, the Populists selected a candidate to run for President. The Populist program included many new ideas:

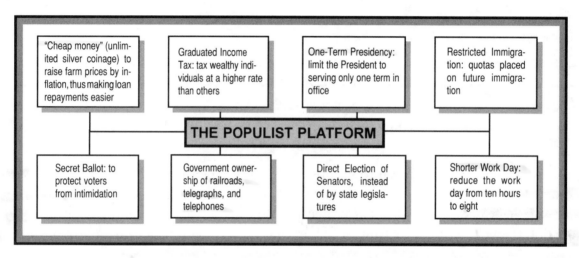

"Cheap money" (unlimited silver coinage) to raise farm prices by inflation, thus making loan repayments easier	Graduated Income Tax: tax wealthy individuals at a higher rate than others	One-Term Presidency: limit the President to serving only one term in office	Restricted Immigration: quotas placed on future immigration

THE POPULIST PLATFORM

Secret Ballot: to protect voters from intimidation	Government ownership of railroads, telegraphs, and telephones	Direct Election of Senators, instead of by state legislatures	Shorter Work Day: reduce the work day from ten hours to eight

ELECTION CAMPAIGNS

With their greatest support in Southern, Northwestern and Mountain states, the Populists turned their attention to getting candidates elected to office. In 1892, the Populists received over a million votes for their Presidential candidate. In 1896, the Democratic Party nominated **William Jennings Bryan** for President after his convention speech, in which he denounced bankers for trying to "crucify mankind on a cross of gold." Bryan supported farmers' interests so strongly that the Populists decided to support him. As a result, the Democrats adopted much of the Populist program, and a separate Populist Party no longer seemed necessary. However, Bryan lost the election to the Republican candidate, **William McKinley**. In 1900, Bryan ran again, but McKinley was re-elected. Bryan's second defeat and better economic times for farmers brought about the end of the Populist movement.

Cartoon attacking William Jennings Bryan's use of religious symbols in his "Cross of Gold" speech

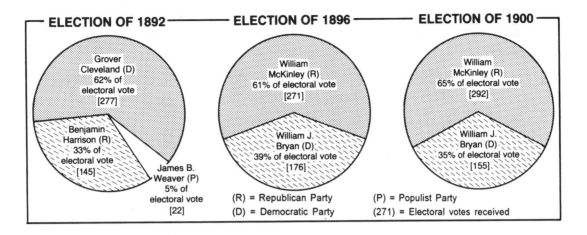

THE ROLE OF THIRD PARTIES

There have been two major political parties in the United States throughout most of its history. Smaller parties have usually been referred to as "**third parties.**" The Populists illustrate the role ◆ often played by third parties in American politics — they provide an outlet for minorities to voice their grievances, generate new ideas, propose new solutions, and educate the public.

- ■ **The Formation of Third Parties.** Third party movements usually are formed when the major political parties ignore a vital public issue. Some issues that third parties have focused on are women's suffrage and abortion.

- ■ **Influence of Third Parties.** If a third party is successful, one or both of the major parties will usually adopt its ideas — much as the Democrats adopted the Populist program. The best evidence of the influence of third parties is that many third party proposals have become laws. Some Populist ideas that later became laws were the **graduated income tax** (*taxing higher-income people at a higher rate than others*), the **direct election of Senators** (*having Senators elected by the voters of a state, rather than by the members of the state legislature.*) and the **secret ballot** (*being able to vote without others knowing how one voted*).

SUMMING UP: THE GRANGE AND POPULIST MOVEMENTS

The period from the 1870s to the early 1900s saw the lives of most farmers change for the worse. They received less money for their crops, and paid more for machinery, supplies and shipping. In an effort to improve their lives, farmers organized the Grange Movement. Eventually, farmers joined with other groups to support a new political party, the Populists. Although no Populist ever became President, many Populist ideas eventually became law.

THINKING IT OVER

Would you now change your tactics in response to a doubling of electricity prices? _____

Explain. _____

_____

CHECKING YOUR UNDERSTANDING

Directions: Complete the following cards. Then answer the multiple-choice questions.

THE GRANGE MOVEMENT

What was it? _____

Identify one demand of the Grangers:

_____

_____

THE POPULIST MOVEMENT

What was it?: _____

List two demands of the Populists:

1. _____
2. _____

---

1 A major aim of both the Grange and the Populist Movements was to
   1 get the government to stop the abuses of railroad owners
   2 require the government to end inflation
   3 pass laws that prevented state regulation of monopolies
   4 support unlimited immigration of Asians

2 A supporter of the Grange Movement would probably have been in favor of
   1 government regulation of railroads
   2 lower food prices
   3 higher bank interest rates
   4 higher protective tariffs for manufactured goods

3 Which statement best describes many of the reforms proposed by the Populist Party?
   1 They were just campaign promises.
   2 Most voters opposed Populist ideas.
   3 They were undesirable for a democracy.
   4 They were later achieved by other political parties.

4 Third parties in the United States have usually led to
   1 less participation in politics by citizens
   2 an end to democratic government
   3 the introduction of new ideas into government
   4 an end to all immigration to the U.S.

5 The Grangers and the Populists were most interested in helping
   1 Native American Indian groups
   2 African Americans
   3 businessmen and politicians
   4 farmers and workers

6 Many of the reforms first proposed by third parties were later adopted by the two major political parties. This suggests that
   1 major political parties support all third parties
   2 third parties can often influence the major political parties
   3 the major political parties will no longer exist in the future
   4 third party issues do not affect the major political parties

7 Presidential nominee William Jennings Bryan would have expected voter support to come from
   1 farmers
   2 bankers
   3 businessmen
   4 factory owners

8 An important characteristic of a graduated income tax is that it is
   1 paid by corporations but not by individuals
   2 charged only by the federal government
   3 paid only by the wealthy
   4 based on an individual's income

THE PROGRESSIVE MOVEMENT, 1900-1920

In this section you will read about the Progressive
Movement and its efforts to introduce new reforms
to local, state and national government.

THINK ABOUT IT

What do you think are some of the wrongs that exist in American society today?

_____

Important Terms and Concepts: As you read this section, look for the following:

- ✦ Progressive Movement
- ✦ Muckrakers
- ✦ Initiative
- ✦ Referendum

- ✦ Recall
- ✦ Pure Food and Drug Act
- ✦ Graduated Income Tax
- ✦ Clayton Anti-Trust Act

THE GOALS OF THE PROGRESSIVES

The period from 1900 to 1920 saw the flowering of the **Progressive Movement**. The Progressives gained their name because their aim was to achieve **progress** by correcting political and economic abuses that had resulted from America's rapid industrialization. Progressives wanted to use the power of government to stop these abuses, so that all Americans could enjoy better lives. To achieve this, Progressives felt they had to reform government, which had been corrupted by big business and political "bosses." Although the Progressives borrowed some Populist ideas, they were a very different group. Progressives were mainly middle-class people from the cities, while the Populists had been mainly farmers from the countryside. Progressive reforms moved the U.S. away from a laissez-faire economy (*with little government interference in business*) to one in which government regulations prevented many of the abuses of economic power.

THE ACCOMPLISHMENTS OF THE PROGRESSIVES

THE PROBLEMS

Some cities had grown so fast that they could not deal with such problems as overcrowded housing, poor schools, and inadequate health services. Looking for a solution, people turned to the local head of one of the political parties, known as a **political boss**. Bosses helped people get jobs, housing and even loans. In return, the boss expected these people to vote for candidates he recommended. Once the candidate was elected, the boss often took advantage of his contacts in government to steal from the public treasury or to make money in other illegal ways.

THE MUCKRAKERS

Among the early Progressives who had the most influence were a group of newspaper reporters and writers known as the **muckrakers**. They got this name because they "raked" through the muck (*dirt*) of American life in search of news. The muckrakers wrote about people who suffered as a result of industrialization. They also let the American people know about the dishonest and corrupt practices of people in government and big business. Some newspaper, magazine and television reporters today act as modern muckrakers, exposing problems to help bring about reforms.

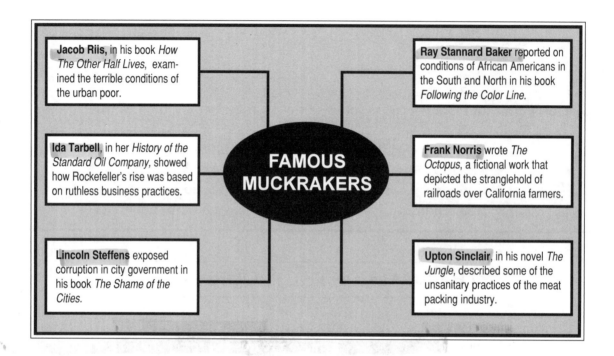

Jacob Riis, in his book *How The Other Half Lives*, examined the terrible conditions of the urban poor.

Ray Stannard Baker reported on conditions of African Americans in the South and North in his book *Following the Color Line*.

Ida Tarbell, in her *History of the Standard Oil Company*, showed how Rockefeller's rise was based on ruthless business practices.

FAMOUS MUCKRAKERS

Frank Norris wrote *The Octopus*, a fictional work that depicted the stranglehold of railroads over California farmers.

Lincoln Steffens exposed corruption in city government in his book *The Shame of the Cities*.

Upton Sinclair, in his novel *The Jungle*, described some of the unsanitary practices of the meat packing industry.

PROGRESSIVE REFORMS

Many Americans believe that society can be made better through reform. The Progressive Movement — like the earlier Abolitionist Movement against slavery, and the Women's Rights Movement — was another example of Americans determined to solve problems through reform.

Progressives believed that big business had a corrupting influence on politicians, preventing meaningful attempts to solve the problems of industrialization. Dishonesty and stealing had become all too common in the federal government. Much of the corruption resulted from the **spoils system**. Under this system, government jobs were given not to the most qualified people, but to those who made contributions or worked for the winning party. Some Presidents began favoring the **merit system** as a way of awarding jobs. In 1883, Congress passed a law creating a **Civil Service Commission**. Afterwards, federal jobs were awarded on the basis of how well people did on special examinations.

Progressives urged still further political and social reform. Following are some of the political reforms passed during the era of the Progressive Movement, at both the state and national levels.

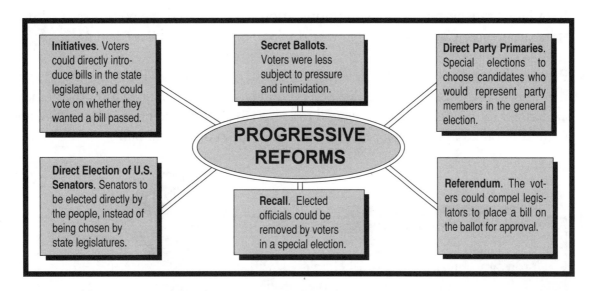

Initiatives. Voters could directly introduce bills in the state legislature, and could vote on whether they wanted a bill passed.

Secret Ballots. Voters were less subject to pressure and intimidation.

Direct Party Primaries. Special elections to choose candidates who would represent party members in the general election.

PROGRESSIVE REFORMS

Direct Election of U.S. Senators. Senators to be elected directly by the people, instead of being chosen by state legislatures.

Recall. Elected officials could be removed by voters in a special election.

Referendum. The voters could compel legislators to place a bill on the ballot for approval.

THE PROGRESSIVE PRESIDENTS

Theodore Roosevelt and Woodrow Wilson were Presidents who identified with the Progressive Movement. They tried to use their Presidential powers to introduce important reforms to correct some of the problems created by industrialization.

THEODORE ROOSEVELT (1901-1909)

Theodore "Teddy" Roosevelt became President in 1901, when President **William McKinley** was assassinated. Roosevelt believed that the President, as the only official who represented *all* the people, should act strongly in their interests.

■ **Roosevelt the "Trust-Buster."** How Roosevelt put his beliefs into action can be seen by the way he treated businesses called **trusts** (*companies that joined together to limit competition*). He believed there were "good" and "bad" trusts. "Bad trusts" acted unfairly against the public interest. For example, Roosevelt took steps to break up John D. Rockefeller's Standard Oil Company because its control of the entire oil industry made it a "bad trust." Roosevelt did not break up many trusts, but he established the idea that the federal government should break up harmful ones. For this reason, Roosevelt earned a reputation as the "trust-buster."

This cartoon calls attention to Roosevelt's role as a trust-buster.

■ **Square Deal Legislation.** Roosevelt promised Americans a "Square Deal." This meant fair play and equal opportunities. In order to do this he acted to:

• **Protect Public Health**. The **Pure Food and Drug Act** and **Meat Inspection Act** were passed in 1906 to protect consumers. They established government inspection of foods, meats, and drugs sold to the public.

- **Regulate Transportation and Communication.** He increased the powers of the Interstate Commerce Commission to protect the interests of the public.

- **Protect the Environment.** Roosevelt was an avid outdoorsman. He drew attention to the need to conserve forests, wildlife and natural resources. He helped form the National Conservation Commission, dedicated to preserving forests and protecting wildlife and natural resources. He helped preserve wilderness areas on federal lands.

FOCUS ON THE ARTS

Upton Sinclair, Novelist

Upton Sinclair, a muckraker, helped to focus the nation's attention on abuses in the meat packing industry. Sinclair's novel *The Jungle* told of rats crawling into sausage-mixing hoppers. Often, these rats were ground up with the sausage meat. His stories shocked the nation. Such an uproar resulted that Congress passed new laws requiring government inspections of all meat and prepared foods.

WOODROW WILSON (1913-1921)

In 1908, Roosevelt's friend **William Taft** was elected President. In 1912, Taft was nominated again by the Republican Party. Roosevelt, who had become dissatisfied with Taft, decided to accept the nomination of a new third party, known as the Progressive or **Bull Moose Party**. This split the Republican Party and allowed the Democratic nominee, Woodrow Wilson, to win the election. Like Roosevelt and other Progressives, Wilson used his powers as President to control big business and to improve the living conditions of the American people. Wilson promised Americans what he called the **New Freedom**. Wilson persuaded Congress to pass several major laws favored by Progressives:

Woodrow Wilson

- ■ **Graduated Income Tax (1913).** A graduated or progressive income tax requires people with higher incomes to pay a higher percentage of their income in tax than people with lower incomes. Wilson introduced the graduated **Federal Income Tax** as a result of the passage of the **Sixteenth Amendment** to the U.S. Constitution.

- ■ **Regulate the Economy.** The **Federal Reserve Act (1913)** established 12 Federal Reserve Banks, to serve as "banker's banks." These banks lend money to other banks. The act regulated the banking industry by fixing the amount of money banks could lend.

■ **New Antitrust Legislation.** Under Wilson, the federal government took further steps to encourage business competition. Congress passed the **Clayton Antitrust Act (1914)**, which outlawed many of the actions being used by some businesses to prevent competition. The **Federal Trade Commission**, a new federal agency, was created to enforce anti-trust laws and to protect consumers against unfair practices by businesses.

THE PROGRESSIVE MOVEMENT COMES TO AN END

In 1914, World War I began in Europe. The U.S. entered the war in 1917. Women's suffrage and "Prohibition" of alcoholic drinks were both passed just after the war. These were the final reforms of the Progressive Era. By then, the best Progressive ideas had passed into law, and Progressivism lost much of its appeal. The war also made many people lose their faith in the ability of government to solve social problems. As a result, the Progressive Movement came to an end.

SUMMING UP: THE PROGRESSIVE MOVEMENT

The Progressive Movement was formed by people who hoped to solve some of the problems caused by industrialization. Progressive writers and government leaders were effective in making people more aware of conditions that needed to be corrected. Progressive Presidents, such as Theodore Roosevelt and Woodrow Wilson, led the fight for the federal government to curb the abuses of big business and to protect those who had suffered the most as a result of industrialization. The Progressive Movement came to an end by 1920.

THINKING IT OVER

Which political reform of the Progressives would you use if you thought there was:

a corrupt official? _____

a bad law? _____

the need for a new law? _____

CHECKING YOUR UNDERSTANDING

Directions: Complete the following cards. Then answer the multiple-choice questions.

PROGRESSIVE MOVEMENT
What were its goals? _____
What reforms were introduced? _____
_____

MUCKRAKERS
Name two: _____
What did they do? _____
_____

1   Which encouraged the growth of the Progressive Movement?
    1   the activities of muckrakers, Populists and reformers
    2   the failure of Reconstruction
    3   the racial conflict in the South
    4   the movement of people from cities to the countryside

2   The reforms of the Progressive Era resulted primarily from the efforts of
    1   the Supreme Court
    2   authors and social activists
    3   political bosses
    4   bankers and industrialists

3   The direct election of Senators, the graduated income tax and the use of national primaries were all measures introduced during the
    1   Civil War
    2   Reconstruction Period
    3   Progressive Era
    4   New Deal

4   The major concern of the Progressives was
    1   protecting U.S. business abroad
    2   improving social and economic conditions
    3   abolishing slavery in the South
    4   settling the American frontier

5   Throughout the history of the United States, the word "reform" has usually referred to
    1   eliminating democracy
    2   achieving greater fairness and justice
    3   suspending the Bill of Rights
    4   lowering food prices

6   The purpose of agencies such as the Federal Trade Commission and the Interstate Commerce Commission is to
    1   regulate business in the public interest
    2   promote government ownership of business
    3   protect the interests of labor unions
    4   increase investment and exports

7   The initiative, recall, and referendum are examples of
    1   types of foreign policies
    2   reforms making government much more democratic
    3   government regulations passed to control big business
    4   abolitionist measures adopted before the Civil War

8   Muckrakers were people who attempted to
    1   prevent immigration into the United States
    2   expose corrupt practices in government and business
    3   decrease the birthrate in the United States
    4   prepare the nation for future wars

9   Which statement is supported by a study of the Progressive Movement?
    1   The Progressives wished to ease immigration requirements.
    2   Progressives supported government attempts to reform certain evils in society.
    3   The Progressives opposed the reforms proposed by the Populists.
    4   Progressives supported the growth of big business.

10 A system of taxation in which the income of wealthy individuals is taxed at a higher rate than others is known as a
    1   protective tariff
    2   luxury tax
    3   progressive income tax
    4   sales tax

11 A major goal of the Progressive Presidents in the early 1900s was to
    1   bring about state ownership of all public utilities
    2   find jobs for people who were unemployed
    3   replace company officials who were corrupt
    4   use the power of government to correct abuses in society

PROFILES IN HISTORY

SUSAN B. ANTHONY
(SUFFRAGETTE)

Susan B. Anthony was a leader in the movement to abolish slavery and to achieve equal rights for women. In 1869, she helped to found the National American Woman Suffrage Association. In 1872, she tested the 14th and 15th Amendments by voting in New York State —

Susan B. Anthony

for which she was fined $100. She was scorned for voting, and accused of acting more like a man than a woman. In her honor, the 19th Amendment is known as the "Susan B. Anthony Amendment."

JANE ADDAMS AND LILLIAN WALD
(SOCIAL REFORMERS)

Jane Addams and Lillian Wald were reformers in the "Settlement House" movement. Settlement houses were places for poor people living in the cities to learn to read and write, and to obtain the social services they needed. In 1889, Jane Ad-dams opened Hull House in a slum area of Chicago. Soon afterwards, Lillian Wald opened the Henry Street Settlement House in New York City. Others followed their example. For many immigrants living in cities, Settlement houses represented a place of safety and self-improvement.

IDA B. WELLS
(REFORMER)

Ida B. Wells was a crusading journalist who worked to stop a form of violence called lynching (*hanging by a mob*) in America. Because of her editorials and speeches against the lynching of African Americans, she faced personal threats, mob violence and bomb at-

tacks, but she persisted in her crusade. She was also a co-founder of the N.A.A.C.P.

JOHN MUIR
(CONSERVATIONIST)

John Muir was a conservationist and a crusader for the protection the beautiful landscape and natural wonders of America. A friend of President Theodore Roosevelt, Muir worked to conserve and protect our natural environment. He is credited with making Yosemite in California a national park. In 1892 he founded the Sierra Club, a group devoted to preserving wilderness areas in their natural state.

ELIZABETH BLACKWELL
(DOCTOR)

In 1849, Elizabeth Blackwell, despite strong male opposition, became the first woman to receive a medical degree in the United States. She founded the first school in America dedicated to training nurses. She became a leader in the movement to encourage women to become professionals — lawyers, doctors, ministers and teachers.

THE CONSTITUTION AT WORK

KEY AMENDMENTS

SIXTEENTH AMENDMENT (1913)
Gave Congress the power to collect income taxes.

SEVENTEENTH AMENDMENT (1913)
Changed the election of U.S. Senators from selection by state legislatures to direct election by voters.

EIGHTEENTH AMENDMENT (1919)
Prohibited the manufacture, sale, importation or transportation of alcoholic beverages. In 1933 it was repealed by the 21st Amendment.

NINETEENTH AMENDMENT (1920)
Gave women the right to vote.

KEY LAWS

INTERSTATE COMMERCE ACT (1887)
Prohibited railroads from charging different rates to customers shipping goods over the same distance. An Interstate Commerce Commission was created to investigate complaints and enforce the act. The act marked the first step towards having the federal government regulate unfair business practices. The I.C.C. was the first of many regulatory agencies created to watch over business.

PURE FOOD AND DRUG ACT (1906)
This act was a direct result of a novel written by Upton Sinclair about unsanitary practices in the meat-packing industry. The act made it illegal to sell mislabeled foods.

THE COURT SPEAKS

MUNN v. ILLINOIS (1877)
Background: Midwestern farmers felt they were overcharged by railroads and grain warehouses. Illinois passed a law limiting the rate railroads and warehouses could charge farmers. The railroads argued that Illinois deprived them of their property without constitutional "due process" of law.

Decision/Significance: The Court upheld the right of a state to regulate railroads and grain warehouses because their rates were closely related to the public interest. The ruling allowed states to regulate businesses which the state believed affected the public interest.

WABASH v. ILLINOIS (1886)
Background: Illinois passed a law penalizing railroads if they charged the same or more for shipping freight for short distances as they did for long distances. The Wabash Railroad said that Illinois had no right to regulate prices on an **interstate** line even if the trip was within the state's borders.

Decision/Significance: The Court ruled that only Congress, not the states, could regulate interstate commerce rates. This ended state regulation of most railroads, but led to increased federal regulation of interstate commerce. The ruling was followed by passage of the Interstate Commerce Act (*see above*).

SUMMARIZING YOUR UNDERSTANDING

Directions: Confirm your understanding of the important terms and concepts in this chapter. Check those you can explain. For those you are not sure of, find the ✦ symbol in the margin next to the term and review it.

Directions: Fill in the information called for in the following organizers.

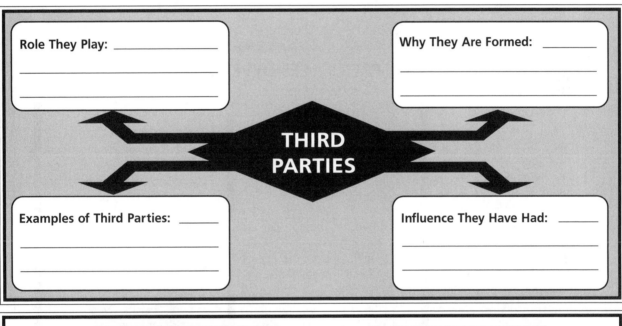

Role They Play: _____
_____
_____

Why They Are Formed: _____
_____
_____

THIRD PARTIES

Examples of Third Parties: _____
_____
_____

Influence They Have Had: _____
_____
_____

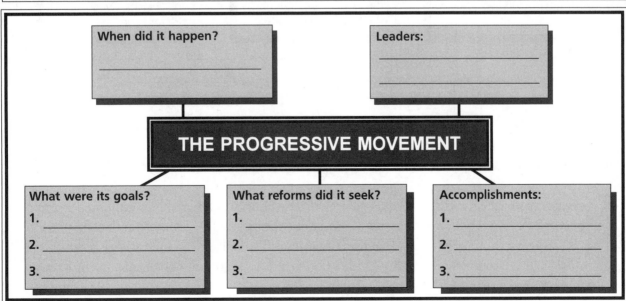

When did it happen?
_____
_____

Leaders:
_____
_____

THE PROGRESSIVE MOVEMENT

What were its goals?
1. _____
2. _____
3. _____

What reforms did it seek?
1. _____
2. _____
3. _____

Accomplishments:
1. _____
2. _____
3. _____

TEST HELPER

Much of your study of American history focused on our nation's leaders — who have traditionally been wealthy white Protestant men. But to truly understand our history, we need to study other groups. We often refer to these groups as **minorities**, even though, if we include women, they actually make up a majority of the population. Let's look at the patterns of prejudice many groups have faced.

THE ROOTS OF PREJUDICE

Prejudice refers to negative attitudes and beliefs about people from other racial, ethnic, or gender groups. What causes people to be prejudiced? Social scientists have identified several factors that explain why people become prejudiced:

— HOW PREJUDICES DEVELOP —

Psychological Factors

People often feel more familiar with those in the same racial, ethnic, class or gender group. Lack of familiarity leads to looking at other groups as "outsiders." This **ethnocentrism** increases a group's self-esteem if they believe they are superior and other groups are inferior.

Influence of Tradition

We are not born with prejudices: we learn them from family and friends. Dominant groups have often looked down on other groups as inferior. For example, many men thought women were incapable of rational decision-making. This often led women to limit their expectations of what they could achieve.

Economic Competition

Often prejudice is increased by fears of economic competition. For example, in the late 1800s poor blacks feared that the flood of new immigrants would take away their jobs by working for less money. Poor whites have also feared competition from poor blacks who might work for lower pay.

THE MANY FACES OF DISCRIMINATION

While prejudice refers to attitudes about members of a group, **discrimination** refers to actual acts against someone from a different group. Discrimination can take many forms.

❖ **Private Acts of Discrimination.** Private discrimination can make it difficult for members of disadvantaged groups to get a good education, a better job, and a decent place to live. This discrimination blocks their economic and social advancement. For example, in the past the residents of some neighborhoods signed agreements promising not to sell their homes to members of certain groups.

❖ **Legal Discrimination and Seg-regation.** In more extreme cases, minorities face public discrimination supported by law. For example, "Jim Crow" laws in the South once prohibited African Americans from attending white public schools and using "whites-only" public facilities.

❖ **Enslavement, Expulsion and Genocide.** Earlier in our history, Africans were brought to the United States by force and enslaved. Native American Indians

Jim Crow laws institutionalized discrimination in the South

were forcibly resettled on reservations during the settlement of the West. There have also been attempts to eliminate a minority through mass murder, known as **genocide** — for example, the Nazi attempt to exterminate the Jews during World War II.

THE CHALLENGE OF A PLURALISTIC SOCIETY

In the 20th century, the leaders of many disadvantaged groups organized reform movements by winning the sympathies of people outside their own group. The atrocities during World War II and the African-American Civil Rights Movement of the 1950s and 1960s were major turning points. The Supreme Court began reading new meaning into the Equal Protection Clause of the Fourteenth Amendment, and Congress passed new laws against discrimination. Women, Native American Indians, Hispanic Americans, and the disabled all followed the example of African Americans by fighting for benefits for their own group. As a result, our nation today is making efforts to create a society in which all groups participate equally. However, this goal has presented two challenges.

THE NEED FOR AGREEMENT
Americans need to agree on how to overcome past prejudice to achieve equality. Should we establish a "color-blind" society in which race is never a factor in any decision, or should we compensate the members of disadvantaged groups for past discrimination?

THE NEED TO PRESERVE DIVERSITY
Americans must find new ways to preserve their identities as members of diverse cultural groups while also cooperating to maintain a common American identity. Will Americans be able to strike a balance between loyalty to their particular group and loyalty to society as a whole? Some scholars fear the recent emphasis on ethnic or group identity threatens to weaken the American commitment to a common culture.

SHARPENING YOUR TEST-TAKING SKILLS

EXAMINING THE "ACTION WORDS" USED IN DOCUMENT-BASED ESSAY QUESTIONS

Document-based essay questions *(which will be discussed fully in the next chapter)* will often require you to understand certain key words. The most common "action words" are *"discuss"* and *"evaluate."* Let's examine each of these action words to see what they require you to do.

DISCUSS

Discuss means "to tell about it." The word *discuss* is used when you are asked for the "who," "what," "when," and "where" of something. Not every *discuss* question requires all four of these elements, but your answer must go beyond just a sentence. It must consist of several paragraphs. The following is an example of a *discuss* question:

Discuss the differences between the Populists and the Progressives.

EVALUATE

Evaluate means "to examine and judge carefully." *Evaluate* questions ask you to make a judgment. For example, you may have to evaluate a government policy or action. First consider its advantages and disadvantages. Then decide whether the advantages outweigh the disadvantages, or the reverse. Similarly, you may have to evaluate the effects of an important historical event. Let's look at a typical *evaluate* question:

Evaluate the positive and negative effects of American industrialization after the Civil War.

Here is what you must do to properly answer this question:

1 DESCRIBE THE RISE OF AMERICAN INDUSTRY AFTER THE CIVIL WAR

2 IDENTIFY THE GOOD AND BAD EFFECTS OF THIS DEVELOPMENT

3 MAKE AN OVERALL JUDGMENT ABOUT WHETHER THE DEVELOPMENT WAS GOOD OR BAD

Let's look at a sample answer to this question:

The industrialization of the United States proceeded rapidly after the Civil War. The number of factories producing cloth and other goods increased. Railroads were built across the nation, connecting factories with farms and cities. Farmers on the Great Plains could now ship their crops and livestock back East. The railroads also increased demand for coal and steel. New inventions such as the telephone, sewing machine, electric power, and automobiles increased communication, transportation, and production.

If you thought that rapid industrialization in America

was mostly beneficial, you might continue as follows:

Although conditions were difficult for early industrial workers, they gradually improved. Many workers in cities were better educated than the average farmer. Eventually, workers organized into unions to improve their conditions. Many farmers moved to cities, where they found new jobs and opportunities. Best of all, Americans could choose from a variety of new products. They became better educated and lived longer. Although industrialization brought problems in its early years, the problems were later solved. We continue to enjoy the benefits of American industry today. Therefore, the advantages of rapid industrialization far outweigh the drawbacks.

brought more problems than benefits, you might continue as follows:

All this was achieved at a terrible cost. While factory owners got wealthy, workers labored for long hours under harsh and dangerous conditions, and earned barely enough to live on. Unlike farmers, industrial workers were totally dependent on their employers. They could be fired at any time, and often faced starvation. Child labor was common. Workers had to live in overcrowded cities with foul air and water, and no medical care. Diseases spread rapidly. When the growth of railroads forced Native American Indians onto reservations, destruction of our wildlife and environment began. All these problems far outweighed the advantages of rapid industrialization in the United States.

Notice how the first part of the answer describes the background and explains the rapid industrialization of America. Each sample response then focuses on the positive or negative effects of rapid industrialization, and makes an overall judgment about the whether the effects were mostly positive or negative. Note how one response emphasizes the beneficial effects, while the other focuses on the problems. Once you take a position, be sure to provide information to support it.

TESTING YOUR UNDERSTANDING

Directions: Circle the number in front of the word or expression that correctly completes the statement or answers the question. Then answer the essay questions.

Base your answers to questions 1 and 2 on the table below and your knowledge of social studies.

1   Since 1820, most immigrants to the United States have come from
1 Europe   3 Asia
2 Americas   4 Africa

2   Based on the information in the chart, which statement is correct?
1 The number of immigrants from Europe has remained constant.
2 Since 1981, most immigrants have come from the Americas.
3 Throughout history, more immigrants came to the United States from Australia than from Africa.
4 Many people left the United States to settle in other countries.

U.S. IMMIGRATION BY CONTINENT OF ORIGIN

Continent	1820-1940	1941-1960	1961-1980	1981-1991
Europe	32,468,776	1,946,874	2,015,820	840,864
Asia	1,074,926	190,277	2,015,828	2,424,988
Americas	4,401,446	1,351,748	3,699,109	4,871,843
Africa	26,060	21,459	109,733	228,391
Australia	54,437	25,311	43,350	22,648

Source: Department of Justice, Immigration and Naturalization Service

3   Which was a common complaint of U.S. nativist groups during the late 1800s and early 1900s?
1 Congress failed to protect U.S. industries.
2 There were too many incoming immigrants.
3 Too many elected officials came from rural backgrounds.
4 Government hiring practices needed reform.

4   Which contributed to the passage of laws limiting immigration to the U.S. in the 1920s?
1 demands of organized labor
2 complaints about welfare costs
3 lack of adequate food supplies
4 demands of Native American Indians

5   A common belief held by most Progressives in the early 1900s was that
1 massive government spending was needed to reform society
2 federal government ownership of industry was needed to correct social problems
3 a return to weak federal government would end abuses of big business
4 legislation could help solve social and economic problems

6   Which was a major problem faced by farmers in the late 1800s?
1 falling prices for crops
2 the lack of the right to vote
3 low railroad rates
4 a shortage of farm workers

7   Elizabeth Cady Stanton and Lucretia Mott were most noted for their efforts to
1 organize national labor unions
2 expose government corruption
3 secure the vote for women
4 limit immigration

8   U.S. immigration laws in the 1920s primarily sought to
1 increase the flow of immigrants
2 encourage cultural diversity
3 reduce the number of immigrants
4 limit the role of the U. S. in foreign affairs

9   Political party primaries help increase public interest in elections by allowing voters to
1 remove corrupt officials
2 select their party candidates
3 attend their party conventions
4 write their party platform

10 Muckrakers of the Progressive Era and investigative reporters today are most similar in that both
1 fight corruption in American society
2 want fewer government controls on the economy
3 try to increase the spirit of patriotism
4 call for more aid to less developed nations

Base your answers to questions 11 and 12 on the chart and on your knowledge of social studies.

U.S. CROP PRICES, 1878-1897

Years	Wheat (per bushel)	Corn (per bushel)	Cotton (per pound)
1878-1881	$1.00	$.43	$.09
1882-1885	$.80	$.39	$.09
1886-1889	$.74	$.35	$.08
1890-1893	$.70	$.41	$.07
1894-1897	$.63	$.29	$.05

11 Which factor was a major cause of the trend shown by the chart?
1 severe droughts   3 crop failures
2 new farm equipment   4 overproduction

12 Because of the trend shown in the chart, American farmers wanted the federal government to
1 reduce regulation of the railroads
2 increase the money supply
3 pay for increased crop yields
4 raise tariffs on foreign goods

13 Which is a primary source of information about immigrants coming to the U.S. in 1880?
1 a textbook chapter on 1880s immigration policy
2 a biography of a famous immigrant who lived during the 1880s
3 a news account of the re-opening of Ellis Island as a museum
4 the diary of an immigrant who came to the U.S. in 1880

14 An experience shared by most immigrants to the U.S. between 1880 and 1920 was that they
1 frequently met with local prejudice
2 mainly settled in rural areas
3 were rapidly assimilated into mainstream lifestyles
4 joined radical political parties to bring about reform

15 Many of Theodore Roosevelt's actions demonstrated his belief that the role of the President was to
1 act vigorously in the public interest
2 follow the lead of Congress
3 remain free from politics
4 free businesses from burdensome government regulation

16 Which contributed to the birth of the Progressive Movement?
1 the influence of muckrakers, Populists, and social reformers
2 the Stock Market Crash of 1929
3 racial conflicts in the South
4 people moving from cities to the countryside

17 Theodore Roosevelt's Square Deal and Woodrow Wilson's New Freedom were primarily designed to
1 increase the power and influence of the United States in foreign affairs
2 reduce the role of government in the economy
3 help Americans cope with the problems caused by industrialization
4 protect the constitutional rights of racial and religious minorities

18 The Federal Reserve System was established to
1 serve as a source for farm loans
2 reform the practices of big business
3 balance the federal budget
4 regulate the circulation of money

19 The Women's Rights Movement of the late 1800s primarily focused its efforts on securing
1 Cabinet positions for women
2 the reform of prisons
3 equal rights for all minorities
4 suffrage for women

THEMATIC ESSAY QUESTION

Directions: Write a well-organized essay that includes an introduction, several paragraphs explaining your position, and a conclusion.

Theme: Laws

> Throughout American history, economic and social problems have prompted the U.S. Congress to pass various laws.

Task:

> Choose any *two* laws from your study of U.S. history and government.
>
> For *each* law:
> * Explain how the law sought to address an economic or social problem in the United States.
> * Describe the main provision or intent of the law.
> * Describe the extent to which the law succeeded in addressing that problem.

You may use any example from your study of U.S. history. Some suggestions you might wish to consider include: Homestead Act (1862), Chinese Exclusion Act (1882), Dawes Act (1887) Interstate Commerce Act (1887), Sherman Anti-Trust Act (1890), Pure Food and Drug Act (1906), Federal Reserve Act (1913), Wagner Act (1935), and Taft-Hartley Act (1947).

You are *not* limited to these suggestions.

INTERPRETING DOCUMENTS

> "We hold these truths to be self-evident: that all men and women are created equal; that they are endowed by their Creator with certain inalienable rights; that among these are life, liberty, and the pursuit of happiness ... The history of mankind is a history of repeated injuries ... on the part of man toward woman, having in direct object the establishment of an absolute tyranny over her."
>
> —*Excerpt from a resolution passed by the Seneca Falls Convention (1848)*

1   What is the main idea of the Seneca Falls Declaration? _____

2   Which earlier document in American history provided the inspiration for the ideas expressed in this document? _____

3   Which amendment to the U.S. Constitution sought to correct the abuses highlighted in this document? _____

CHAPTER 8

AMERICA REACHING OUT

Early American Foreign Policy
  A. Foreign Policy to 1812
  B. America Secures its Borders: 1812- 1898
  C. The Spanish-American War

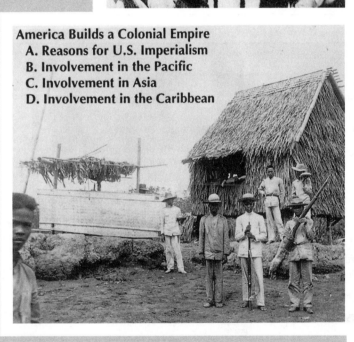

America Builds a Colonial Empire
  A. Reasons for U.S. Imperialism
  B. Involvement in the Pacific
  C. Involvement in Asia
  D. Involvement in the Caribbean

The U.S. in World War I
  A. European Causes of the War
  B. The U.S. Enters the War: 1917
  C. The U.S. at War: 1917-1918
  D. The Peace Settlement

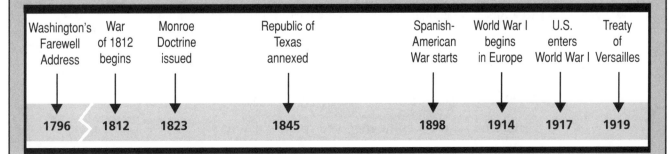

Washington's Farewell Address	War of 1812 begins	Monroe Doctrine issued	Republic of Texas annexed	Spanish-American War starts	World War I begins in Europe	U.S. enters World War I	Treaty of Versailles
1796	1812	1823	1845	1898	1914	1917	1919

WHAT YOU SHOULD FOCUS ON

In this chapter, you will learn how United States foreign policy developed from its beginnings, under President George Washington, through the end of World War I.

You will read how under President Washington American foreign policy initially sought to avoid all entanglements in foreign alliances and overseas wars. This policy shifted in the later 1800s as the nation became an industrial giant, leading to the emergence of the United States as a major world power.

In this chapter you should focus the following:

U.S. Marines arriving in China in 1900 to put down the Boxer Rebellion

U.S. Foreign Policy to 1898	America Builds a Colonial Empire	The United States in World War I
During its early years as a nation, the United States sought to avoid alliances and military involvement with Europe and other nations. Much of early U.S. foreign policy was focused on expanding the nation's borders westward.	To halt atrocities in Spanish-held Cuba and to help Cubans win their independence, America went to war with Spain in 1898. As a result of winning the war, the United States acquired Spanish possessions in the Caribbean and Pacific, and became a colonial empire.	To protect freedom of the seas, the United States was drawn into World War I in Europe. U.S. involvement in the war led to Allied victory, as well as the end of Progressivism in America. After the war, the nation retreated into isolationism.

In studying this period, you should focus on the following questions:

❖ What factors helped to determine America's early foreign policy goals?

❖ How did U.S. involvement in the Spanish-American War lead to important foreign policy changes?

❖ What factors led to America's becoming a colonial power?

❖ Why did the United States become involved in World War I?

SECTION 1

EARLY AMERICAN FOREIGN POLICY

When the United States was a young country, it sought to avoid military involvement with Europe and other nations. When America became a global power in 1898, its foreign policy changed dramatically.

THINK ABOUT IT

What advice would you give to a small, new country for dealing with other countries?

_____

_____

What would your advice be if the country were a large, well-established country?

_____

_____

Important Terms and Concepts: As you read this section, look for the following:

◆ **Louisiana Purchase**   ◆ **Manifest Destiny**
◆ **Monroe Doctrine**   ◆ **Spanish-American War**

To help you find these terms, the ◆ symbol will appear in the margin where the term is first explained.

U.S. FOREIGN POLICY TO 1812

NOTE: *Foreign policy consists of the actions of one nation towards other nations.*

In its first years after independence, the United States was quite weak and feared attacks by more powerful European nations. As a result, Americans generally followed a policy of **neutrality** — they avoided taking sides in conflicts between other nations. During this period two important foreign policy developments took place.

WASHINGTON'S FAREWELL ADDRESS (1796)

When George Washington addressed the nation for the last time as President of the United States, he warned Americans against entering into long-term agreements with other countries or getting involved in disputes among European nations. He said that it was important for the United States, as a new nation, to develop its own economy and ties with the Western Hemisphere, rather than to get entangled in developments in other parts of the world.

◆ LOUISIANA PURCHASE (1803)

When the United States became independent in 1776, it controlled only the lands east of the Mississippi River. The U.S. Constitution did not directly give the President permission to buy new territories. This became an issue when France offered to sell the area it controlled west of the Mississippi River (*see map, p. 176*). The purchase of this territory removed France, a European power, from the western border of the United States. Although President Jefferson was uncertain if the purchase was constitutional, he went ahead with the purchase of Louisiana Territory for $15 million. The Louisiana Purchase doubled the size of the United States.

AMERICA SECURES ITS BORDERS, 1812-1898

THE WAR OF 1812

From 1793 to 1815, Britain and France were locked in a series of wars. British sailors sometimes deserted the British navy to become sailors on American ships. As a result, British warships would often stop American ships to search for deserters from the British navy. Going against its policy of neutrality, the United States went to war with Great Britain in 1812 to stop the British from taking their sailors off American ships on the high seas, and thus protecting the freedom of the seas. Some Americans also wanted to use the war as an excuse to invade and conquer Canada. The war ended in 1815 with no clear winner. Things remained as they had been; not an inch of territory changed hands.

James Monroe

◆ THE MONROE DOCTRINE (1823)

Between 1810 and 1822, most of Spain's Latin American colonies rebelled against Spanish rule. These former colonies established independent nations. The United States supported these nations, but feared that Spain or other European nations might try to re-conquer them. As a result, President Monroe issued the Monroe Doctrine: The U.S. would oppose any attempt by European nations to establish new colonies in the Western Hemisphere (*North America, Central America, the Caribbean and South America*) or to reconquer former colonies that had already become independent. However, the U.S. would not interfere with older European colonies still in existence, such as Canada and Cuba.

> ### The Monroe Doctrine
>
> *The American continents are henceforth not to be considered as subjects for future colonization by any European powers ... [W]e should consider any attempt on their part to extend their system to any portion of this hemisphere as dangerous to our peace and safety.*

The Monroe Doctrine was meant to show the world that the United States had special interests in the Western Hemisphere. The Doctrine was later used to justify U.S. interference in the affairs of countries in Central and South America. It served as the cornerstone of U.S. foreign policy in Latin America for many years.

ANALYSIS

The Monroe Doctrine suggests that the United States has a right to control the Western

Hemisphere. Do you agree? _____

If yes, why? _____

_____

If not, why not? _____

_____

MANIFEST DESTINY

By the 1840s, the western boundary of the United States was at the edge of the Rocky Mountains. Many Americans wanted to expand the nation to the shores of the Pacific Ocean. They claimed that it was the **Manifest Destiny** — the future of the United States — to extend its borders from the Atlantic to the Pacific. Supporters of expansion believed that Americans would benefit others by spreading democracy and other American values. However, westward expansion meant taking risks, such as battling Native American Indians on the Plains, going to war against Mexico, and a possible conflict with the British on the Pacific coast.

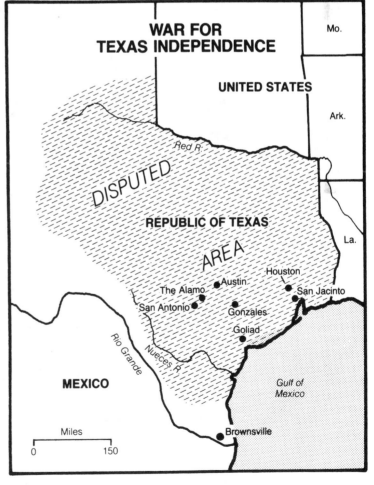

■ **Annexation of Texas (1845).** When Mexico became independent from Spain, its government invited Americans to settle the Mexican province of Texas. Soon the 20,000 settlers in Texas outnumbered the Mexicans living there. A series of disagreements led Americans in Texas to declare independence from Mexico. After some fighting, Mexico recognized Texan independence. In 1845, Congress voted to annex Texas (*make it part of the United States*).

■ **Mexican-American War (1846-1848).** A dispute broke out between the United States and Mexico over the southern border of Texas. In the war that followed, Mexico was defeated. Under the terms of the peace treaty, Mexico ceded to the United States the territory now occupied by California, Nevada, Utah, Arizona, and parts of Colorado and New Mexico. The United States paid Mexico $18 million for these areas.

■ **Additional Acquisitions.** Other acquisitions that helped the United States grow to its present size included:

• **Gadsden Purchase (1853).** This small strip of land, bought from Mexico, completed American expansion in the southwest.

• **Oregon Territory (1846).** In an agreement with Great Britain, the line dividing Canada and the United States was extended westwards to the Pacific. Land south of the line was given to the United States.

• **Alaska (1867).** The United States purchased Alaska from Russia for $7.2 million. Alaska later became the 49th state, in 1959.

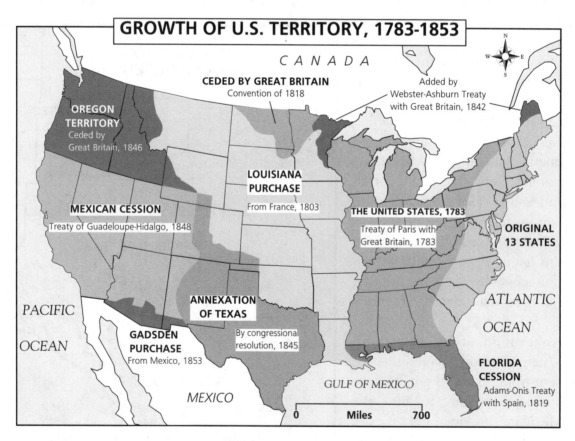

THE SPANISH-AMERICAN WAR OF 1898

Cuba, an island only 90 miles from the coast of Florida, was one of the last of Spain's colonial possessions in Latin America. Cubans were heavily taxed and treated harshly under Spanish rule. In 1894, Cubans rebelled against Spain to obtain their independence. The Spanish army sent to

Cuba used brutal force to put down the rebellion. The American public was shocked at this treatment and pressured the President and Congress to step in. Several factors finally led the United States to go to war with Spain:

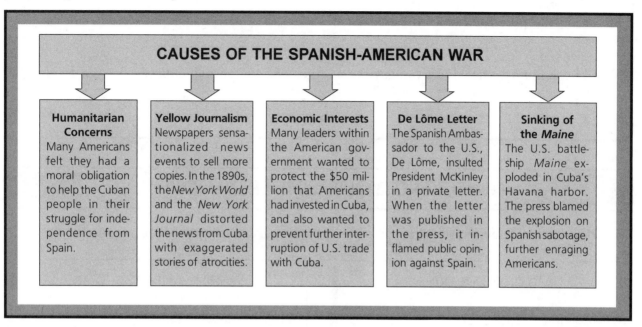

CAUSES OF THE SPANISH-AMERICAN WAR

Humanitarian Concerns	Yellow Journalism	Economic Interests	De Lôme Letter	Sinking of the Maine
Many Americans felt they had a moral obligation to help the Cuban people in their struggle for independence from Spain.	Newspapers sensationalized news events to sell more copies. In the 1890s, the *New York World* and the *New York Journal* distorted the news from Cuba with exaggerated stories of atrocities.	Many leaders within the American government wanted to protect the $50 million that Americans had invested in Cuba, and also wanted to prevent further interruption of U.S. trade with Cuba.	The Spanish Ambassador to the U.S., De Lôme, insulted President McKinley in a private letter. When the letter was published in the press, it inflamed public opinion against Spain.	The U.S. battleship *Maine* exploded in Cuba's Havana harbor. The press blamed the explosion on Spanish sabotage, further enraging Americans.

The Battleship Maine

The wreckage of the Maine

RESULTS OF THE SPANISH-AMERICAN WAR

The Spanish-American War marked an important turning point in U.S. foreign policy. The United States quickly defeated Spain, and acquired the Philippines and Guam — in the Pacific — and Puerto Rico — in the Caribbean — as a result of the war. Officially, Cuba became independent, but in reality the United States took control over Cuban affairs. The United States changed from being a nation without colonies to one that controlled an overseas empire.

SUMMING UP: EARLY AMERICAN FOREIGN POLICY

For most of their first century as a nation, Americans followed the advice of George Washington to avoid involvement in European alliances and wars. The Spanish-American War marked an important change in U.S. foreign policy. In just over 100 years, the United States was transformed from being a colony itself into a nation with its own overseas empire.

THINKING IT OVER

Would you change your earlier advice to a new country? _____ Explain. _____

_____

Would you change the advice you gave to a large, well-established country? _____ Explain.

_____

CHECKING YOUR UNDERSTANDING

Directions: Complete the following cards. Then answer the multiple-choice questions.

MONROE DOCTRINE

What was it? _____

What role did it play in U.S. foreign policy?

_____

SPANISH-AMERICAN WAR

What were its causes? _____

List two results: 1. _____

2. _____

---

1 A major reason for the Monroe Doctrine was to
   1 halt the slave trade from Africa to the Caribbean
   2 prevent European intervention in the Western Hemisphere
   3 keep the United States out of World War I
   4 protect American sailors

2 Which term identifies the desire of many Americans to expand westward in the 1800s?
   1 neutrality   3 manifest destiny
   2 balance of power   4 appeasement

3 A major reason for U.S. involvement in the affairs of Cuba in the 1890s was
   1 fear of growing Russian power
   2 humanitarian concern over the treatment of Cubans
   3 fear of increased Cuban immigration to the United States
   4 a desire to help Spain keep its Caribbean colonies

4 Believers in Manifest Destiny felt that the general direction of U.S. expansion should be from
   1 the East coast to the Pacific Ocean
   2 Texas to Canada
   3 the Canadian border to Florida
   4 California to New York

5 Information on subjects such as the De Lôme letter, the sinking of the battleship *Maine*, and "yellow journalism" would be found in a history textbook chapter on the
   1 Abolitionists   3 Spanish-American War
   2 Reconstruction Era 4 Populist Party

6 U.S. involvement in the Spanish-American War demonstrates that
   1 nations will fight only when they are attacked
   2 government policies in a democracy may be affected by the press
   3 advanced weapons do not guarantee victory
   4 all nations need nuclear weapons

SECTION 2

AMERICA BUILDS A COLONIAL EMPIRE

In this section you will read about how the
United States reversed its traditional policies
by becoming an imperialist nation.

THINK ABOUT IT

Some Americans believed that in obtaining colonies we went against our democratic tradition of allowing people to govern themselves. What do you think? _____

_____

Important Terms and Concepts: As you read this section, look for the following:

✦ Imperialism   ✦ Big Stick Policy
✦ Open Door Policy   ✦ Good Neighbor Policy
✦ Boxer Rebellion   ✦ Organization of American States

REASONS FOR U.S. IMPERIALISM

The United States was once a British colony. Americans declared their independence in 1776 on the basis of democratic beliefs. Thereafter, many Americans felt it was wrong to force colonial rule on others. They believed that taking over other countries was undemocratic. Nevertheless, a majority of Americans in the late 1800s and early 1900s supported the policy of **imperialism** (*the* ✦ *control of one country by another*). This support came about for several reasons:

WHY AMERICANS SUPPORTED COLONIAL EXPANSION

Economic Reasons	Desire To Be A Great Power	Belief In Moral Superiority
The United States had recently become an industrial power. Colonies would provide needed raw materials for factories, and a guaranteed market for manufactured goods.	Some people believed that in order to be a great and powerful nation, the United States had to control areas around the world, just as the European powers were doing.	Many Americans believed they were a superior people and should rule "less able" peoples overseas by spreading Christianity and the American way of life.

AMERICAN INVOLVEMENT IN THE PACIFIC

THE PHILIPPINES

The Philippine Islands were Spanish colonies when the Spanish-American War began. The Filipinos had expected their independence at the end of the war. When the United States **annexed** (*took over*) their islands, they revolted. After several years of fighting for their independence, the Filipinos were defeated. From 1902 until 1946, the Philippines were controlled by the United States. Finally, following World War II, the Philippines were granted their independence.

Filipino soldiers in the early 1900s

HAWAII, GUAM, SAMOA, AND MIDWAY

The United States also gained control of Hawaii. American landowners living there successfully rebelled against the Hawaiian Queen and persuaded Congress to annex the islands. Smaller Pacific islands like Guam, Samoa and Midway also were annexed by the United States. These islands became valuable naval bases and refueling stations for American ships traveling back and forth between Asia and the United States. In 1960, Hawaii became the 50th state.

AMERICAN INVOLVEMENT IN ASIA

U.S. trade with China and Japan increased after the United States gained the Philippines and Guam in the Spanish-American War.

THE UNITED STATES AND CHINA

In 1899, the United States was concerned that European powers were taking over parts of China and cutting off these areas from American trade. In reaction, the U. S. announced the
◆ **Open Door Policy**, which declared that all nations should have equal trading rights in China. Many Chinese opposed this increased European and American involvement. A Chinese group called the "Boxers" attacked foreigners living in China. An in-
◆ ternational army was organized to put down the **Boxer Rebellion**. After the rebellion was crushed, the United States stepped in to prevent China from being carved up by the European powers.

A Chinese "Boxer" in 1900

THE UNITED STATES AND JAPAN

Japan's rulers feared the influence of foreign nations, and had not allowed its people to have contact with other countries for nearly 200 years. In 1853, U.S. Commodore **Matthew Perry** was sent to Japan with a fleet of gunships to demand that Japan open its ports to trade with the United States. Fearing American military power, Japanese leaders gave in.

Landing of Commodore Perry in Japan, 1853

After opening its ports to the world, Japan quickly adopted Western ideas and technology, and became a strong military and industrial power. In 1905, to the surprise of much of the world, Japan defeated Russia in the **Russo-Japanese War**. President Theodore Roosevelt helped bring both sides to a peace settlement.

THE IMPACT OF GEOGRAPHY ON HISTORY

Admiral **Alfred Thayer Mahan**, President of the Naval War College, became America's leading advocate of imperial expansion. In his book *The Influence of Sea Power Upon History*, Mahan argued that the examples of Greece, Rome and Great Britain showed that naval power was the key to national greatness. To achieve world power, a country needed a powerful navy, a large merchant marine, colonies, and naval bases.

Because other nations would compete for naval supremacy and world markets, Admiral Mahan believed it essential for Americans to seize control of the Pacific trade routes, to construct a canal through Central America, and to dominate the Caribbean region. Geographically, the United States would control the sea lanes from the Caribbean Sea across the Pacific as far as China and Japan.

Admiral Alfred Thayer Mahan

AMERICAN INVOLVEMENT IN THE CARIBBEAN

The United States had special interests in the Caribbean region. After the Spanish-American War, the United States gained direct control of Puerto Rico and indirect control of Cuba. The construction of the Panama Canal and the rise of American business interests in the Caribbean further contributed to U.S. involvement. American leaders acted to keep other foreign powers out of the region because they might pose a threat to the United States.

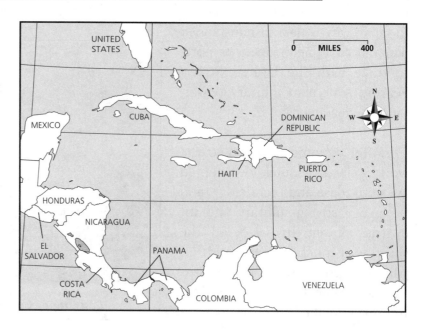

THE PANAMA CANAL

The Spanish-American War had shown the importance of building a **canal** (*a man-made waterway that connects two bodies of water*) between the Atlantic and Pacific Oceans. It took a U.S. battleship six weeks to sail 14,000 miles from the west coast down around the tip of South America, and then north to Cuba. By 1903, the U.S. decided to build a canal across Panama, in Central America. At the time Panama was part of Colombia. The U.S. offered Colombia $10 million for the land to build a canal. When Colombia delayed giving its acceptance, President Theodore Roosevelt bargained with a group of rebels in Panama. He sent warships to help Panama gain its independence from Colombia, and the rebels agreed to sell the United States the land to build the canal. The actions of the United States against Colombia angered many Latin American countries. Panama gained its independence and the canal was completed after ten years of construction (1903-1914). The U.S. was given control of the Panama Canal Zone.

The Panama Canal

CARIBBEAN SEA

CANAL ZONE
PANAMA RAILROAD
LOCKS

Limon Bay
Colon

Madden Lake

GATUN LOCKS

REPUBLIC OF PANAMA

Gatun Lake

PEDRO MIGUEL LOCKS

Panama City

MIRAFLORES LOCKS

Balboa

REPUBLIC OF PANAMA

PACIFIC OCEAN

0   15
Miles

CUBA

Following the Spanish-American War, Cuba became an American **protectorate** (*a territory under the protection and control of another country*). U.S. military forces remained on the island, and American businesses invested heavily in Cuba.

PUERTO RICO

Puerto Rico became an American possession after 1898. Since 1952, Puerto Rico has governed itself as a U.S. "Commonwealth." However, there is a great deal of disagreement as to how Puerto Rico should be governed in the future.

THREE VIEWS ON THE FUTURE STATUS OF PUERTO RICO		
COMMONWEALTH: Puerto Rico has been a U.S. Commonwealth for almost 100 years, and should continue in that position. Puerto Ricans are American citizens, free to move anywhere in the United States that they wish. In Puerto Rico, they pay no federal tax, and they can serve in the U.S. military.	**STATEHOOD:** If Puerto Rico becomes a state, its people will be able to vote in U.S. elections, will be represented in Congress, and will receive more federal aid and other social services. However, Puerto Ricans will have to pay federal taxes; businesses may leave the island, since they will have to pay federal tax on their profits.	**INDEPENDENCE:** Puerto Ricans identify strongly with Latin America and the culture of the Caribbean. If Puerto Rico becomes independent, its citizens will have a true cultural identity, instead of feeling like "second-class citizens" in a larger country. Spanish would become the official language of the island, instead of English.

U.S. POLICY IN THE CARIBBEAN

In the early 1900s, the U.S. government began to take a more active part in the affairs of Latin America. In 1904, President Theodore Roosevelt declared that the United States would act as a policeman in the Western Hemisphere. This expansion of United States power in Latin America was known as the **Roosevelt Corollary** to the Monroe Doctrine, or the "**Big Stick Policy.**" It was often used by the United States to justify sending troops to the West Indies and Central America. Haiti, Nicaragua, Honduras and the Dominican Republic became American protectorates like Cuba. President Weilson even sent U.S. troops to Mexico. These frequent interventions caused many Latin American nations to resent the United States.

United States Marines in Nicaragua, 1927

THE GOOD NEIGHBOR POLICY (1930-1945)

By the late 1920s, American leaders saw the need to improve U.S. relations with Latin American countries. Presidents Herbert Hoover and Franklin D. Roosevelt replaced the Big Stick Policy
◆ with the "**Good Neighbor Policy**," under which the United States agreed not to interfere in Latin America's internal problems. Friendly relations between the United States and Latin American countries began to grow.

THE ORGANIZATION OF AMERICAN STATES (O.A.S.)

◆ The **Organization of American States** (O.A.S.) was created in 1948 as a means for peacefully solving problems in the Western Hemisphere. It continues to serve as an organization for resolving disputes in the Americas and for increasing its members' knowledge of each other's cultures.

SUMMING UP: AMERICA BUILDS A COLONIAL EMPIRE

By the early 1900s, the United States had interests and possessions in the Caribbean, Asia and the Pacific. American overseas expansion led to some hostility against the U.S., especially in the Philippines, China and Latin America. Eventually, the U.S. changed its policies to help bring about better relations, particularly with its Latin America neighbors.

THINKING IT OVER

Now that you have read this section, how do you think the United States should treat its Latin American neighbors? _____

_____

CHECKING YOUR UNDERSTANDING

Directions: Complete the following cards. Then answer the multiple-choice questions.

IMPERIALISM
Define it: _____
What effect did it have on the United States?
_____

GOOD NEIGHBOR POLICY
What was it? _____
What was its effect on U.S.-Latin American relations? _____

1 Which headline best reflects the concept of "imperialism"?
1 "The Supreme Court Bans Segregation in Public Schools."
2 "President Theodore Roosevelt Meets with Russian Leaders."
3 "The United States Buys Cars from Japan."
4 "President McKinley Announces the Take-over of the Philippines."

2 An important aim of the "Open Door Policy" was to
1 encourage Chinese people to emigrate to the United States
2 prevent European powers from dividing up China
3 develop China's industries and factories
4 introduce democratic government into China

3 The primary reason for constructing the Panama Canal was to
1 increase the security of the United States
2 spread the U.S way of life to less developed nations
3 encourage economic development in Latin America
4 stop the spread of communism

4 Which was a major feature of President Franklin Roosevelt's foreign policy in the 1930s?
1 improving relations with Latin American nations
2 trying to overthrow several elected governments in South America
3 encouraging unlimited immigration from all Latin American nations
4 attracting Spanish Jews to settle in the United States

5 A "protectorate" can best be defined as
1 protecting women workers
2 a territory under the protection and control of another country
3 protection of an individual's liberties
4 a tax protecting U.S. exports

6 The annexation of Hawaii, the Philippines and Samoa showed U.S. interest in
1 Central and South America
2 Asia and the Pacific
3 Europe and Africa
4 the Middle East

7 The United States tried to improve its relations with Latin American nations in the 1930s through the
1 Good Neighbor Policy
2 Open Door Policy
3 Big Stick Policy
4 Monroe Doctrine

8 Which statement about the Organization of American States is most accurate?
1 It seeks greater U.S. control over Latin American nations.
2 It is a military organization devoted to defeating the United States.
3 It seeks peaceful solutions to problems in Latin America.
4 It is an organization with many colonies in Latin America.

9 The Boxer Rebellion primarily involved the United States in its relations with
1 China   3 Belgium
2 Panama   4 Mexico

10 The United States sent Commodore Perry to Japan in order to
1 sell natural resources to the Japanese
2 help Japan recover from the damages of its war with Russia
3 open Japanese ports to U.S. trade
4 build naval bases in Japan

11 Which entry would be the main topic in an outline of major developments in U.S. foreign policy during the late 1800s and early 1900s?
1 The development of U.S. imperialism
2 Building the Panama Canal
3 Expansion in the Pacific
4 The Spanish-American War

SECTION 3

THE UNITED STATES IN WORLD WAR I

In this section you will read how the United States, despite its best efforts, could not avoid involvement in World War I in Europe.

THINK ABOUT IT

How should a victorious nation treat a defeated nation? _____

Important Terms and Concepts: As you read this section, look for the following:

- ✦ Nationalism
- ✦ Freedom of the Seas
- ✦ Fourteen Points
- ✦ Treaty of Versailles
- ✦ League of Nations
- ✦ Isolationism

CAUSES OF WORLD WAR I IN EUROPE

The assassination of **Archduke Francis Ferdinand**, a member of Austria-Hungary's ruling family, was the spark that ignited **World War I**. This development provides a classic example of how one event can trigger multiple results. A group in neighboring Serbia helped carry out the assassination, which led Austria-Hungary to invade Serbia. The invasion brought in Russia, which had a treaty to help Serbia. Next, Germany came to the aid of Austria-Hungary. France and Great Britain then joined to help Russia. Within a few weeks, all of Europe was drawn into the war. Although the assassination sparked the war, there were many underlying causes:

✦ ■ **Nationalism.** Pride in one's country is called nationalism. However, nationalism also describes the idea that each **nationality** is entitled to its own homeland. Both types of nationalism contributed to the outbreak of World War I. France, Germany, Austria-Hungary and Russia each tried to prove their nation's importance by building up armies. The other type of nationalism existed in the Austro-Hungarian Empire, where many national groups wanted their own countries and were willing to use violence to get their way.

■ **Economic Competition and Imperialism.** Many European nations were struggling to become great economic powers. This led to much conflict. For example, the growing industrial strength of Germany threatened the British. Russian interests in Central Europe threatened the Austro-Hungarian Empire. European leaders also believed that one way of making a nation's economy stronger was **imperialism** (*the taking of colonies*). Frequently European nations competed over the same colonies.

■ **The System of Alliances.** In order to protect themselves in case of war, Europe divided into two large alliances in the 1890s. On one side stood Germany, Austria-Hungary and Italy, which formed the **Triple Alliance** (*without Italy, these later became the "Central Powers"*). On the other side stood Russia, France and Great Britain, known as the **Triple Entente** (*later called the "Allies"*). The members of each alliance promised to help the other members if they were attacked. Any dispute involving a nation in these alliances threatened to involve all the others.

EUROPE AT THE START OF WORLD WAR I

The Allies
The Central Powers

THE U.S. ENTERS WORLD WAR I, 1917

During the period leading up to World War I, the United States chose not to side with either of the two European alliance systems. When the war finally did break out in 1914, America attempted to continue its traditional policy of neutrality. Although most Americans favored the Allies because of long-standing ties with Great Britain, President Woodrow Wilson called on the American people not to take sides. In fact, during Wilson's campaign for the Presidency, he had pledged to keep the United States out of war.

Despite Wilson's best efforts, however, the United States eventually became involved in World War I. This occurred when German submarines violated the principle of **freedom of the seas** — that neutrals have a right to ship non-war goods to nations at war.

U.S. soldier says goodbye to his sweetheart, 1917

REASONS FOR U.S. INVOLVEMENT IN WORLD WAR I

Close Ties with the Allies. Many Americans traced their roots to Great Britain. A common language and traditions tied Americans to the British. The United States, Great Britain, and France also shared similar democratic political systems.

German Actions. Americans were shocked at Germany's violations of international law. Its invasion of neutral Belgium, destruction of civilian buildings, and sinking of unarmed passenger ships turned American public opinion against Germany.

Submarine Warfare. Germany began to sink U.S. ships that were supplying materials to England, in violation of the principle of freedom of the seas. In 1915 a German submarine sank the British passenger ship *Lusitania*, killing over 1000 passengers, 128 of them Americans.

The **Zimmerman Telegram**, in which German leaders offered U.S. territory to Mexico if it would side with Germany, was leaked to the U.S. press and infuriated the American public. When German leaders began using submarines to sink all U.S. ships on route to England, President Wilson finally asked Congress to declare war.

THE UNITED STATES AT WAR, 1917-1918

President Woodrow Wilson told the American people that the war was being fought to "make the world safe for democracy." Involvement in an overseas war led to many important changes at home. Congress gave President Wilson sweeping powers over businesses and workers so that they would quickly make weapons and other war goods. A military draft brought millions of men into the army.

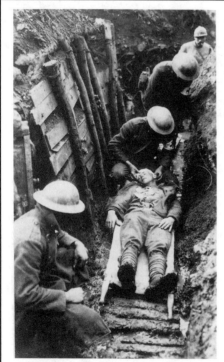

Wounded U.S. Marine in a trench in France, 1918

Because many men went off to war, their jobs were often filled by women. Taxes increased and government war bonds were sold to raise money. Some basic rights, like the freedom to criticize the war effort, were limited. The U.S. Supreme Court upheld these limits to free speech in *Schenck v. U.S.* (see *The Constitution at Work*, page 192).

World War I was a global war fought with new and destructive technology. Weapons such as machine guns, poison gas, airplanes and submarines were preventing either side from gaining a quick victory. However, the entrance of the United States into the war on the side of the Allies helped swing the tide of battle in their favor. Germany surrendered in November 1918.

THE PEACE SETTLEMENT

When the U.S. entered the war, President Wilson announced America's war aims in a famous speech. He hoped these goals would provide the terms for securing a just and lasting peace.

THE FOURTEEN POINTS (1918)

Wilson referred to America's war aims as the **Fourteen Points**. One of the major points was that each nationality should have its own country. The Fourteen Points also called for freedom of the seas, reduced armaments and an end to secret dealings between countries. Wilson suggested the creation of a **League of Nations** to peacefully settle future disputes between countries.

Wilson (r.) and other leaders, at Versailles

THE VERSAILLES TREATY (1919)

The terms of the peace settlement, established in the **Versailles Treaty** and related treaties, were very different from those proposed in Wilson's Fourteen Points. The settlement was extremely harsh on Germany, which had to pay a huge penalty for supposedly starting the war. The Austro-Hungarian empire was divided into smaller national states. However, the treaty did adopt Wilson's idea of a League of Nations.

KEY TERMS OF THE 1919 PEACE SETTLEMENT

Germany lost territory to France and Poland, and all of its colonies

Germany had to accept blame for starting the war and pay a huge reparation (payment for damages) to the Allies

A League of Nations was established

Germany lost its navy and its powerful army was reduced to the size of a police force

Austria-Hungary was divided up into new, smaller national states

THE UNITED STATES REFUSES TO JOIN THE LEAGUE OF NATIONS

Wilson hoped the League of Nations would be an international peace organization, providing a place for nations to discuss their problems rather than going to war. The League of Nations had no army of its own, and depended on its member nations to provide troops to stop aggressive countries. The League of Nations failed, however, because many major world powers, including the United States, refused to join.

According to the U.S. Constitution, all treaties must be approved by a two-thirds vote of the Senate. Wilson thought that the Senators would approve the Versailles Treaty and the League of Nations, but most of the Senators were concerned that U.S. troops might be called upon to stop acts of aggression overseas. Wilson rejected any compromises suggested by the Senate. The Senate voted against the treaty, and the U.S. never joined the League.

THE UNITED STATES RETURNS TO ISOLATION

The refusal of the United States to join the League of Nations marked the return of the American policy of **isolationism** (*refusing to become involved in the affairs of other countries*). Many Americans favored this policy because they were unhappy with the huge costs of the war and the small benefits that the United States had obtained from its involvement. They felt protected by the oceans and did not want to get involved in European conflicts again.

ANALYSIS

If you had been a U.S. Senator, would you have voted for or against joining the League of Nations? _YES_ Explain the reasons for your vote: _because discusing problems instead of using violence by going to war, problems would get solved quicker_

THINKING IT OVER

Now that you have read this section, how do you think a victorious nation should treat a defeated one? _equally_ Explain: _because whoever gets defeated would want to be treated equally_

CHECKING YOUR UNDERSTANDING

Directions: Complete the following cards. Then answer the multiple-choice questions.

THE TREATY OF VERSAILLES

Its major provisions included:
1. _hold Germany responsible_
2. _Germany lost territory_
3. _looses navy_
4. _reduce army_

THE LEAGUE OF NATIONS

What were its goals? _avoid war._

Why did the United States refuse to join? _dont wanna get involved_

1 During the late 19th and early 20th centuries, U.S. foreign policy was marked by
  1 declining interest in the Far East
  2 increased enforcement of the Monroe Doctrine
  3 acceptance of the principle of collective security
  4 formation of military alliances with European nations

2 During World War I, a major goal of the United States was to
  1 limit the spread of communism
  2 invade Latin American nations
  3 defend freedom of the seas
  4 eliminate the need for allies

3 A major goal of the United States in both the War of 1812 and World War I was to
  1 acquire more territory
  2 defeat the British
  3 protect the freedom of the seas
  4 increase U.S. trade with Asia

4 The United States entered World War I as an ally of
  1 Germany and Austria-Hungary
  2 Russia and Germany
  3 Great Britian and France
  4 Great Britain and Austria-Hungary

5 Why did President Wilson's power increase during World War I?
  1 Congress refused to meet during the war
  2 fast action was necessary for conducting the war
  3 the Constitution only allows the President to act during wartime
  4 the courts ruled that Congress may not conduct foreign policy

6 The status of women changed as a result of World War I mainly because
  1 large numbers of women served in the armed forces
  2 many women were sent to relocation centers
  3 greater job opportunities were suddenly available for women
  4 women were accepted to colleges for the first time

7 United States participation in World War I resulted in
  1 a stable peace for the remainder of the century
  2 an end to conflicts among the American people
  3 racial and religious harmony in Europe
  4 a return to a policy of American isolationism after the war

8 Which statement best describes American public opinion when World War I started in Europe in 1914?
  1 America must fight communism even if it means going to war with Russia.
  2 The United States should not get involved in European wars.
  3 Germany should win the war.
  4 Great Britain and France were responsible for starting the war.

9 Information on subjects such as the sinking of neutral ships, freedom of the seas, and the assassination of Archduke Francis Ferdinand would be found in a textbook dealing with which period of history?
  1 the period before the Civil War
  2 the Reconstruction Era
  3 the Industrial Revolution
  4 World War I

10 United States foreign policy developments immediately after World War I included
  1 membership in the United Nations
  2 refusal to join the League of Nations
  3 issuance of the Monroe Doctrine
  4 following the policy of Manifest Destiny

11 Roosevelt's "Big Stick Policy" assumed the right of the United States to
  1 intervene in the internal affairs of a country in the exercise of international police power
  2 grant special privileges to big business in economic transactions in Latin America
  3 grant financial aid to less developed countries
  4 disregard any or all parts of the Monroe Doctrine

PROFILES IN HISTORY

WILLIAM H. SEWARD
(SECRETARY OF STATE)

In 1867, Secretary of State William Seward was informed that Russia wanted to sell Alaska. Seward arranged to buy the 600,000 square miles of territory for $7.2 million. Unable to anticipate the future discovery of gold and oil in Alaska, people ridiculed Seward for his purchase, calling it "Seward's icebox." However, Alaska proved to be very valuable. In 1959, it became the 49th state of the Union.

QUEEN LILIUOKALANI
(QUEEN OF HAWAII)

In 1893, Queen Liliuokalani (lee LEE OO oh kah LAH nee) tried to halt the growing influence of American settlers living in Hawaii and return control of the islands to her people. In response, some American business leaders led a revolt against her rule. They seized power and removed her from the throne. The new leaders of Hawaii persuaded the U.S. Congress to annex the islands, making Queen Liliuokalani Hawaii's last ruling monarch.

WILLIAM RANDOLPH HEARST
AND JOSEPH PULITZER (PUBLISHERS)

Hearst's *New York Journal* and Pulitzer's *New York World* were pioneers in **yellow journalism**. Both newspapers sensationalized stories about the treatment of Cubans living under Spanish control. Their stories aroused public opinion and helped push the U.S. into war with Spain in 1898. Pulitzer left funds

W. R. Hearst

now used for the "Pulitzer Prize," the most prestigious award in writing and journalism.

WALTER REED
(ARMY SURGEON)

Americans in Cuba and the Panama Canal Zone were often stricken by yellow fever. In 1900, Walter Reed led a medical team sent to find the cause, and discovered that it was spread by the bites of certain mosquitoes. Within a year, most of the mosquito-breeding swamps were drained and the disease was practically eliminated.

THE CONSTITUTION AT WORK

SCHENCK v. U.S. (1919)

Background: During World War I, Schenck was arrested and convicted for handing out literature encouraging Americans not to fight in World War I. Schenck claimed his First Amendment rights to freedom of speech and freedom of the press had been violated.

Decision/Significance: The Court ruled that the right to free speech is not absolute — that this right does not protect someone who shouts "fire" in a crowded theater when there is no fire. The government can limit speech when faced with a "clear and present danger." The decision became a guide for the Court to measure the limits of free speech.

THE COURT SPEAKS

SUMMARIZING YOUR UNDERSTANDING

Directions: Confirm your understanding of the important terms and concepts in this chapter. Check those you can explain. For those you are not sure of, find the ✦ symbol in the margin next to the term and review it.

- ❑ Louisiana Purchase
- ❑ Monroe Doctrine
- ❑ Manifest Destiny
- ❑ Spanish-American War
- ❑ Imperialism
- ❑ Open Door Policy
- ❑ Good Neighbor Policy
- ❑ O.A.S.
- ❑ Nationalism
- ❑ Freedom of the Seas
- ❑ Submarine Warfare
- ❑ Fourteen Points
- ❑ Treaty of Versailles
- ❑ League of Nations
- ❑ Isolationism

Directions: Fill in the information called for in the following organizer.

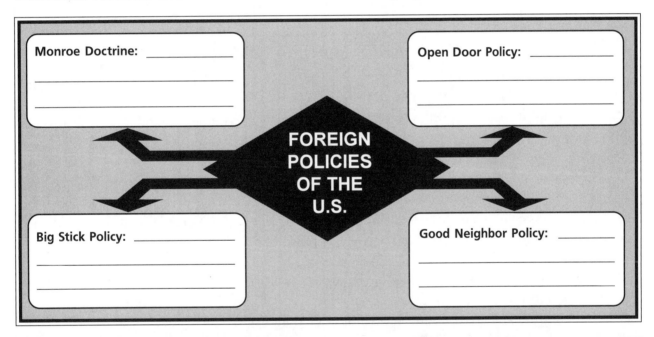

Monroe Doctrine: _____
_____
_____

Open Door Policy: _____
_____
_____

FOREIGN POLICIES OF THE U.S.

Big Stick Policy: _____
_____
_____

Good Neighbor Policy: _____
_____
_____

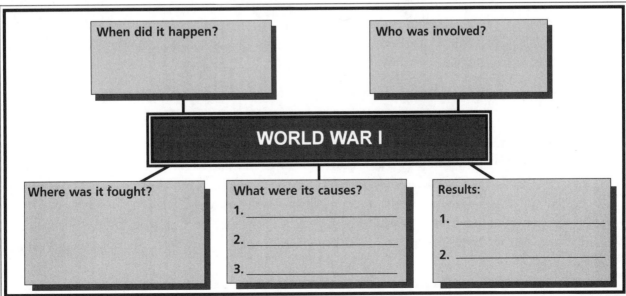

When did it happen?

Who was involved?

WORLD WAR I

Where was it fought?

What were its causes?
1. _____
2. _____
3. _____

Results:
1. _____
2. _____

TEST HELPER   LOOKING AT FOREIGN POLICY

Many questions on American history examinations ask about foreign policy. This section will help give you an overview of the nature of foreign policy.

WHAT IS FOREIGN POLICY?

Foreign policy is the conduct of one nation towards other nations. An example of foreign policy would be President Clinton's decision to provide money to help Russia after the collapse of communism. Domestic policy, on the other hand, refers to a government's actions within the borders of its own country, such as Congress's passing a new income tax law.

WHO MAKES FOREIGN POLICY?

THE PRESIDENT AND CONGRESS

The Constitution gave control of foreign policy to the federal government. To prevent one branch of government from becoming too strong, the Constitution divided control over foreign policy between the President and Congress. The President has the day-to-day control of foreign policy. The President is assisted in making foreign policy by the Secretary of State (*a member of the Cabinet*), and by other officials in the State Department. The President also has the assistance of the Central Intelligence Agency (C.I.A.), the National Security Council, and the Joint Chiefs of Staff. The foreign policy powers of the President include:

- serving as commander-in-chief of the armed forces
- negotiating treaties with foreign countries
- appointing ambassadors and receiving foreign ministers.

Congress was also given some important control over foreign policy. Primarily, this was done to act as a check or control on the President's powers over foreign policy. The foreign policy powers of Congress include:

- declaring war
- approving treaties and Presidential appointments (*a 2/3rds vote of the Senate is required to ratify a treaty*)
- deciding how much money the President may spend on defense.

Generally, the President's ability to act quickly has allowed the Presidency to become the major player in making United States foreign policy. However, Congress often attempts to re-establish its control over foreign policy in times when the United States is not faced with a military crisis.

OTHER INFLUENCES ON FOREIGN POLICY

The President and Congress are often influenced in their decisions by:

- **Special Interest Groups**. Businesspeople, political action groups and others often lobby Congress or contact the President's staff to press their views.

- **The News Media**. Newspapers, television and radio are very influential, since they decide what foreign news to report and how to report it.

- **Public Opinion**. Congress and the President are sensitive to public opinion, knowing that the public elected them.

FOREIGN POLICY GOALS

The main objective of American foreign policy has always been to act according to the nation's best interests. Many factors determine what our leaders believe those interests are:

NATIONAL SECURITY

The first and highest goal of U.S. foreign policy is to protect the American way of life. Every nation claims the right to protect itself against other nations. The United States protects its security through military preparedness and by participating in international organizations. Today, nuclear weapons protect the United States from attack.

PROTECTION OF U.S. CITIZENS AND INVESTMENTS

The United States acts to protect its citizens overseas. For example, in the 1970s, concern for American hostages in Iran had a strong influence on foreign policy.

PROMOTION OF AMERICAN TRADE

The United States acts to promote the American economy. For example, the promotion of trade has been crucial to U.S. support for freedom of the seas.

PROMOTION OF DEMOCRACY

The United States actively seeks to spread its political system, democracy. For example, it consistently fought the spread of communism in the world.

PROMOTION OF HUMAN RIGHTS AND PEACE

The United States supports the causes of morality and peace in international affairs. It realizes that the survival of the human species depends on the actions of individual countries. For this reason, the United States is a member of the United Nations.

SHARPENING YOUR TEST-TAKING SKILLS

LEARNING TO WRITE GOOD PARAGRAPHS

Because of the importance of good writing in answering essay questions, this section looks more closely at the process of writing. What you learn in this section will apply to what you write in both thematic and document-based essay questions.

After you develop an outline or plan for your essay, you must put it into written form. Each major heading of your outline will become one or more paragraphs. As you know, a paragraph is a group of related sentences that deal with the same topic or theme. A good paragraph displays three important characteristics:

UNITY   COMPLETENESS   ORDER

Because of the importance of good paragraphs to writing well, let's examine each of these characteristics in greater detail.

UNITY

Every paragraph should be unified — all the sentences in the paragraph should deal with a single topic, even if they deal with different aspects of that topic. Sentences that are not directly related to the topic of the paragraph should be moved to other paragraphs.

Writers use several techniques to give a paragraph unity. They use topic sentences which identify — in a *single sentence* — what the main idea of each paragraph is. Through proper planning, all the sentences in a paragraph should be related to the topic sentence. Read the paragraph below, and notice how many sentences use the word "slavery" to unify the paragraph:

> *One of the most important causes of the Civil War was the disagreement over the future of slavery. Slavery was an important economic institution in the South, where plantation owners used slave labor to grow cotton and other crops. It was less important to the North, where the economy was based on free laborers. Southerners did not think slavery was wrong or immoral. They pointed to slavery in the Bible and in other societies. Slave owners also felt their slaves were better treated than many factory workers in the North. But most Northerners detested slavery. They did not see how the nation could continue half-slave and half-free. Eventually, the existence of conflicting attitudes over slavery led to the outbreak of war.*

COMPLETENESS

A second characteristic of a good paragraph is completeness. Each paragraph should thoroughly develop the idea expressed in its topic sentence. How much explanation is needed will depend on the subject. In general, you should provide enough details and supporting facts that, after reading your paragraph, your reader:

❖ will understand the main idea of your thesis statement, and
❖ will have enough details to conclude that your main idea could be correct.

To see if your explanation is complete, pretend you are the reader and re-read the paragraph. Does it meet the above criteria for completeness, or do you have to add information to make your point to the reader?

How long should a paragraph be? Again, the answer depends. If there is not enough information in the paragraph to support the main idea, then the paragraph is too short. If the paragraph is very long, it may deal with too many aspects of the same topic and should be broken up. Following is a paragraph with a thesis statement and details that support it:

> *The Spanish-American War of 1898 was a major turning point in American foreign policy. Until this time, Americans had expanded westward across the North American continent, but possessed no overseas colonies. The United States had also tried to avoid war with any European power. Now America showed that it was a world power. It not only helped the Cuban people by fighting and defeating the Spanish there, but took direct control of Puerto Rico, the Philippines and Hawaii after the war, as well as indirect control of Cuba. America had become an imperial power.*

Do you think this paragraph is complete? Do the details show that the Spanish-American War was a major turning point in U.S. foreign policy?

ORDER

All the sentences of the paragraph should be presented in a logical order. In other words, the paragraph should move in a consistent direction. This is one of the most essential aspects of writing. The direction in which the paragraph moves depends on the purpose of the paragraph. Here are some the most common ways for logically presenting information in a paragraph.

❖ **Sequential (*Chronology*).** This type of paragraph presents a series of events or steps in a process in the order in which they have occurred, or should occur.

❖ **From General to Specific.** This kind of paragraph opens with a general thesis statement and then provides examples or details to explain it. The examples could be organized from the most important to the least, or from the least important to the most. Sometimes the thesis statement is restated in different words as a conclusion at the end of the paragraph.

❖ **From Specific to General**. A paragraph may also start with a series of examples or details that lead to a more general conclusion. The conclusion at the end of the paragraph can serve as the topic sentence.

❖ **Parts to a Whole**. Here, the purpose of the paragraph is to identify or describe a number of "parts" to something. The parts should be described in any order that will make sense to the reader. If describing the details of a scene, you might describe items in the scene moving from right to left, or from the least to most important. Often, we start with the least important so we can end the paragraph with the item having the most importance.

❖ **Cause and Effect**. Another way to organize a paragraph is to begin with an effect, stated in the topic sentence, followed by its causes. The topic sentence could be stated either as a question, such as "Why did Americans go to war in 1917?" or as a thesis statement: "There were many reasons why Americans went to war in 1917." The rest of the paragraph would then list the major causes of American involvement in World War I.

In addition to organizing their sentences into the most logical order, good writers rely on **transition words** to help make this order more obvious. Transition words serve as signposts, letting your readers know exactly what to expect. This enables them to process new information more easily as they read.

FUNCTION	TRANSITION WORD OR PHRASE
To explain a new point about the topic	*Moreover, in addition, also, furthermore, then, similarly, again, next, secondly, finally*
To introduce an example	*For example, thus, to illustrate, in this case*
To introduce a conclusion or effect	*Therefore, in conclusion, thus, to sum up, as a result, in consequence*
To mention a contrast or qualification	*Nevertheless, on the other hand, nonetheless, however, despite*

TESTING YOUR UNDERSTANDING

Directions: Circle the number preceding the word or expression that correctly answers the statement or question. Following the multiple-choice questions, answer the essay questions.

Base your answers to questions 1 and 2 on the following cartoon and on your knowledge of social studies.

1 The policeman in the cartoon most likely represents
   1 George Washington   3 Theodore Roosevelt
   2 Thomas Jefferson   4 Woodrow Wilson

2 Which U.S. foreign policy goal is depicted in the cartoon?
   1 increased control of the Americas
   2 spread of democracy
   3 decreased foreign trade
   4 moves toward world peace

3 Which was a basic cause of United States entry into World War I?
   1 a desire to obtain colonies
   2 the defense of freedom of the seas
   3 tensions between the U.S. and Soviet Union
   4 the German invasion of Poland

4 Which was a major result of World War I?
   1 American troops occupied Japan.
   2 A League of Nations was created.
   3 Russia controlled most of Europe.
   4 Germany gained colonies.

5 The most accurate statement about United States foreign policy is that it has
   1 been guided by the nation's self-interest
   2 consistently supported imperialism
   3 always followed an isolationist policy
   4 used military force to solve all disputes

6 Which news headline provides an example of the use of the Monroe Doctrine?
   1 "U.S. Declares Independence from England"
   2 "U.S. Issues Open Door Policy"
   3 "U.S. Announces 'Big Stick' Policy"
   4 "U.S. Enters War In Europe"

7   A major reason for the Senate's refusal to support the League of Nations was its opposition to
    1 lower tariffs
    2 freedom of the seas
    3 nuclear weapons
    4 future military commitments

8   Which of the following is evidence that the United States followed a policy of isolationism in the period after World War I?
    1 The U.S. condemned German aggression.
    2 The U.S. rejected communism.
    3 The U.S. did not join the League of Nations.
    4 The U.S. signed the Treaty of Versailles.

9   In gaining colonies in the early 1900s, the United States was following the policy of
    1 isolationism
    2 imperialism
    3 neutrality
    4 containment

10 The United States established the "Good Neighbor Policy" in order to
    1 sell natural resources to Latin American nations
    2 build air and naval bases in South America
    3 improve relations between the United States and Latin America
    4 help rebuild Asia after years of imperialism

11 An important result of the "Open Door Policy" was that
    1 China was saved from being taken apart by foreign powers
    2 the U.S. took control of Canada
    3 the U.S. expanded to the Pacific Ocean
    4 Mexico was allowed to keep part of Texas

12 Which was a major result of the Spanish-American War?
    1 The United States emerged with a colonial empire.
    2 The power of the U.S. government decreased.
    3 Cuba became a new state of the United States.
    4 All U.S. expansion overseas came to an end.

13 In *Schenck v. United States*, the Supreme Court decided that a "clear and present danger" to the United States permitted
    1 an expansion of Presidential power
    2 restrictions on First Amendment rights
    3 establishment of a peacetime draft
    4 limitations on the right to vote

14 The Fourteen Points proposed by President Woodrow Wilson are best described as a
    1 statement of principles that would govern the postwar world
    2 program the United States could follow to achieve victory in World War I
    3 list of reasons for the United States to remain neutral in World War I
    4 policy dealing with the threat of international communism

15 Which argument was used to support United States acquisition of overseas possessions in the late 1800s?
    1 The United States needed raw materials and new markets.
    2 Communism had to be stopped since it threatened world peace.
    3 The United States should be the first world power to build a colonial empire.
    4 The doctrine of Manifest Destiny had become obsolete.

16 "I took the Canal and let Congress debate."
                                    — *Theodore Roosevelt*
    This quotation best demonstrates
    1 an effort by a President to maintain a policy of isolationism
    2 a decline in the use of militarism as a defense policy
    3 an increased reliance on the legislative process
    4 a Presidential action that achieved a foreign policy goal

    _____

Read the following Skill Builder, and base your answers to questions 17 and 18 on the speakers' statements and on your knowledge of American history:

SKILL BUILDER: INTERPRETING SPEAKERS

Occasionally a history examination will contain questions about speakers' statements.

Interpreting a Speaker-Type Question
Ask yourself the following questions about each speaker's statement:

- What term, concept or situation is being described by the speaker?

- What is the speaker saying about the term, concept or situation?

- Is the speaker in favor of or opposed to this concept or situation?

- Does the speaker's opinion remind you of the views held by any other groups or individuals?

Now that you know what to look for, read the following explanations of two sample questions, and then answer questions 17 and 18 below.

Speaker A: Americans must be careful to guard against entering into permanent alliances with foreign countries.

Speaker B: The U.S. will not allow any European nation to establish new colonies in the Western Hemisphere.

Speaker C: I believe it is America's destiny to extend its borders to the Pacific.

Speaker D: Since the U.S. is now an industrial power, we need colonies to supply us with raw materials and provide markets for our manufactured goods.

1 Which speaker would favor the policy known as the Monroe Doctrine?
1 Speaker A   3 Speaker C
2 Speaker B   4 Speaker D

> **Speaker B's** views favor a policy which was first stated in the Monroe Doctrine. This doctrine announced to the world that since America had special interests in the Western Hemisphere, it would not permit European nations to have any new colonies there.

2 Which speaker would most likely have supported the purchase of Louisiana from France and the annexation of Texas in 1845?
1 Speaker A   3 Speaker C
2 Speaker B   4 Speaker D

> **Speaker C** argues in support of Manifest Destiny, under which the U.S. was urged to expand its territory across the continent.

Speaker A: The United States has enough problems of its own. We should keep out of the affairs of other countries.

Speaker B: We must expand our borders to the Pacific Ocean and not stop until we have achieved our true destiny.

Speaker C: American businesses are producing more than they can sell. We need to acquire overseas markets.

Speaker D: We must not join this international organization. If we do, Congress will lose its power to declare war.

17 Which speaker is most likely an American imperialist of the early twentieth century?
1 Speaker A   3 Speaker C
2 Speaker B   4 Speaker D

18 Which speaker's advice is most similar to that given by President George Washington in 1796?
1 Speaker A   3 Speaker C
2 Speaker B   4 Speaker D

THEMATIC ESSAY QUESTION

Directions: Write a well-organized essay that includes an introduction, several paragraphs explaining your position, and a conclusion.

Theme: Foreign Policy Goals

> Throughout American history, the nation
> has pursued a variety of foreign policy goals.

Task:

Choose *two* foreign policy goals from your study of American history.

For *each* foreign policy goal:
- Define the goal.
- Identify an action taken by the United States to carry out that goal.
- Describe the specific historical circumstances that led to that action.

You may use any example from your study of American history. Some suggestions you might wish to consider include: isolationism, territorial expansion, humanitarianism, global involvement, and neutrality.

You are *not* limited to these suggestions.

INTERPRETING DOCUMENTS

This World War I poster was created by James Montgomery Flagg for the U.S. Army.

1   What is the main idea of the poster?

     _____

     _____

2   How does Flagg communicate this idea in his poster?

     _____

     _____

     _____

CHAPTER 9

PROSPERITY, DEPRESSION, AND WAR

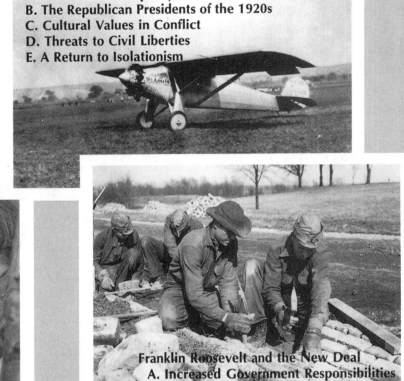

Boom Times: the 1920s
  A. Reasons for Prosperity
  B. The Republican Presidents of the 1920s
  C. Cultural Values in Conflict
  D. Threats to Civil Liberties
  E. A Return to Isolationism

The Great Depression: 1929-1940
  A. The Stock Market Crash
  B. Causes of the Depression
  C. President Hoover Fails

Franklin Roosevelt and the New Deal
  A. Increased Government Responsibilities
  B. Legislation: Relief, Recovery, Reform
  C. Reactions to the New Deal

World War II: 1941-1945
  A. Origins in Europe
  B. The U.S. Enters the War
  C. War Against Germany and Japan
  D. Treatment of Defeated Nations

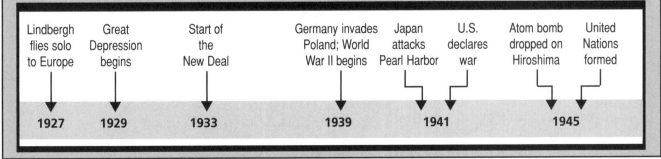

Lindbergh flies solo to Europe	Great Depression begins	Start of the New Deal	Germany invades Poland; World War II begins	Japan attacks Pearl Harbor	U.S. declares war	Atom bomb dropped on Hiroshima	United Nations formed
1927	1929	1933	1939	1941		1945	

WHAT YOU SHOULD FOCUS ON

In this chapter, you will learn how the nation entered a new age of prosperity in the 1920s. Unfortunately, this prosperity was cut short by the Stock Market Crash of 1929 and the Great Depression that followed — the worst economic crisis in U.S. history. President Hoover proved unable to restore economic growth.

Under President Franklin D. Roosevelt, the federal government intervened to stimulate the economy on a massive scale. However, it was not until the United States entered World War II that the nation fully recovered from the depths of the Great Depression.

A photograph taken by Dorothea Lange during the Great Depression

In this chapter, you will learn about the following:

Boom Times: the 1920s	**The Great Depression**	**The New Deal**	**The U.S. in World War II**
In the 1920s, the automobile and other new technologies contributed to growing prosperity. Mass consumption also led to changes in cultural values, such as new roles for women.	When the New York Stock Market crashed in 1929, banks failed, markets vanished and businesses went bankrupt. Soon millions of people were out of work.	President Franklin D. Roosevelt introduced policies of relief, recovery and reform to revive the economy. The New Deal greatly increased the size, power and responsibilities of the federal government.	Despite the outbreak of World War II in Europe in 1939, the United States remained neutral. On December 7, 1941, Japanese planes bombed Pearl Harbor. This attack brought the United States into the war against Germany, Italy, and Japan.

In studying this period, you should focus on the following questions:

❖ What factors contributed to the economic prosperity of the 1920s?

❖ What were the causes of the Great Depression?

❖ What has been the impact of the New Deal?

❖ What impact did World War II have on the United States and Europe?

SECTION 1

BOOM TIMES: THE 1920s

In this section you will read about the 1920s, a period in America of good economic times, changing values and Presidents who believed that government should not interfere too much in the nation's economy.

THINK ABOUT IT

The period of the 1920s has been known by many names: the "Roaring Twenties," the "Golden Twenties," and the "Jazz Age." Based on these phrases, what you think it was like to live in the 1920s?

_____

_____

Important Terms and Concepts: As you read this section, look for the following:

- ✦ Assembly Line
- ✦ Laissez-faire
- ✦ Rugged Individualism
- ✦ Harlem Renaissance

- ✦ Prohibition
- ✦ Red Scare
- ✦ Nativism
- ✦ Isolationism

To help you find these terms, the ✦ symbol will appear in the margin where the term is first explained.

After World War I was over, Americans were ready to concentrate on making money and enjoying themselves.

REASONS FOR THE PROSPERITY OF THE 1920s

For many Americans, the 1920s were good times. Wages rose and job opportunities increased, while business profits and production soared. There were many factors underlying this prosperity.

THE RISE OF THE AUTOMOBILE

Probably the single most important factor in creating prosperity was that the automobile came into widespread use. In the 1920s, ownership of cars jumped from 7 million to 23 million. This enormous growth in automobile ownership greatly affected many aspects of American life. Automobile production helped stimulate other industries, since cars required vast amounts of steel, glass, and rubber. By 1929, one out of every nine workers in America was employed in an auto-related industry.

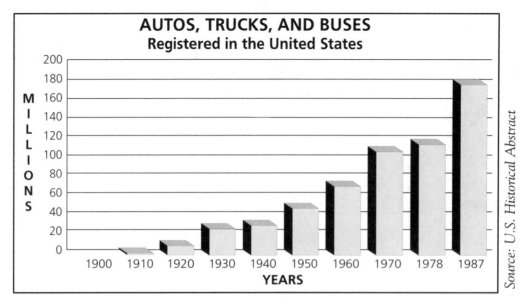

THE DEVELOPMENT OF OTHER INDUSTRIES

The widespread use of electricity led to the development of other new products, such as vacuum cleaners, refrigerators and toasters. The radio and motion picture industries became businesses. Commercial air travel began. These new industries created jobs, produced large profits, and changed the ways Americans lived.

MORE EFFICIENT PRODUCTION TECHNIQUES

During World War I, improved production techniques were developed. These improvements were soon applied to manufacturing and industrial production. The
◆ **assembly line** (*where workers stay in one place doing the same job, as products came to them on a conveyor belt*), the use of interchangeable standardized parts and other labor-saving devices made American industry more efficient and productive.

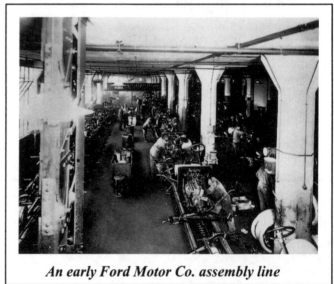

An early Ford Motor Co. assembly line

Although these were prosperous times for many, some groups did not share in the good times of the 1920s. Farmers, African Americans, Native American Indians and workers in some industries suffered from declining incomes and unemployment.

THE REPUBLICAN PRESIDENTS OF THE 1920s

Part of the reason for the business boom of the 1920s can be found in the policies of the government. From 1921 to 1933, three Republicans (Harding, Coolidge, and Hoover) served as Presidents of the United States. In general, these Presidents followed policies favorable to American
◆ business. Each believed in **laissez-faire** — the principle that the government should interfere as little as possible in the affairs of business.

REPUBLICAN PRO-BUSINESS POLICIES: 1920-1932

High Tariffs
Congress raised **tariffs** (*taxes on goods imported into the U.S.*) to protect American manufacturers. This discouraged foreigners from selling their goods here.

Lax Enforcement
Existing laws against monopolies were not enforced. As a result, big businesses grew larger and wealthier.

Tax Cuts
Taxes on big business and the wealthy were reduced. This put a greater tax burden on middle class and working class people.

WARREN HARDING AS PRESIDENT (1921-1923)

Warren Harding was elected President in 1920. He captured the national spirit with his call for a "return to normalcy" — bringing America back to a time when the government was less involved with foreign affairs and business. Under Harding, the U.S. refused to join the League of Nations, placed limits on immigration and raised tariffs. His administration became infamous for corruption in the **Teapot Dome Scandal**, in which government officials were bribed by businessmen.

CALVIN COOLIDGE AS PRESIDENT (1923-1929)

When Harding died of a heart attack in 1923, Vice President Calvin Coolidge became President. He came to symbolize old-fashioned values like honesty and thrift. Continuing Harding's pro-business policies, Coolidge's motto was: "The business of America is business." During Coolidge's Presidency, business expanded. Because he received much of the credit for the nation's prosperity, Coolidge was re-elected President in 1924. He was still very popular in 1928, when he decided not to seek another term.

Herbert Hoover fishing in the Klamath River, Oregon

HERBERT HOOVER AS PRESIDENT (1929-1933)

In campaigning for the Presidency in 1928, Herbert Hoover predicted that poverty in the United States would soon end. He believed that the nation's prosperity was the result of the American spirit of "**rugged individualism.**" Hoover was convinced that people did best when they were given a free education and individual opportunity, and when they had a will to succeed. Like Harding and Coolidge, Hoover believed that too much government interference in business could threaten future progress and prosperity. These ideas seemed reasonable in 1928, but they left Hoover badly prepared for the crisis he would face soon after his election as President.

CULTURAL VALUES IN CONFLICT

The way Americans lived and what they believed in was strongly affected by new inventions such as automobiles and radios, by new discoveries in science, and by greater contact with other nations after World War I. As a result, the 1920s saw the appearance of new and conflicting values. Some groups — such as women, young people and African-Americans — felt a new sense of power and freedom. African Americans and women especially benefited from new job opportunities created by industrialization and the war.

Young linotyper, 1920

■ **Women.** Work on the home front during World War I and the passage of the 19th Amendment gave women a greater sense of equality. New appliances reduced housework, allowing more women to go to college and to work outside the home. This new equality and economic independence brought about changes in manners and morals, such as smoking and drinking in public. Many women wore shorter skirts and had their hair cut short, earning them the nickname "flappers."

■ **Youth and the "Lost Generation."** Young adults were responsible for fads like flagpole sitting and marathon dancing. A group of writers known as the "Lost Generation" rejected the desire for material wealth. One of its leading writers was F. Scott Fitzgerald.

Langston Hughes, poet

■ **The Harlem Renaissance.** African Americans began migrating from the rural South to Northern cities, where they developed a new pride in their culture and asserted new demands for equality. African American writers such as Langston Hughes expressed these new views in what became known as the Harlem Renaissance. Jazz music, with its roots in black spirituals, flourished in Harlem (in New York City). The 1920s is often called the **Jazz Age**, reflecting the importance of this variety of African-American music.

■ **Popular New Heroes.** More leisure time gave people greater opportunity for entertainment. They turned to spectator sports, radio, movies and magazines. This had a great impact on popular culture and values. New popular heroes emerged, such as the pilot Charles Lindbergh, the boxer Jack Dempsey and the movie star Rudolph Valentino.

Some people were upset by these changes. Many Americans felt traditional values were being threatened by the growth of cities and the development of different values.

■ **Prohibition.** Many people believed that alcohol was the cause of poverty, crime and the breakdown of families. In 1919, the states approved the **Eighteenth Amendment**, banning the manufacture or sale of alcoholic drinks. However, by 1933 it was obvious that

Prohibition had failed. The law was unpopular, and a large part of the population refused to accept the ban on alcoholic drinks. The ban was lifted with the passage of the **Twenty-first Amendment**, demonstrating that unpopular laws are often unenforceable.

■ **Scopes "Monkey Trial."** In 1925, John Scopes, a biology teacher in Tennessee, was brought to trial for teaching the theory of evolution. State law required that the theory of Creation, as described in the Bible, should be taught instead of the modern theory of evolution. Scopes was convicted and forced to pay a small fine. The trial spotlighted the conflict between science and traditional religious teachings.

THREATS TO CIVIL LIBERTIES

The development of new values and ideas sometimes led to unfortunate reactions. The 1920s saw new attacks on some people's basic rights. Some Americans feared that foreign ideas and problems would "infect" the United States. Newly arriving immigrants and racial and religious minorities became special targets of hostility.

RISE OF NATIVISM

One reason for attacks on foreign immigrants was the **Red Scare** — a fear that communists would take over the United States as they did in Russia in 1917. Thousands of people who were thought to be communist supporters were arrested in 1919-1920. Two Italian immigrants, **Sacco and Vanzetti**, were executed for murder in 1927 after being convicted with little evidence. Many believed Sacco and Vanzetti were executed more for their political beliefs than for any crime they had committed. Their trial, as well as the Red Scare, contributed greatly to the rise of **nativism** (*a distrust and dislike of foreigners*). New laws were passed restricting immigration.

RISE OF RACISM

Racism (*a belief that one's race is superior to other races*) also increased. Many Americans felt threatened by the changes of the1920s. They distrusted those who looked, spoke or worshipped differently. African Americans became the victims of racial prejudice and mob-lynchings. The **Ku Klux Klan**, which had been quiet for many years, became active again during the 1920s. Its influence spread rapidly throughout the Midwest and the South. The Klan, declaring that African Americans, Catholics, Jews and immigrants were inferior, gained significant public support.

A RETURN TO ISOLATIONISM

In World War I, ten million people had been killed and twenty million wounded. Some of these casualties were Americans. By 1920, Americans felt let down by the results of the war. Although the United States had been on the winning side, the world was not "safe for democracy," as President Wilson had promised. In the 1920s, the United States returned to its traditional policy of isolationism — keeping away from involvement in Europe's troubles. Americans focused more on events at home, feeling safe behind the oceans that separated them from Europe and Asia. This was one major reason why the United States never joined the League of Nations.

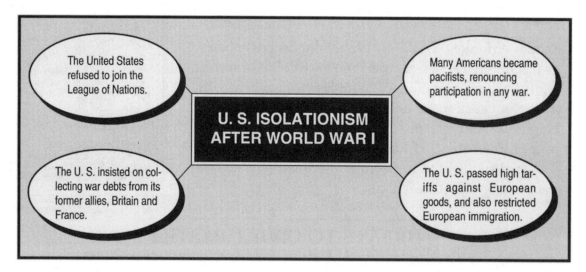

There were some exceptions to this trend towards isolationism. In 1921, the United States hosted the **Washington Naval Conference**, in which European and Asian powers agreed to limit the number of naval weapons and the size of their navies. In 1928, the United States also promoted the **Kellogg-Briand Pact**, in which 62 countries said they would give up war and settle their disputes by peaceful means only. But Americans were reluctant to become any more involved than this, and were especially opposed to being caught up in any future wars in Europe.

ANALYSIS

Some historians have criticized the United States for following a policy of isolationism after World War I. They claim that America acted like an ostrich burying its head in the sand. Do you think this policy was a good idea for Americans? ❑ Yes ❑ No   Explain:

_____

_____

SUMMING UP: BOOM TIMES OF THE 1920s

Americans in the 1920s were eager to put World War I behind them. This caused a return to a foreign policy of isolationism. The 1920s were also marked by economic prosperity and new opportunities for many groups. These developments gave rise to conflicts between traditional and modern values, and a growing distrust of people who were different.

THINKING IT OVER

Now that you have read this section, what do you think it was like to live in the 1920s?

_____

Do you think the expressions: "Roaring Twenties," "Golden Twenties," and "Jazz Age" were

good descriptions of this period? _____ Explain. _____

_____

CHECKING YOUR UNDERSTANDING

Directions: Complete the following cards. Then answer the multiple-choice questions.

HARLEM RENAISSANCE

What was it? _African American pride._

Name a writer associated with it: _Langston Hughes_

PROHIBITION

Define it: _banning of alchcol_

What lesson did it teach Americans? _unless theres popular support for a movement it wont work_

---

1 Which generalization is best supported by a study of Prohibition?
   (1) People's attitudes can often make some laws difficult to enforce.
   2 Increased taxes can affect consumer spending.
   3 People's morality can be successfully legislated.
   4 People will sacrifice willingly for the common good.

2 The "Harlem Renaissance" refers to the
   1 artistic style of the first settlers in New York
   2 African American soldiers in World War I
   (3) re-awakening of African American pride in the 1920s
   4 rise of Hispanic culture in New York during the 1920s

3 Which invention brought about the greatest change in American lifestyles in the 1920s?
   1 railroad   (3) automobile
   2 steam engine   4 computer

4 The boom years of the 1920s were characterized by
   1 decreases in agricultural surpluses
   2 limited investment capital and declining jobs
   (3) widespread use of the automobile and an increase in consumer purchases
   4 increased government regulation of the economy

5 Which was an immediate effect of the use of new production techniques from 1900 to 1929?
   1 a loss of commitment to the work ethic
   (2) a flood of new consumer products
   3 an increase in the rate of inflation
   4 a decline in business profits

SECTION 2

THE GREAT DEPRESSION, 1929-1940

In this section you will read about the worst economic period in American history, which started with the Stock Market Crash of 1929 and lasted until 1940.

THINK ABOUT IT

When you hear the term the Great Depression, what images come to mind? _____

_____

Important Terms and Concepts: As you read this section, look for the following:

✦ **Business Cycle**   ✦ **New York Stock Market Crash**
✦ **Great Depression**   ✦ **Dust Bowl**

Market economies go through good and bad periods that repeat themselves over time. Economists call these up-and-down periods the **business cycle**. In the good times, businesses are growing and it is easy to find a job. The bad times are called depressions, when many businesses close down and people lose their jobs for a long period of time. Because people have less money, less goods are bought. This leads to more and more businesses closing, and more and more people losing their jobs. One of these down periods, the **Great Depression**, was the worst economic period in the history of the United States.

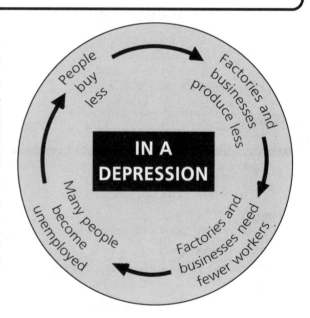

THE NEW YORK STOCK MARKET CRASH

In 1929, the prices of stocks on the New York Stock Exchange turned sharply downward. On October 29th, the market "crashed" as prices went into free fall. Everyone wanted to sell stocks but nobody wanted to buy them. Within a few days the total market value of stocks fell by more than 30 billion dollars. The **New York Stock Market Crash** marked the beginning of the Great Depression. Corporations found it hard to raise money, and many went out of business. As a result, people lost their jobs. Unemployed people had very little money to spend, so more companies went out of business. People went hungry. Millions depended on soup kitchens and bread provided by private charities. People who lost money in the stock market could not repay their loans to banks; this forced banks to close, and thousands of people lost their life savings.

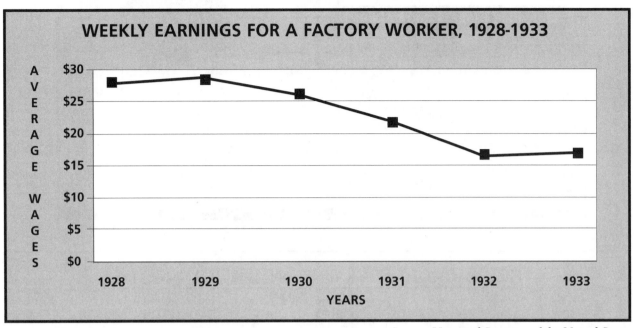

Source: Historical Statistics of the United States

CAUSES OF THE GREAT DEPRESSION

The crash of the stock market in 1929 set off a chain reaction that toppled the American economy and became a national nightmare. Soon the Great Depression spread to Europe, showing that conditions in one part of the world are affected by conditions in another part. This connection is known as **global interdependence**.

FACTORS LEADING TO THE GREAT DEPRESSION

In addition to the New York Stock Market Crash, many underlying factors helped cause the Great Depression:

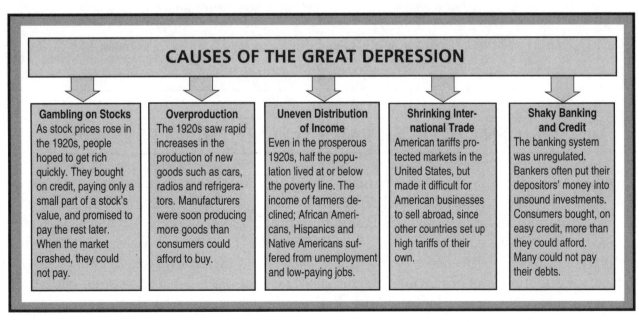

FOCUS
ON THE
ARTS

Dorothea Lange, Photographer

When the Depression hit, Dorothea Lange was working as a photographer in San Francisco. Soon after, she obtained a job as a photographer for the Farm Security Administration. She became famous for capturing the despair of everyday life and the brutal effects of the Depression. One of her best known photos, called "Migrant Mother," (see pg. 203) shows a poverty-stricken young woman holding her exhausted children. This picture was selected by the University of Missouri as one of the fifty best photographs of the twentieth century.

THE IMPACT OF GEOGRAPHY ON AMERICAN HISTORY

The Dust Bowl. During the 1930s, in addition to financial disaster, the farmers of the Great Plains faced a natural catastrophe. Since the 1870s, farmers had been plowing the Great Plains, removing the grasses that held the topsoil, and tapping underground water supplies. A series of droughts (*long periods without rain*) in the early 1930s dried up crops. Soon the topsoil turned into dust. Fierce winds blew the dust across hundreds of miles, burying homes and destroying harvests. Farmers, unable to grow enough crops to pay their bills,

Farm machinery buried under a sea of dust

were forced to abandon their land. Over one million farmers were driven from their lands by the "dust bowl." Many of these farmers moved west to California.

PRESIDENT HOOVER FAILS TO END THE DEPRESSION

President Hoover felt strongly that government should not interfere in the economy. He believed the economy would eventually fix itself. Hoover thought that when prices got low enough, people would start to buy again, leading businesses to start hiring more workers. Therefore, at the beginning of the Great Depression, President Hoover did not respond to requests that the federal government provide money for the unemployed and needy. Hoover felt that voluntary and private organizations would provide enough help. Eventually, when things did not get better, Hoover changed his mind. He met with business leaders and asked them not to lay off workers. He cut taxes and increased spending on projects in which the unemployed could work. He established the **Reconstruction Finance Corporation** to give emergency loans to banks and businesses. Unfortunately, Hoover's policies were too little, too late. The amount of money which he made available was not enough to deal with the problem. Many Americans became frustrated with Hoover for failing to stop the Depression. The shanty towns that sprang up all across America, sheltering unemployed homeless people, became known as "Hoovervilles."

SUMMING UP: THE GREAT DEPRESSION, 1929-1940

The period of the Great Depression saw Americans facing the most difficult of times. A variety of factors brought about the Great Depression. Once it began, millions of people became unemployed and faced homelessness and starvation. The public became frustrated when President Hoover did not seem to be doing enough to stop things from getting worse.

THINKING IT OVER

Now that you have read this section, if someone mentioned the Great Depression, what things would come to your mind?

1. _____

2. _____

CHECKING YOUR UNDERSTANDING

Directions: Complete the following cards. Then answer the multiple-choice questions.

NEW YORK STOCK MARKET CRASH

Why did it happen? _____

What impact did the crash have on the nation?

_____

_____

THE GREAT DEPRESSION

Define it: _____

What were its major causes? _____

_____

_____

1 Which was one of the basic causes of the Great Depression?
   1 over-extension of credit
   2 labor shortages
   3 shortages of consumer goods
   4 a rise in oil prices

2 Which situation is most likely to develop when an economy is in a depression?
   1 new jobs are created by private businesses
   2 the government raises taxes to all-time highs
   3 there is a sharp decrease in available jobs
   4 many new companies open for business

3 An economy suffering from a depression is one in which there is a high rate of
   1 employment   3 business failures
   2 interest   4 production

4 Information on subjects such as business cycles, the Dust Bowl, and Hoovervilles would be found in a history textbook section on
   1 the Abolitionist Movement
   2 World War I
   3 the Roaring Twenties
   4 the Great Depression

5 When the Great Depression first began, President Hoover believed that
   1 depressions are a useful part of economic life
   2 the government should provide jobs for the unemployed
   3 voluntary organizations should provide relief to the needy
   4 the federal government should give food and shelter to the poor

SECTION 3

FRANKLIN D. ROOSEVELT AND THE NEW DEAL

In this section you will read about the new programs President Franklin D. Roosevelt introduced to lift the nation out of the Great Depression. Roosevelt's "New Deal" greatly increased the size, power and responsibilities of the federal government.

THINK ABOUT IT

If you had been President during the Great Depression, what measures would you have taken to improve conditions in the nation?

_____

_____

Important Terms and Concepts: As you read this section, look for the following:

♦ New Deal
♦ Social Security Act
♦ Federal Deposit Insurance Corp.
♦ Court Packing Plan

During the Great Depression, the main problem facing Americans was widespread unemployment. In the 1932 election, Democratic candidate **Franklin D. Roosevelt** promised that no one would starve, and that new programs would put people back to work. Roosevelt easily defeated Herbert Hoover in the election.

THE NEW DEAL INCREASES GOVERNMENT RESPONSIBILITIES

Over thirteen million people were jobless; thousands stood on bread lines waiting for a free meal; banks were failing; and hundreds of farmers were losing their farms for failure to pay their mortgages. Under these conditions, President Franklin D. Roosevelt (*also known as F.D.R.*) took office in March, 1933.

U.S. UNEMPLOYMENT RATE: 1920-1932

Roosevelt saw the Great Depression as a national emergency as serious as any war. He believed that the President's task was to find a way for the country to get back to prosperity. Unlike Hoover, F.D.R. believed that the federal government was primarily responsible for managing the nation's economy. He immediately began to push through a series of laws designed to get people and businesses back to work.

Jobless men in Texas seeking work, 1934

Roosevelt called his program the **New Deal**. It was a major turning point in American history. It established the idea that the federal government has the major responsibility for intervening in the American economy to help it regain its balance and run smoothly.

NEW DEAL LEGISLATION: RELIEF, RECOVERY, REFORM

Roosevelt brought together a group of extremely talented people as advisers, who suggested new ways of dealing with the economy. Roosevelt explained these ideas to the American people in radio talks known as "**fireside chats.**" He tried to build people's confidence by telling them that things would get better, hoping his listeners would begin buying and investing again. F.D.R.'s legislation was new, both in size and in its idea that the federal government had to take a more active role in running the economy. He explained the New Deal measures in terms of three R's: "**Relief, Recovery,** and **Reform.**"

One of F.D.R.'s "Fireside Chats"

RELIEF, RECOVERY, AND REFORM

RELIEF measures were short-term steps designed to tide people over until the economy recovered. There was no unemployment insurance as there is today, and many people were without food or shelter. They needed immediate help. Giving people money to spend also increased demand for products.

➤ **Civilian Conservation Corps, or** C.C.C. (1933) provided relief by giving young people jobs, such as planting trees, cleaning up forests and draining swamps.

➤ **Public Works Administration** (1935) provided relief by giving people jobs building public works projects such as schools, courthouses, roads, post offices and bridges.

RECOVERY measures were designed to stimulate production and restore the economy by increasing production incentives and rebuilding people's purchasing power. Roosevelt hoped to "prime the pump," getting the national economy going again.

➤ **Agricultural Adjustment Act** (1933) promoted the economic recovery of farmers by paying them to limit their production of crops.

Young men age 18 to 25 were employed by the C.C.C. for many outdoor jobs, and earned $30 a month.

➤ **National Recovery Administration** (1933) promoted recovery by drawing up codes for businesses which set prices, limits on production, a reduced work week and a minimum wage. These codes were later declared unconstitutional by the Supreme Court.

REFORM measures sought to correct defects in the economy to ensure that a depression would never strike again. Reforms protected people against risks they could not handle on their own.

➤ **Federal Deposit Insurance Corporation, or** F.D.I.C. (1933) provided reform by insuring bank deposits so that people would not lose their savings if their bank failed.

➤ **Tennessee Valley Authority**, or T.V.A. (1933) built government-owned dams along the Tennessee River to prevent floods and generate electricity.

➤ **Securities and Exchange Commission**, or S.E.C. (1934) was created to prevent fraud in the stock market and guard against another stock market crash.

➤ **National Labor Relations Act**, or **Wagner Act** (1935) gave workers the right to form unions and to bargain collectively.

➤ **Social Security Act** (1935) insured Americans against unemployment and provided them with limited retirement benefits. (See *The Constitution At Work*, page 233.)

REACTIONS TO THE NEW DEAL

POPULARITY OF F.D.R. AND THE NEW DEAL

Although the New Deal did not immediately end the Great Depression, people were happy to see the President doing something. Things gradually did get better, although the Depression did not end until 1940. Some business owners opposed F.D.R., accusing him of acting like a dictator. They said he gave the government too much power over the economy. But Roosevelt was re-elected by landslides in 1936, 1940 and 1944 — the only President ever elected for more than two terms.

F.D.R. campaigning for president, 1932

ROOSEVELT'S COURT PACKING PLAN (1937)

The greatest threat to the New Deal came from the Supreme Court. In 1935-1936, the Court ruled two New Deal programs — the N.R.A. and A.A.A. — unconstitutional. Roosevelt feared the Court might soon declare all of his New Deal programs unconstitutional. In the 1930s, as today, the Supreme Court consisted of nine Justices. Roosevelt believed that if he could appoint more Justices, his programs would be safe. Most of the Justices were relatively old, and in 1937 Roosevelt proposed that he be allowed to appoint one new Justice for each one 70 years or older. This would have given his appointees control of the Court. Most people saw the plan as a dangerous attempt to undercut the independence of the judiciary and to upset the traditional separation of powers. As a result, Congress defeated the plan. Although Roosevelt failed to "pack" the Supreme Court, the Justices stopped overturning New Deal legislation.

SUMMING UP: F.D.R. AND THE NEW DEAL

Franklin D. Roosevelt was a very popular president. His New Deal programs greatly changed the role of the federal government in the economy, giving it new powers and responsibilities. F.D.R's opponents objected to greater government interference in the free market economy. However, Roosevelt was elected to four terms because he gave people confidence that things were getting better. The Supreme Court overturned some early New Deal legislation. When Roosevelt tried to "pack" the Court with more Justices, Congress defeated the plan, but the Court stopped overturning New Deal programs.

THINKING IT OVER

What additional steps would you have taken, besides those of the New Deal, to help bring the United States out of the Great Depression? _____

_____

CHECKING YOUR UNDERSTANDING

Directions: Complete the following cards. Then answer the multiple-choice questions.

NEW DEAL

What was it? _____

List three major New Deal programs:

1. _____
2. _____
3. _____

COURT PACKING PLAN

What was it? _____

_____

Why did F.D.R. suggest it? _____

_____

1 The major problem facing Franklin D. Roosevelt when he took over the Presidency was
   1 the high cost of consumer goods
   2 an overseas trade imbalance
   3 factory overproduction
   4 widespread unemployment

2 A major result of the New Deal was that it
   1 eliminated poverty in the United States
   2 extended the merit system in the civil service
   3 destroyed the free enterprise system
   4 expanded the federal government's power

3 The Social Security Act of 1935 sought to
   1 achieve integrated public schools
   2 provide old age and unemployment insurance
   3 limit international trade
   4 guarantee the creation of labor unions

4 Which best describes New Deal programs?
   1 They reduced the number of government employees.
   2 They expanded the role of the government in the economy.
   3 They called for local government leadership.
   4 They greatly increased big business power.

5 Which action was viewed as an attempt to undercut the independence of the judiciary?
   1 Wilson's attempt to decrease the salaries of Supreme Court Justices
   2 Taft's appointment as a Supreme Court Justice
   3 Hoover's appointments to the Supreme Court
   4 F.D.R.'s plan to reorganize the Supreme Court

6 Which branch of the U.S. government declared some New Deal legislation unconstitutional?
   1 President   3 Supreme Court
   2 Senate   4 House of Representatives

7 Many business failures, high unemployment, and low production are usually found in a period of
   1 depression   3 expansion
   2 prosperity   4 recovery

8 The New Deal established the idea that
   1 Presidents have little power to correct social problems
   2 the government must own the nation's major industries
   3 government is ultimately responsible for correcting problems in the nation's economy
   4 imperialism is the fastest method to rebuild a colonial empire

9 Which is a correct conclusion, based on a study of the New Deal?
   1 Labor and businesses were unaffected.
   2 It resulted in government budget surpluses.
   3 It influenced U.S. economic policy for many years.
   4 It made individuals solely responsible for their own economic welfare.

10 The popular belief in the 1920s that prosperity would never end promoted
   1 a renewed interest in hand-made goods
   2 stricter enforcement of government regulations
   3 government efforts to increase the incomes of farmers
   4 heavy speculation on the stock market

SECTION 4

WORLD WAR II, 1939-1945

In this section you will read about attempts by the United States to avoid involvement in another foreign war. However, Japan's attack on Pearl Harbor ended U.S. neutrality.

THINK ABOUT IT

What reasons do you believe justify a nation in going to war?

1._____   3._____

2._____   4._____

Important Terms and Concepts: As you read this section, look for the following:

◆ World War II   ◆ Hiroshima / Nagasaki
◆ Pearl Harbor   ◆ Nuremberg Trials
◆ Korematsu v. U.S.   ◆ United Nations

THE ORIGINS OF WORLD WAR II IN EUROPE

World War II began in 1939, when Germany invaded Poland. This act led to a war that eventually pitted the **Axis Powers** (*Germany, Italy and Japan*) against the **Allied Powers** (*Britain, France, the Soviet Union and the United States*). Although the invasion of Poland was the spark that began the war, there were many underlying causes. In particular, new political ideas promoted war.

THE RISE OF DICTATORS

In Europe, the Great Depression caused the rise of new political beliefs and systems. In Italy, **Benito Mussolini** established **fascism** — a totalitarian system in which the government controlled all aspects of life and used terror to enforce its policies. In Germany, **Adolf Hitler** and the Nazis gained power. **Nazism** was a type of fascism that encouraged strong feelings of national pride, **anti-Semitism** (*hatred of Jews*) and the use of violence. Under Nazism, human rights were crushed. Rival political parties and criticism of the government were banned. Once in power, these dictators demanded more territory from neighboring countries.

The Nazis march into Austria, 1938

THE CAUSES OF WORLD WAR II

Failure of the League of Nations. When Hitler built up Germany's military power in violation of the Versailles Treaty, members of the League of Nations did nothing to stop him. Hitler then annexed Austria, making it part of Germany.

German Expansion. Next, Hitler threatened war unless he could annex western Czechoslovakia. At the **Munich Conference** in 1938, British Prime Minister Neville Chamberlain gave in. This was an example of **appeasement** (*giving in to a potential aggressor in order to avoid war*).

Attacks by Axis Powers. In 1939, Hitler signed a non-aggression pact with Soviet dictator Stalin, and invaded Poland. Britain and France declared war, and World War II began. In 1941, Hitler broke the pact with Stalin and invaded the Soviet Union. Meanwhile, Japan invaded China and Southeast Asia.

WORLD WAR II IN EUROPE, 1941

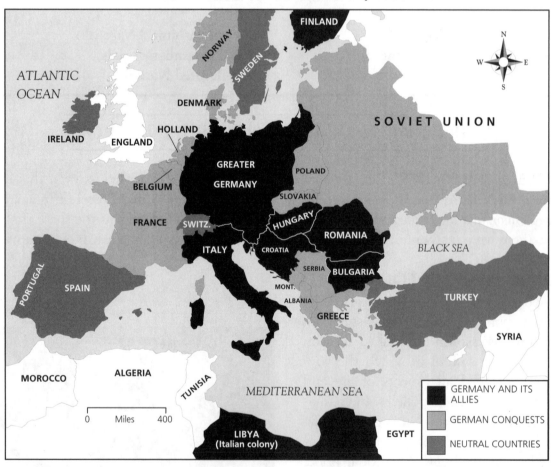

As the map shows, by late 1941 the Axis powers controlled most of Europe, the western Soviet Union and part of North Africa.

History examinations often contain questions about maps. Knowing how to read and interpret a map is the focus of the following Skill Builder.

SKILL BUILDER: UNDERSTANDING MAPS

What Is a Map?

A map is a diagram showing a much larger area. Most maps show the political divisions between countries, or the major geographic features of an area, but there is almost no limit to the kinds of information that can be shown on a map. Different types of maps can be found in a special reference book called an **atlas**.

Keys to Understanding a Map

Start by looking at its major parts:

Title. The title indicates what information will be found in the map. For example, the title of the map on page 222 is "WORLD WAR II IN EUROPE, 1941". The map shows the extent of conquests by Germany and its allies during World War II.

Direction. To find directions on a map, look at the direction indicator, often shown as a small compass. The indicator shows the four basic directions: north, south, east and west. Most maps show north at the top and south at the bottom. The direction indicator on the map on page 222 is in the upper right-hand corner.

Scale. A scale indicates distances. It is usually shown as a marked line. For example, the lower left-hand corner of the map on page 222 has a line indicating the

scale. The line is one inch long. The map maker has shown that the actual distance between two points 1 inch apart on the map is 400 miles. If two points are 2 inches apart on the map, they are 800 miles apart in the real place.

Legend or Key. The legend or "key" unlocks the information in a map. It lists the symbols used and tells what each represents. From the key on the map on page 222 we can see that the black areas represent Germany and its allies (the Axis powers).

■ Germany and its allies

Interpreting a Map

The title gives you an idea of the type of map it is. If it is a political map, the lines show the political boundaries between countries; dots or circles are often used to show major cities:

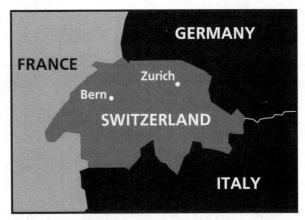

Maps also may be used to show population density, climate, geographical features, or information about a nation's history. Whatever type of map it is, the legend or symbols will unlock its meaning.

THE UNITED STATES TRIES TO REMAIN NEUTRAL

With fascists in control of much of Europe in the late 1930s, war became increasingly likely. Congress passed a series of laws to keep America out of a new European war. In 1917, the United States had become involved in World War I when Germany attacked American ships bringing supplies to Great Britain and France. To avoid a similar situation, Congress passed the **Neutrality Acts** (1935-1937). These prohibited Americans from traveling on the ships of nations at war or from selling arms to countries at war.

F.D.R. signing draft law

Despite public opposition to war, President Roosevelt began making preparations in case the United States was dragged into the conflict. Congress increased spending on the army and navy. In 1940, it set up the first peacetime **draft** for men between the ages of 21 and 35. In 1941, Congress passed a law that allowed the U.S. government to send or lend war materials to countries fighting against Germany, Italy and Japan. Soon U.S. battleships began protecting British ships carrying supplies. It seemed that American involvement in the war was just a matter of time.

AMERICA ENTERS WORLD WAR II, 1941

Surprisingly, events in Asia, not Europe, finally brought the United States into the war. In 1937, Japan had invaded China. Later, Japan took over parts of Southeast Asia. President Roosevelt felt that American interests in Asia and the Pacific were threatened by Japan's expansion. He cut off all U.S. trade with Japan, agreeing to resume trade only if Japan withdrew its forces. Late in 1941, Japanese military leaders decided to launch a surprise attack against the United States, believing that they would catch Americans unprepared and eliminate U.S. naval power in the Pacific. On **December 7, 1941**, Japanese planes attacked the U.S. Pacific Fleet stationed at **Pearl Harbor**, Hawaii. They destroyed 200 planes, sank 19 ships, and killed over 2,400 Americans. The following day, President Roosevelt asked Congress to declare war on Japan. Soon after, Japan's allies, Germany and Italy, declared war on the United States.

The U.S.S. Shaw during the Japanese attack on Pearl Harbor

THE HOME FRONT

The United States now faced fighting a war on two fronts: the Atlantic and Pacific. Americans had to ready themselves quickly for war. They had to greatly increase the size of their armed forces and to step up production to meet enormous wartime needs. This production finally ended the unemployment of the Great Depression.

MEETING WAR NEEDS

In order to fight the war, the United States set up a draft requiring all able-bodied men between 18 and 45 to serve in the armed forces. Fifteen million people served in the military during the war. Among them were 1 million African Americans, who were forced to serve in segregated units. Also, for the first time in U.S. history, women could enlist. These men and women in uniform served and fought on the Pacific and Atlantic Oceans, the Pacific islands, North Africa, and Europe. Many gave their lives for their country.

American industry rapidly retooled for full-time production of armaments.

Women building fighter planes, 1943

American factories quickly changed from producing consumer goods to wartime production. As a large number of men went into the armed services, many women and African Americans took their places. In order to pay for the huge cost of the war, taxes were raised. Americans also bought war bonds, which were to be repaid with interest by the government after the war. The ability of the U.S. economy to produce large numbers of ships, tanks, airplanes and guns was an important factor in helping the Allies to win the war.

THE FORCED RELOCATION OF JAPANESE AMERICANS

One unfortunate side effect of the war was the forced relocation of innocent Japanese Americans. The attack on Pearl Harbor created a fear, especially on the West Coast, that Japanese Americans might serve as spies for Japan or interfere with the U.S. war effort. Although there was no evidence that Japanese Americans were guilty of disloyalty, President Roosevelt ordered the removal of all Japanese Americans to relocation centers. Roosevelt justified this order as a military necessity, even though German Americans and Italian Americans did not face similar treatment. This demontrates how Presidential power often increases during wartime. Most Japanese Americans were forced to sell their property and belongings on short notice. In the relocation camps, they lived in primitive and crowded conditions. The Supreme Court upheld these relocations in **Korematsu v. U.S.** (see *The Constitution at Work*, page 233). ◆

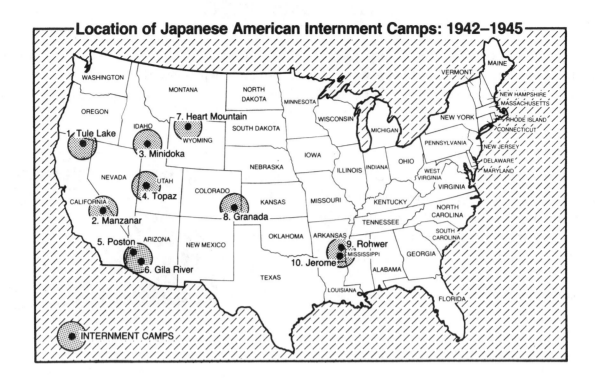

Location of Japanese American Internment Camps: 1942–1945

1. Tule Lake
2. Manzanar
3. Minidoka
4. Topaz
5. Poston
6. Gila River
7. Heart Mountain
8. Granada
9. Rohwer
10. Jerome

INTERNMENT CAMPS

THE WAR AGAINST GERMANY

When the United States entered the war, Hitler controlled most of Europe and North Africa. Roosevelt decided to commit most U.S. forces to defeating Nazi Germany first, because he believed that Germany was a greater military threat than Japan.

HITLER'S PLAN

Hitler planned to reorganize Europe along racial lines. Germans were to be the new ruling class, and other peoples would be turned into slaves. Jews, Gypsies, Poles, the elderly, the disabled and mentally ill people would be exterminated through mass murder. These plans led to the **Holocaust** — the murder of over six million Jews and six million other people in concentration camps, where they were tortured, starved, gassed, and their bodies burned in large ovens.

THE WAR IN EUROPE

By the end of 1940, Hitler had defeated France and was in control of most of Western Europe. He had also signed a pact of non-aggression with Joseph Stalin, the leader of the Soviet Union. Hitler went back on his word when he suddenly invaded the Soviet Union in 1941. This proved to be one of Hitler's greatest mistakes. The Ger-

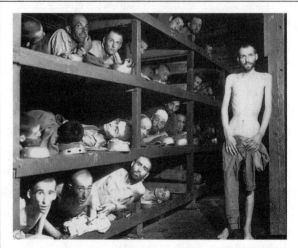

Jewish slave laborers at Buchenwald Concentration Camp in 1945

man invasion was stopped by the bitter cold of the Russian winter and the refusal of the Russian people to surrender. After two years of fighting, Soviet troops started pushing the Germans back in 1943. Meanwhile, Roosevelt and British Prime Minister Winston Churchill promised Stalin that they would open a second front against Germany in the west, to relieve the pressure on the Soviet army. Late in 1942, British and American troops landed in North Africa.

THE COLLAPSE OF NAZI GERMANY

After defeating German forces in North Africa, the Allies landed troops in Italy. Finally, on **D-Day** (*June 6, 1944*) Allied troops landed on the French coast. They advanced quickly to free Paris from Nazi control. American, British and French forces then invaded Germany from the west, while the Soviets attacked from the east. By the spring of 1945, the Soviet army captured Berlin, the German capital. Hitler committed suicide and Germany surrendered.

THE WAR AGAINST JAPAN

Meanwhile, fighting was also raging in the Pacific and in Asia. After its successful attack on Pearl Harbor, Japan had taken over the Philippines and other territories in Asia and the Pacific.

THE WAR BEGINS TO TURN AGAINST JAPAN

In 1943, the tide started to turn against the Japanese when the U.S. Navy began to overpower them in the Pacific. American forces began freeing Pacific islands from Japanese control. Once Germany was defeated, the United States prepared for a massive invasion of Japan.

THE ATOMIC BOMB AND THE JAPANESE SURRENDER (1945)

The United States had begun development of an atom bomb even before it entered the war. American leaders had feared Nazi Germany might develop an atom bomb first. Although the bomb was expected to be a weapon against Hitler, Germany surrendered before it could be used.

Atom bomb dropped on Nagasaki

When President Truman learned that an invasion of Japan might result in a million American casualties, he decided to use the new bomb against Japan. Truman selected the cities of **Hiroshima** and **Nagasaki** as targets, since both of them were centers of military production. Nearly 100,000 people were killed by the enormous ball of fire at Hiroshima; 36,000 died at Nagasaki. Thousands of others died later from burns, wounds and radiation sickness. As a result of these bombings, and the fact that the United States agreed to let the Japanese Emperor remain on his throne as a symbol, Japan surrendered.

THE INFLUENCE OF GEOGRAPHY ON AMERICAN HISTORY

Geography played a critical role in the Pacific campaign during World War II. The United States and Japan were separated by the vast Pacific Ocean. After they attacked Pearl Harbor, the Japanese conquered Malaya, Burma, Indonesia, the Philippines, and the western Pacific Islands. They now threatened Australia, India and Hawaii.

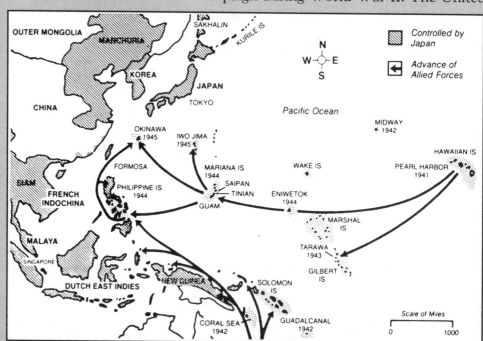

The Japanese used their control of the western Pacific as a barrier to fortify Japan and their vast new empire. The Americans, who had deciphered the Japanese codes, attacked them at **Midway** and destroyed many of their aircraft carriers. The Americans then halted the Japanese advance, draining their resources through a series of assaults on Pacific islands like Guadalcanal. However, it was not until June 1944 that American forces had captured islands close enough to use as bases to launch air attacks against the Japanese home islands. Meanwhile, the Pacific campaign had caused a delay in the all-out Allied assault on Germany.

TREATMENT OF THE DEFEATED NATIONS

✦ THE NUREMBERG TRIALS (1945-1946)

The discovery of millions of dead bodies in concentration camps provided clear evidence of Nazi crimes. The Allies put leading Nazis on trial for "crimes against humanity" in Nuremberg, Germany. The defendants claimed they had only been following orders. The judges ruled that people should disobey orders that are obviously immoral, establishing the principle that individuals are responsible for their own actions even in wartime. Most of the Nazi leaders were found guilty: some were hanged, and others were imprisoned for life.

THE DIVISION OF GERMANY

Germany was occupied by the armies of the United States, Great Britain, France and the Soviet Union. They divided Germany into four occupation zones. This eventually led to the division of Germany into two states — East and West Germany — which lasted for the next 45 years.

THE OCCUPATION OF JAPAN

American forces also occupied postwar Japan. Japan's overseas empire was taken away, and her military leaders were put on trial in Tokyo. Top officials in Japan were charged with war crimes and other atrocities. Japan's premier and other former leaders were executed, but Emperor Hirohito remained on the throne. **General Douglas MacArthur** was assigned the task of rebuilding the Japanese government and economy.

Under MacArthur's leadership, important changes were introduced. Japan renounced war and the use of nuclear weapons. Japan was forbidden from having a large army or navy. A new constitution went into effect in May 1947, making Japan a democracy.

A Japanese Vice Admiral on trial for war crimes

THE RESULTS OF WORLD WAR II

World War II proved to be a disaster for much of the world. More than 50 million people lost their lives. After fighting in both the Pacific and Europe, U.S. casualties were also high: 405,000 Americans were killed and 671,000 wounded.

THE GLOBAL IMPACT OF WORLD WAR II

Mass Destruction	Defeat of Dictatorships	Decline of Colonialism	Rise of Superpowers
The war was fought in North Africa, East Asia, Europe and the Soviet Union. It left much of Europe destroyed and more than 50 million people dead.	Germany was divided into 4 Allied occupation zones. The postwar governments of West Germany and Japan became democratic.	The European powers exhausted themselves in the war. Afterwards they were too weak to prevent their overseas colonies from gaining independence.	Europe's collapse left the U.S. and the Soviet Union as **superpowers**. Their different political and economic systems led to future tensions and conflicts.

World War II brought about important changes in the United States and the world. America had demonstrated its ability to supply almost unlimited goods during the war, and now became the economic superpower of the world. Americans also came to realize that they could no longer retreat into isolationism as they had done in the past. The war had social effects, too. As men were called into the armed forces, women had replaced them in the workforce — dramatically increasing the number of women working outside the home. High-paying jobs in Northern factories increased the flow of African Americans moving away from rural areas in the South.

FORMATION OF THE UNITED NATIONS

By 1945, most world leaders recognized the need for an international peace-keeping organization. This led to the creation of the **United Nations**. Its major goals were to preserve peace, promote international cooperation, end hunger and disease, and improve education around the world.

The U.N. has many advantages over the former League of Nations. Unlike the League, the U.N. has its own peacekeeping forces. Also, the major world powers, such as the United States and the Soviet Union, all chose to become members. U.N. membership has grown from its original 51 nations to include almost every nation in the world.

THE ORGANIZATION OF THE UNITED NATIONS

General Assembly: Provides a place to discuss problems affecting world peace and international issues. It also recommends actions to the Security Council.

Security Council: Acts as the U.N.'s executive branch, and carries out U.N. decisions. Five permanent members have power to veto U.N. actions; ten non-permanent members, without veto power, serve two-year terms.

Secretariat: Headed by a Secretary General chosen by the General Assembly. The Secretary General serves for five years, oversees the day-to-day running of the U.N., and brings before the Security Council matters which threaten world peace.

Agencies: Include the World Health Organization, UNICEF and the World Bank. They work to improve health, education, and human welfare worldwide.

SUMMING UP: WORLD WAR II

The rise of dictators in Germany and Italy in the 1930s tested the will of Americans to avoid war. In Asia, aggression by Japan brought it into conflict with American interests. Japan's attack on Pearl Harbor in 1941 brought America into the war. U.S. involvement changed the course of the war in favor of the Allies. American economic and military power led to the defeat of Germany, Italy and Japan. World War II was the most destructive war in world history. After the war, the Allies created the United Nations to help prevent future wars.

THINKING IT OVER

Do you think the United States was justified in entering World War II? _____

Explain. _____

_____

CHECKING YOUR UNDERSTANDING

Directions: Complete the following cards. Then answer the multiple-choice questions.

NUREMBERG TRIALS

Who was put on trial? _____

What did the trials teach about individual responsibility? _____

_____

UNITED NATIONS

What are its major aims? _____

_____

How does it differ from the League of Nations?

_____

1 Which was a basic cause of World War II?
   1 tensions between the United States and the Soviet Union
   2 nationalistic rivalries within Austro-Hungary
   3 the rise of fascism in Germany and Italy
   4 European competition for colonies in Africa

2 America's failure to join the League of Nations signaled to the world that the United States was adopting a foreign policy of
   1 imperialism   3 fascism
   2 isolationism   4 militarism

3 The belief that the United States should mind its own business and not become involved in Europe's wars helped promote the passage of the
   1 Monroe Doctrine
   2 Open Door Policy
   3 Good Neighbor Policy
   4 Neutrality Acts

4 Which event pushed the United States to declare war in 1941?
   1 the surprise attack on Pearl Harbor
   2 Germany's invasion of Poland
   3 the rise of fascism in Italy
   4 German attacks on U.S. merchant ships

5 Which statement most accurately describes U.S. policy toward Japan before 1941? The United States
   1 supported Japan's territorial expansion
   2 felt threatened by Japan's growth and power
   3 lacked interest in Japan's policies
   4 was militarily allied to Japan

6 In the 1930s, the United States responded to the rise of fascism in Europe by
   1 invading Germany and Italy
   2 forming alliances with Germany and France
   3 joining the League of Nations
   4 adopting a series of neutrality laws

7 Which U.S. citizens suffered the greatest loss of constitutional rights during World War II?
1 Italian Americans
2 Japanese Americans
3 German Americans
4 Chinese Americans

8 The bombing of Hiroshima and Nagasaki marked
1 the start of World War II
2 the beginning of the Atomic Age
3 U.S. entry into World War II
4 the end of world communism

9 Which was a major result of World War II?
1 Great Britain and France helped to rebuild the Soviet Union.
2 The United Nations was created.
3 Germany gained control of Eastern Europe.
4 Italy was divided into two countries.

10 The principal defense used by Nazi leaders at the Nuremberg trials was that they had been
1 following the orders of their superiors
2 serving the good of all humanity
3 trying to prevent the loss of innocent lives
4 reflecting the popular will of their society

11 The United States joined the United Nations after World War II to
1 limit the spread of communism in Europe
2 improve American social and economic conditions
3 help prevent future wars
4 seek allies against the Japanese government

12 Presidential powers often increase during wartime mainly because
1 Congress is not in session
2 the U.S. Constitution is suspended
3 quick action is often needed
4 the President uses his veto power

13 A major cause of World War II was
1 U.S. violation of the rights of German Americans
2 the expansion and aggressiveness of Germany and Japan
3 the forced relocation of Japanese Americans
4 the participation of the United States in the League of Nations

PROFILES IN HISTORY

HENRY FORD (AUTOMAKER)
Henry Ford's goal was to build cars that everyone could afford. He introduced the assembly line in 1914, increasing the efficiency of workers. By 1924, Ford was producing 1.6 million cars a year. As production and efficiency increased, Ford reduced the price of his cars from $850 in 1908 to under $300 by 1926.

MARCUS GARVEY (POLITICAL LEADER)
Jamaican-born Marcus Garvey was a spokesman for "Negro Nationalism." He stressed unity through education, self-help and pride in being black. He set up loans for black businesses, and encouraged African Americans to shop in black-owned stores. He later planned a "Back-to-Africa Movement," believing that African Americans would never find justice in the United States.

CHARLES LINDBERGH (AVIATOR)
In 1927, Charles Lindbergh was the first person to fly across the Atlantic Ocean to Europe. He made his flight in *The Spirit of St. Louis*, a single-engine plane. It lacked a radio and Lindbergh had only a compass to guide him. The trip made him a national hero and worldwide celebrity.

(continued...)

(Profiles in History, continued)

ELEANOR ROOSEVELT (REFORMER)

Eleanor Roosevelt was the wife of President Franklin D. Roosevelt. As First Lady, she served as her husband's eyes and ears, traveling around the country and the world. She promoted women's rights, programs to help the poor, and world peace. One of her greatest contributions was her role in creating the United Nations. From 1946 to 1948 she was chairperson of the U.N. Commission on Human Rights.

ALBERT EINSTEIN (SCIENTIST)

Einstein was one of the greatest scientists of all time. His "Theory of Relativity" provides the basis for much of modern physics. A German Jew, Einstein came to the U.S. to escape Nazi persecution. His work helped develop nuclear fission — the splitting of atoms to release enormous energy. In 1939, Einstein wrote to President Roosevelt warning him that Nazi Germany was developing an atom bomb. As a result, Roosevelt decided to develop the bomb in the United States.

THE CONSTITUTION AT WORK

TWENTY-SECOND AMENDMENT (1951)

Franklin Roosevelt was the only President to be elected to more than two terms. After his death, an amendment was passed limiting future Presidents to two elected terms.

KEY AMENDMENT

SOCIAL SECURITY ACT (1935)

This act is often considered the most important New Deal law. Before this Act, Americans had no "safety net" to prevent them from being thrown into poverty by unemployment, illness, or a death in the family. The Act provided unemployment insurance for workers without jobs — paid for by a tax on employers. Workers who lose their jobs now receive payments until they either find work or their benefits run out. In addition, employees now receive monthly payments after retiring, paid for by a special tax on their wages and by employer contributions.

KEY LAW

KOREMATSU V. U. S. (1944)

Background: After World War II began, some feared that Japanese Americans would become spies. There was very little evidence to support this, but F.D.R. ordered that Americans of Japanese ancestry be moved inland from the West Coast to "relocation camps." Korematsu was convicted of violating the order when he refused to move.

Decision/Significance: Korematsu claimed that his constitutional rights as an American citizen had been violated. The Court ruled against Korematsu, stating that constitutional freedoms may be limited in wartime. The Court upheld the government's actions because of military necessity. Almost 50 years later, Congress apologized and voted to pay compensation to the Japanese-American families involved.

THE COURT SPEAKS

SUMMARIZING YOUR UNDERSTANDING

Directions: Confirm your understanding of the important terms and concepts in this chapter. Check those you can explain. For those you are not sure of, find the ◆ symbol in the margin next to the term and review it.

CHECKLIST

- ❑ Assembly line
- ❑ Laissez-faire
- ❑ Rugged Individualism
- ❑ Harlem Renaissance
- ❑ Prohibition
- ❑ Red Scare
- ❑ Nativism

- ❑ Business Cycle
- ❑ Great Depression
- ❑ Stock Market Crash
- ❑ Dust Bowl
- ❑ New Deal
- ❑ Social Security Act
- ❑ Court Packing Plan

- ❑ World War II
- ❑ Appeasement
- ❑ Pearl Harbor
- ❑ *Korematsu v. U.S.*
- ❑ Hiroshima/Nagasaki
- ❑ Nuremberg Trials
- ❑ United Nations

Directions: Fill in the information called for in the following organizers.

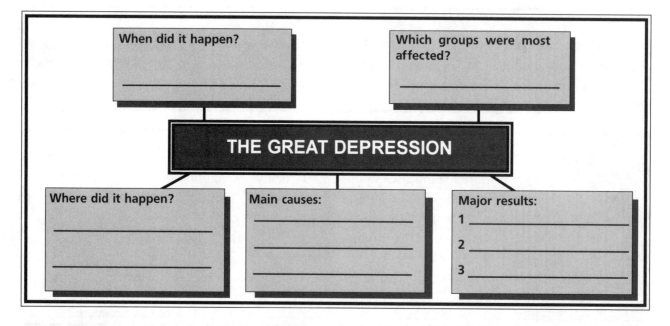

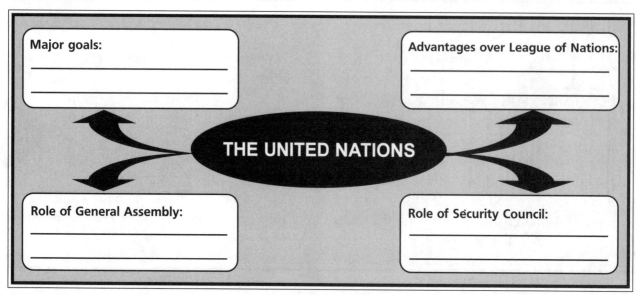

When did it happen?

_____

Who was involved?

_____

_____

WORLD WAR II

Where was it fought?

_____

_____

_____

What were its causes?

1. _____

2. _____

3. _____

Results:

1. _____

2. _____

3. _____

TEST HELPER   LOOKING AT HISTORICAL EVENTS

In the movie *Back to the Future*, the main character travels back in time and meets his mother while she is still a teenager. This threatens to change things that happen so that in the future he will never be born. Such time travel is a fantasy, but part of the excitement of the film is that it suggests something true: if we could change even *one* past thing that happened, we might change the *entire* course of history. Why is this so?

CAUSE AND EFFECT

Every **event** (*a thing that happens*) has effects, and these effects have still further effects. Some events affect the entire development and direction of a society — its organization, government or economy. These changes then influence later developments in society. At key times, choices by leaders can be especially important. For example, if a leader decides to go to war, it can change a country's political, social and economic system. Historians are particularly interested in examining how events are connected by causes and effects.

- The **causes** of something are the conditions or factors that brought it about. An event would not have happened except for this cause. For example, turning the switch on a lamp is the *cause* of the light's going on.

- The **effects** of something are the things that happened because of it — the results of a particular decision or event. For example, the light's going on was the *effect* of turning the switch.

Cause	$\longrightarrow$	Effect
I turned the switch.		The light went on.

ANSWERING AN ESSAY QUESTION ABOUT HISTORICAL EVENTS

Often history examinations contain questions about historical events and their effects. One possible question might ask you to discuss the causes or effects of the New Deal. Causes and effects are linked: the Great Depression caused the New Deal; the New Deal led to a new relationship between the federal government and the economy. With this type of question, first think about the event itself. Write about the *who*, *what*, *when*, and *where*. Then, think about the results (or causes) of the event. For each result (or cause), also try to think about the who, what, when, and where. For example, you might write your answer as follows:

(*Cause*) During the *Great Depression*, millions of Americans were unemployed. They faced poverty, hunger and homelessness. When Franklin D. Roosevelt was elected President in 1932, he promised to do something to help Americans and end the suffering caused by the Great Depression.

(*Effect*) Roosevelt proposed a series of laws known as the *New Deal*, which had important effects on American society. Under the New Deal, the federal government began to take steps to improve the economy and put Americans back to work. Congress also passed the Social Security Act, providing a safety net for all Americans. Ever since the New Deal, the federal government has tried to keep the economy running smoothly.

Now you do the same thing with the subject of World War II. On a separate sheet of paper, begin an essay with this topic sentence: **"World War II had many important effects."**

Follow the guidelines of *who*, *what*, *when*, and *where* explained above, and write about World War II (*the event*) and its effects.

SHARPENING YOUR TEST-TAKING SKILLS

ANSWERING A DOCUMENT-BASED ESSAY QUESTION

As you know, some U.S. history examinations will require you to answer a document-based essay question, also known as a "D.B.Q." This type of question tests your ability to interpret historical documents. Let's look at a typical D.B.Q.:

> **This task is based on the accompanying documents (1-5). Some of these documents have been edited for the purposes of this task. This task is designed to test your ability to work with historical documents. As you analyze the documents, take into account both the source of each document and the author's point of view.**
>
> *Directions:* Read the documents in Part A and answer the questions after each document. Then read the directions for Part B and write your essay.
>
> *Historical Context:*
> Beginning in the 1890s, Americans set out to correct the problems caused by rapid industrial growth. Reformers worked to eliminate a wide range of abuses.
>
> *Task:*
> Discuss **three** specific problems caused by rapid industrial growth, and explain how reforms sought to eliminate them.
>
> ## TURN TO PART A

NOTE: Most document-based questions will present five to eight documents. At least two will be documents other than reading passages, such as cartoons, graphs, or pictures. (You may want to review pages 166-167 before reading the following documents.)

Part A
Short Answer

Directions:
Analyze the documents on the following pages, and answer the questions that follow each document in the space provided.

DOCUMENT 1

Old sausages that had been rejected and were moldy would be [sprayed] with borax and glycerine, and dumped into the hoppers for home sale as sausages. In the factory, sausage meat would be used that had fallen on the floor, in the dirt and sawdust, where workers had trampled and spit their billions of germs. The sausage meat was stored in great piles in rooms where water from leaky roofs would drip on it, and thousands of rats would race about on the piles of meat. It was too dark in these storage places to see well, but a man could run his hand over these piles of meat and sweep off handfuls of dried rat dung.

— *Excerpt from* The Jungle, *a novel by Upton Sinclair describing conditions at a Chicago meat-packing plant*

1. According to the document, what was the condition of the meat being prepared for sale as sausages? _____

DOCUMENT 2

[This law]... prohibits the manufacture, sale, or transportation of adulterated or misbranded or poisonous or deleterious [harmful] foods, drugs, medicines, and liquors.

— *The Pure Food and Drug Act of 1906*

2. How did this law help American consumers? _____

_____

DOCUMENT 3

Boy working in glass factory, 1911

3. What problems are revealed in this photograph of working conditions in the United States?

_____

_____

_____

_____

DOCUMENT 4

> *My boss paid me three dollars [a week], and for this he hurried me from early [morning] until late [at night]. He gave me only two coats at a time to do. When he handed me new work he would say quickly and sharply, "Hurry!" Late at night when the people would stand up and begin to fold their work away, and I too would rise, feeling stiff in every limb and thinking with dread of our cold empty little room and the uncooked rice, he would come over with still another coat.*
>
> *— Rose Cohen describing her first job at a sweatshop when she was 12 years old*

4a. Why did Ms. Cohen's boss want her to "hurry"? _____

4b. How would you describe Ms. Cohen's job conditions? _____

_____

DOCUMENT 5

> *Resolved: That we sympathize with the efforts of organized workingmen to shorten the hours of labor, and demand a rigid enforcement of the existing eight-hour law on work, and ask that a penalty clause be added to the said law.*
>
> *— From the Populist Platform of 1892*

5. How did this proposal in the Populist Platform try to eliminate one of the abuses of rapid industrial growth? _____

_____

Part B — Essay

Directions:
- Write a well-organized essay that includes an introduction, several paragraphs, and a conclusion.
- Use evidence from the documents to support your response.
- Do not simply repeat the contents of the documents.
- Include specific related outside information.

Task:

Using information from the documents and your knowledge of American history and government, write an essay in which you:

- Discuss **three** specific problems caused by rapid industrial growth.
- Explain how reformers sought to eliminate these problems.

Notice that this document-based question has the following parts:

(1) directions on how to write the essay;
(2) a historical generalization that sets the stage for the essay question;
(3) a task you must perform, stated in the form of a question;
(4) Part A, with five documents to analyze and questions to answer; and
(5) Part B, where you write the final essay.

To do well on a document-based essay question, you need to focus on three areas: (1) <u>L</u>ook at the Task; (2) <u>A</u>nalyze the documents and answer the questions; and (3) <u>W</u>rite the essay. An easy way to remember this method is to think of the word "L • A • W." Let's use the L • A • W approach to answer the sample question on page 237.

"L" — LOOK AT THE TASK

Let's start by looking at the Task.

Historical Context
Beginning in the 1890s, Americans set out to correct the problems caused by rapid industrial growth. Reformers worked to eliminate a whole range of abuses.

Task:
Discuss **three** specific problems caused by rapid industrial growth, and explain how reformers sought to eliminate them.

Notice that the Task contains two important directions:

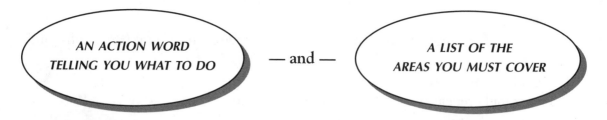

Action Words	— *Discuss* — — *Explain how* —
Areas to Cover	• You must *discuss* **three** specific problems caused by rapid industrial growth, and • You must *explain how* reformers sought to eliminate these problems.

This information gives you an indication of how many paragraphs you should write. All essays must have an introduction and a conclusion. What varies from one essay to another is the number of paragraphs needed in the body of the essay to answer *the requirements in the Task*.

In this example, you need at least three paragraphs in the body of the essay: one paragraph for each problem created by industrial growth and how reformers sought to eliminate it. If you have a lot to write about one of these problems, you may want to divide your discussion of that problem into two paragraphs.

Your final written essay should contain at least five paragraphs:

PARAGRAPH 1	This should include your thesis statement and a transition sentence.
PARAGRAPH 2	This should deal with one problem created by rapid industrial growth and how reformers sought to eliminate it.
PARAGRAPH 3	This should deal with a second problem created by rapid industrial growth and how reformers sought to eliminate it.
PARAGRAPH 4	This should deal with a third problem created by rapid industrial growth and how reformers sought to eliminate it.
PARAGRAPH 5	This should end the essay with your conclusion that reaffirms the thesis statement.

Some students find it helpful to jot down what they know about the topic in note form before turning to the documents.

"A" — ANALYZE THE DOCUMENTS

You are now ready for the second part of the **L • A • W** approach — analyzing the documents. A document-based question will contain up to eight documents, which may include short quotations, timelines, cartoons, tables and readings. Each document also has a question that is related to the Task. With such a large amount of data, you need a way to organize your analysis. One recommended method is to use an **Analysis Box**. As you answer the questions following each document, you fill in the boxes. A sample Analysis Box is provided on the following page.

SAMPLE ANALYSIS BOX

DOCUMENT	MAIN IDEA	PROBLEM	REFORM
The Jungle	Describes a meat packing plant — reusing spoiled food, food on the floor, leaky roof water dripping on food, rat droppings.	Unsanitary conditions in sausage plant	
Pure Food Act	Congress outlawed many abuses exposed by Sinclair in *The Jungle*.		Protect against harmful products
Photo	Young boy working in a factory with broken glass all around.	Child labor	
Rose Cohen's testimony	Rose worked long hours for low pay, under miserable conditions.	Poor conditions and long hours for workers	
Populist Platform	Part of the Platform demanding that the work day be reduced to eight hours.		Institute an eight-hour work day
Related outside information:			

- Samuel Gompers formed the American Federation of Labor, a union that fought against long hours, low wages, and poor working conditions.
- The Progressives called for legislation that would abolish child labor.

Let's examine each of the items of information in the Analysis Box above:

- In the **Document** column, you should write a brief phrase to identify each document. Since the first document was from Upton Sinclair's book *The Jungle*, you might identify it by writing "The Jungle" in the first box.

- In the **Main Idea** column, briefly describe the main idea of each document.

- The number of additional columns will depend on what you must cover in your essay answer. In this example, since you must cover a *problem* and also a *reform* that sought to correct it, you need two additional columns. The questions accompanying the documents will help you identify what you need to know to complete the Task.

- The directions ask you to use **additional information**. This is where you need to draw on your outside knowledge, as shown in the bottom section of the Analysis Box.

"W" — WRITE THE ESSAY

In the last part of the **L • A • W** approach, you must plan and write your essay. You should follow the same general rules as you do for writing thematic essays, except that now you will also include references to the documents in your answer.

OPENING PARAGRAPH

In a document-based essay, you need an opening sentence that identifies the historical context (*sets the time and place*). The next sentence is your thesis statement, based on the question. For example, your opening sentence and thesis statement might be:

> *During the late 1800s and early 1900s, American industry expanded greatly. Rapid industrial growth caused new problems, which reformers sought to eliminate.*

MAIN PARAGRAPHS

Each paragraph should deal with one aspect stated in the Task. You must also use your analysis of the documents and related outside knowledge to support your conclusions, just like a good lawyer would refer to evidence in court.

CONCLUSION

How you close your essay will depend on the action word used in the Task.

❖ **Discuss.** If the task asks you to *discuss* a topic, your conclusion should restate your thesis statement. For example,

> *Thus, we can see that during the late 19th and early 20th centuries, American reformers helped eliminate new problems caused by rapid industrial growth.*

You might add a short summary of what you have written already, to reinforce your case:

> *Intervention by the government showed that in a democracy, legislation can be an effective tool in helping to resolve certain social problems.*

❖ **Evaluate.** If the task asks you to *evaluate* a policy or program, you should weigh its positive and negative effects, and then make a final judgment. For example, if you had to evaluate the reforms sponsored by Populists and Progressives, you might conclude as follows:

> *In conclusion, the reforms sponsored by Populists and Progressives had a positive impact in curbing the worst abuses of rapid industrialization.*

TESTING YOUR UNDERSTANDING

Directions: Circle the number preceding the word or expression that correctly answers the statement or question. Following the multiple-choice questions, answer the essay question.

Base your answer to question 1 on the following cartoon and your knowledge of social studies.

1 Which statement best expresses the main idea of the cartoon?
  1 There are many wild animals in the nation.
  2 There is no justice in America.
  3 Animals should be caged to prevent damage.
  4 There are limits to the President's power.

2 President Franklin D. Roosevelt's main purpose in his "Court Packing" Plan was to
  1 increase the Court's power
  2 prepare the nation for war
  3 limit the seats on the Court
  4 gain control of the Supreme Court

3 Which is an accurate statement concerning F.D.R.'s New Deal program?
  1 It depended on rapid military growth.
  2 It benefited all groups in the nation equally.
  3 It reduced the power of the national government.
  4 It attempted to get the nation out of a depression.

4 Unpopular laws are sometimes unenforceable. Which evidence best supports this statement?
  1 Most people refuse to pay their income taxes.
  2 Some people will not vote if they do not like the candidates.
  3 The amendment banning the sale of alcoholic beverages was repealed.
  4 Improvements in production techniques are often rejected.

5 A major result of the New Deal has been
  1 decreased government alliances
  2 resistance to joining labor unions
  3 increased regulation of the economy
  4 an increased number of farms

6 Which factor contributed to the Red Scare in the United States in 1919-1920?
  1 Germany's attack of U.S. merchant ships
  2 widespread hatred of big business
  3 fear of a communist revolution in the U.S.
  4 rise of the automobile industry

7 The major significance of the Social Security Act of 1935 was that it
  1 banned business trusts in the United States
  2 raised tariffs at the start the Great Depression
  3 provided help to the elderly and unemployed
  4 established price codes for certain industries

8 A basic idea of the New Deal programs was that
  1 government is primarily responsible for correcting economic problems
  2 an increase in the power of big business was needed
  3 the United States must remain neutral in all future wars
  4 an equal rights amendment was needed to achieve equality for women

9 Which period witnessed a major increase in the federal government's role in the economy?
1 Reconstruction Era of the 1870s
2 Imperialism of the late 1890s
3 Republican prosperity of the 1920s
4 New Deal in the 1930s

10 The Harlem Renaissance encouraged African Americans to
1 demand an end to segregation
2 support the League of Nations
3 take pride in their culture
4 rebel against the government

11 The main reason for the creation of the United Nations was to
1 allow nations to resolve disputes peacefully
2 limit the amount of trade between nations
3 end the spread of communism
4 regulate monopolies in developing nations

12 The Nuremberg Trials established the principle that
1 people in power are responsible for their wartime actions
2 national policies during wartime cannot be criticized after the war
3 individuals cannot be prosecuted for their actions
4 a violent act is not a crime when it happens during wartime

13 Which statement best describes the experience of American women during World War II?
1 They were required to serve in combat.
2 They achieved economic equality with men.
3 They entered the workforce in large numbers.
4 They refused to support American policy during the war.

14 What was an important effect of the growth of the automobile industry after World War I?
1 It stimulated other new industries.
2 There were fewer employment opportunities.
3 There was in increase in the number of railroad passengers
4 It encouraged government operation of major industries.

15 Which characterized world politics just before the outbreak of World Wars I and II?
1 the existence of opposing alliances
2 the growth of Communist influence in Western nations
3 acts of aggression by Western democracies
4 a decline in imperialism

16 The U.S. Supreme Court decision in the case of *Korematsu v. U.S.* (1944) is important because it shows that
1 the Supreme Court is always a firm upholder of personal liberty
2 racial prejudice often increases in times of national danger
3 the right to protest against the draft is limited in wartime
4 racial discrimination is unconstitutional

Base your answer to question 17 on the graph and your knowledge of social studies.

BANK FAILURES IN THE UNITED STATES, 1926-1937

1926
1931
1933
1937

KEY: = 250 banks

17 Which factor best explains the decline in bank failures by 1937 shown in this graph?
1 New banking laws restored public confidence in banks.
2 Most people were too poor to have any bank savings.
3 The government operated the nation's banks.
4 Most Americans had transferred their savings to foreign banks.

18 Someone who supported immigration quotas, the execution of Sacco and Vanzetti, and the rebirth of the Ku Klux Klan would be called
1 a rugged individualist
2 an imperialist
3 a nativist
4 a mercantilist

THEMATIC ESSAY QUESTION

Directions: Write a well-organized essay that includes an introduction, several paragraphs explaining your position, and a conclusion.

Theme: Economic Problems

> **Economic problems have been a major concern of Americans, especially since the Civil War.**

Task:

Choose **two** economic problems from your study of U.S. history.

For *each* economic problem:
- Describe how it presented a problem.
- Show how that problem was dealt with by the federal government
- Discuss how successful the federal government was in resolving the problem.

Suggestions: You may use any examples from your study of U.S. history. Some suggestions you might wish to consider include: rebuilding the Southern economy after the Civil War, the rise of monopolies, the problems of farmers in the late 1800s, unemployment during the Great Depression, and the poor working conditions for industrial laborers.

You are *not* limited to these suggestions.

INTERPRETING DOCUMENTS

1. How many Americans were unemployed in 1937? _____

2. What event led to the dramatic increase in unemployment between 1929 and 1932? _____

3. What factors helped to lower unemployment in the mid-1930s? _____

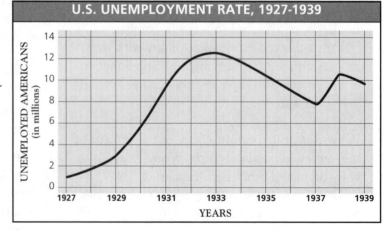

U.S. UNEMPLOYMENT RATE, 1927-1939

(Graph: UNEMPLOYED AMERICANS (in millions) vs. YEARS, 1927–1939)

CHAPTER 10

AMERICA IN UNCERTAIN TIMES

The Cold War
  A. Roots of the Cold War
  B. Containment in Europe and Asia
  C. Effects on U.S. Security

The Age of Civil Rights
  A. The Eisenhower Years
  B. The Civil Rights Movement
  C. African-American Militancy

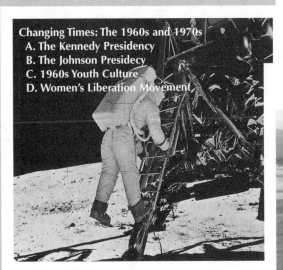

Changing Times: The 1960s and 1970s
  A. The Kennedy Presidency
  B. The Johnson Presidecy
  C. 1960s Youth Culture
  D. Women's Liberation Movement

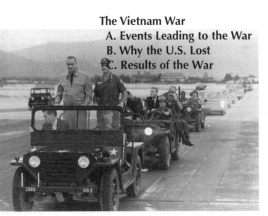

The Vietnam War
  A. Events Leading to the War
  B. Why the U.S. Lost
  C. Results of the War

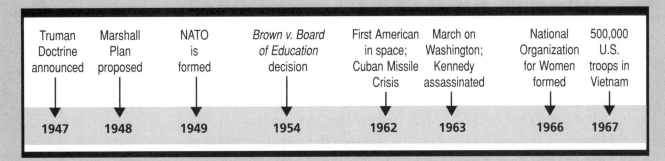

Truman Doctrine announced	Marshall Plan proposed	NATO is formed	*Brown v. Board of Education* decision	First American in space; Cuban Missile Crisis	March on Washington; Kennedy assassinated	National Organization for Women formed	500,000 U.S. troops in Vietnam
1947	1948	1949	1954	1962	1963	1966	1967

WHAT YOU SHOULD FOCUS ON

The 1950s and 1960s were a time of prosperity and social reform, in which our current pluralistic society was created. Americans were also concerned about the spread of communism abroad.

Dr. Martin Luther King, Jr.

The Civil Rights Movement sought equality for African Americans. The Women's Liberation Movement achieved greater rights for women. Presidents John F. Kennedy and Lyndon Johnson introduced programs to help the poor. The Supreme Court expanded individual rights. Young people all over the United States organized protests concerning environmental pollution, materialism, and poverty.

This period of reform was brought to a close by American involvement in the Vietnam War. This involvement began under President Kennedy. The war escalated dramatically during President Johnson's term in office. It was not until President Nixon's administration that the United States finally withdrew from Vietnam.

In this chapter you will learn about the following:

The Cold War	**The Age of Civil Rights**	**Changing Times: the 1960s and 1970s**	**The Vietnam War**
Immediately after World War II, the United States and the Soviet Union became rivals in the "Cold War," which quickly spread from Europe to Asia. American leaders took a number of steps in an attempt to contain the spread of Communism around the world.	Through demonstrations, court challenges, and legislation, African Americans succeeded in ending racial segregation in public schools and other public places, and obtained equal civil rights. Their success helped inspire other minority groups, as well as women.	John Kennedy brought a new style to the Presidency. President Johnson introduced Civil Rights legislation and Great Society programs to help the poor. Women sought greater equality. The 1960s were also a time of rebellion by young people.	America became involved in defending the government of South Vietnam from attacks by communist North Vietnam. Despite massive aid, heavy bombing, and a half a million troops, the U.S. was unable to win the Vietnam War. Soon after the U.S. withdrew, the North Vietnamese took over South Vietnam.

In studying this period, you should focus on the following questions:

❖ What were the causes of the Cold War?
❖ What were the achievements of the Civil Rights Movement?
❖ What factors led to the Women's Liberation Movement?
❖ How did Johnson's "Great Society" attempt to extend social reform?
❖ How did Americans become divided during the Vietnam War?

THE COLD WAR

In this section you will read about the the rivalry that developed between the United States and the Soviet Union. This rivalry, called the Cold War, lasted nearly half a century — from 1945 to 1991.

THINK ABOUT IT

What does the term "Cold War" mean? _____

_____

How do you think it was different from other types of warfare?

_____

Important Terms and Concepts: As you read this section, look for the following terms:

- ✦ Cold War
- ✦ Iron Curtain
- ✦ Truman Doctrine
- ✦ Marshall Plan

- ✦ NATO
- ✦ Korean War
- ✦ Rosenberg Trial
- ✦ McCarthyism

To help you find these terms, the ✦ symbol appears in the margin where the term is first explained.

The "Soviet Union" was created by Communist revolutionaries after they took over the Russian empire in 1917. The United States and the Soviet Union were allies during World War II. Soon after 1945, however, they became rivals in a **Cold War**. The war was "cold" only in the sense that the two superpowers never fought one another directly in open warfare. However, their global competition led to frequent crises and conflicts on every continent.

THE ROOTS OF THE COLD WAR

The roots of the Cold War lay in the differences between two political and economic systems — the democratic, capitalist system of the United States, and the dictatorial communist system of the Soviet Union. When World War II ended, the United States and the Soviet Union each sought new opportunities to spread its system and way of life. Each country looked with suspicion and alarm at attempts by the other country to spread its beliefs. Many Americans became convinced that communists were trying to take over the world.

The systems of the two countries were very different. Let's take a look at some of their features.

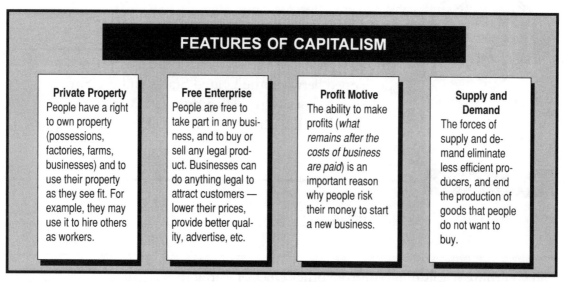

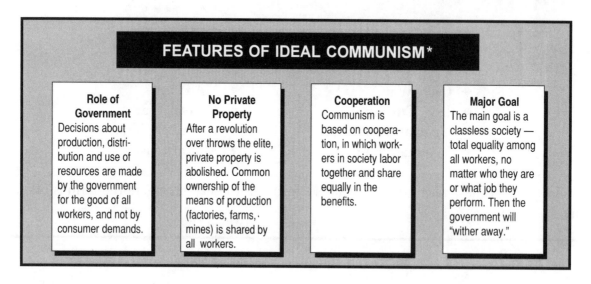

* Note: Although these were the ideals of communism, in reality the Soviet government controlled all aspects of life: the workers never owned the factories, benefits were not shared equally, and the government kept on growing instead of "withering away."

WARTIME ALLIES BECOME COLD WAR ENEMIES

In 1945, President Roosevelt, British Prime Minister Winston Churchill and Premier Joseph Stalin of the Soviet Union met at Yalta (a city in the Soviet Union) to plan for the future of Europe after the war. The **Yalta Conference** was the most important wartime meeting of the "Big Three." They agreed that Germany would be divided into four separate zones, and that the troops of the United States, Soviet Union, Britain and France would each occupy one zone. They also agreed to hold free elections in all the countries liberated from Nazi rule. Stalin gave his pledge to withdraw Soviet troops and to allow free elections in Eastern Europe after the war. Soon after the war ended, a second conference of Allied leaders was held at Potsdam, Germany. Even though the United States and Soviet Union had fought on the same side, serious differences between them began to develop at the **Potsdam Conference** over the future of Eastern Europe.

Who was to blame for starting the Cold War?

THE AMERICAN VIEWPOINT	THE SOVIET VIEWPOINT
American leaders felt that Eastern European countries wanted to become democratic like the United States, but that the Soviet Union was preventing this. They also believed that it would be a mistake for them to turn their back on European affairs as they had done after World War I. Americans felt that Stalin could not be trusted, since he had promised elections in Poland and other countries in Eastern Europe and seemed to be backing away from his promise. Communism was seen as a dangerous system that needed to be stopped before it spread.	Soviet leaders believed they had a right to control Eastern Europe. They felt that just as the U.S. controlled Latin America through the Monroe Doctrine, the Soviet Union should have the final say over its Eastern European neighbors. Stalin believed that the Western powers had no direct interests in Eastern Europe and should not interfere. Soviet leaders also believed they could not trust the U. S. and other Western countries because they had delayed the invasion of France during World War II, resulting in very heavy losses suffered by the Soviet Union.

THE IRON CURTAIN FALLS ON EASTERN EUROPE

In 1946, Stalin refused to allow the promised elections in Poland. The United States also refused to share the secret of the atomic bomb, and the Cold War began in earnest. The Soviet army had

occupied Eastern Europe while fighting Germany, and now Stalin refused to withdraw these troops. Instead, Soviet officers placed local communists in power in all the governments of Eastern Europe, making these countries "satellites" of the Soviet Union. Trade and communications between Eastern and Western Europe were cut off. It seemed that an **Iron Curtain** had fallen, closing off Eastern Europe from the democracies of the West. Travel and contact between East and West was limited, and Eastern European leaders followed the dictates of the Soviet government.

SOVIET SATELLITES, 1946

The Iron Curtain remained in place for the next forty years. At various times, Soviet troops were sent to crush democratic uprisings in Hungary, Czechoslovakia and other nations in Eastern Europe.

THE POLICY OF CONTAINMENT IN EUROPE

American leaders responded to the Soviet control of Eastern Europe by developing a policy of **containment** — the United States would prevent communism from spreading to additional countries, even though it would not challenge communism where it already existed.

✦ THE TRUMAN DOCTRINE (1947)

Vice President Harry Truman became President when Franklin D. Roosevelt died in 1945. Truman had met Stalin at Potsdam, and had made the decision to drop the atomic bomb on Japan, ending the war. Truman became alarmed about the rapid expansion of communism in Eastern Europe after the war. When communist rebels threatened the governments of Greece and Turkey in 1947, President Truman gave these countries military aid. With this help, the Greek and Turkish governments were able to defeat the communist rebels. Truman declared that America would support any country that was fighting communism. This announcement, known as the **Truman Doctrine**, marked the start of America's policy of containment.

British Prime Minister Attlee, (l.) Truman (c.) and Stalin (r.) meeting at Potsdam after the defeat of Germany, 1945

✦ THE MARSHALL PLAN (1948)

Truman was convinced that communism was attractive to people only when they were desperate and miserable. Therefore, he believed that by fighting poverty in Europe he could make Europeans more resistant to communism. As a result, Secretary of State George Marshall proposed that aid be given to the countries of Western Europe to help them rebuild their economies. Marshall and Truman hoped to avoid the economic chaos that had followed World War I. They believed that economic aid would create strong European allies and future trading partners for the United States. The **Marshall Plan**, as it became known, was extremely successful: it speeded the economic recovery of Western Europe and created new good will towards the United States.

THE DIVISION OF GERMANY AND THE BERLIN AIRLIFT (1948)

After World War II, Germany was divided into four zones of occupation. In 1948, the French, British and Americans united their zones into a single West German state. Berlin, the former

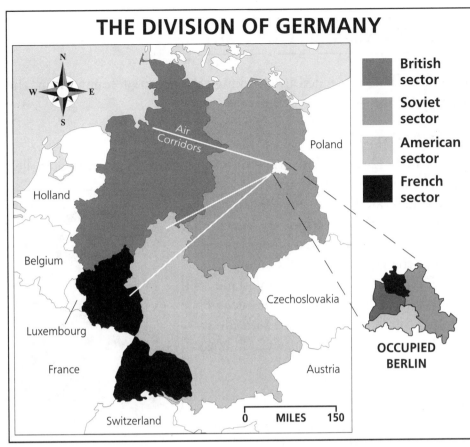

THE DIVISION OF GERMANY

British sector

Soviet sector

American sector

French sector

Holland

Belgium

Luxembourg

France

Switzerland

Air Corridors

Poland

Czechoslovakia

Austria

OCCUPIED BERLIN

0   MILES   150

capital of Germany, was located 110 miles within the Soviet zone. Because of the importance of the city, Berlin had also been divided into four sectors, each occupied by a different power. Stalin reacted to the merging of the Western zones of Germany by announcing a blockade of West Berlin, and closed all its highway and railroad links. The Western Allies refused to abandon the two million West Berliners, and began a massive airlift to feed and supply the city. Every few minutes, day and night, Allied planes landed in Berlin with supplies. After 11 months, Stalin admitted defeat and lifted the blockade.

THE FORMATION OF NATO AND THE WARSAW PACT

In response to the tensions of the Cold War, the United States, Canada, and ten Western European countries formed the North Atlantic Treaty Organization (**NATO**) in 1949. NATO's ✦

purpose was to protect Western Europe from communist aggression. The alliance was based on the idea of **collective security** — each NATO member pledged to defend every other member if it was attacked. The Soviet Union responded to the formation of NATO by creating the **Warsaw Pact** in 1955 with the Eastern European countries that were under its control.

MEMBERS OF NATO AND THE WARSAW PACT

MEMBERS OF NATO

MEMBERS OF WARSAW PACT

NORWAY   FINLAND

NORTHERN IRELAND   North Sea   SWEDEN

IRELAND   GREAT   DENMARK

BRITAIN   NETH.   EAST GER.   POLAND   SOVIET UNION

English Channel   BEL.   WEST GERMANY   CZECHOSLOVAKIA

Bay of Biscay   LUX.   SWITZ.   AUSTRIA   HUNGARY

FRANCE   ITALY   YUGOSLAVIA   RUMANIA   Black Sea

PORTUGAL   SPAIN   BULGARIA   TURKEY

GIBRALTAR   ALBANIA

Mediterranean Sea   GREECE

AFRICA

CONTAINMENT IN ASIA

Just when Americans believed they had succeeded in checking the spread of communism, the world's most populated nation — China — became communist.

THE CIVIL WAR IN CHINA (1949)

China had become a democracy in 1912, but its government was unstable. Warlords controlled parts of the country, most people were poor, and Japan had taken over large areas of China in World War II. Since the 1920s, communists had been trying to overthrow the government, and after World War II, the struggle grew more intense. The communists, led by **Mao Zedong**, finally defeated the government of **Chiang Kai-Shek** in 1949. Chiang and his followers fled to the nearby island of Taiwan. The United States refused to extend diplomatic recognition to the communist government in China, and vetoed its admission to the United Nations. The U.S. pledged to protect Chiang's government in Taiwan from communist attacks.

Mao Zedong

◆ THE KOREAN WAR (1950-1953)

Korea is a peninsula extending out of northern China. It was ruled by Japan from 1910 to 1945. After World War II, it was taken away from Japan and divided into northern and southern parts. In the north, a communist government was established. Elections in the south led to the creation of a non-communist government there. In 1950, North Korea invaded South Korea in an attempt to unify the country under communist rule. President Truman, using his emergency powers and without a declaration of war from Congress, ordered U.S. forces into South Korea to resist the invasion. United Nations troops joined the Americans; it was the first time that an international peace organization used military force to oppose aggression. In 1951, U.N. forces entered North Korea and advanced close to the Chinese border. China entered the war in support of its ally North Korea.

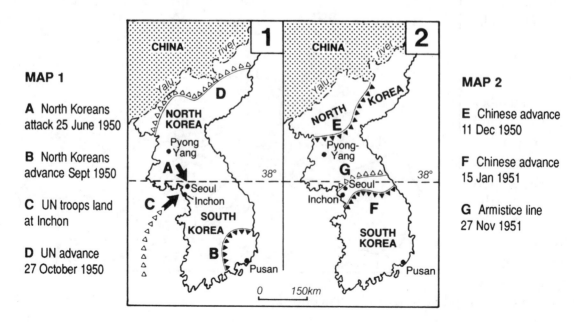

MAP 1

A North Koreans attack 25 June 1950

B North Koreans advance Sept 1950

C UN troops land at Inchon

D UN advance 27 October 1950

MAP 2

E Chinese advance 11 Dec 1950

F Chinese advance 15 Jan 1951

G Armistice line 27 Nov 1951

General Douglas MacArthur was in command of American troops. He urged President Truman to use the opportunity to invade China and overthrow its communist government. MacArthur was even willing to use atomic weapons if necessary. Truman refused, and when MacArthur criticized the President in the press, Truman removed him from his command. The war soon reached a stalemate (*standstill*). Neither side could force the other to move. In 1952, **Dwight Eisenhower** was elected President on a pledge he would end the war in Korea. Fighting ended when a peace agreement was signed in 1953. The agreement left Korea divided exactly as it had been before the North Korean invasion three years earlier.

THE EFFECT OF THE COLD WAR ON U.S. SECURITY

In 1945, America was the only atomic power. By 1949 the Soviet Union developed its own atom bomb, leading to a nuclear arms race. The U.S. and the Soviet Union began developing more and more powerful bombs. Both countries believed nuclear weapons were cheaper than large armies.

THE SOVIETS LAUNCH SPUTNIK (1957)

In World War II, German scientists had greatly improved rocket technology. After the war, both the U.S. and the Soviet Union had programs to develop this technology still further. In 1957, the Soviet Union launched **Sputnik**, the first man-made space satellite. Not only did this mark the beginning of the **"Space Race,"** but it had great military importance. With missiles that could travel into space, the Soviet Union clearly had the ability to fire nuclear weapons at the United States from great distances. The United States launched its own space satellite in 1958.

INTERNAL THREATS AND McCARTHYISM

The rise of the Cold War had serious effects on life inside the United States. Americans became concerned about the possibility of a communist threat at home. Some people were accused of "un-American" acts. Often these accusations were based on little or no evidence. Some people lost their jobs and a few others faced even more serious problems. In 1950, **Julius and Ethel Rosenberg** were arrested and charged with selling atom bomb secrets to the Soviet Union. They were brought to trial, found guilty, and executed as spies.

Joseph McCarthy

In 1950, a Senator from Wisconsin, **Joseph McCarthy**, shocked the nation by claiming that he knew the names of hundreds of communists working in the State Department. Although McCarthy never proved any of his claims, he frightened Americans and destroyed the careers and reputations of many people whom he accused of being communists. The term **McCarthyism** has come to mean making charges about a person's loyalty without having any supporting evidence or proof. The Rosenberg trial and the accusations made by Senator McCarthy sent a wave of panic across the nation, similar to the "Red Scare" of the 1920s.

ANALYSIS

In 1949, the U.S. Supreme Court upheld the conviction of several Communist Party members for their belief that social change could only be achieved through the use of force. The Court ruled that people who are willing to use force to overthrow the government are not protected by the right to free speech. Do you think citizens who are members of the Communist Party should enjoy the same constitutional protections as other U.S. citizens? ❏ Yes ❏ No. Explain your answer.

_____

_____

SUMMING UP: THE COLD WAR

When World War II ended, the United States and the Soviet Union had very different ideas about the future of Europe. Each country wanted to spread its own form of government and way of life around the world. When the Soviet Union used its army to establish communist governments in Eastern Europe, American leaders became alarmed, and the Cold War began. To prevent the spread of communism in Europe and Asia, Americans developed a policy of containment and entered into a rivalry with the Soviets. The United States gave aid to Europe, fought in Korea, and built nuclear bombs and missiles. Both the United States and the Soviet Union developed space programs, which furthered the arms race. Fear of communism at home resulted in McCarthyism, a time of reckless and unproven accusations, when some Americans were denied their basic rights.

THINKING IT OVER

Do you think the policy of containment was a wise one for the United States to follow during the Cold War? ❏ Yes ❏ No.   Explain. _____

_____

_____

CHECKING YOUR UNDERSTANDING

Directions: Complete the following cards. Then answer the multiple-choice questions.

COLD WAR

What was it? _____

What were its major causes? _____

_____

MARSHALL PLAN

Why was it proposed? _____

What was its goal? _____

Effects: _____

TRUMAN DOCTRINE

Why was it proposed? _____

What was its goal? _____

Effects: _____

NATO

Why was it formed? _____

What were its goals? _____

Effects: _____

---

1 The term "cold war" refers to
  1 U.S. neutrality before World War II
  2 attempts to appease Hitler
  3 disputes between the Soviet Union and China
  4 hostility between the U.S. and Soviet Union

2 One result of the Cold War in the United States was that
  1 people became more isolated from world events
  2 minorities gained full civil rights
  3 industrial growth declined sharply
  4 some people were accused of "un-American" activities

3 The Truman Doctrine and NATO were similar in that both sought to
  1 increase U.S. power in Latin America
  2 punish Germany for starting World War II
  3 stop the expansion of communism
  4 gain military control of European nations

4 A main purpose of American economic aid to Western Europe after World War II was to
  1 create a tariff-free Common Market
  2 rebuild the economies of European nations
  3 provide the United States with raw materials
  4 bring about the unification of Europe

5 A study of the Red Scare of the 1920s and the McCarthy Era of the 1950s shows that
  1 communists infiltrated the U.S. government
  2 fears of a foreign threat can lead to violations of constitutional freedoms
  3 communism advances in good economic times
  4 loyalty oaths can help to prevent spying by government employees

6 Following the Soviet occupation of Eastern Europe, the U.S. adopted a foreign policy known as
  1 isolationism   3 imperialism
  2 containment   4 neutrality

7 Which governmental action is consistent with a "Cold War" mentality?
  1 establishing Loyalty Review Boards
  2 reducing military spending
  3 eliminating the C.I.A.
  4 adopting the G.I. Bill of Rights

8 One major cause of the Cold War was
  1 trade competition between the U.S. and Europe
  2 differences in ideology between the U.S. and the Soviet Union
  3 rejection of Soviet membership in the U.N.
  4 internment of Soviet-Americans in camps

SECTION 2

AMERICA IN THE AGE OF CIVIL RIGHTS

In this section you will read about the many changes that occurred in America during the 1950s and 1960s, especially as a result of the Civil Rights Movement.

THINK ABOUT IT

The 1950s and 1960s have been the subject of many different television shows, movies, and books. What things do you associate with the 1950s and 1960s in America?

1950s	1960s
1._____	1._____
2._____	2._____
3._____	3._____

Important Terms: As you read this section, look for the following terms:

- ✦ Civil Rights Movement
- ✦ Brown v. Board of Education
- ✦ Civil Rights Act of 1964
- ✦ Voting Rights Act
- ✦ Affirmative Action
- ✦ Black Power Movement

THE EISENHOWER YEARS, 1953 -1961

The Presidency of Dwight Eisenhower was a time of prosperity and social change. The period was marked by several important developments:

■ **Economic Expansion.** The United States continued to be the world's largest producer of goods. Americans bought millions of automobiles, television sets, refrigerators and other appliances.

■ **Baby Boom.** As a result of economic prosperity, people settled down to work and started having families. Birth rates were extremely high.

■ **Growth of Suburbs.** The G.I. Bill made it easy for war veterans to obtain loans to buy houses. This led to an increase in home ownership and the growth of **suburbs** (*loosely-populated areas just outside of cities*). People living in the suburbs were able to commute by car to work in city centers.

Dwight Eisenhower

■ **Conformity**. There was an emphasis on conformity (*being like everyone else*). Fear and distrust of communism increased hostility towards unusual or different ideas.

■ **Containment**. In foreign affairs, the U.S. contained communism by stopping the Soviets from gaining additional territory. In 1957, the **Eisenhower Doctrine** stated the U.S. would send troops to any Mideast nation defending itself against communism.

■ **The Civil Rights Movement.** This major turning point in American history is more fully described below. President Eisenhower gave some support to the Civil Rights Movement when he sent federal troops to Little Rock, Arkansas in 1957 to enforce a Supreme Court decision against racial segregation in public schools.

THE EMERGENCE OF THE CIVIL RIGHTS MOVEMENT

A hundred years earlier, the Civil War and Reconstruction had held out the promise to African Americans of equality with other citizens. But in the aftermath of Reconstruction, black Americans had lost the right to vote in Southern states, and "Jim Crow" laws had **segregated** (*separated*) blacks and whites in many areas of public life. The Civil Rights Movement did not spring up overnight, but was based on a hundred years of struggle against these unjust laws. Nevertheless, there were several reasons why the fight for civil rights reached a climax in the 1950s and 1960s.

Segregation in the South

THE IMPACT OF AFRICAN-AMERICAN ORGANIZATIONS

The **N.A.A.C.P.** and the **Urban League** were both founded in the first decade of the twentieth century to promote equality for African Americans. Getting the courts to enforce constitutional rights provided one way to promote non-violent change in American society. The N.A.A.C.P. developed a strategy for achieving school desegregation by starting a series of court challenges to state laws that enforced segregation.

Jackie Robinson

THE IMPACT OF WORLD WAR II

During World War II (1941-1945), more than one million African Americans joined the armed services. Their efforts and sacrifices during the war played an important role in leading President Harry Truman to order the desegregation of the armed forces in 1948. At the same time, Truman also ended discriminatory hiring practices in the federal government. In 1947, **Jackie Robinson** became the first African-American major league baseball player, when he was hired by the Brooklyn Dodgers.

THE COLD WAR

The Cold War made American leaders sensitive to criticisms that the United States was undemocratic, since it claimed to be the champion of the "free world." American Presidents looked to preserve the nation's reputation abroad. Racism and discrimination hurt the American image.

◆ BROWN v. BOARD OF EDUCATION OF TOPEKA, KANSAS (1954)

The *Brown* decision was central to the emergence of the Civil Rights Movement. As early as 1896, African Americans had challenged segregation in the South. In *Plessy v. Ferguson*, the Supreme Court had upheld the constitutionality of segregation laws which separated whites and blacks, so long as the facilities were "separate but equal."

Thurgood Marshall, the first African American to be appointed to the U.S. Supreme Court

- ■ **Background**. Starting in the 1930s, the N.A.A.C.P. began challenging the exclusion of black Americans from white schools in the South. In 1953, the N.A.A.C.P. argued a case before the Supreme Court involving Linda Brown, an African-American student who was denied admission to an all-white public school near her home. The N.A.A.C.P.'s lawyers, led by **Thurgood Marshall**, claimed that segregated public schools denied African-American children the "equal protection" of the law that they were entitled to under the Fourteenth Amendment. They further argued that the education received by African-American students was inferior, since it held a hidden message that they were not good enough to be schooled with white students.

- ■ **The Decision**. Chief Justice Earl Warren wrote the decision for a unanimous Supreme Court, which ruled that segregation in public schools was unconstitutional. The "separate-but-equal" doctrine first established in *Plessy v. Ferguson* had no place in public education. The Supreme Court left the enforcement of the decision to the lower federal courts, which were instructed to see that local school districts carried out the desegregation order.

- ■ **Significance**. Although it was to take many years before the decision was fully implemented, this case was the first step on the road to racial equality in America. The decision showed that the Supreme Court was willing to become involved in a controversial social issue. It also indicated how the federal Constitution can control what is allowable under state law. Finally, the case illustrated how changing social, political, and economic conditions can often affect the decisions of the Supreme Court.

THE LEADERSHIP OF DR. MARTIN LUTHER KING, JR.

Dr. Martin Luther King, Jr., was a young minister who headed the Southern Christian Leadership Conference (S.C.L.C.), a group dedicated to ending segregation. King assumed the role of leader of the Civil Rights Movement in the mid-1950s.

- ■ **Beliefs**. King was influenced by the work of Mohandas Gandhi in India, as well as by his own Christian training. Like Gandhi, King believed in **non-violence**. By this he meant that the best way to change the attitudes of racists was to protest or disobey unjust laws, without using force or violence.

- ■ **Actions and Methods**. King carried out his resistance through **civil disobedience** — if the government passed an unjust law, King and others opposed it with boycotts, picketing, sit-ins, marches and demonstrations. For example, King became the leader of the **Montgomery Bus Boycott** (1955-1956) started by **Rosa Parks**. African Americans refused to use the public bus company in Montgomery, Alabama, where they were required to sit at the back of the bus. King's followers also conducted sit-ins at "whites only" lunch counters. King

Dr. King leading the March on Washington, August 1963

and his followers often faced violence from those who opposed them. When King was arrested in Birmingham, Alabama in 1963, he wrote a letter from jail which was published in the newspapers. In his letter he explained to all Americans why African Americans could wait no longer for their rights.

"I have a dream. It is a dream deeply rooted in the American dream. I have a dream that one day this nation will rise up and live out the true meaning of its creed: 'We hold these truths to be self-evident, that all men are created equal.' I have a dream that one day..the sons of former slaves and the sons of former slave owners will be able to sit down together at the table of brotherhood."

In 1963, King delivered his famous "I Have A Dream" speech at the Lincoln Memorial as part of the **March On Washington**. King spoke to a crowd of almost 250,000 people, and to millions of others watching on television. The speech stirred the nation's conscience by focusing attention on the problems faced by African Americans who were being deprived of their civil rights. For his work in promoting peaceful social change, Dr. King was awarded the Nobel Peace Prize in 1964.

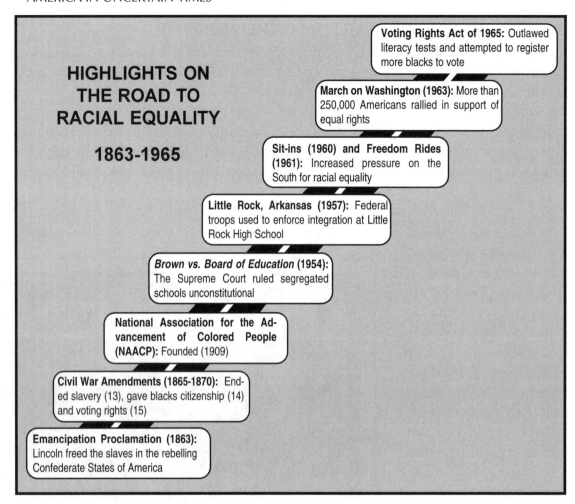

HIGHLIGHTS ON THE ROAD TO RACIAL EQUALITY

1863-1965

Voting Rights Act of 1965: Outlawed literacy tests and attempted to register more blacks to vote

March on Washington (1963): More than 250,000 Americans rallied in support of equal rights

Sit-ins (1960) and Freedom Rides (1961): Increased pressure on the South for racial equality

Little Rock, Arkansas (1957): Federal troops used to enforce integration at Little Rock High School

***Brown vs. Board of Education* (1954):** The Supreme Court ruled segregated schools unconstitutional

National Association for the Advancement of Colored People (NAACP): Founded (1909)

Civil War Amendments (1865-1870): Ended slavery (13), gave blacks citizenship (14) and voting rights (15)

Emancipation Proclamation (1863): Lincoln freed the slaves in the rebelling Confederate States of America

✦ THE CIVIL RIGHTS ACT OF 1964

As a result of the Civil Rights Movement, President Lyndon Johnson pushed this act through Congress in 1964. The law prohibited discrimination based on race, color, religion or ethnic origin in hotels, restaurants, and places of employment doing business with the federal government or engaged in interstate commerce. It also banned discrimination in employment on the basis of gender (*sex*). The act cut off federal aid to school districts with segregated schools.

✦ THE VOTING RIGHTS ACT OF 1965

Most African Americans in the South were still denied the right to vote through poll taxes (*payment of a fee to vote*), literacy tests, and fear of attack. In 1965, Martin Luther King, Jr. went to Selma, Alabama to organize a march demanding the vote for African Americans. When demonstrators were attacked, President Lyndon Johnson introduced a federal Voting Rights Bill. The act ended poll taxes and suspended literacy tests where they were used to prevent African Americans from voting.

✦ AFFIRMATIVE ACTION (1965)

In 1965, President Johnson signed an order requiring employers and institutions with federal contracts to raise the number of minority and female employees, to correct imbalances caused by past discrimination. **Affirmative action** programs have done much to increase minority representation in colleges and the professions. Under affirmative action programs, minorities and women have sometimes been given preferential treatment over equally or better qualified people. Critics have challenged these programs as "reverse discrimination," saying that they favor some groups unfairly by discriminating against others.

ANALYSIS

Americans often disagree on how to best achieve equality among all groups.

1. Should we establish a "color-blind" society in which race is never a factor in any decision? ❏ Yes ❏ No.

2. Should we take specific steps to help members of disadvantaged groups, to make up for the effects of past discrimination? ❏ Yes ❏ No.

Explain your answers: _____

_____

INCREASING AFRICAN-AMERICAN MILITANCY

Despite the achievements of the Civil Rights Movement in the 1950s and early 1960s, by the mid-1960s many African Americans believed that even faster changes were needed. They felt that they still had limited opportunities in many areas of American life. Some of these African Americans, known as militants, disagreed with Dr. King's policy of cooperation with sympathetic whites and his program of non-violence.

URBAN VIOLENCE (1965-1968)
In the North, segregation was often the product of residential patterns of whites and blacks, who lived in different neighborhoods, rather than the result of any public laws. Starting in 1965, African-American anger over racism erupted in a series of riots that shook Northern cities three summers in a row. The climax of these disturbances occurred in the spring of 1968 after Dr. King was **assassinated** (*killed for political reasons*) in Memphis, Tennessee. In cities across the nation, rioters smashed windows, overturned cars, and started fires. A commission appointed by President Johnson blamed the violence on the lack of job opportunities, urban poverty, and racism.

Riot in Detroit, Michigan, 1967

THE BLACK POWER MOVEMENT

Not satisfied with imitating whites or being absorbed into mainstream American culture, many African Americans began to search for the roots of their own cultural identity. They asserted that "black is beautiful," and that African Americans should be proud of their unique heritage. This led to the rise of the **Black Power Movement**. Supporters of the movement believed that African Americans should take control of their own communities, shop in black-owned stores, vote for black candidates and identify more closely with traditional African culture. The spread of these feelings also led to the emergence of new militant leaders:

Malcolm X giving a speech

- **Malcolm X** questioned the effectiveness of non-violent resistance. He thought that African Americans should meet violence with violence and not depend on the cooperation of whites. Malcolm X also believed that blacks should control their own businesses, schools and communities. He was assassinated in 1965 by members of the Black Muslims.

- **New Groups Emerge**. Traditional groups like the Urban League and the N.A.A.C.P. had favored non-violent methods and an end to segregation. New militant groups challenged these traditional organizations. The **Black Muslims** believed that Islam should be the religion of African Americans and that they should form their own separate nation, since cooperation with whites was impossible. The **Black Panthers** called on African Americans to arm themselves, and also favored forming a separate black nation.

AFRICAN-AMERICAN ORGANIZATIONS

Organization	Formed In	Leaders	Major Goal
N.A.A.C.P.	1909	W.E.B. Du Bois Thurgood Marshall	To achieve equality, especially through legal actions
Urban League	1911	Whitney Young	To end economic and social abuses of urban blacks
Black Muslims	1930	Elijah Mohammed	To spread Islam, achieve black self-sufficiency, and form a separate nation
Southern Christian Leadership Conference (SCLC)	1957	Dr. Martin L. King, Jr.	To end segregation through civil disobedience and non-violent protest
Black Panthers	1966	Huey Newton	To help poor blacks, halt police brutality, and demand reparations from "white America."

SUMMING UP: AMERICA IN THE AGE OF CIVIL RIGHTS

In the 1950s and early 1960s, America experienced an increase in its population and growth in its economy. African Americans began to make important gains in their struggle for equality. Many forms of public discrimination were made illegal. By the late 1960s, some African Americans demanded faster change and proposed new approaches for dealing with racism.

THINKING IT OVER

In your opinion, what was the most significant event of the 1950s and 1960s?

_____ Explain._____

_____

CHECKING YOUR UNDERSTANDING

Directions: Complete the following cards. Then answer the multiple-choice questions.

BROWN V. BOARD OF EDUCATION

Background of the case: _____

What did the Court say? _____

Importance of decision: _____

DR. MARTIN LUTHER KING, JR.

What were his major beliefs? _____

List two of his accomplishments: 1. _____

_____ 2. _____

1 Which conclusion could best be drawn from a study of the Civil Rights Movement in the United States?
   1 Racial prejudice can make some laws difficult to enforce.
   2 Racism was not a problem in the North.
   3 African Americans have enjoyed full equality since the Civil War.
   4 Supreme Court decisions have no effect on race relations.

2 The major goal of the Civil Rights Movement in the 1950s and 1960s was to
   1 gain voting rights for women
   2 stop the spread of communism
   3 end racial segregation in the United States
   4 discourage African Americans from traveling to Africa

3   The decision in *Brown v. Board of Education* was important because it established
1   greater rights for accused persons
2   the "separate but equal" principle
3   women's right to have abortions
4   an end to segregated public schools

4   Which development was the result of the other three?
1   African Americans were barred from voting in a number of states.
2   State laws supported racial segregation in schools and housing.
3   The Federal Civil Rights and Voting Rights Acts were passed.
4   Civil Rights advocates held boycotts, demonstration and sit-ins.

5   Dr. Martin Luther King Jr.'s "I have a dream" speech was important because it
1   led to improved living standards for immigrants
2   called for a violent revolution in America
3   drew attention to the inequalities faced by African Americans
4   demanded voting rights for 18-year-olds

6   The major goal of the Voting Rights Act of 1965 was to
1   end to discrimination against retired voters
2   train officials to administer state elections
3   increase the use of literacy tests in voting
4   increase the number of African-American voters

7   Since World War II, integration in the United States has been most stimulated by
1   decisions of federal and state courts
2   passage of constitutional amendments
3   actions by state legislatures
4   Southern school boards

8   What conclusion can be drawn from a study of the Civil Rights Movement since 1954?
1   There was little support for the movement among African Americans.
2   The media usually avoids controversial issues.
3   Governments often react to public pressure.
4   Legislatures usually ignore public pressure.

9   The views of Mohandas Gandhi of India and Dr. Martin Luther King, Jr. were similar in that both attempted to achieve change through
1   civil disobedience
2   new social controls
3   violent uprisings
4   a suspension of civil liberties

Base your answers to questions 10 and 11 on the following quotation from a Supreme Court decision and on your knowledge of social studies.

"We conclude that in the field of public education the doctrine of 'separate but equal' has no place. Separate educational facilities are inherently unequal. Therefore, ... the plaintiffs ... are, by reason of the segregation ..., deprived of the equal protection of the laws guaranteed by the Fourteenth Amendment."

10 This quotation marked the reversal of principles earlier stated in
1   *Plessy v. Ferguson*   3   *Roe v. Wade*
2   *Gideon v. Wainwright*   4   *Miranda v. Arizona*

11 This Supreme Court decision was based on the idea that public school segregation
1   creates unnecessary problems in the administration of schools
2   places excessive burdens on school transportation systems
3   results in unfair tax increases to support dual school systems
4   denies individuals the equal rights to which they are guaranteed under the Constitution

SECTION 3

CHANGING TIMES: THE 1960S AND 1970S

In this section you will read about the 1960s and 1970s,
a period of unsettled and changing times.

THINK ABOUT IT

President John F. Kennedy set a new tone for the nation in his inaugural address by challenging Americans to "ask not what your country can do for you, but what you can do for your country." Explain what you think he meant by this.

_____

_____

Important Terms and Concepts: As you read this section, look for the following:

- ✦ Bay of Pigs Invasion
- ✦ Cuban Missile Crisis
- ✦ Great Society
- ✦ Youth Culture
- ✦ Women's Liberation Movement
- ✦ Roe v. Wade

THE KENNEDY PRESIDENCY, 1961-1963

In 1960, a young Senator from Massachusetts named John F. Kennedy was elected President. Kennedy told Americans that he represented a "new generation" and would bring a different and more youthful spirit to the nation.

DOMESTIC POLICY

Kennedy promised Americans a **New Frontier**. He meant that the nation had reached a dramatic turning point in which it faced important challenges and opportunities. Like Franklin D. Roosevelt, Kennedy believed in using the powers of the federal government to help solve the nation's problems. He focused on creating programs to help the cities, improve education, provide health care for the aged, and aid the poor. Kennedy also gave his support to civil rights leaders like Dr. King, and proposed a civil rights bill. Although he was often unable to get Congress to pass bills he introduced, many became laws under the next President, Lyndon Johnson.

John F. Kennedy

Kennedy also believed it was important for America to win the "space race" with the Soviet Union, and proposed the **Apollo Program** to land the first person on the moon.

FOREIGN POLICY

Foreign policy under Kennedy, as under Truman and Eisenhower, was dominated by the problems of the Cold War. Kennedy saw the United States as the world's defender of democracy and freedom. He was especially troubled by the rise of a communist nation close to the United States. In 1959, Fidel Castro had established a communist government in Cuba, only 90 miles from Florida. This alarmed Kennedy, who believed that communism might spread in Latin America.

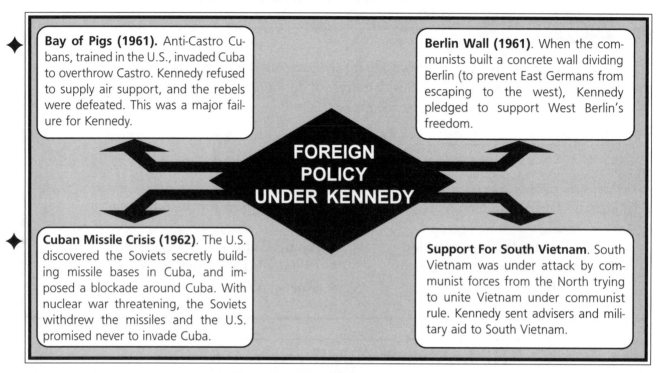

Bay of Pigs (1961). Anti-Castro Cubans, trained in the U.S., invaded Cuba to overthrow Castro. Kennedy refused to supply air support, and the rebels were defeated. This was a major failure for Kennedy.

Berlin Wall (1961). When the communists built a concrete wall dividing Berlin (to prevent East Germans from escaping to the west), Kennedy pledged to support West Berlin's freedom.

FOREIGN POLICY UNDER KENNEDY

Cuban Missile Crisis (1962). The U.S. discovered the Soviets secretly building missile bases in Cuba, and imposed a blockade around Cuba. With nuclear war threatening, the Soviets withdrew the missiles and the U.S. promised never to invade Cuba.

Support For South Vietnam. South Vietnam was under attack by communist forces from the North trying to unite Vietnam under communist rule. Kennedy sent advisers and military aid to South Vietnam.

Kennedy believed in lending poorer nations a helping hand, to improve their living standards and to better resist the temptations of communism. In 1961, he created the **Alliance For Progress**, which offered economic aid and promoted social reform among Latin American nations. Kennedy also created the **Peace Corps** for American volunteers to go to developing countries in Africa, Asia and Latin America and apply their skills to improve living conditions.

The nation was shocked when President Kennedy was assassinated by **Lee Harvey Oswald** on November 22, 1963 in Dallas, Texas. Lyndon B. Johnson became the next President of the U.S.

Vice President Lyndon B. Johnson being sworn in as President on Air Force One, immediately after the assassination of John F. Kennedy

THE JOHNSON PRESIDENCY, 1963-1968

DOMESTIC POLICY

A Democrat from Texas, Johnson had been a follower of F.D.R. as a young Congressman. Soon after becoming President, Johnson proposed a far-ranging program of social legislation. Johnson's aim was to open up opportunities and to improve the quality of life for all Americans. His **Great Society** was the most ambitious program of social reform since Roosevelt's New Deal. Johnson believed that America was so rich and prosperous, it could become the first nation to eliminate poverty within its borders.

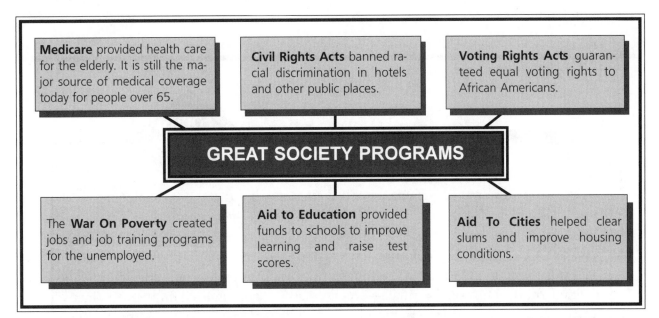

Medicare provided health care for the elderly. It is still the major source of medical coverage today for people over 65.

Civil Rights Acts banned racial discrimination in hotels and other public places.

Voting Rights Acts guaranteed equal voting rights to African Americans.

GREAT SOCIETY PROGRAMS

The **War On Poverty** created jobs and job training programs for the unemployed.

Aid to Education provided funds to schools to improve learning and raise test scores.

Aid To Cities helped clear slums and improve housing conditions.

Despite massive federal spending, many Americans remained poor. Meanwhile, U.S. involvement in the Vietnam War became increasingly costly, forcing Johnson to cut Great Society programs.

FOREIGN POLICY

The major foreign policy event of the Johnson Administration was the increasing involvement of American troops in the Vietnam war. (*This topic is more fully discussed in the next section.*)

THE YOUTH CULTURE OF THE 1960s

In the 1950s, most young Americans had followed traditional lifestyles and focused on their families and careers. In the 1960s, many young people challenged this tradition. They questioned whether it was important to make a lot of money. They prized individual freedom and having a social conscience. They were shocked that America's leaders seemed not to care about poverty, pollution and other world problems. The **Youth Culture** was especially influenced by rock music. The Beatles, an English rock group, introduced new fashions and long hair for men. The Youth Culture was equally affected by greater sexual freedom and by the availability of drugs like marijuana and LSD. Groups who called themselves **hippies** organized communities based on their new values. In the late 1960s, young people became active in the movement against U.S. involvement in the Vietnam War; they persisted until the U.S. withdrew from the war in 1973.

ANALYSIS

Are young people different today than they were in the 1960s? What ideas do young people have today about:

- their role in society? _____

- making a lot of money? _____

- patriotism? _____

Bob Dylan, Folk Singer

FOCUS ON THE ARTS

Bob Dylan was a leading singer and songwriter whose music became associated with the youth culture of the 1960s. When he wrote that "the times they are a-changin'," he could not have been more accurate. Many of his songs typified the feelings of the time — rejecting conformity and material wealth. His song "Blowin' In The Wind" came to symbolize the restlessness of the younger generation. His music captured the spirit of a generation uncomfortable with a nation founded on democratic principles but still practicing racism. His music influenced many 1960s rock artists such as the Beatles, the Byrds and Jimi Hendrix.

THE WOMEN'S LIBERATION MOVEMENT

Like young people, women also were influenced by the new spirit of individual freedom that appeared in the 1960s. Despite having achieved the right to vote with the passage of the Nineteenth Amendment in 1920, women's progress towards gaining equality had been slow.

THE WOMEN'S LIBERATION MOVEMENT IS BORN

Many women were dissatisfied in their role as mothers and housewives. They wanted careers and the ability to earn as much money as men did. Unlike the earlier Women's Suffrage Movement, which had focused on voting rights, the Women's Liberation Movement was directed at achieving full equality in the workplace and in society at large. Movement leaders such as **Betty Friedan** and **Gloria Steinem** learned a great deal from the legal and political methods used by the Civil Rights Movement.

IMPACT OF THE WOMEN'S LIBERATION MOVEMENT

Education
Affirmative Action programs promoted the hiring of more women professors. Colleges offered courses on women's history and contributions. More women were admitted into military academies, law schools and medical schools.

Employment
Equal job opportunities for women were introduced, along with maternity leave, and federal aid for child care. A new law required women to be paid equally with men if they did equal work. Working wives also urged that men and women should share household chores.

Sexist Language
The title Ms. replaced Miss and Mrs., which revealed a woman's marital status. Women fought against sexist language (such as police*man*, fire*man*), and ads that used women as sex objects. Men who treated women as inferiors were called "male chauvinists."

Focus On Women's Problems
Women lobbied for more funds for research on women's diseases such as ovarian and breast cancer, and on the social problems of women, such as rape and domestic violence.

Betty Friedan, Writer

FOCUS ON THE ARTS

In 1957, Betty Friedan completed a study of the lives of her former Smith College classmates. She discovered that many of them were unhappy and unfulfilled. In 1963, she wrote *The Feminine Mystique*, attacking the idea that all women were content simply to be mothers and housewives. She pointed out that many women felt "empty" and "useless." She stated that women were as capable as men and should be permitted to compete for the same jobs and careers. In 1966, Friedan and others formed the National Organization for Women (**NOW**), which became the chief voice of the Women's Liberation Movement.

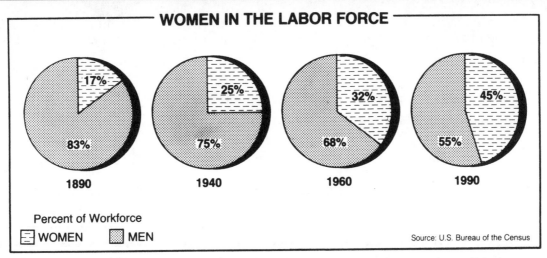

WOMEN IN THE LABOR FORCE

1890	1940	1960	1990
17% / 83%	25% / 75%	32% / 68%	45% / 55%

Percent of Workforce
☐ WOMEN   ☐ MEN

Source: U.S. Bureau of the Census

Having trouble understanding these pie charts? The following Skill Builder section will help.

What Is a Pie Chart?

A pie chart is a circle divided into slices (*sections*) of different sizes. Its purpose is to show the relationship between a whole and its parts.

Keys to Understanding a Pie Chart

To understand a pie chart you should look for certain helpers:

Title. This tells you the overall topic of the pie chart. For example, the title of the pie chart on page 271 is: "**Women In The Labor Force.**" It shows the percentage of women in the workforce for various years.

Legend. The legend shows what each slice of the pie represents. In our pie charts the shaded slices refer to men, and the hatched slices refer to women. (In some charts no legend is needed because each slice is fully labeled.)

Slices of the Pie. Each slice of the pie tells us what information is shown, and its size or relationship to the whole pie. Our first pie chart shows that in 1890 women made up 17% of the circle. This means that in 1890, out of every 100 people in paid employment (*the whole pie*), 17 of them were women (*the slice*).

Interpreting a Pie Chart

Start by looking at the title; it provides the overall meaning. To find specific information, you must examine a particular piece of the pie and its relationship to the other pieces. For example, in 1940 what percentage of the workforce were women? In our 1940 pie chart, the shaded piece marked "75%" represents the number of men in the workforce. You can see by the hatched piece that the rest of the people in the workforce — 25% — were women.

ANALYSIS

These pie charts can also help you draw other conclusions about women in the workforce. For example:

* The pie charts show that in seventy years — from 1890 to 1960 — the number of women in the workforce almost doubled.

What other conclusions can you draw from information in the pie charts?

* _____

* _____

THE EQUAL RIGHTS AMENDMENT FAILS

One of the failures of the Women's Liberation Movement was its inability to get the **Equal Rights Amendment (E.R.A.)** passed. This constitutional amendment sought to guarantee women equal rights with men. Opponents of the amendment argued that women already had equal rights because of the 14th Amendment. Others feared that ratification of the E.R.A. might require women to be eligible for the military draft. In 1972, the amendment failed to gain the approval of the required number of states needed for ratification.

THE ABORTION ISSUE

In the 1960s, some states had laws that prohibited abortion *(a medical operation that ends a pregnancy)*. The Supreme Court became involved in this controversial issue in the case of **Roe v. Wade** (1973). Jane Roe *(a fictitious name)* wanted to end her pregnancy. She challenged a state law that made abortion a crime unless the pregnant woman's life was in danger. The Supreme Court ruled that the state law against abortion was unconstitutional, since it violated a woman's constitutional right to privacy. This decision overturned all state laws that prohibited abortions during the first three months of pregnancy.

Should Women Be Allowed or Denied the Right to an Abortion?	
RIGHT-TO-LIFE	PRO-CHOICE
Those who want to make abortion illegal argue that every life is precious. They believe that human life begins at conception, that abortion is murder, and that to abort a fetus is to put it through a painful death. Abortion opponents believe that only God should determine who lives and who dies, and that the state has an obligation to protect the fetus. If a pregnant woman wants to have an abortion, then the state, on behalf of the fetus, should prevent it.	Pro-choice advocates believe an abortion decision is a private matter best left to a woman and her doctor. They argue that it is unclear at what point human life begins, and object to religious beliefs of certain groups being imposed on others. They believe that women should have the right to determine what happens to their own bodies, and that this control is a basic human right. If abortions are banned, they argue, it will only prevent safe, legal abortions and increase the dangerous "back alley" abortions of the past.

SUMMING UP: CHANGING TIMES — THE 1960s AND EARLY 1970s

President Kennedy sought to breathe new life and a sense of youthful optimism into American government. Both Kennedy and Johnson introduced new programs to promote greater opportunity, eliminate poverty and to encourage positive social change. They were also strong supporters of civil rights. Their desire to promote freedom and democracy led them to take a strong stand against communism. Kennedy nearly threatened nuclear war to get the Soviet Union to remove its missiles from Cuba, and both Kennedy and Johnson involved the United States in the Vietnam War. By the late 1960s, the spirit of individual freedom and equality started by the Civil Rights Movement was affecting other parts of American society; young people and women rebelled against traditional beliefs and roles.

THINKING IT OVER

Now that you have read more about the 1960s, would you call this period a "decade of change?"

_____

Explain why or why not._____

CHECKING YOUR UNDERSTANDING

Directions: Complete the following cards. Then answer the multiple-choice questions.

WOMEN'S LIBERATION MOVEMENT

What were its goals? _____

How did it differ from the earlier Women's Rights

Movement? _____

ROE V. WADE

Background of the case: _____

What did the Supreme Court decide?

_____

1 Which statement best reflects one of President Kennedy's foreign policy goals?
   1 Communism should be encouraged in some Latin American republics.
   2 The extension of European influence in Latin America must be prevented.
   3 The United States has no interest in Latin American affairs.
   4 The spread of communism in Latin America must be stopped.

2 The formation of the Alliance For Progress was intended to help nations in
   1 Europe   3 Asia
   2 Latin America   4 the Middle East

3 An accurate conclusion based on a study of the "Great Society" programs is that they
   1 helped to develop China's industrial capacity
   2 were federal laws encouraging social reforms
   3 eased tensions with the Soviet Union
   4 encouraged people to help themselves and not depend on government

4 Both the New Deal and the Great Society shared the idea that
   1 foreign trade should be cut to a minimum
   2 the federal government should help those unable to help themselves
   3 key industries should be nationalized
   4 taxes should be raised to increase consumer spending

5 One effect of the Women's Liberation Movement has been
   1 that women gained the right to vote
   2 that more women entered the workforce
   3 a decrease women's salaries
   4 the passage of an Equal Rights Amendment

6 Affirmative Action programs seek to correct past discrimination by
   1 giving food stamps to the poor
   2 giving preference to minorities and women
   3 encouraging poor people to vote
   4 providing low cost public housing

SECTION
4

THE VIETNAM WAR, 1954-1973

In this section you will learn how Vietnam, a country
in Southeast Asia, had an important impact on the
affairs of the United States in the 1960s and 1970s.

THINK ABOUT IT

Many Americans protested against the Vietnam War. Is it unpatriotic for citizens to protest
involvement in a war they oppose? _____

Explain. _____

Important Terms and Concepts: As you read this section, look for the following:

◆ Vietnam War   ◆ Paris Peace Accords
◆ Domino Theory   ◆ War Powers Act

To help you find these terms, the ◆ symbol appears where the term is first explained.

EVENTS LEADING TO THE VIETNAM WAR

American involvement in the war in Vietnam did not occur suddenly, as in World War II. It ◆
evolved slowly, over a period of time, and through several U.S. Presidencies.

BACKGROUND

During the 1800s, France colonized Vietnam. When World War II ended in 1945, Vietnam declared its independence. France refused to recognize Vietnamese
independence, and a war followed. After nine years of fighting, the
Vietnamese finally defeated the French in 1954. At the **Geneva
Peace Conference**, Vietnam was divided in two. The Vietnamese
communist leader, **Ho Chi Minh**, was given control of the north,
and a non-communist state was established in the south. The country was to be reunited after elections in 1956. However, when the
time came to hold the elections, South Vietnam refused. Its leaders
claimed that the communists in the north would not conduct a fair
election. When elections were not held, Vietnamese communists,
called **Vietcong**, supported by the North Vietnamese, began a
guerrilla war (*a war fought by irregular troops who take cover in the
countryside or jungle*) against South Vietnam, to reunite the country
under communist rule.

Ho Chi Minh

THE WAR UNDER
PRESIDENT KENNEDY (1961-1963)

Responding to requests from South Vietnam for help, President Kennedy sent military and economic aid to assist in fighting the Vietcong. Kennedy and the Presidents who succeeded him believed that if South Vietnam fell to communism, other nations in Southeast Asia would quickly follow. This belief was called the **"Domino Theory"** — countries would fall to communism one after another, like a row of dominoes. Kennedy also felt a moral duty to defend South Vietnam, believing it could develop into a democratic nation and serve as a model for other developing countries in Asia, Africa and Latin America.

*President Kennedy meeting
with members of his Cabinet*

THE WAR UNDER
PRESIDENT JOHNSON (1963-1968)

A major turning point occurred in 1964, when Congress passed the **Tonkin Gulf Resolution**, giving President Johnson authority to take emergency steps to halt North Vietnamese aggression. Over the next three years, Johnson sent large numbers of troops to Vietnam; more than 500,000 U.S. soldiers were eventually stationed there. Despite this, the Vietcong were able to launch major attacks throughout South Vietnam in 1968. These attacks, known as the **Tet Offensive**, showed that despite the large number of U.S. forces, the Vietcong could still mount major military offensives. The Tet Offensive demonstrated to the American public that victory was far off.

THE WAR UNDER PRESIDENT NIXON (1969-1973)

President Nixon campaigned for the Presidency in 1968 on the promise that he would bring about "peace with honor" in Vietnam. However, the war dragged on for five more years. Nixon began his Presidency by increasing the bombing of North Vietnam and invading neighboring Cambodia, a country from which the Viet Cong often attacked. When this had little impact, Nixon began gradually withdrawing U.S. forces from South Vietnam. In 1973, Nixon's representatives signed a cease-fire agreement with the North Vietnamese, known as the **Paris Peace Accords**. Under its terms, the United States simply withdrew its remaining forces from South Vietnam. Two years later, South Vietnam was taken over by North Vietnam, and Vietnam was reunited under communist leadership.

*U.S. soldiers relaxing after a battle
in the jungles of Vietnam*

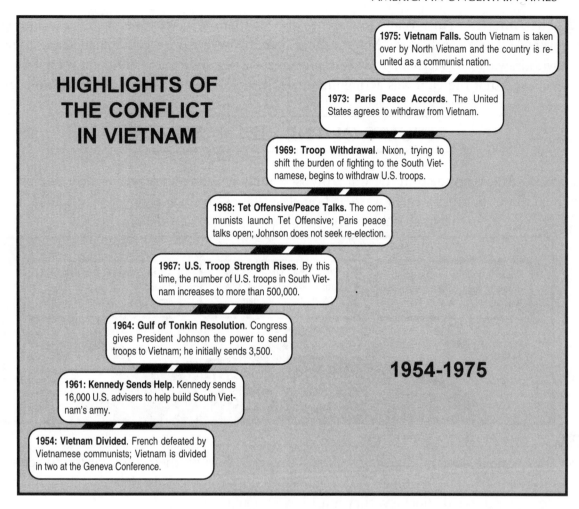

HIGHLIGHTS OF THE CONFLICT IN VIETNAM

1954-1975

1975: Vietnam Falls. South Vietnam is taken over by North Vietnam and the country is reunited as a communist nation.

1973: Paris Peace Accords. The United States agrees to withdraw from Vietnam.

1969: Troop Withdrawal. Nixon, trying to shift the burden of fighting to the South Vietnamese, begins to withdraw U.S. troops.

1968: Tet Offensive/Peace Talks. The communists launch Tet Offensive; Paris peace talks open; Johnson does not seek re-election.

1967: U.S. Troop Strength Rises. By this time, the number of U.S. troops in South Vietnam increases to more than 500,000.

1964: Gulf of Tonkin Resolution. Congress gives President Johnson the power to send troops to Vietnam; he initially sends 3,500.

1961: Kennedy Sends Help. Kennedy sends 16,000 U.S. advisers to help build South Vietnam's army.

1954: Vietnam Divided. French defeated by Vietnamese communists; Vietnam is divided in two at the Geneva Conference.

WHY THE U.S. WAS UNABLE TO WIN THE WAR

By the end of 1968, the United States had dropped more bombs in Vietnam than during all of World War II. The war was costing $25 billion a year. Despite these efforts, America was still losing the war, for a number of reasons:

- ■ **Guerrilla War.** Vietnam's jungles provided an ideal cover for guerrilla war. American soldiers were not trained in guerrilla warfare. The Vietcong often hid among the South Vietnamese people and had the support of many of them.

- ■ **International Support for North Vietnam.** The North Vietnamese received large amounts of supplies from the communist governments of China and the Soviet Union. This prompted American leaders to reject an invasion of North Vietnam, fearing it might lead to Chinese and Soviet intervention.

- ■ **Popularity of the Nationalist Cause.** Since Ho Chi Minh had led the fight for independence from the French, many Vietnamese saw him as the father of their country. The North Vietnamese were willing to suffer large losses to reach their goals; the South Vietnamese government was unable to command the same respect and loyalty from their people.

■ **The American Anti-War Movement.** The Vietnam War was one of the most unpopular wars in American history. Marches and demonstrations in the U.S. called for complete withdrawal from Vietnam. Many Americans saw the conflict as a Vietnamese civil war, and believed that the U.S. was acting immorally by bombing civilians and burning villages.

RESULTS OF THE VIETNAM WAR

Over 58,000 Americans died in the war. Almost 2 million Vietnamese were killed, and over half the population of South Vietnam was left homeless. Cities and rice paddies were ruined, leaving the Vietnamese economy in shambles. The war also left Americans deeply divided.

Public support is needed to successfully fight a war: Spanish-American War, WW II, Vietnam

Presidential power expands greatly in time of war: WW I, WW II, Korea, Vietnam

Often there is frustration following a war, and a return to isolationism: WW I, Vietnam

LESSONS LEARNED FROM WAR

IMPACT OF PUBLIC OPINION

Universities became centers of protest. Some young men burned their draft cards and refused to serve in the military. The Vietnam War demonstrated to America's leaders that for government policies to succeed in a democracy, they must have popular support.

LIMITS ON PRESIDENTIAL WARTIME POWERS

The President is often in a position to act quickly. In the Vietnam War, as in the Korean War, Presidential powers greatly expanded. In response, Congress passed the **War Powers Act** (1973), limiting the ability of the President to send troops overseas. The President must inform Congress within 48 hours; Congress must approve within 60 days, or the troops must be withdrawn.

CONCERN OVER U.S. OVERSEAS INVOLVEMENT

American leaders became less willing to involve U.S. military power abroad. Just as after World War I, many Americans again became opposed to an active role in world affairs. As a result, U.S. leaders adopted a more cautious foreign policy. avoiding overseas commitments.

ANALYSIS

The Vietnam War again raised questions over how much control   over foreign policy the President or Congress should have. What are the advantages of Presidential control?

_____

What are the advantages of Congressional control? _____

_____

Maya Lin, Architect

In the late 1970s, the government decided to build a memorial in Washington, D.C. to the 58,724 Americans killed and the 2,487 listed as missing during the Vietnam War. A contest was held to determine the design of the monument. Hundreds of proposals were submitted. The winner was an unknown 21-year-old Chinese-American student, Maya Lin. Her design was a V-shaped 500-foot-long wall rising out of the ground. On its polished black granite surface appear the names of every American killed or missing in the Vietnam War. Since its dedication in 1984, millions of people have visited the memorial. In 1988, another of her designs was chosen for the Civil Rights Memorial in Montgomery, Alabama.

THINKING IT OVER

What do you now think is the best way to protest involvement in a war that you disapprove of? _____

SUMMING UP: THE VIETNAM WAR

In 1954, Vietnam was divided into two states: communist North Vietnam and non-communist South Vietnam. When Vietnamese communists began attacking South Vietnam, the U.S. sent troops to help. At one point, over 500,000 U.S. troops were fighting in support of South Vietnam. Eventually, many Americans came to believe that U.S. troops should be withdrawn. The war became one of the most divisive and unpopular causes in U.S. history. In 1973, a cease-fire agreement with North Vietnam was signed and U.S. forces withdrew. Two years later, Vietnam was reunited under communist rule. Congress passed the War Powers Act, requiring Congressional support when the President sends U.S. troops abroad.

CHECKING YOUR UNDERSTANDING

Directions: Complete the following cards. Then answer the multiple-choice questions.

VIETNAM WAR

When did it take place? _____

State one major cause: _____

State one major effect: _____

WAR POWERS ACT

What were its main provisions? _____

_____

Why was it passed? _____

1 The conflicts in Korea and Vietnam were similar in that in both the United States
1 was protecting freedom of the seas
2 sought to encourage religious freedom
3 tried to stop the spread of communism
4 restored kings to power in Asia

2 U.S. actions in the Vietnam War demonstrated that
1 the domino theory cannot prevent the spread of communism
2 in a democracy, popular opinion affects government policies
3 advanced technology can guarantee victory
4 use of nuclear weapons can be successful

3 Which was an eventual result of American involvement in the Vietnam War?
1 South Vietnam was taken over by North Vietnam.
2 South Vietnam remained non-communist.
3 Vietnam was annexed by China.
4 Vietnam was taken over by the United Nations.

4 The War Powers Act of 1973 sought to limit the power of the
1 President   3 Supreme Court
2 Congress   4 states

5 Presidents Kennedy, Johnson, and Nixon sent U.S. troops to Vietnam in an effort to
1 prevent violations of U.S. neutrality
2 support the policy of containment
3 protect freedom of the seas
4 create a new colonial empire

6 Which developments were part of U.S. foreign policy during the Vietnam War?
1 isolationism and the issuance of the Monroe Doctrine
2 imperialism and the Big Stick Policy
3 Manifest Destiny and the announcement of the Marshall Plan
4 containment and the passage of the War Powers Act

7 According to the domino theory
1 war is popular with the American people
2 when one nation falls to communism, nearby nations will soon follow
3 military power alone does not always insure victory
4 America's allies must act as "dominoes" in support of U.S. foreign policy

8 Vietnam is a country located in
1 Africa   3 the Middle East
2 Southeast Asia   4 Latin America

PROFILES IN HISTORY

JACKIE ROBINSON
(BASEBALL PLAYER)

Jackie Robinson broke the "color barrier" by becoming the first African American to play major league baseball. Before Robinson was hired by the Brooklyn Dodgers in 1947, African Americans were limited to playing only in the "Negro League." At first, Robinson met with resistance and hostility, but his talent and skill helped him to achieve eventual acceptance. In 1962, he was voted into the Baseball Hall of Fame at Cooperstown.

CESAR CHAVEZ
(UNION ORGANIZER)

Migrant farm workers were among the most poorly paid and badly treated workers in the nation. Cesar Chavez, a union organizer for Mexican-American farm workers in California, led a non-violent strike against California grape-growers. His leadership in a 1965 strike and boycott of California grapes won national attention and support. Chavez's methods succeeded in obtaining better working conditions and higher pay for migrant workers.

THURGOOD MARSHALL
(SUPREME COURT JUSTICE)

Thurgood Marshall became the first African American on the Supreme Court when he was appointed by President Lyndon Johnson in 1967. His selection to the Court capped a distinguished career as a lawyer for the N.A.A.C.P. Legal Defense Fund, which he had helped to establish. As a lawyer, Thurgood Marshall had argued the famous case of *Brown v. Board of Education* before the Supreme Court in 1954.

S.I. HAYAKAWA
(SENATOR)

S.I. Hayakawa, a Japanese-American, was a noted scholar and expert on the English language. Hayakawa served as a President of the University of California. He was also elected by the voters of California to the United States Senate.

RACHEL CARSON
(ENVIRONMENTALIST)

Rachel Carson was a leader in alerting Americans to the dangers of pesticides. Her 1962 book, *Silent Spring*, sounded the alarm for Americans to wake up to the destruction of plant and animal life caused by using insecticides and pesticides. She warned  that with the continued use of pesticides and the resulting chemical pollution, a time would come when wildlife would die off and the food supply would be unfit for human use.

THE CONSTITUTION AT WORK

CIVIL RIGHTS ACTS OF 1964 AND 1968 One of the most significant achievements of President Lyndon Johnson's Great Society was the Civil Rights Act of 1964, which forbid discrimination in employment and public accommodations (hotels, restaurants, buses, etc.). It also established the Equal Employment Opportunity Commission to make sure that all minorities were fairly treated. The Civil Rights Act of 1968 extended the prohibition on racial discrimination to house sales and rentals.

KEY LAWS

WAR POWERS ACT (1973) This act was passed to set limits on the war-making powers of the President, in response to widespread concern that Presidents had involved the nation in several wars without Congressional approval. Presidents had sent troops to fight in Korea and Vietnam without declaring war. Under the Act, the President must inform Congress within 48 hours of sending troops into combat. If Congress does not approve the use of the troops within 60 days, the President must withdraw them.

KEY LAWS

THE WARREN COURT

The events of the Kennedy and Johnson years, especially with regard to the Civil Rights Movement, cannot be understood without reference to the "Warren Court." During the 1950s and 1960s, the United States Supreme Court under Chief Justice **Earl Warren** became a strong defender of civil rights in cases such as *Brown v. Board of Education*. The Warren Court also acted as a vigorous supporter of the rights of defendants in criminal cases. Some people criticized the Warren Court for going too far in protecting the rights of the accused, making it more difficult for the police to capture and convict criminals. But supporters of the Warren Court argued that the Court had a constitutional duty to protect individual rights. The Court, under Warren, became a major instrument of social change, protecting rights that other institutions of government were unwilling to defend.

Earl Warren

GIDEON V. WAINWRIGHT (1963)

Background: Clarence Gideon was arrested for robbing a pool hall. He was too poor to afford a lawyer, and was not provided with a lawyer by the trial court. His request for a lawyer was denied because under Florida law the government appointed a lawyer for poor defendants only in death penalty cases.

Decision/Significance: The Supreme Court ruled that Gideon's Sixth Amendment rights to a lawyer had been violated, even though this was not a death penalty case. The decision required all states to provide free legal services to any defendant who cannot afford them. As a result, states today have public defenders who provide legal services to the poor.

MIRANDA V. ARIZONA (1966)

Background: Ernesto Miranda was arrested for kidnapping and raping a young woman. After appearing in a police line-up, Miranda confessed. The police never told him that he had a right to remain silent, that he did not have to answer their questions, and that he could have a lawyer present to advise him.

Decision/Significance: The Court overturned Miranda's conviction. The police now must warn all suspects that their statements can be used against them, and inform them of their constitutional rights to remain silent and to have a lawyer present during questioning. These are known as "Miranda rights," and were again upheld by the Court in 2000.

THE COURT SPEAKS

SUMMARIZING YOUR UNDERSTANDING

Directions: Confirm your understanding of the important terms and concepts in this chapter. Check those you can explain. For those you are not sure of, find the ♦ symbol in the margin next to the term and review it.

CHECKLIST

- ❏ Cold War
- ❏ Iron Curtain
- ❏ Truman Doctrine
- ❏ Marshall Plan
- ❏ NATO
- ❏ Korean War
- ❏ McCarthyism

- ❏ Civil Rights Movement
- ❏ *Brown v. Board of Education*
- ❏ Civil Rights Act
- ❏ Affirmative Action
- ❏ Bay of Pigs Invasion
- ❏ Cuban Missile Crisis
- ❏ Great Society

- ❏ Women's Liberation Movement
- ❏ Vietnam War
- ❏ Domino Theory
- ❏ Tet Offensive
- ❏ Paris Peace Accords
- ❏ War Powers Act
- ❏ *Roe v. Wade*

Directions: Fill in the information called for in the following organizers.

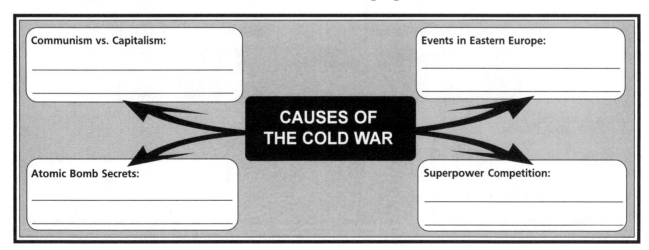

Communism vs. Capitalism:
_____
_____

Events in Eastern Europe:
_____
_____

CAUSES OF THE COLD WAR

Atomic Bomb Secrets:
_____
_____

Superpower Competition:
_____
_____

MILESTONES IN THE CIVIL RIGHTS MOVEMENT

March on Washington:

_____
_____
_____
_____
_____

Role Played By Dr. King:

_____
_____
_____
_____
_____

Civil Rights Act of 1964:

_____
_____
_____
_____
_____

Voting Rights Act of 1965:

_____
_____
_____
_____
_____

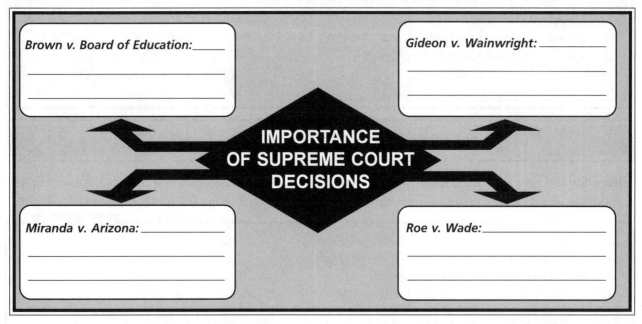

*Brown v. Board of Education:*_____
_____
_____

*Gideon v. Wainwright:*_____
_____
_____

IMPORTANCE OF SUPREME COURT DECISIONS

Miranda v. Arizona: _____
_____
_____

*Roe v. Wade:*_____
_____
_____

When did it develop?

_____

Who were some of its leaders?

_____
_____

THE WOMEN'S LIBERATION MOVEMENT

Why did it begin?

_____
_____

Its main goals:

_____
_____

Results:

1. _____
2. _____

TEST HELPER   LOOKING AT OUR LEGAL SYSTEM

Americans live under the rule of law — a system that protects us from random or oppressive acts by government or unfair treatment by neighbors. This section briefly reviews how our system works.

WHAT IS LAW?

A **law** is a rule that tells people to do something or not to do something. Usually there is a **penalty** or other consequence for breaking the law. There are several law-making bodies in our legal system. The most familiar are **legislatures**, such as the U.S. Congress or your state legislature. Your county or town may also have a legislative body with law-making authority.

WHAT DO THE COURTS DO?

You have often heard that courts "apply" or "interpret" the law, but what does this mean? No law can ever be so precise that it can tell in advance all the kinds of situations that might arise. That is why we need courts to determine whether or not a law applies to a particular circumstance. For example, a sign reads:

> **NO VEHICLES
> IN THE PARK**

We are fairly sure this means no cars or trucks in the park, but what about bicycles? What about baby strollers or wheel chairs? Are they "vehicles" in the sense intended by the sign? As you can see, courts must interpret the *words* of a law to decide just what the law means. Sometimes they might want to consider the purpose of the law (or what was said about the law when it was made) to determine whether it applies to a particular situation or not. A court might say that the purpose of "NO VEHICLES IN THE PARK" is to avoid danger to pedestrians. Since wheel chairs and baby strollers are not dangerous to pedestrians, they are not "vehicles" in the sense intended by the rule.

Because we live under the "rule of law," we want each person in the same situation to be treated similarly. In any court proceeding, each party has rights — the right to an attorney, the right to hear the opposing evidence, the right to present its case, and the right to appeal the decision. In criminal cases and some civil cases, the defendant also has the right to be tried by a **jury** — a panel of unbiased citizens. These guarantees — known as "due process" rights — give each side a fair opportunity to persuade the judge or jury that it should win the case.

THE APPEALS PROCESS

Often the losing side in a trial is unhappy with the result. They can then ask a special court, known as a court of appeals, to reconsider the decision. In general, an appeals court will only change the decision if the trial court made some error in interpreting or applying a law.

THE ROLE OF THE SUPREME COURT

The United States Supreme Court is the highest court in the land, hearing appeals from both federal and state courts. The Supreme Court plays two roles. First, it determines how a law should be applied to a particular case. For example, has the law been applied as Congress intended? Second, the Supreme Court can decide whether the law itself is constitutional. If the Court decides that a law violates the Constitution, it voids the law. In that case, the only way to override the Court's decision is to amend the Constitution itself.

The Supreme Court has had an important impact in a number of areas. This chart will help you review some of the major cases you have studied.

CASE	IMPORTANCE OF DECISION
Judicial Review (Decisions establishing the power of the Court)	
Marbury v. Madison (1803)	Established the Supreme Court's power to declare laws unconstitutional.
The "necessary and proper" clause	
McCulloch v. Maryland (1819)	Upheld Congressional power to create a national bank on the basis of the "necessary and proper" clause.
Free Speech (First Amendment)	
Schenck v. U.S. (1919)	Limited an individual's right to free speech if it presented a "clear" and present danger" to others.
Rights of Criminal Defendants (Fifth and Sixth Amendments)	
Gideon v. Wainwright (1963)	A state must provide a defendant with a free lawyer if that person is too poor to afford one.
Miranda v. Arizona (1966)	Persons in legal custody must be informed of their constitutional rights.
Rights of Privacy (Fifth and Fourteenth Amendments)	
Roe v. Wade (1973)	Established a woman's right to an abortion during the first three months of pregnancy.
Equal Protection of the Laws (Fifth and Fourteenth Amendments)	
Plessy v. Ferguson (1896)	As long as states provided "separate but equal" facilities, they could separate blacks from whites.
Korematsu v. U.S. (1944)	Upheld the relocation and detention of Japanese Americans in World War II on the basis of military need.
Brown v. Board of Education (1954)	Overturned *Plessy*, by ruling that segregated public schools were "inherently unequal."

TESTING YOUR UNDERSTANDING

Directions: Circle the number preceding the word or expression that correctly answers the statement or question. Following the multiple-choice questions, answer the essay questions.

Base your answers to questions 1 and 2 on the following charts and on your knowledge of social studies.

1 According to the information on the pie charts
  1 in general, women earn less than men
  2 more women than men are paid a salary of over $50,000 a year
  3 the number of women in the workforce is increasing
  4 in general, women earn more than men

2 Which statement best explains the information shown on the pie charts?
  1 There has been a large increase in divorces.
  2 Women do not receive equal pay for equal work, or have the same job opportunities.
  3 Men and women are starting to share domestic chores.
  4 Women have achieved economic and social equality with men.

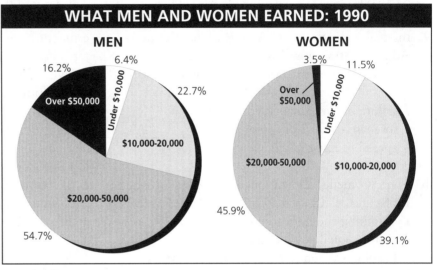

WHAT MEN AND WOMEN EARNED: 1990

Source: Bureau of the Census

3 In *Roe v. Wade*, the Supreme Court ruled that
  1 racial segregation in public schools is unconstitutional
  2 the Court can declare federal laws to be unconstitutional
  3 women deserve equal pay for equal work
  4 women have a constitutional right to an abortion in early pregnancy

4 Which person is correctly paired with the movement with which she is associated?
  1 Harriet Beecher Stowe / Progressive Movement
  2 Betty Friedan / Women's Liberation Movement
  3 Rachel Carson / Right-to-Life Movement
  4 Eleanor Roosevelt / Environmental Movement

5 The terms "hippies" and "Youth Culture" would most likely be discussed in an essay dealing with the decade of
  1 the 1920s   3 the 1950s
  2 the 1930s   4 the 1960s

6 One basic difference between the beliefs of Malcolm X and Martin Luther King, Jr. was over
  1 whether violence could ever be used to achieve racial equality
  2 the desirability of racial equality
  3 the issue of U.S. commitments in Africa
  4 the issue of pride in being American

7 With which statement would a follower of Dr. Martin Luther King be most likely to agree?
  1 All laws must be obeyed.
  2 Demonstrations against unjust laws are morally correct.
  3 Civil disobedience is damaging to society.
  4 Violence is an acceptable form of protest if the cause is just.

8   Which example best illustrates the idea of Affirmative Action?
   1   A company actively recruits minority members for a training program.
   2   A corporation hires people on a first come, first served basis.
   3   A college admits students based solely on their entrance examination scores.
   4   A college accepts all students who apply.

9   In dealing with Latin America, the Kennedy Administration was most concern about
   1   refusal of some nations to join the Organization of American States
   2   failure of the Alliance For Progress
   3   increased threat of communism
   4   spread of imperialism

10 The Women's Liberation Movement of the 1960s and 1970s focused primarily on
   1   obtaining the right to vote
   2   getting equal pay for equal work
   3   keeping women as homemakers and wives
   4   environmental issues

11 A major cause of the Cold War was
   1   discovery by the United States of Soviet missiles in Cuba
   2   the Soviet attempt to enter World War II on the side of Japan
   3   Soviet control of Eastern Europe after World War II
   4   U.S. military action in the Middle East

12 Which statement is most clearly illustrated by the Supreme Court decision in *Brown v. Board of Education*?
   1   The Constitution ensures federal control of education in the states.
   2   Racial prejudice no longer exists in America.
   3   Non-whites have gained economic and political equality with whites.
   4   The Court's interpretation of the Constitution can change over time.

13 The decisions of the U.S. Supreme Court in *Miranda v. Arizona*, *Gideon v. Wainwright*, and *Mapp v. Ohio* all advanced
   1   the voting rights of minorities
   2   free speech
   3   the rights of accused persons
   4   women's rights

14 The Equal Protection Clause of the Fourteenth Amendment has been used by the federal government to justify its intervention in state matters concerning
   1   civil rights
   2   appointment of judges
   3   granting of corporation charters
   4   regulation of currency

15 Johnson's Great Society programs illustrated
   1   the increased power of the states to deal with economic problems
   2   direct federal action to address poverty
   3   laissez-faire capitalism
   4   decreased support for minority groups

16 When the Vietnam War began, many Americans favored U.S. policy there because they
   1   feared Vietnam would invade the U.S.
   2   believed communism must be prevented from spreading in Asia
   3   did not like the Vietnamese people
   4   wanted to conquer Vietnam

17 Presidential power increased during the Vietnam War because
   1   Congress was afraid to exercise its Constitutional powers
   2   the Constitution was suspended
   3   the President was in a position to act quickly
   4   the Constitution puts all the power into the President's hands

18 As a result of the Vietnam War, Congress attempted to
   1   increase the number of men in the military
   2   take a larger role in shaping foreign policy
   3   recall most U.S. troops stationed overseas
   4   increase economic aid to Southeast Asia

THEMATIC ESSAY QUESTION

Directions: Write a well-organized essay that includes an introduction, several paragraphs explaining your position, and a conclusion.

Theme: Issues Facing the U.S. Supreme Court

> **Throughout American history, the U.S. Supreme Court has often been called onto resolve major issues confronting the nation.**

Task:

> Choose *two* Supreme Court cases from your study of American history and government.
>
> For *each* Supreme Court case:
> - Identify the Supreme Court case.
> - Explain the important issue that the case dealt with.
> - Describe how the Supreme Court decided the issue.

You may use any example from your study of American history. Some suggestions you might wish to consider include: *McCulloch v. Maryland, Dred Scott v. Sandford, Plessy v. Ferguson, Schenck v. U.S., Korematsu v. U.S., Brown v. Board of Education,* and *Roe v. Wade.*

You are *not* limited to these suggestions.

INTERPRETING DOCUMENTS

"His legislative leadership was remarkable. No President since Lincoln has done more for civil rights. Yet much of this has been forgotten as American society became increasingly divided over U.S. participation in a bloody, undeclared war."

1. Which President does this statement best describe? _____

2. Describe one piece of legislation proposed by this President in the field of civil rights.

_____

_____

_____

SHARPENING YOUR TEST-TAKING SKILLS

ANSWERING A DOCUMENT-BASED ESSAY QUESTION

A document-based essay question appears on the next few pages. Before you answer it, let's review the main highlights of the "L • A • W" approach for this type of question.

"L" — LOOK AT THE TASK

Start by looking at the "Historical Context" and the "Task." Focus on (1) the **topic**, and (2) the **action words**, to determine how you will answer the question.

"A" — ANALYZE THE DOCUMENTS

As you read each document, think about (1) who wrote it; (2) the time period in which it was written; (3) the purpose for which it was written; and (4) what it says. Next, answer the question following each document. Then create your Analysis Box.

> **Note:** Two important keys to writing a successful document-based essay are to:
> (1) link the information in the documents to the topic, and
> (2) use your own words instead of simply copying text from the document.

In your Analysis Box, summarize the information in each document and indicate how it supports the thesis statement. Remember to add other information, from your own knowledge, that is not found in the documents.

"W" — WRITE THE ESSAY

In writing your essay answer, remember that you need the following:

❖ **Opening Paragraph.** Your first sentence should state the historical context and set the time and place. The next sentence is your thesis statement, which you obtain from the question. Then write a transition sentence that leads into your supporting paragraphs.

❖ **Supporting Paragraphs.** In these paragraphs you provide evidence that supports your thesis statement. The evidence must include references to the documents, in your own words, as well as additional information from your own knowledge of the topic.

❖ **Closing Paragraph.** The last paragraph should restate the thesis statement. Here is where you may want to summarize your most important evidence or ideas about the general topic.

DOCUMENT-BASED ESSAY QUESTION

Directions: Read the documents in Part A and answer the questions after each document. Then read the directions for Part B and write your essay.

Historical Context:
The decision to go to war is one of the gravest choices made by any nation. Throughout their history, Americans have made this choice for a variety of reasons.

Task:
Compare and contrast various reasons why Americans have decided to go to war.

Part A — Short Answers

Directions:
Analyze the documents and answer the questions that follow each document.

DOCUMENT 1

"Whenever any form of government becomes destructive [of the people's rights], it is the right of the people to alter or abolish it ... The history of the present King of Britain is the history of repeated injuries ... all having in direct object the establishment of an absolute tyranny over these states. He has obstructed the administration of justice. He has kept among us ... standing armies, without the consent of our legislatures."
— Declaration of Independence, July 4, 1776

1a. According to the Declaration, why were Americans justified in fighting Britain?

_____

1b. Give one example of the "tyranny" the colonists were complaining of. _____

_____

DOCUMENT 2

"My [main] object in this struggle is to save the Union, and is not either to save or destroy slavery. If I could save the Union without freeing any slaves, I would do it; if I could save it by freeing all the slaves, I would do it; and if I could do it by freeing some and leaving others alone, I would also do that."
— Abraham Lincoln's reply to the *New York Tribune,* August 22, 1862

2. What did Lincoln see as the main reason for the Civil War? _____

_____

DOCUMENT 3

3a. What is the main idea of this cartoon?

_____

3b. How did political cartoons like this contribute
    to the outbreak of the Spanish-American War?

_____

_____

"The Spanish Brute"

DOCUMENT 4

> **ADMIRALTY PROCLAMATION**
> *The waters surrounding Great Britain and Ireland including the whole English Channel are hereby declared to be within the war zone and all enemy merchant vessels found in those waters after the eighteenth of February, 1915 will be destroyed. In addition, it may not always be possible to save crews and passengers ... Danger to neutral vessels within this zone of war cannot be avoided and neutral vessels may suffer from attacks intended to strike enemy ships.*
>
> —German Admiralty, February 4, 1915

4. How did the policy announced in this proclamation eventually bring the United States
    into World War I? _____

_____

DOCUMENT 5

> *"Yesterday, December 7, 1941 — a date which will live in infamy — the United States of America was suddenly and deliberately attacked by naval and air forces of the Empire of Japan ... the distance of Hawaii from Japan makes it obvious that the attack was deliberately planned ... I ask that Congress declare that since the unprovoked and dastardly attack by Japan on Sunday, December 7, a state of war has existed between the United States and the Japanese Empire."*
>
> —President Franklin D. Roosevelt, Address to Congress, December 8, 1941

5a. What did Roosevelt ask Congress to do in this address? _____

5b. What evidence Roosevelt point to as proof of Japanese aggression? _____

_____

DOCUMENT 6

6a. Why did the division of Vietnam eventually involve the United States in war?

_____

_____

_____

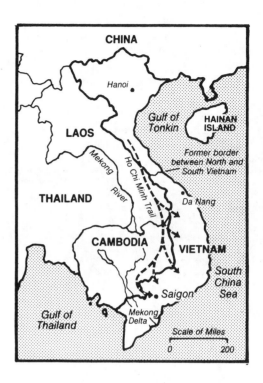

6b. Why did American leaders invade Cambodia in 1969 in order to try to win the war in Vietnam?

_____

_____

Part B
Essay

Directions:
- Write a well-organized essay that includes an introduction, several paragraphs, and a conclusion.
- Use evidence from the documents to support your response.
- Do not simply repeat the contents of the documents.
- Include specific related information.

Historical Context:
The decision to go to war is among the gravest choices made by any nation. Throughout their history, Americans have made this choice of war for a variety of reasons.

Task:
Using information from the documents and your knowledge of American history and geography, write an essay in which you:
- Compare and contrast various reasons why the United States has gone to war.
- Evaluate the effects of *one* of the wars related to these documents.

CHAPTER 11

CONTEMPORARY AMERICA

The Presidency in Crisis
  A. The Nixon Presidency
  B. The Ford Presidency
  C. The Carter Presidency

The Recent Presidents
  A. The Reagan Presidency
  B. The George H.W. Bush Presidency
  C. The Clinton Presidency
  D. The George W. Bush Presidency

Living in a Global Age
  A. Technology
  B. The Global Economy
  C. The Environment

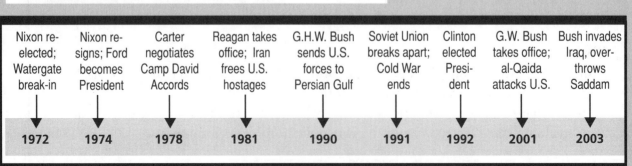

Nixon re-elected; Watergate break-in	Nixon resigns; Ford becomes President	Carter negotiates Camp David Accords	Reagan takes office; Iran frees U.S. hostages	G.H.W. Bush sends U.S. forces to Persian Gulf	Soviet Union breaks apart; Cold War ends	Clinton elected President	G.W. Bush takes office; al-Qaida attacks U.S.	Bush invades Iraq, overthrows Saddam
1972	1974	1978	1981	1990	1991	1992	2001	2003

WHAT YOU SHOULD FOCUS ON

In this chapter, you will learn about U.S. history during the past 35 years. Under President Nixon, the country coped with the Vietnam War, inflation, and the Watergate crisis, which led to the first Presidential resignation in the nation's history. President Ford was unable to solve "stagflation" *(inflation and a stagnant economy)*, or to save Vietnam and Cambodia from Communism. As the 1970s progressed, the nation sank into an economic recession. During the Carter Administration, U.S. prestige in the world community suffered when radical students in Iran seized American embassy personnel as hostages.

Russians watch as a statue of Lenin — the founder of Communism in the Soviet Union — is toppled at the end of the Cold War

Under Presidents Reagan and G.H.W. Bush, America moved toward greater conservatism in government. Communism collapsed in Eastern Europe and the Soviet Union, bringing the Cold War to an abrupt end. Under President Clinton, Americans enjoyed unparalleled prosperity. President George W. Bush pushed through huge tax cuts and initiated a "War on Terrorism" after the September 11, 2001 attacks on America.

In this chapter you will learn about the following:

The Presidency in Crisis	The Presidency from Reagan to the Present	Living in a Global Age
Under Richard Nixon, failure to achieve "peace with honor" at the end of the Vietnam War, as well as the Watergate scandal, tarnished the Presidency. Nixon was forced to resign. Presidents Gerald Ford and Jimmy Carter had to struggle with skyrocketing oil prices, a recession, inflation, and new acts of Soviet aggression.	Reagan's policies restored prosperity but greatly increased the national debt. G.H.W. Bush led a coalition that defeated Iraq in the Gulf War. Then the Soviet Union collapsed, ending the Cold War. Under Clinton, the economy surged. George W. Bush's first term was defined by massive tax cuts, the terrorist attacks on New York and Washington, and the invasion of Afghanistan and Iraq.	Long-term changes in technology, the world economy and the environment have greatly affected Americans in the past thirty years. Advances in computers and medicine have increased opportunities. However, threats to the environment and the gap between rich and poor nations continues to be a problem that requires complex solutions.

In studying this period, you should focus on the following questions:

❖ How have recent Presidents coped with our nation's domestic problems?

❖ How well have recent Presidents protected U.S. interests in foreign affairs?

❖ What changes can Americans expect in the 21st century?

SECTION 1

THE PRESIDENCY IN CRISIS

In this section you will learn about the domestic and foreign crises that occurred under Presidents Nixon, Ford and Carter

THINK ABOUT IT

Who would you rate as the best President of the 1970s: Nixon, Ford, or Carter? _____

Explain your reasons. _____

_____

Important Terms and Concepts: As you read this section, look for the following:

✦ Détente   ✦ Camp David Accords
✦ Watergate Affair   ✦ Iranian Hostage Crisis

THE NIXON PRESIDENCY, 1969-1974

President Richard Nixon introduced a number of significant changes to U.S. foreign policy. However, the Watergate scandal dominated his second term in office and brought about his sudden resignation.

NIXON AND THE GROWTH OF PRESIDENTIAL POWER

The authors of the Constitution separated the powers of government among the President, Congress and the Supreme Court. This was done to prevent any one branch of government from dominating the other two branches. However, over the last sixty years Presidential powers have grown more rapidly than the powers of the other legislative and judicial branches. Many people believed that the expansion of Presidential power went too far during Nixon's Presidency. Some of his major decisions, such as the invasion of Cambodia during the Vietnam War, were made without consulting Congress. This led Congress to pass the War Powers Act, which limited the ability of the President to send troops overseas without Congressional approval. Nixon's decision to open relations with Communist China — a major change in U.S. foreign policy — was also made without the prior approval of Congress.

Richard M. Nixon

There were several reasons for this growth in Presidential power:

- **Economic Developments**. During the Great Depression, the nation turned to the President to solve the nation's economic problems. The New Deal gave the President greatly increased power over the economy.

- **Foreign Policy Developments**. Two world wars and the Cold War made foreign affairs, over which the President has more influence than either of the other branches of government, very important.

- **Mass Communication**. Radio and television allowed the President to appeal directly to the public for support.

FOREIGN POLICY UNDER NIXON

Nixon believed the President's major role was to direct the country's foreign policy. His program included American withdrawal from Vietnam, opening diplomatic relations with Communist China, and developing better relations with the Soviet Union:

HIGHLIGHTS OF NIXON'S FOREIGN POLICY

Ending the Vietnam War (1969-1973)
Nixon shifted the fighting from American troops to the South Vietnamese army, and began withdrawing U.S. forces. In 1973, Nixon agreed to the Paris Peace Accords, pulling the U.S. out of the war.

Re-Opening Relations With China (1972)
Ever since the communist takeover of China in 1949, the United States had refused to establish diplomatic relations with the government there. Nixon visited Communist China and began to restore normal diplomatic relations.

Détente with the Soviet Union (1972)
Nixon introduced **détente** (*a relaxing of strained relations*) with the Soviet Union. In 1972, he became the first U.S.President to visit Moscow. He also agreed to sell American grain to the Soviet Union to ease a severe food shortage there.

DOMESTIC POLICY UNDER NIXON

In domestic affairs, Nixon wanted to reduce the role of the federal government. He believed that programs such as welfare should be in the hands of state and local officials instead of the federal government. Under his **New Federalism**, he proposed giving local governments greater responsibilities and providing them with federal funds to deal with the problems affecting their citizens.

As a result of the Vietnam War and increased oil prices, serious **inflation** (*rising prices*) occurred in the early 1970s. To combat inflation, Nixon cut government spending on social programs such as education and welfare. He also tried to limit inflation by announcing a sudden freeze on wages and prices; however, this policy was unsuccessful, and the freeze was soon ended.

CORRUPTION IN NIXON'S GOVERNMENT

Despite Nixon's successes in foreign policy, his administration was eventually brought down by internal corruption.

- ■ **Agnew Resigns.** In 1973, **Spiro Agnew** was forced to resign as Nixon's Vice President when it was discovered that he had taken bribes while he was the Governor of Maryland. With Congressional approval, Nixon appointed **Gerald Ford** to replace Agnew.

- ◆ ■ **The Watergate Affair.** In 1972, a group of former government employees, working for Nixon's re-election, was caught breaking into Democratic Party headquarters at the Watergate (*a building in Washington, D.C.*). Nixon denied any knowledge of the break-in, but he also hindered the subsequent investigation, saying that any discussion of the details would endanger American security. During Senate hearings, it was revealed that Nixon had secretly tape-recorded all of his White House conversations. At first, Nixon refused to turn over these tapes, claiming that Congress could not question members of the executive branch without Presidential approval. However, in *United States v. Nixon* (1974) the Supreme Court ordered Nixon to turn over the tapes, confirming the principle that no one, not even the President, is above the law.

When the tapes were finally made public, they showed that Nixon had lied about the break-in and cover-up. Congress took steps to **impeach** Nixon (*remove him from office*). Fearing impeachment, Nixon resigned, and Gerald Ford became President.

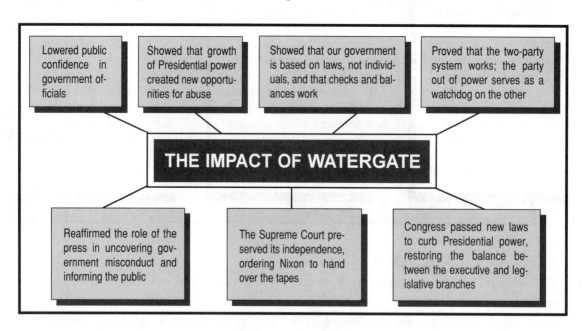

THE IMPACT OF WATERGATE

Lowered public confidence in government officials

Showed that growth of Presidential power created new opportunities for abuse

Showed that our government is based on laws, not individuals, and that checks and balances work

Proved that the two-party system works; the party out of power serves as a watchdog on the other

Reaffirmed the role of the press in uncovering government misconduct and informing the public

The Supreme Court preserved its independence, ordering Nixon to hand over the tapes

Congress passed new laws to curb Presidential power, restoring the balance between the executive and legislative branches

THE FORD PRESIDENCY, 1974-1977

Gerald Ford faced a special challenge on taking office. He had never been elected either as Vice-President or President. Ford had been appointed by Nixon, a man who had resigned in disgrace. When Ford became President, one of his first acts was to **pardon** Nixon (*officially excuse someone who may have committed a criminal act*). This action was heavily criticized.

■ **Economic Worries.** Ford's main concerns were economic. The nation was suffering from **stagflation** — high unemployment combined with inflation. One of the biggest problems that plagued President Ford was high oil prices. By the 1970s America had become dependent on other nations — particularly in the Middle East — for much of its oil. In 1973, oil-producing nations in the Middle East, to protest America's friendship with Israel and its economic support of the Israelis, imposed an **oil embargo** (*refusal to ship oil*) on the United States and other countries. After the Vietnam War ended, nations in **OPEC** (*the Organization of Petroleum Exporting Countries*) continued to limit oil production to keep prices high. This made it very difficult for the Ford Administration to control the soaring inflation in the United States.

Gerald Ford

■ **Foreign Policy.** Ford was unable to get Congress to provide funds to help save the South Vietnamese government. In 1975, South Vietnam fell to the Communists. Cambodia also fell to the Communist Khmer Rouge, which massacred millions of civilians. However, Ford continued Nixon's policy of improving relations with the Soviet Union, and the United States and the Soviet Union signed an important agreement promising to respect human rights.

THE CARTER PRESIDENCY, 1977-1981

Many Americans blamed the Republican party for the Watergate Affair, and Ford lost the 1976 Presidential election to Democrat Jimmy Carter. Carter, a former Governor of Georgia, promised that he would change the way politics in Washington were conducted.

CARTER'S DOMESTIC POLICY

Oil prices continued to climb, and Carter suggested a number of solutions to deal with the energy crisis.

Carter created a Department of Energy, proposed a special tax on cars that wasted gasoline, and encouraged the use of substitute fuels. He also cut federal spending in order to fight escalating prices. However, inflation, oil shortages and high unemployment continued throughout the Carter years.

Jimmy Carter addressing a joint session of Congress

300 300 CONTEMPORARY AMERICA

FOREIGN POLICY UNDER CARTER

Carter enjoyed several triumphs in foreign policy. However, he also suffered major defeats.

- **Human Rights.** Carter wanted America to assert world leadership by setting a moral example. He made human rights a high priority. He condemned apartheid in South Africa, pressured the Soviet Union to allow Soviet Jews to emigrate, and cut U.S. aid to dictatorships (such as Chile and Argentina) that violated human rights.

- ◆ **The Camp David Accords.** Carter's greatest foreign policy achievement was the Camp David Accords. Egypt and Israel had fought wars in 1948, 1956, 1967, and 1973. Carter invited Egypt's President **Anwar Sadat** and Israel's Prime Minister **Menachem Begin** to Camp David, where a peace agreement between the two nations was reached in 1978. Under the Camp David Accords, Israel agreed to return the Sinai Peninsula to Egypt (*see map*), in exchange for a peace treaty and normal diplomatic relations between the two countries. The Accords asserted America's leadership role and its interest in stability in the Middle East.

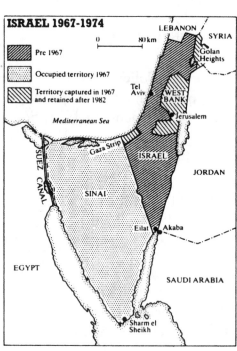

- **The Panama Canal Treaty (1977).** Carter felt the United States should set an example for the world by doing what was right and respecting local feelings. Since 1903, the U.S. had controlled the Panama Canal Zone. In 1977, Carter negotiated a new treaty, which was ratified by the Senate. In it, the United States agreed to turn the canal over to Panama in 1999.

- **Iranian Revolution.** The **Shah** (*ruler*) of Iran was modernizing his country, and was a loyal ally of the United States. But he was also a dictator who used secret police and brutal measures against his opponents. In 1978, widespread demonstrations broke out against him. The Shah, who was ill, fled the country and went to the United States for medical treatment. An Islamic fundamentalist religious leader, **Ayatollah Khomeini**, became Iran's new ruler. Khomeini rejected the Western cultural and technological changes introduced by the Shah. He was determined to return the people of Iran to the "fundamental" (*basic*) beliefs, laws and values of Islam.

- ◆ **The Iran Hostage Crisis (1979-1981).** Soon after coming to power, Ayatollah Khomeini broke off diplomatic relations with the United States. Iran's leaders decided to punish the United States for helping the Shah and supporting Israel. Their supporters took over the U.S. Embassy in Iran. Fifty-two staff members were held hostage for 444 days. Although Carter tried to free the hostages, all of his attempts failed. America's image abroad suffered because of Carter's inability to obtain the hostages' release. They were finally freed just as Ronald Reagan was sworn in as President.

■ **U.S.-Soviet Relations.** Carter continued the policy of détente with the Soviet Union. However, when the Soviet Union invaded Afghanistan in 1979, détente came to a temporary halt. Carter stopped all U.S. grain sales to the Soviet Union and refused to permit American participation in the 1980 Olympics, held in Moscow.

THE IMPACT OF GEOGRAPHY ON HISTORY

Until the 1970s, most Americans lived in the Northeast and Midwest, with hot summers and cold winters. The Southeast was considered too humid and hot in the summer, while the West was too dry and remote. Technological developments changed this situation. Government-built dams made water available to western cities. Hydroelectric power and air conditioning made it possible to keep homes, offices, and factories cool in summer.

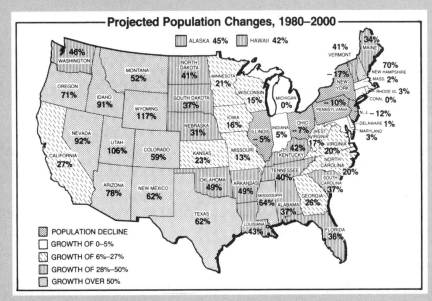

The result has been a shift of population to the West and South — known as the "Sunbelt." With rising oil prices, Americans chose warm winters over snow and cold. California and Texas are now the states with the largest populations, while Atlanta and Las Vegas are among the nation's fastest growing urban regions. As the nation moves into the 21st century, population declines in the Northeast and Midwest continue. The Southeast has become the fastest growing section of the nation.

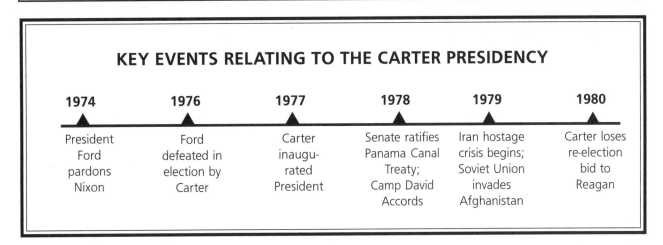

KEY EVENTS RELATING TO THE CARTER PRESIDENCY

1974	1976	1977	1978	1979	1980
President Ford pardons Nixon	Ford defeated in election by Carter	Carter inaugurated President	Senate ratifies Panama Canal Treaty; Camp David Accords	Iran hostage crisis begins; Soviet Union invades Afghanistan	Carter loses re-election bid to Reagan

Having trouble understanding this timeline? The Skill Builder on the next page will help.

SKILL BUILDER: UNDERSTANDING TIMELINES

On occasion, American history examinations may ask you to interpret information on a timeline. It is helpful to know what to look for in answering this type of question.

What Is a Timeline?

A timeline lists a group of events arranged in chronological order along a line. **Chronological order** means the order in which the events occurred, so that the first event that took place is also the first event to appear on the line. The span of the timeline can be anything from a short period to several thousand years. The main function of a timeline is to show how events in a given time period are related to each other.

Keys to Understanding a Timeline

To understand a timeline, look at its major components:

Title. The title tells you what the topic is. For example, the title of the timeline on the previous page is "Key Events Relating to the Carter Presidency." The line lists important events just before and during Carter's Presidency.

Special Terms. To understand questions about timelines or chronology, you must learn some special terms. A **decade** refers to a ten-year period. A **century** is a one-hundred-year period. Thus, the 20th century refers to the 100 years from 1901 to 2000. Counting centuries may seem confusing at first. For example, the 1900s are known as the twentieth century. This came about because the first 100 years after what many believe to have been the birth of Jesus

were the years 1-100. That was the first century.

1-100	First Century
101-200	Second Century
201-300	Third Century
301-400	Fourth Century

Which century includes the years 1601 - 1700? _____

What will the century including the years 2001 - 2100 be called? _____

Measuring the Passage of Time. To measure the passage of time from one date to another, subtract the smaller from the larger date. How long ago was 1776? If the present year is 2000, just subtract 1776:.

$$
\begin{array}{r}
2000 \quad \text{(2000 years since year 1)} \\
-1776 \quad \text{(1776 years since year 1)} \\
\hline
224 \quad \text{years ago}
\end{array}
$$

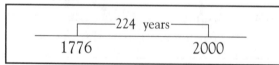

How much time passed between the end of the Civil War in 1865 and the 1954 *Brown v. Board of Education* decision? _____ years.

Interpreting a Timeline

Events on a timeline relate to the title. For questions about time *span*, the events are usually arranged from the earliest on the left to the most recent on the right. Timelines are used to make a point. For example, in our timeline the events show the achievements and problems of Carter's Presidency.

SUMMING UP: THE PRESIDENCY IN CRISIS

In the 1970s, American Presidents faced both foreign and domestic challenges. President Nixon had foreign policy successes, but was forced to resign over the Watergate Affair. After President Ford's pardon of Nixon, the problems of stagflation cast doubt on Ford's ability to lead. President Carter was not able to solve these economic problems either, and his inability to free U.S. hostages in Iran led many to believe the U.S. needed a stronger leader.

THINKING IT OVER

Now that you have read about the 1970s, whom would you rate as the best President of this period: Nixon, Ford or Carter? _____

Explain. _____

_____

CHECKING YOUR UNDERSTANDING

Directions: Complete the following cards. Then answer the multiple-choice questions.

THE WATERGATE AFFAIR

What happened?_____

Why was the affair important?_____

_____

CAMP DAVID ACCORDS

Who was involved? _____

Why were the Accords important?_____

_____

1 A major foreign policy change made by President Nixon was the
1 end of United States participation in NATO
2 establishment of diplomatic relations with communist China
3 closing of all military bases around the Soviet Union
4 boycott of the Moscow Olympics

2 During the Ford Presidency, the United States experienced
1 a booming economy
2 a lowering of oil prices
3 stagflation
4 a deflation of the currency

3 Which of the following events did *not* occur during the Carter Administration?
1 the Camp David Accords
2 U.S. participation in the 1980 Olympics in Moscow
3 the Panama Canal Treaty
4 the Iranian hostage crisis

4 Information on subjects such as the Watergate Affair, Vice President Agnew's resignation and détente would be found in a book on the
1 Nixon Administration
2 Reagan Administration
3 Carter Administration
4 Bush Administration

SECTION 2

THE PRESIDENCY FROM REAGAN TO THE PRESENT

In this section you will learn about the
presidencies of Ronald Reagan, George H.W. Bush,
Bill Clinton, and George W. Bush

THINK ABOUT IT

What do you think were the most important differences among Presidents Ronald Reagan,
George H. W. Bush, Bill Clinton and George W. Bush?

_____

Important Terms and Concepts: As you read this section, look for the following:

✦ **Reagan Doctrine**   ✦ **Persian Gulf War**
✦ **Iran-Contra Affair**   ✦ **Terrorism**

THE REAGAN PRESIDENCY, 1981-1989

President Ronald Reagan introduced far-reaching changes in both domestic affairs and foreign
policy.

DOMESTIC POLICIES UNDER REAGAN

President Reagan believed that individuals, businesses and local governments were able to solve
problems better than federal government programs could. He set out to reduce the role of the federal government in American life. Reagan reversed the trend that had begun with the New Deal:
that the federal government should help to solve all major domestic problems.

■ **Tax Cuts and Domestic Spending**. When Reagan took office, the key problems facing
   the nation were rising prices and high unemployment. Reagan tried to ease unemployment by cutting taxes on businesses and the wealthy. He believed that this would result
   in more investment in new businesses, leading to production of more goods and the creation of more jobs. To help pay for his tax cuts, Reagan reduced spending on government welfare and education programs.

■ **Increased Military Spending**. While cutting taxes, Reagan increased military spending
   sharply. He believed the armed forces were not strong enough to confront the Soviet
   Union. New military spending created a demand for many goods and services, which
   helped the economy to grow. However, the government did not collect enough taxes to
   pay for this military buildup and had to borrow money. The **national debt** doubled under President Reagan.

In order to curb inflation, which had plagued the economy throughout the 1970s, the Federal Reserve tightened credit sharply. This caused a deep recession in 1981-1982, but then the economy rebounded and continued to grow with low inflation.

FOREIGN POLICY UNDER REAGAN

As President, Reagan set out to restore American confidence. He believed that the United States should act as the world's defender of freedom and democracy.

Ronald Reagan

- **The Reagan Doctrine.** Reagan announced that the United States would go beyond trying to stop communism from spreading. Instead, the U.S. would aid rebels fighting to free their countries from communist control. Under this policy, the U.S. sent weapons to groups fighting communism in Afghanistan and other countries. In 1983 Reagan sent U.S. marines to **Grenada** in the Caribbean, just after communists had taken control, and defeated them. This prevented Cuba and the Soviet Union from using Grenada to spread communism to other areas.

- **Terrorism** (*bombings, assassinations or kidnappings by groups or individuals, either for revenge or to get publicity for their views*). Reagan was determined to show that America would not give in to terrorist demands, but he did not want to take any action that would permit them to kill innocent people. In 1983, Muslim extremists blew up a U.S. barracks in Lebanon, killing 241 marines; the U.S. withdrew from Lebanon. In 1986, Reagan received proof that Libya's dictator was aiding terrorists, and had his headquarters bombed.

- **The Iran-Contra Affair.** In 1986, the Reagan Administration secretly sold weapons to Iran, in exchange for the release of U.S. hostages being held in Lebanon by pro-Iranian groups. Profits from the weapons sales were then used to support rebels (*called "contras"*) who were fighting the communist government in Nicaragua. This violated a U.S. law forbidding further aid to the Nicaraguan rebels. Although an investigation by Congress cleared the President of wrongdoing, several government officials were convicted of lying to Congress and went to prison.

- **The Thawing of the Cold War.** When Reagan became President, the Soviet Union was still a dangerous enemy. To help protect the nation, Reagan approved spending for research on anti-missile devices, known as the **Strategic Defense Initiative** or "Star Wars." The failures of the Soviet economic and political system finally forced the communist leadership to introduce changes, giving their citizens a larger voice in government. Soviet President **Mikhail Gorbachev** agreed to allow peaceful change in Eastern European countries like Poland, East Germany and Czechoslovakia. Presidents Reagan and Gorbachev held a number of meetings, and in 1987 they signed a major agreement to dismantle thousands of intermediate range nuclear missiles.

THE GEORGE H.W. BUSH PRESIDENCY, 1989-1993

George H.W. Bush had served as Vice President under President Reagan. In 1988, Bush successfully campaigned on a promise to continue Reagan's policies. He also pledged to help the homeless and the poor, to improve education, and to step up the war on illegal drugs.

DOMESTIC POLICIES UNDER BUSH

Bush's experience had mainly been in the area of foreign policy. Some critics believed that President Bush should have paid more attention to domestic matters like the economy.

■ **Recession.** Bush's greatest challenge was to reduce the growing budget debt, which was costing U.S. taxpayers billions of dollars in interest payments. Some economists believe that this debt helped push the economy into a recession by 1990. Many companies went bankrupt and thousands of workers lost their jobs. As a result of the recession President Bush's approval ratings began to drop.

■ **Civil Rights and Civil Unrest.** Bush promoted civil rights when he signed into law the **Americans with Disabilities Act of 1990**, guaranteeing rights and accessibility to disabled Americans. However, many African Americans accused the Bush administration of doing little to help them. Bitterness boiled over into riots in Los Angeles and other cities when a jury found four policemen not guilty of beating **Rodney King**, an African American, even though the incident had been videotaped by a bystander.

FOREIGN POLICY UNDER BUSH

President Bush focused much of his attention on foreign affairs.

■ **The Invasion of Panama (1989).** President Bush acted against dictator and drug dealer **Manuel Noriega**. He sent American forces to invade Panama, restore democratically elected leaders, and bring Noriega to the U.S. He was convicted on drug charges.

◆ ■ **The Persian Gulf War (1990).** The Gulf War was George H.W. Bush's greatest foreign policy success. Iraqi dictator Saddam Hussein ordered his army to invade Kuwait, capturing Kuwait's vast oil wealth. Hussein refused a United Nations demand to withdraw. When all attempts at negotiating a peaceful solution failed, American and United Nations coalition forces launched air attacks against Iraq. In early 1991, coalition ground forces invaded Kuwait and forced Hussein's troops back into Iraq. Hussein agreed to pay damages to Kuwait, and President Bush declared a cease-fire.

President Bush addresses the U.N.

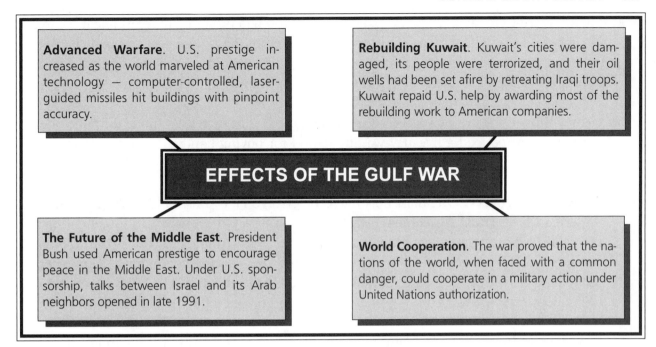

Advanced Warfare. U.S. prestige increased as the world marveled at American technology — computer-controlled, laser-guided missiles hit buildings with pinpoint accuracy.

Rebuilding Kuwait. Kuwait's cities were damaged, its people were terrorized, and their oil wells had been set afire by retreating Iraqi troops. Kuwait repaid U.S. help by awarding most of the rebuilding work to American companies.

EFFECTS OF THE GULF WAR

The Future of the Middle East. President Bush used American prestige to encourage peace in the Middle East. Under U.S. sponsorship, talks between Israel and its Arab neighbors opened in late 1991.

World Cooperation. The war proved that the nations of the world, when faced with a common danger, could cooperate in a military action under United Nations authorization.

THE END OF THE COLD WAR00

Within two years of Bush's inauguration, Eastern Europe moved from communism to democracy, the Berlin Wall was torn down and Germany was reunited. In addition, democratic changes swept through the Soviet Union. These changes eventually led to the breakup of the Soviet Union in 1991, which was replaced by a looser arrangement known as the **Commonwealth of Independent States**. Bush recognized the newly independent nations and offered them economic assistance.

THE CLINTON PRESIDENCY, 1993-2001

In the Presidential election of 1992, Bill Clinton successfully united different groups within the Democratic Party to end twelve years of Republican rule. The public believed President Bush had not done enough to fight the recession. The criticisms of third-party candidate **Ross Perot** regarding the national debt helped weaken Bush's prestige. Clinton was elected with 43% of the popular vote.

CLINTON'S DOMESTIC POLICY

Clinton had an ambitious agenda of reform, but like many Presidents, he was often unable to obtain Congressional support.

Bill Clinton taking the oath of office

- **The Budget Deficit**. Clinton's first budget limited federal spending, increased income taxes for wealthy Americans, raised the gasoline tax, and increased the Earned Income Tax Credit for working families. Throughout his term in office, Clinton and the Congress agreed on annual budgets that reduced spending. This debt reduction was so successful that, combined with strong economic growth, the nation began to have budget surpluses for the first time in many years.

- **Health Care Reform**. During the campaign, Clinton had promised to reform health care. He appointed his wife, **Hillary Clinton,** to head a task force whose goal was to give every American guaranteed health insurance. Although many alternative plans were proposed, none were acceptable to Congress. This marked a major defeat for Clinton.

- **Crime Bills**. Clinton was successful in passing a bill that increased funds for police departments, introduced a five-day waiting period for buying handguns, increased federal money for prisons, and banned sales of assault weapons.

- **Economic Recovery**. Originally negotiated by George H.W. Bush, **NAFTA (the North American Free Trade Agreement)** was pushed through Congress by Clinton, creating a favorable trade association with Mexico and Canada. Tariffs among the three countries are being gradually phased out. Clinton's policies and the growing computer and Internet-related industries restored the economy. In his second term, employment rose to historic highs, consumer spending and business profits soared, and inflation was low.

- **Scandal and Impeachment**. Clinton was elected to a second term in 1996. In less than a year he became the subject of a major scandal. A federal prosecutor, who had been investigating Clinton's financial affairs during his governorship of Arkansas, was given information about a sexual encounter between the President and a White House intern. The prosecutor later determined that the President had lied under oath about the matter, and recommended **impeachment** *(indictment for a crime while holding office)*. The Republican-dominated House of Representatives voted to impeach the President, but the vote in the Senate fell short of the two-thirds majority required to remove him from office.

CLINTON'S FOREIGN POLICY

Unlike George H.W. Bush, Clinton came to the White House with little experience in foreign affairs. Nevertheless, some of his greatest successes were achieved in foreign policy.

- **Russia**. Clinton followed Bush's policy of maintaining friendly relations with Russian President **Boris Yeltsin**, the first democratically-elected president in that nation's history. Clinton also encouraged the growth of free markets in Russia.

- **Yugoslavia, Bosnia, and Kosovo**. The end of the Cold War renewed ethnic tensions in Yugoslavia, which had split into several separate states. Serbs nationalists attacked Croatia, as well as Muslims in Bosnia. When Serbs persecuted Muslims in Kosovo, Clinton spearheaded the use of NATO forces, which bombed Serbia and brought an end to the bloodshed. International peacekeepers were deployed in Bosnia and Kosovo.

- **China**. At first, Clinton tried to promote human rights by threatening to link U.S.-China trade with moves toward democracy in China. He abandoned this policy, but continued to encourage reform. In 1999, U.S. missiles accidentally hit the Chinese embassy in Serbia during the bombing there. Chinese demonstrators attacked the U.S. embassy in Beijing, throwing rocks and chanting anti-U.S. slogans, but there was no attempt to halt U.S.-China trade. By the end of the year, the U.S. had helped China to join the World Trade Organization, further strengthening economic ties.

THE GEORGE W. BUSH PRESIDENCY, 2001 - PRESENT

The election of 2000 was one of the most extraordinary in the history of the United States. The Governor of Texas, George W. Bush (son of former president George H.W. Bush) ran against Al Gore, Clinton's Vice President. Gore won the popular vote, but in Florida the vote tally was so close that it was not clear who had won the electoral vote. After several weeks of indecision, election officials in Florida certified Bush as the winner, giving him Florida's electoral votes. Gore disputed this result in the Florida Supreme Court and won the right to have the votes in several counties recounted. However, Bush's attorneys went to the U.S. Supreme Court to stop the recount. In a 5-4 decision, the Court agreed, thus making Bush the winner.

President George W. Bush

BUSH'S DOMESTIC POLICY

■ **Recession**. A recession began in 2001, and President Bush pushed a series of tax cuts through Congress to simulate the economy. In addition, the Federal Reserve Board lowered interest rates to levels not seen in decades. These measures increased the GDP, and slowly the economy began to recover. However, they also wiped out a large budget surplus that had accumulated during Clinton's last year in office and caused a return to deficit spending.

■ **Education**. As Governor of Texas, Bush had taken an active role in reforming education. As President, he introduced the **No Child Left Behind Act**, which required states to give standardized tests in English and math, starting in third grade. Students who fail the tests are to be given special help to catch up with their classmates.

■ **Faith-Based Initiatives**. Noting that many religious groups had been successful in treating drug addicts and reforming prisoners, Bush got Congress to pass a law allowing faith-based groups to compete with secular organizations for federal funding of these and other programs. Some people believe this violates the "separation of church and state" principle of the First Amendment, and have challenged it in court.

■ **Employment**. During the first three years of Bush's term, the economy failed to create enough jobs to absorb the 300,000 new workers who enter the job market each month. Among the causes of this were: Outsourcing (sending computer and other technology jobs to countries with low-wage labor, where the work is done over the Internet); free trade agreements that encourage manufacturers to close factories and move their operations to foreign countries, in order to cut their labor costs; and high levels of immigration. In 2004 there was a surge in jobs, but employment insecurity is still widespread.

■ **Terrorists Attack the U.S.** On the morning of September 11, 2001, nineteen Islamic fundamentalists boarded four different jet planes in Boston and Washington, D.C. Once airborne, they hijacked the airliners and took control. Two of the planes flew into the World Trade Towers in New York City, and one plane hit the Pentagon in Washington. On the fourth plane (whose target was later discovered to be either the White House or the Capitol Building), the hijackers were fought by passengers who had learned of the other attacks by cell phone. The plane crashed in a field in Pennsylvania, killing all those on board. Almost 3,000 people died at the hands of terrorists that day — the worst attack ever on American soil.

The Trade Towers burning

BUSH'S FOREIGN POLICY

During the campaign, Bush had pledged to conduct a more humble foreign policy, and to avoid attempts at "nation-building" such as Clinton had pursued in Bosnia and Kosovo. Bush had expected to focus mainly on domestic policy, but the 9/11 attacks drastically changed his priorities.

■ **The War on Terrorism.** President Bush launched a worldwide "war" on terrorists, and declared that nations harboring or financing terrorists would be targets as well. The prime suspects in the 9/11 attacks were **Osama bin Laden** and his terrorist group **Al-Qaeda**. They were protected by the **Taliban**, the Islamic fundamentalist government of Afghanistan. When the Taliban refused to turn over bin Laden and the other terrorists, Bush ordered air and ground assaults that toppled the Taliban and destroyed bin Laden's training bases. Although many members of Al-Qaeda were caught, bin Laden escaped into the mountains. In 2004 free elections were held in Afghanistan, and a new government took office.

■ **The War in Iraq.** In 1991, U.N. inspectors had discovered weapons of mass destruction (WMDs) in Iraq — biological and chemical weapons, and a nuclear program. Although they destroyed these WMDs, dictator **Saddam Hussein** had the capability to make them again. Bush feared he might sell them to terrorists, and got a U.N. resolution forcing him to submit to more WMD inspections. France, Germany and Russia favored a cautious approach, but in March 2003, Bush gave Saddam 24 hours to leave Iraq. When he refused, the U.S., Britain and Spain launched air strikes and an invasion. Saddam's regime quickly collapsed, and he went into hiding. No WMDs were found after the war, but Saddam was captured and is awaiting trial for crimes against humanity.

A powerful insurgency (*resistance movement*) has been ambushing and bombing the occupying troops and Iraqis who cooperate with them.

In 2004, Bush ran for a second term against Senator John Kerry. Kerry criticized the war in Iraq, but Bush won both the popular vote and the electoral vote in another narrow contest.

SUMMING UP: THE PRESIDENCY FROM REAGAN TO THE PRESENT

The Reagan presidency limited government's role in American life. Prosperity was fueled by government borrowing and a rising debt. George H.W. Bush's greatest success was defeating Iraq in the Gulf War. Although the Cold War ended in 1991, Bush's defeat in the 1992 election was partly due to the recession. Clinton promised major domestic reforms, but got few of them through Congress. However, his policies produced the best economic times since the 1960s. George W. Bush's presidency is marked by tax cuts and the war on terrorism.

THINKING IT OVER

Now that you have read about Presidents Reagan, George H.W. Bush, Clinton, and George W. Bush, what were their most important differences and similarities?

Differences: _____

Similarities: _____

CHECKING YOUR UNDERSTANDING

Directions: Complete the following cards. Then answer the multiple-choice questions.

IRAN-CONTRA AFFAIR

What did the government do? _____

What resulted after it was revealed? _____

_____

THE IRAQ WAR

Why did it begin? _____

What are some of the results? _____

_____

1 President Reagan's federal budgets were criticized because they
   1 lowered interest rates
   2 produced very large budget deficits
   3 increased social welfare spending
   4 increased income taxes

2 A major difference between the Presidencies of Lyndon Johnson and Ronald Reagan was that President Reagan
   1 had a good relationship with labor unions
   2 followed an isolationist foreign policy
   3 called for local governments and businesses to take on a larger role in domestic programs
   4 supported allowing women to serve in combat

3 The U.S. took military action after Iraq's invasion of Kuwait in 1990 because that region of the world
   1 supplies the U.S. with computer technology
   2 is a major source of oil for the U.S.
   3 provides most of the coal used in the U.S.
   4 supplies the U.S. with wheat

4 Which of the following was a major reason for the collapse of the Soviet Union and the end of the Cold War?
   1 the OPEC oil embargo
   2 a violent revolution by people in the Soviet Union
   3 the failure of the Soviet economic system
   4 the reunification of Germany

SECTION
3

LIVING IN A GLOBAL AGE

In this section you will learn about the
long-term changes that have affected
Americans in recent years.

THINK ABOUT IT

Since 1970, Americans have experienced important changes in technology, the global economy and the environment. Which of these changes do you think will have the greatest impact in your lifetime? _____

Explain: _____

Important Terms and Concepts: As you read this section, look for the following:

◆ Internet   ◆ Global Warming
◆ Multinational Corporations ◆ Acid Rain

Perhaps even more important than recent government policies have been several long-term technological, economic and environmental developments. Over the past thirty years, these changes have gradually altered the American way of life.

TECHNOLOGY

Modern technology is based on the application of science to meet our needs. Leading the revolution in technology today are developments in computers and genetics.

THE SHIFT TO A SERVICE ECONOMY

America began as an agricultural nation, with most if its citizens engaged in farming. After the Industrial Revolution, millions of Americans worked in manufacturing. In the past 50 years, however, this nation has experienced a shift from a manufacturing economy to a service or "post-industrial" economy. An American is now more likely to find work in a store, office or school as a salesperson, computer programmer or teacher, rather than as a factory worker.

THE COMPUTER REVOLUTION

The use of silicon chips in place of large transistors launched a technological revolution. Each year computers become smaller, yet are capable of faster processing. Computers now make possible the use of countless labor-saving machines in manufacturing, and have added millions of jobs in the service sector. Much of the increased productivity of American workers in the 1990s was due to the huge increase in the use of computers. The **Internet**, a world-wide linking of computers, makes it much easier to communicate and to find information. **E-commerce** (*buying and selling on the Internet*) is replacing many traditional "brick and mortar" forms of business.

MEDICINE AND HEALTH

Since World War II, the development of antibiotics, vaccines and other medicines have increased life spans and cured many deadly diseases. Americans have become more health-conscious, limiting fat in their diets, drinking less alcohol, and cutting down on the use of tobacco. Cigarette advertising is banned on television, and some states have raised the age for buying alcohol to 21.

Americans are also more aware of the importance of exercise in maintaining good health. Scientists have now mapped the human genome (the 25,000 genes in our 46 chromosomes), and are beginning to use gene therapy to treat Parkinson's Disease and cystic fibrosis. Thousands of other diseases, such as sickle-cell anemia, cancer, diabetes and Alzheimer's, may be cured in this century through **genetic engineering**.

Clean energy: Inside a hydro-electric power plant

ENERGY

Population growth and rising living standards have led to ever-increasing demands for energy. It was once thought that nuclear power was the solution to producing energy without air pollution. However, the 1979 **Three Mile Island** accident in Pennsylvania, in which a nuclear power plant had a partial meltdown, showed the dangers of that technology. It has also proven very difficult to store nuclear waste, since the radioactivity lasts for thousands of years. New sources of oil in Alaska and the Gulf of Mexico have helped meet our energy demands, but Americans look to conservation and new, non-polluting energy sources such as wind, solar and hydro (*water*) power for future needs.

THE GLOBAL ECONOMY

Today, countries around the world have become economically **interdependent**. Huge **multinational corporations** (*corporations with local companies in many countries*) make and sell their products in every corner of the world. By the 1990s, these multinationals controlled half of the industrial assets of the United States and employed millions of workers here and abroad.

Competition among American and foreign multinational corporations is intensifying. The United States, once a manufacturing giant, now produces just a fraction of the world's steel, clothing, toys, and other goods. American automobile manufacturers, once the world's largest, now face stiff competition from corporations in Japan, Germany, Britain, and South Korea, who have captured a large share of the American car market.

GLOBAL INEQUALITIES

Vast differences separate the "have" and "have-not" nations of the world. About one-fourth of the world's population lives in developed countries like the United States, where people are relatively well-fed, have access to good medical care, consume great quantities of energy, are wealthier, and live longer. However, three-fourths of the world's people still live in the developing nations of the "Third World."

The gap between the developed countries and the poorer nations is very stark, and poses a challenge for the future. Although the United States is sensitive to the problems of developing nations, this gap has created international tensions.

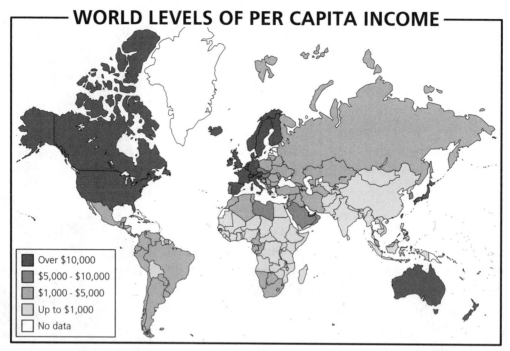

WORLD LEVELS OF PER CAPITA INCOME

- Over $10,000
- $5,000 - $10,000
- $1,000 - $5,000
- Up to $1,000
- No data

To help these poorer nations, the United States contributes money to established international relief agencies which strive to improve education and raise living standards in the Third World. The U.S is the major contributor to the World Bank, which provides loans to developing nations.

In the late 1990s, there was a growing realization that interest payments on the debts owed by Third World nations were hampering their efforts to develop. Discussions began among the industrialized nations about forgiving (*cancelling*) a considerable portion of the debts, to give these "have-not" countries a fresh start.

THE ENVIRONMENT

In the past thirty years, Americans have become increasingly aware of dangers to our environment. As more countries develop and the world's population grows, pollution of the air, water and other resources becomes an ever-increasing threat to the future survival of humankind.

✦ ■ **Global Warming.** Some pollutants in the atmosphere prevent heat from escaping into space. This "**greenhouse effect**" may permanently raise temperatures enough to cause farmland to become deserts, or polar ices to melt, raising seas to dangerous levels. The U.S. is the leading polluter, producing 25% of the world's "greenhouse" gases.

✦ ■ **Acid Rain.** When coal and oil are burned to create energy, they pour pollutants into the atmosphere. Many pollutants released by factories and automobile exhausts turn into acids. These acids get washed out of the air when it rains. They are highly toxic, killing fish, destroying forests, eroding soil, and further endangering the environment.

■ **Shrinking of the Ozone Layer.** The ozone layer absorbs ultraviolet rays passing through the earth's atmosphere. Over-exposure to ultraviolet radiation causes skin cancer. The ozone layer has been rapidly eroded by fluorocarbons used in refrigeration, air conditioners and spray cans. These fluorocarbons are being replaced by safer substances.

■ **Water Pollution.** As cities become more crowded, it is harder for them to handle the increased sewage. Raw sewage is often dumped into rivers and lakes, contaminating people's drinking water. Toxic waste products from factories also pollute waterways.

■ **Solid Waste.** Modern societies generate millions of tons of garbage: bottles, cans, plastic and other waste. Some waste is recycled, but much is put into landfills, which are now filling up. Burning waste or dumping it into oceans and rivers creates pollution. The disposal of toxic chemical by-products and radioactive materials also pose special dangers.

■ **New Efforts.** To deal with these problems, the **Environmental Protection Agency** (E.P.A.) and many state agencies set standards for permissible pollution levels. New projects of any size must now go through detailed environmental impact reviews before being approved. The United States is also cooperating with other countries for a global strategy to reduce pollution and conserve the environment.

SUMMING UP: LIVING IN A GLOBAL AGE

In recent years, changes in technology, the global economy and the environment have been as important as developments in domestic and foreign policy. More powerful computers and the Internet have made possible a global sharing of information. Advances in medicine are improving health and extending life. Americans also benefit from the global economy, which brings us low-cost products from all over the world. However, this means that U.S. companies must compete against overseas producers with much lower labor costs. Globalization also means we are affected by problems in countries around the globe. Americans are concerned about worldwide environmental threats such as global warming, acid rain, air and water pollution, and the shrinking ozone layer.

THINKING IT OVER

What do you now think is the most important recent development that will affect you during your lifetime?

_____

Explain. _____

_____

CHECKING YOUR UNDERSTANDING

Directions: Complete the following cards. Then answer the multiple-choice questions.

GLOBAL WARMING

What is it? _____

Why is it a threat? _____

_____

THE INTERNET

What is it? _____

What are two of its main uses? _____

_____

---

1 Based on recent trends, which statement is most accurate?
1 The pace of technological change can be expected to slow down.
2 The demand for educated, highly skilled workers will increase.
3 The U.S. population will decrease.
4 Future industries will be less automated.

2 Future breakthroughs in finding cures for many inherited diseases is most likely to result from
1 better sanitation standards in cities.
2 genetic engineering.
3 new surgical techniques.
4 preventive medicine.

3 "Emergency Evacuation Ordered in Area around Pennsylvania Plant"
This newspaper headline from 1979 most probably refers to
1 a tornado in Pennsylvania.
2 an accident at the Three Mile Island nuclear power plant.
3 a fire at a Pennsylvania paper factory.
4 major flooding on the Susquehanna River.

4 Russian grain purchases from the United States, sales of Japanese cars in Latin America, and European reliance on Middle Eastern oil are examples of
1 the trend toward higher tariffs on imports.
2 economically self-sufficient nations.
3 the rise of economic interdependence.
4 a worldwide spirit of imperialism.

5 Per capita income in much of the developing world is less than $1000 a year, while in the developed nations it is more than $10,000 a year. Which of the following is a major cause of this income gap?
1 lack of funds for education, technology and medical care in many developing countries.
2 global warming and other environmental problems.
3 the policies of the World Bank.
4 an unwillingness of people in developing countries to work hard.

6 A textbook chapter discusses "acid rain," "the ozone layer" and "the greenhouse effect." The chapter most likely concerns
1 new children's toys.
2 20th-century weapons.
3 the environment.
4 indoor plants.

7 The agency of the federal government that is responsible for dealing with pollution control in the United States is the
1 Food and Drug Administration
2 Environmental Protection Agency
3 Federal Bureau of Investigation
4 National Recovery Administration

8 Acid rain is caused by
1 dumping acids into waterways.
2 unusual weather patterns.
3 air pollution from burning coal and oil.
4 radiaton from nuclear power plants.

PROFILES IN HISTORY

NEIL ARMSTRONG AND EDWIN ALDRIN (ASTRONAUTS)

For thousands of years, people have gazed up at the moon. In July 1969, six hundred million television viewers watched Neil Armstrong and Edwin "Buzz" Aldrin step out of their lunar module — the first humans to walk on the surface of the moon. This was an enormous achievement for U.S. technology and helped boost American prestige around the world. The U.S. continued to send astronauts to the moon for several years. This magnificent photo of Earth was taken by the astronauts of the last Apollo moon mission from their spacecraft.

CARL BERNSTEIN AND BOB WOODWARD (REPORTERS)

Carl Bernstein and Bob Woodward were reporters for the *Washington Post*. Their newspaper columns were responsible for uncovering the connection between the Watergate break-in and the Nixon Administration. Their daily reports in the newspapers prompted an investigation of the entire Watergate Affair, and eventually led to the resignation of President Nixon.

COLIN POWELL (SECRETARY OF STATE, 2001-2005)

The son of Jamaican immigrants and a decorated officer in the Vietnam War, Colin Powell later became President Reagan's national

security adviser. In 1989, President George H. W. Bush appointed Powell, a four-star general, to be Chairman of the Joint Chiefs of Staff. He provided inspiring military leadership during the Persian Gulf War. Under President George W. Bush, Powell was confirmed as the nation's 65th Secretary of State in 2001.

SANDRA DAY O'CONNOR (SUPREME COURT JUSTICE)

Sandra Day O'Connor served in various elective posts in the state of Arizona —

as assistant Attorney General, as a state senator and as superior court judge. In 1981, she was nominated by President Reagan to the U.S. Supreme Court. She became the first woman in American history to serve on the Court.

THE CONSTITUTION AT WORK

AMERICANS WITH DISABILITIES ACT (1990)

KEY LAWS

This act, signed by President George Bush, prohibits discrimination against the disabled in employment, public accommodations, transportation and telecommunications. The act defines as disabled anyone who has a physical or mental impairment. The act guarantees that they be treated equally in their jobs, and be given easy access to stores, office buildings, theaters, restaurants, stadiums, trains and buses.

THE BURGER COURT

The Supreme Court is often known by the name of its Chief Justice. The Warren Court had seen itself as an instrument of social change. For example, in *Tinker v. Des Moines S.D*, it upheld the right of a student to wear a black armband in school to protest the Vietnam War. The **Burger Court** (1969-1986) usually ruled to safeguard the Constitution against violations by other branches of government. In *Roe v. Wade*, the Burger Court overturned all state laws that made abortions illegal. However, in *New Jersey v. T.L.O*, it ruled that a search of a student's locker without a warrant did not violate the 4th Amendment. In *U.S. v. Nixon*, the Court ordered the President to turn over tapes on the Watergate break-in. The following decision was also made by the Burger Court:

NEW YORK TIMES V. U.S. (1971)

THE COURT SPEAKS

Background: The government tried to block publication in *The New York Times* of a secret study of its Vietnam policy, commonly called the *Pentagon Papers*. The government argued that freedom of the press could be suspended when national security was at stake.

Decision/Significance: The Supreme Court supported the right of *The New York Times* to publish the *Pentagon Papers*. The Court ruled that since the national security of the United States was not threatened, the government's attempt at censorship was unconstitutional.

THE REHNQUIST COURT

The **Rehnquist Court** (1986-present) has produced a shift in the Supreme Court's views. Justices appointed by Presidents Nixon, Reagan and George H.W. Bush have tended to be more conservative than most of the members of the two previous Courts. The Rehnquist Court has reversed or altered some of the decisions of the Warren and Burger Courts, especially in the matters of abortion rights, affirmative action programs, and the rights of defendants in criminal cases. More recent appointees by President Clinton have been less conservative, moving the Court to the "middle of the road."

SUMMARIZING YOUR UNDERSTANDING

Directions: Confirm your understanding of the important terms and concepts in this chapter. Check those you can explain. For those you are not sure of, find the ✦ symbol in the margin next to the term and review it.

- ❏ Détente
- ❏ Stagflation
- ❏ Watergate Affair
- ❏ Camp David Accords
- ❏ Panama Canal Treaty
- ❏ Iran Hostage Crisis

- ❏ Reagan Doctrine
- ❏ Iran-Contra Affair
- ❏ Saddam Hussein
- ❏ Gulf War
- ❏ Osama bin Laden
- ❏ War on Terrorism

- ❏ Internet
- ❏ Genetic Engineering
- ❏ Global Warming
- ❏ Three Mile Island
- ❏ Acid Rain
- ❏ Economic Interdependence

Directions: Fill in the information called for in the following organizers.

Nixon Administration:
_____
_____
_____
_____

Carter Administration:
_____
_____
_____
_____

Reagan Administration:
_____
_____
_____
_____

KEY FOREIGN POLICY DECISIONS DURING RECENT PRESIDENCIES

George H.W. Bush Administration:
_____
_____
_____
_____

Clinton Administration:
_____
_____
_____
_____

George W. Bush Administration:
_____
_____
_____
_____

Nixon Administration:

_____
_____
_____
_____

Carter Administration:

_____
_____
_____
_____

Reagan Administration:

_____
_____
_____
_____

KEY DOMESTIC POLICIES OF RECENT PRESIDENTS

George H.W. Bush Administration:

_____
_____
_____
_____

Clinton Administration:

_____
_____
_____
_____

George W. Bush Administration:

_____
_____
_____
_____

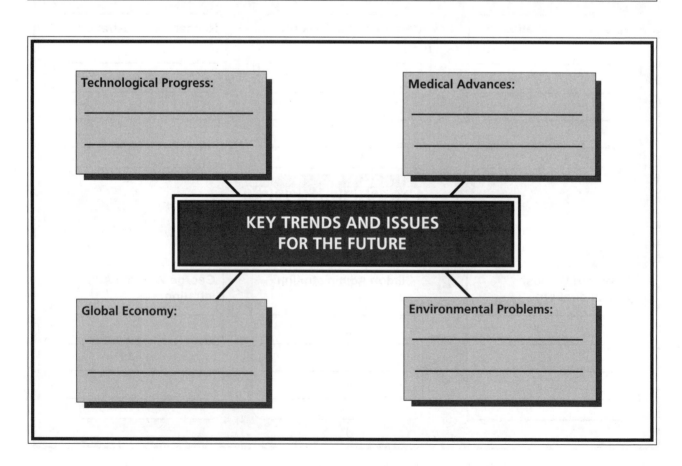

Technological Progress:

_____
_____

Medical Advances:

_____
_____

KEY TRENDS AND ISSUES FOR THE FUTURE

Global Economy:

_____
_____

Environmental Problems:

_____
_____

TEST HELPER

Throughout American history, our national leaders have made decisions that have had important effects on the lives of others. What makes a person a great leader? What makes someone into a person whom others are willing to follow? A leader needs a vision for the future, an ability to communicate this vision to others, and the power to motivate others to act.

TYPES OF LEADERS

Many types of leaders have had a significant impact on U.S. history. Some of the most important have been Presidents, leaders of social movements or economic enterprises, and authors.

PRESIDENTS OF THE UNITED STATES

The President is the chief executive of the federal government. The President has charge of foreign policy, military preparedness and national economic policy. Today, the President is also the leader of a major political party and can communicate to millions of Americans through television. Both the political skills that help a person attain the Presidency, as well as the powers of the Presidency itself, make the President an important national leader. Presidents have been personally responsible for many changes in the United States.

Some of the Presidents you should know:

- ❏ George Washington
- ❏ Thomas Jefferson
- ❏ Andrew Jackson
- ❏ Abraham Lincoln
- ❏ Theodore Roosevelt
- ❏ Woodrow Wilson
- ❏ Warren Harding
- ❏ Herbert Hoover
- ❏ Franklin D. Roosevelt
- ❏ Harry Truman
- ❏ John F. Kennedy
- ❏ Lyndon Johnson
- ❏ Richard Nixon
- ❏ Jimmy Carter
- ❏ Ronald Reagan
- ❏ George H.W. Bush
- ❏ Bill Clinton
- ❏ George W. Bush

Check those Presidents whom you need to read about again.

SOCIAL REFORMERS AND BUSINESS LEADERS

Unlike Presidents, leaders of major social movements or economic enterprises do not hold political office or have the powers of the U.S. government at their disposal. Instead, they share the ability to manage and mobilize people. Great reformers and social leaders are able to organize people into groups that urge social changes and better conditions for their supporters. Great leaders of business — like Henry Ford — are similarly able to organize people and direct their activities towards a common purpose: the production of goods and services in the most efficient way possible. In their different ways, both the social reformer and the business leader have an important influence on society. Some of the economic, social and political leaders who are frequently asked about in U.S. history examinations are:

❑ Susan B. Anthony   ❑ Samuel Gompers
❑ Andrew Carnegie   ❑ Martin Luther King, Jr.
❑ Frederick Douglass   ❑ Eleanor Roosevelt
❑ Marcus Garvey   ❑ Elizabeth Cady Stanton
❑ John D. Rockefeller   ❑ Henry Ford

Check those leaders whom you need to read about again.

AUTHORS

Writers also act as leaders by introducing the rest of us to new ideas and ways of doing things. New ideas and powerfully-expressed communications can have a major impact on the course of history. Some authors frequently asked about on state examinations are:

❑ Rachel Carson   ❑ Upton Sinclair
❑ Betty Friedan   ❑ Harriet Beecher Stowe

Check those authors whom you need to read about again.

ANSWERING AN ESSAY QUESTION ON LEADERS

Often a state examination will include a thematic essay question dealing with the influence of a President or some other prominent leader or writer.

WHAT TO DISCUSS IN ANSWERING QUESTIONS ON PRESIDENTS

Questions on Presidents expect you to be familiar with the main problems of the period and the chief policies of several Presidents. Usually you must either evaluate decisions made by Presidents, or rate their performance. To answer these questions, you have to:

(1) identify the problems faced by a particular President during his term of office
(2) describe the policies favored by that President to deal with those problems
(3) evaluate the effectiveness of these policies by discussing their effects

WHAT TO DISCUSS IN ANSWERING QUESTIONS ON SOCIAL REFORMERS AND BUSINESS LEADERS

Although the information you provide in your answer will depend on whether you are asked about the leader of a social movement or an economic enterprise, your essay should focus on:

(1) What group or enterprise did this person lead?
(2) What problems did the group or enterprise face?
(3) What policies or programs did this leader favor?
(4) What were the effects of these policies?

WHAT TO DISCUSS IN ANSWERING QUESTIONS ON AUTHORS

Writers use words to influence the way people think. Often, they call attention to a problem or issue, focusing the nation on that problem. Frequently they also suggest new solutions. Your answer about a writer should focus on the following:

(1) What topics did this person write about?
(2) What did people believe about this subject before reading this author?
(3) What changes took place as a result of this author's writings?

HOW THIS BOOK HELPS YOU TO ANSWER QUESTIONS ABOUT LEADERS

This book contains several unique and important features designed to help you answer any question that concerns leaders. For example, the names of Presidents, important leaders and writers always appear in **bold** print. In addition, each chapter contains the following:

PROFILES IN HISTORY

In these sections are short paragraphs about some important people who lived during the period covered by the chapter. Each paragraph contains the background information, experiences and accomplishments of the person and discusses his or her impact on the nation and the world.

ANALYSIS

These sections ask you to explore more fully a person's ideas or impact on the nation.

FOCUS ON THE ARTS

These sections feature important people who contributed to American culture. Each Focus looks at a particular person's work and what impact it had on the nation.

SUMMARIZING YOUR UNDERSTANDING

These sections have graphic organizers to fill in, covering several of the most important events discussed in the chapter. This helps you to review essential information about any important leaders discussed in the chapter.

TESTING YOUR UNDERSTANDING

These sections contain multiple-choice questions and essay questions that test your knowledge about influential people. These questions are designed to mirror the type of question you will typically find on comprehensive school and state examinations.

TESTING YOUR UNDERSTANDING

Directions: Circle the number preceding the word or expression that correctly answers the statement or question. Following the multiple-choice questions, answer the essay questions.

Base your answer to question 1 on the following cartoon and on your knowledge of social studies.

1   The main idea of the cartoon is that
   1   President Nixon was toppled from power by the Watergate Affair.
   2   the Watergate Affair is ancient history.
   3   the President holds the key to the nation's future.
   4   President Nixon's social programs were unpopular.

2   During the administration of President Nixon, U.S. policy toward China was characterized by
   1   acts of aggression and war.
   2   the signing of a defense pact.
   3   increasing hostility and isolation.
   4   a relaxation of strained relations.

3   Gerald Ford was the first President who
   1   won the office by running on a third-party ticket.
   2   resigned from the Presidency.
   3   was impeached.
   4   was neither elected to the Presidency nor the Vice-Presidency.

4   The Camp David Accords negotiated by President Carter were significant because they represented
   1   the first peace agreement between Israel and an Arab nation.
   2   the establishment of a worldwide human rights policy.
   3   a lasting arms-reduction treaty.
   4   the end of the hostage crisis in Iran.

5   Which event took place during the administration of George H.W. Bush?
   1   the invasion of Panama
   2   the invasion of Grenada
   3   the Cuban Missile Crisis
   4   the Watergate scandal

6   The Watergate Affair reinforced the idea that
   1   no one, not even a President, is above the law.
   2   the President has unlimited powers.
   3   Congress is not effective during a crisis.
   4   the Supreme Court is afraid to make difficult decisions.

7   One direct result of the Gulf War was that the United States
   1   gained control of oil resources in the Middle East.
   2   liberated Kuwait by driving out Iraq's military forces.
   3   promoted peaceful relations between Iran and its neighbors.
   4   used its military forces to seize colonies in the Middle East.

8   A major reason for the ending of the Cold War was that
   1   economic problems seriously weakened the Soviet Union.
   2   East and West Germany were reunited.
   3   the U.S. was forced to cut military spending.
   4   the U.S. proved to be unable to destroy the Soviet Union.

9 Which statement best reflects President Reagan's views?
1 The federal government needs more power.
2 Taxes should be raised to reduce the federal budget deficit.
3 The federal government should give power back to the states.
4 Military spending should be cut, to provide more funds for social programs.

10 One similarity between the "Open Door Policy" and NAFTA is that both were intended to
1 raise tariffs among nations.
2 expand economic links among nations.
3 Improve relations between the United States and nations in East Asia.
4 relax restrictions on immigration into the United States.

Base your answer to question 11 on this timeline and on your knowledge of social studies.

IMPORTANT EVENTS OF THE CLINTON PRESIDENCY

Bill Clinton defeats George Bush in Presidential election	Clinton inaugurated; pushes NAFTA through Congress	Clinton health care bill defeated; Republicans gain control of Congress	Clinton defeats Dole, is re-elected to second term as President	House of Representatives impeaches (indicts) Clinton	Senate acquits the President; U.S. forces bomb Serbia
1992	1993	1994	1996	1998	1999

11 Which event would the author of this timeline probably consider an important success of the Clinton Administration?
1 Republicans gain control of Congress
2 the passage of NAFTA
3 the impeachment of the President
4 defeat of the health care bill

12 "Lyndon Johnson Decides Not to Run"
"Richard Nixon Resigns Presidency"
"George H.W. Bush Defeated by Clinton"

Based on these headlines, a valid conclusion about the contemporary Presidency is that
1 incumbent Presidents are guaranteed success when seeking re-election.
2 Vice Presidents seldom become Presidents.
3 Presidents are accountable to the voters for their performance.
4 Presidential power is nearly unlimited.

13 President Theodore Roosevelt's Russo-Japanese Treaty at Portsmouth, President Woodrow Wilson's Fourteen Points, and President Jimmy Carter's Camp David Accords are all examples of U.S. actions aimed at promoting
1 international trade.
2 world peace and order.
3 improved environmental standards.
4 effective communications networks.

14 In the close Presidential race of 2000 between George W. Bush and Al Gore, which branch of government prevented a recount?
1 the Legislative Branch
2 the Executive Branch
3 the Judicial Branch
4 an independent government commission

15 During President George W. Bush's first term, which was the most important event?
1 Democrats gained control of the Senate.
2 Al-Qaeda terrorists attacked the U.S.
3 A Constitutional amendment defining marriage was proposed.
4 The U.S. forced Iraq to withdraw from Kuwait.

THEMATIC ESSAY QUESTION

Directions: Write a well-organized essay that includes an introduction, several paragraphs explaining your position, and a conclusion.

Theme: Change

> Special names have sometimes been used to characterize particular time periods in American history.

Task:

Choose the special names given to **two** time periods from your study of American history.

For *each* time period:

- Identify the time period.
- Describe some of the major events that occurred during that time period.
- Explain how a special name for that time period accurately describes social, political, or economic events that took place during that time period.

You may use any examples from your study of U.S. history. Some suggestions you might wish to consider include: the Critical Period (1781-1789), the Reconstruction Era (1865-1877), the Gilded Age (1880-1900), the Progressive Era (1900-1920), the Roaring Twenties (1920-1929), the New Deal Era (1933-1940), and the Decade of Change (1960-1970).

You are *not* limited to these suggestions.

INTERPRETING DOCUMENTS

"Government is not the solution to our problem. Government is the problem."

Place a check next to the President most likely to have made this statement.

- ❏ Franklin D. Roosevelt
- ❏ Ronald Reagan
- ❏ Lyndon B. Johnson
- ❏ Bill Clinton

Describe some of the programs or policies of this President that reflect his belief in the idea expressed in the quotation. _____

DOCUMENT-BASED ESSAY QUESTION

This task is based on the accompanying documents (1-6). Some of these documents have been edited for the purposes of this task. This task is designed to test your ability to work with historical documents. As you analyze the documents, take into account both the source of each document and the author's point of view.

Directions: Read the documents in Part A and answer the question after each document. Then read the directions for Part B and write your essay.

Historical Context:
Throughout American history, decisions by U.S. Presidents have had an impact on American society and affected events abroad.

Task:
Discuss the decisions of some U.S. Presidents by describing the effects those decisions have had on American society or on other countries.

Part A
Short Answer

Directions: Analyze the documents and answer the question that follows each document in the space provided.

DOCUMENT 1

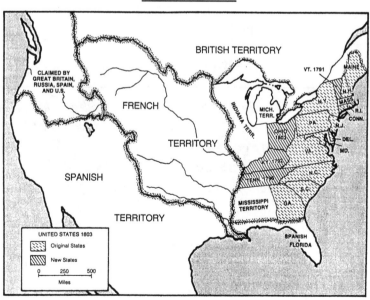

1. How did President Thomas Jefferson's decision to purchase the Louisiana Territory from France in 1803 affect the future development of the United States? _____
_____

DOCUMENT 2

> *"That on the first day of January, in the year of our Lord one thousand eight hundred and sixty-three, all persons held as slaves within any State ... in rebellion against the United States, shall be then, ... and forever free; and the Executive Government of the United States will recognize and maintain the freedom of such persons ..."*
>
> —Abraham Lincoln, *The Emancipation Proclamation,* 1862

2. What were the effects of this Presidential proclamation? _____

_____

DOCUMENT 3

"The program of the world's peace ... as we see it, is this:

1. Open covenants (agreements) of peace, openly arrived at ...

4. Adequate guarantees ... that national armaments will be reduced to the lowest point consistent with domestic safety ...

5. A free, open-minded and absolutely impartial adjustment of all colonial claims ...

14. A general association of nations must be formed ... for the purpose of affording guarantees of independence to great and small states alike."

— President Woodrow Wilson, excerpts from The "Fourteen Points," 1918

3a. Why did President Wilson first issue these Fourteen Points?_____

_____

_____

3b. What role did Wilson envision for the League of Nations, as outlined in Point 14?

_____

_____

_____

DOCUMENT 4

> *"There are ... an additional 3.5 million people who are on relief. This group was the victim of a nationwide depression caused by conditions which were not local but national. The federal government is the only government with sufficient power and credit to meet this situation. We have assumed this task, and we shall not shrink from it. It is the duty of national policy to give employment to these 3.5 million people now on relief, pending their absorption by private employment."*
>
> —President Franklin D. Roosevelt, 1935

4a. How did Roosevelt's message indicate a change in the responsibility of the federal government?

_____

4b. What did Roosevelt do to carry out the "task" he refers to?

_____

DOCUMENT 5

𝕿𝖍𝖊 𝕹𝖊𝖜 𝖄𝖔𝖗𝖐 𝕿𝖎𝖒𝖊𝖘

Price 15¢   *August 7, 1945*

FIRST ATOMIC BOMB DROPPED ON JAPAN; MISSILE IS EQUAL TO 20,000 TONS OF TNT; TRUMAN WARNS FOE OF A "RAIN OF RUIN"

"Impenetrable" Cloud of Dust Hides City After Single Bomb Strike

5. What were some of the long-term effects of the Presidential decision announced in this headline?

_____

_____

_____

_____

DOCUMENT 6

"[O]ur new beginning is a continuation of that beginning created two centuries ago. That system has never failed us, but for a time, we failed the system. We asked things of government that government was not equipped to give. We yielded authority to the National Government that properly belonged to States or to local governments, or to the people themselves. We allowed taxes and inflation to rob us of our earnings. By 1980, we knew it was time to renew our faith, to strive with all our strength toward the ultimate in individual freedom consistent with an orderly society. And we were right to believe that. Tax rates have been reduced, inflation cut dramatically, and more people are employed than ever before in our history."

—Ronald Reagan, Second Inaugural Address, January 1985

6a. In what ways does Reagan claim to have shaped American society since his first election in 1980?

_____

_____

6b. What does Reagan identify as the main goal of American society?

_____

_____

Part B
Essay

Directions:
- Write a well-organized essay that includes an introduction, several paragraphs, and a conclusion.
- Use evidence from the documents to support your response.
- Do not simply repeat the contents of the documents.
- Include specific related information.

Historical Context:

Throughout American history, decisions by U.S. Presidents
have had an impact on American society and affected events abroad.

Task:

Using information from the documents and your knowledge of American history, write an essay in which you:

Discuss the decisions of some U.S. Presidents by describing the effects those decisions have had on American society or on other countries.

Be sure to include specific historic details. You must also include additional information from your knowledge of American history and government.

A FINAL REVIEW

This chapter will help you to continue your preparation for an examination in American history and government by reviewing some important items that may appear on the test. Filling in the graphic organizers will help you remember these items, and will draw attention to those you may need to review further. In addition, charts with brief descriptions of milestones in U.S. political, social, and economic history, as well as foreign policy, will refresh your memory about the most important events and people in American history.

PRINCIPLES OF THE U.S. CONSTITUTION

The system of government established by the U.S. Constitution rests on a series of fundamental principles. Summarize your knowledge of these principles by completing the following chart. The last column indicates the page where you can read about the item if you have trouble recalling it.

CONSTITUTIONAL PRINCIPLE	DEFINE THE PRINCIPLE	HOW THE PRINCIPLE PROMOTES FREEDOM	PAGE
POPULAR SOVEREIGNTY			46
FEDERALISM			46
SEPARATION OF POWERS			49
CHECKS AND BALANCES			49
LIMITED GOVERNMENT			50

MAJOR SUPREME COURT DECISIONS

U. S. Supreme Court decisions have often had a major impact on American government and society. Summarize your knowledge of some of these key decisions by completing the following chart:

CASE	IMPORTANCE OF THE DECISION	PAGE
Marbury v. Madison (1803)		96
McCulloch v. Maryland (1819)		96
Plessy v. Ferguson (1896)		96
Korematsu v. United States (1944)		233
Brown v. Board of Educ. (1954)		260
Roe v. Wade (1973)		273
Gideon v. Wainwright (1963)		283
Miranda v. Arizona (1966)		283

U.S. PRESIDENTS

A number of U.S. Presidents have had a special impact on American history. Summarize your knowledge of their actions by completing the following chart:

PRESIDENT (term of office)	MAJOR SUCCESS OR FAILURE OF THAT PRESIDENT	PAGE
George Washington (1789-1797)		73
Andrew Jackson (1829-1837)		84
Abraham Lincoln (1861-1865)		157
Theodore Roosevelt (1901-1909)		158
Woodrow Wilson (1913-1921)		217
Franklin D. Roosevelt (1933-1945)		267
Lyndon B. Johnson (1963-1969)		296
Ronald Reagan (1981-1989)		304
George W. Bush (2001-present)		309

MILESTONES OF U.S. POLITICAL AND SOCIAL HISTORY

Milestone	Description
The American Revolution (1775-1783)	Colonists became alarmed when the British imposed new taxes without their consent. On July 4, 1776, members of the Continental Congress issued the Declaration of Independence, proclaiming that the purpose of government is to protect the rights of the governed. The Continental Army, led by Gen. George Washington, defeated Britain.
The Constitutional Convention and Bill of Rights (1787-1791)	After independence, the Articles of Confederation created a central government which could not prohibit states from taxing each other's goods or defend against rebellion or invasion. States sent delegates to Philadelphia to write a new Constitution with a national President, Congress, and Supreme Court. The states ratified the Constitution in 1788. A Bill of Rights was added in 1791.
Westward Expansion (1804-1848)	After the American Revolution, settlers streamed over the Appalachian Mountains to settle the Northwest Territory. The Louisiana Purchase (1804) doubled the size of the nation. Americans next annexed California and the Southwest after victory in the Mexican-American War — giving them territory from the Atlantic to the Pacific.
The Civil War (1861-1865)	Sectionalism grew as different ways of life emerged. Southerners relied on slavery, while abolitionism grew stronger in the North. The acquisition of new territories created a crisis as Americans debated whether to extend slavery to these areas. When Lincoln was elected in 1860, Southern states seceded. Determined to preserve the Union, Lincoln led the nation into the Civil War. The North achieved victory but only after four long years of war.
Reconstruction (1865-1877)	During Reconstruction, Americans had to reunify the nation and rebuild the South. Radical Republicans in Congress refused to recognize Southern state governments and imposed military rule. Reconstruction ended in 1877 when Northern troops were withdrawn. White Southerners then deprived African Americans of their voting rights and introduced racial segregation.
Industrialization and the Settlement of the West	After the Civil War, America was transformed by industrialization, urbanization, immigration, the expansion of railroads, and the settlement of the Great Plains and Far West. Native Americans were forced onto reservations.
Grangers and Populists (1867-1896)	High railroad charges and falling food prices led farmers to organize into Grange associations. Later farmers joined the Populist Party, which sought many reforms, including party primaries and a graduated income tax, which were later adopted by the other political parties.

Milestone	Description
The Progressive Era (1900-1920)	Muckrakers and other middle-class reformers exposed the abuses caused by the rise of big business and rapid industrialization. Progressive state governments and Presidents Theodore Roosevelt and Woodrow Wilson helped curb some of the worst abuses.
The Roaring Twenties (1920s)	The passage of the 19th Amendment and the prosperity of the 1920s saw the rise of new cultural values. Women, African Americans and youths enjoyed greater freedom than ever before.
Depression, the New Deal, and World War II (1930s-1940s)	The Stock Market Crash of 1929 led to the Great Depression. President Roosevelt's "New Deal," experimented with new programs to find people work and introduced Social Security and many other reforms. World War II restored full employment as the nation fought for victory.
Post-War Prosperity (1950s-1960s)	After World War II, America emerged as the world's leading economic superpower. Americans bought millions of autos, refrigerators, and other appliances. War veterans moved to suburbs and started families, creating the baby boom. With the onset of the Cold War, America became concerned with internal security.
Civil Rights Movement (1950s-1960s)	The *Brown* decision (1954) and the Montgomery Bus Boycott (1955) inaugurated the Civil Rights Movement. Under Martin Luther King, Jr. and others, African Americans ended racial segregation and made tremendous strides towards racial equality.
The 1960s: A Decade of Change	The Civil Rights Movement was followed by the Women's Liberation Movement, in which women achieved greater equality in the workplace and the home. President Johnson attempted to eliminate poverty with his "Great Society" Programs. A new youth culture emerged in which young people experimented with sexual freedom, new fashions and music, and drugs. The war in Vietnam led to the disillusionment of many with the so-called establishment.
The Presidency in Crisis (1968-1980)	The New Deal, World War II, the Cold War, and the Vietnam War led to tremendous increases in Presidential power. The failure in Vietnam and President Nixon's resignation over the Watergate Scandal led to widespread doubts about the capabilities of our nation's leaders. Presidents Ford and Carter had difficulties copying with rising oil prices, stagflation, and foreign crises.
America Today (1981 - Present)	Under Presidents Reagan, Bush and Clinton, Americans enjoyed a return to prosperity, followed by recession, and then the longest period of economic expansion the nation has ever seen. The Reagan and Bush Presidencies also witnessed the end of the Cold War and the collapse of the Soviet Union. Under President Clinton, Americans have benefited from increased foreign trade and improvements in the computer industry.

MILESTONES OF U.S. ECONOMIC HISTORY

Milestone	Description
Creation of the National Economy	The Commerce Clause of the Constitution and the Supreme Court decision in *Gibbons v. Ogden* (1824) helped create a national economy in which citizens could do business in other states on equal terms — encouraging the free movement of goods, money, and people. This greatly speeded up the growth of the American economy.
Industrial Revolution	Factories, and the use of new machines and sources of power greatly increased the scale of production, changed where people lived, and altered what they produced and consumed.
Abolition of Slavery (1865)	After the Civil War, the plantation system of the South was replaced by sharecropping and light industry; the South fell behind the North in economic power and influence.
The Transcontinental Railroad (1869)	The construction of railroads opened the interior of the nation for settlement, speeded up the pace of industrialization, and linked production centers to large city markets. In addition, railroads helped settle the prairies, leading to the availability of cheaper food to feed the people living in cities.
Urbanization and Immigration (late 1880s)	A new urban culture developed as America was transformed into a nation of city dwellers. Cities became crowded and faced housing shortages. As the need for labor increased, immigrants filled jobs in factories and sweatshops. Despite many hardships, they contributed greatly to the creation of a prosperous economy.
Business Consolidation in the Gilded Age (late 1880s)	The rise of corporations allowed companies to undertake vast enterprises such as the construction of steel mills. The trend toward unfair business practices was limited by federal anti-trust laws like the Sherman Anti-Trust Act of 1890.
Rise of Labor Unions (late 1800s - early 1900s)	Workers gained the right to bargain collectively with their employers over pay and working conditions. Unions obtained better conditions for U.S. workers. The Wagner Act (1935) gave a decisive push to the growth of unions.
Progressive Reforms (early 1900s)	At the state and federal level, Progressives introduced reforms like the Pure Food and Drug Act (1906) to protect consumers and prevent the worst abuses by Big Business.

Milestone	Description
Establishment of the Federal Reserve and the Income Tax (1913)	President Woodrow Wilson introduced a Federal Reserve System to provide stability and flexibility to our national monetary system, and a progressive income tax to raise revenue. The Federal Reserve helped stabilize the economy, while income taxes became the main source of federal revenue, replacing tariffs.
Mass Production of the Automobile	Henry Ford began mass production of the Model T in 1908. The rise of afforable automobiles created a new industry employing millions of Americans. Cars, buses and trucks increased personal mobility, brought different parts of the country closer together, and transformed the American way of life.
The Great Depression and the New Deal (1929-1939)	The Great Depression of 1929 to 1939 was the greatest economic disaster in American history. People were thrown out of work, families lost their homes and farms, banks failed, and national production dropped 50%. The crisis led to increased federal involvement in the economy. President Roosevelt's New Deal introduced Social Security, created jobs, and made the federal government responsible for supervising the performance of the national economy.
World War II and the Post-War Prosperity (1940s-1950s)	The federal government directed national wartime production. Wartime research developed atomic energy, aircraft and computers. Following the war, America prospered as the world's leading producer of manufactured goods.
The Great Society (1960s)	President Johnson introduced new social programs such as Medicare, federal aid to education, and Affirmative Action. These new programs and the costs of the war in Vietnam led to increased federal spending and inflation.
Reaganomics (1980s)	President Reagan's deficit spending and easing of government regulations led to economic prosperity for many Americans. However, minority and low income groups suffered from reduced spending on social programs. Deregulation led to stockbroker scandals and the Savings and Loan crisis; increased military spending created a vast national debt.
The Computer Revolution (1990s)	Almost every part of modern life has been affected by the "computer revolution" — from manufacturing techniques to children's toys. Writers are now more productive because of word processing; lawyers and doctors have immediate access to large computerized databases. The Internet offers new ways to access information worldwide, and to buy and sell goods. Much of the prosperity of the 1990s was due to increases in computer-generated productivity, in which Americans led the world.

MILESTONES OF U.S. FOREIGN POLICY

Milestone	Description
Washington's Farewell Address (1796)	President Washington advised Americans to avoid entangling alliances with European nations. This policy helped the United States keep out of war between France and England until 1812.
War of 1812	In 1812, Congress declared war against Britain in order to stop the impressment of American sailors, to halt Native American raids in the Northwest, and to try to conquer Canada. British troops burned the White House, but the Americans drove them back out to sea. The war ended in 1815.
Monroe Doctrine (1823)	President Monroe announced that America would oppose any attempt by European powers to reconquer former colonies in Latin America that were independent, or to establish new colonies. As a result, the newly independent countries of Latin America preserved their freedom. Later, the Monroe Doctrine was used by the U.S. to justify its interference in the Caribbean region.
Manifest Destiny (mid-1800s)	In the mid-19th century, many Americans held the belief that the United States was destined to expand from the Atlantic to the Pacific coast. The desire for territorial expansion led to the Mexican-American War (1846-1848). Mexico was defeated and forced to give up much of its territory to the United States.
Spanish-American War (1898)	After the DeLôme letter and the sinking of the *U.S.S. Maine*, Americans went to war with Spain to help Cuban rebels win their independence. After the war, Cuba became independent but fell under U.S. control. Spain lost the Philippines and its possessions in the Western Hemisphere.
American Imperialism (1898-1900)	After the Spanish-American War, the United States became an imperialist power by annexing the Philippines, Puerto Rico, Hawaii and Samoa. Americans also developed overseas trade with China and Japan.
The Panama Canal and the "Big Stick" Policy (1902-1914)	Theodore Roosevelt helped Panamanian rebels and reached an agreement with newly-independent Panama to build the Panama Canal. Roosevelt used his "Big Stick" Policy to assert a greater U.S. presence in the Caribbean. The Caribbean became, in effect, an "American lake" under the control of the United States.
World War I (1914-1918)	Events in Europe led to war in 1914. America remained neutral, but entered the war in 1917 after German submarines attacked American ships in the Atlantic. American entry led to an Allied victory by 1918. Germany surrendered, and a revolution in Germany turned that country into a republic.
The Fourteen Points and the Treaty of Versailles (1918-1919)	President Wilson announced his Fourteen Points, which sought to create new states in Europe on the basis of national groups. The Fourteen Points also proposed creating a League of Nations, an international peace organization. Many of the Wilson's ideas were accepted in the Treaty of Versailles but the U.S. Senate, fearing another foreign war, rejected the treaty and the League of Nations. The United States became isolationist.

Milestone	Description
World War II (1939-1945)	World War II broke out when Nazi Germany invaded Poland in 1939. At first, America stayed neutral. Germany conquered much of Western Europe and attacked Russia in June 1941. In December 1941,Germany's ally, Japan, bombed Pearl Harbor, bringing America into the war. World War II was the most destructive war in history. Racial and religious hatred led to the mass murder of European Jews and others in the Holocaust. In the U.S., Japanese Americans were relocated to internment camps in desolate areas. America and its allies landed in France on D-Day (June 6, 1944) and Germany surrendered in May of 1945. The war ended in August 1945, after the U.S. dropped atomic bombs on two Japanese cities. Nazi leaders were brought to trial at Nuremberg. Germany and Japan were occupied by Allied forces and turned into democracies.
The Cold War (1946-1991)	After World War II, America and the Soviet Union emerged as superpowers. When the Soviets imposed Communist governments on Eastern Europe, the "Cold War" began. The U.S. countered Soviet Communism by trying to spread its system of democracy. Germany was divided in two, and an "Iron Curtain" fell between Eastern and Western Europe. The Western allies formed NATO, and the Soviet Union and its satellites formed the Warsaw Pact. Although the superpowers never went to war with each other, they stockpiled nuclear weapons and missiles and became involved in regional crises.
Korean War (1950-1953)	In 1950, Communist North Korea invaded South Korea. The U.S., under a U.N. resolution, sent troops to South Korea to repel the North's attack. When U.S. forces entered North Korea, Communist China entered the war. After three years a truce was signed, leaving Korea divided exactly as before the war.
Vietnam War (1963-1975)	Vietman overthrew French rule in 1954, and was divided in two. Communist North Vietnam began a war against the non-Communist South to reunite Vietnam under Communism. Half a million U.S. troops were sent to aid the South Vietnamese government, but they were unable to defeat the Viet Cong and North Vietnamese. The U.S. finally withdrew, after tens of thousands of Americans had been killed. A million Vietnamese died, and millions more were homeless. Fighting spread to neighboring Cambodia, where local Communists massacred several million innocent civilians. Difficulties in Vietnam led President Nixon to open relations with Communist China and pursue détente with the Soviet Union.
Persian Gulf War (1990)	Iraqi dictator Saddam Hussein invaded oil-rich Kuwait. President George H.W. Bush, with U.N. support, formed a large military coalition that invaded Kuwait and forced the Iraqis to withdraw. The Gulf War was the first example of multinational military cooperation after the end of the Cold War. The allies liberated Kuwait, but decided against toppling the Saddam Hussein regime in Iraq.
Wars in Afghanistan and Iraq (2001-present)	On Sept. 11, 2001 terrorists crashed airliners into the Trade Towers and the Pentagon. President George W. Bush declared a "War on Terrorism." When Afghanistan's Taliban government refused to hand over al-Qaeda leader Osama bin Laden, U.S. forces overthrew the Taliban. The U.S., Britain and Spain, believing Iraq had WMDs they might sell to terrorists, invaded in 2003. The coalition toppled the regime and captured Saddam Hussein. Despite early success, insurgents fighting the occupation are terrorizing the population with bombs and ambushes.

CHAPTER 13

A PRACTICE
FINAL EXAMINATION

Now that you have had an opportunity to review the material in this book, you should take a practice examination to measure your progress. Before you begin, let's look at some common-sense tips for taking such tests:

❖ **Answer All Questions.** Don't leave any questions unanswered. Since there is *no* penalty for guessing, answer all questions — even if only making a guess.

❖ **Use the Process of Elimination.** After reading a multiple-choice question, even if you don't know the right answer, it may be clear that certain choices are wrong. Some choices may be irrelevant because they relate to a different time or place. Other choices may have no connection with the question or may be inaccurate statements. After you have eliminated all the wrong choices, select the *best* choice that remains and write the *number* of that choice on the separate answer sheet.

❖ **Read the Question Carefully.** Underline key words or expressions that are central to the question. If you encounter a word you don't know, look at the prefix (*start of the word*), the root, or the suffix (*ending*) for clues to the word's meaning.

Taking the practice examination that follows will help you to identify any areas that you still need to study. Good luck!

U.S. HISTORY AND GOVERNMENT REGENTS

This New York State Regents Examination was given in August, 2004. It has three parts:

Part I has 50 multiple-choice questions

Part II has one thematic essay

Part III has one document-based essay

PART 1:
ANSWER ALL QUESTIONS IN THIS PART

1 In its economic relationship with its North American colonies, Great Britain followed the principles of 18th-century mercantilism by
   (1) outlawing the African slave trade
   (2) limiting the colonies' trade with other nations
   (3) encouraging the development of manufacturing in the colonies
   (4) establishing laws against business monopolies

2 The principles of government that Thomas Jefferson included in the Declaration of Independence were most influenced by
   (1) John Locke's social contract theory
   (2) Adam Smith's ideas of free enterprise
   (3) Louis XIV's belief in divine right
   (4) William Penn's views on religious toleration

3 The necessary and proper clause, the amendment process, and the unwritten constitution are evidence that our constitutional system of government provides for
   (1) popular sovereignty
   (2) equal representation
   (3) flexibility
   (4) ratification

4 What economic change resulted from the transportation revolution before the Civil War?
   (1) The Northeast became better connected to the western section of the country.
   (2) Trade between the United States and Europe was sharply reduced.
   (3) The system of slavery on southern plantations began to disappear.
   (4) The federal government began to regulate new businesses.

5 In 1788 and 1789, a major controversy between the Federalists and the Antifederalists focused on
   (1) expansion of slavery into the territories
   (2) the wisdom of creating a two-house legislature
   (3) division of power among different levels of government
   (4) the issue of allowing women the right to vote

6 Anti-federalist objections to the ratification of the Constitution led to the
   (1) addition of a Bill of Rights
   (2) seven-year delay in the ratification of the Constitution
   (3) rewriting of major parts of the Constitution
   (4) elimination of states' rights

7 In 1853, Commodore Matthew Perry's visit to Japan was important to the United States because it
   (1) ended the United States policy of neutrality
   (2) opened new trading opportunities in Asia
   (3) began a military alliance between the two nations
   (4) acquired cheap labor for America's factories

8 As the Civil War began, President Abraham Lincoln stated that his primary goal was to
   (1) end slavery
   (2) set new national boundaries
   (3) increase congressional powers
   (4) preserve the Union

9 The Civil War affected the northern economy by
   (1) causing a severe depression
   (2) increasing unemployment rates
   (3) decreasing demand for agricultural products
   (4) stimulating industrialization

10 During the 19th century, New York was one of the most powerful states in the nation because it
   (1) became the financial and industrial center of the nation
   (2) led the nation in achieving political reforms
   (3) produced more presidents than any other state
   (4) offered more civil liberties than any other state

11 During the late 19th century, which practices were used by employers against workers?
   (1) boycotts and lockouts
   (2) picketing and walkouts
   (3) blacklists and yellow-dog contracts
   (4) mass rallies and sit-down strikes

12 The term *robber baron* was used to criticize the
   (1) tactics of big-business leaders
   (2) corruption of government officials
   (3) dishonesty of carpetbaggers
   (4) unskilled labor of illegal immigrants

13 What major trend related to population occurred during the industrialization boom of the late 1800s?
   (1) Immigration decreased.
   (2) Suburbanization decreased.
   (3) Urbanization increased.
   (4) Migration to rural areas increased.

14 The Gentlemen's Agreement, literacy tests, and the quota system were all attempts by Congress to restrict
   (1) immigration   (3) voting rights
   (2) property ownership   (4) access to education

15 One result of the Spanish-American War of 1898 was that the United States was
 (1) recognized as a world power
 (2) committed to isolationism
 (3) drawn into World War II
 (4) forced into an economic depression

16 During the Progressive Era, muckrakers published articles and novels primarily to
 (1) advance their own political careers
 (2) make Americans aware of problems in society
 (3) help the federal government become more efficient
 (4) provide entertainment for readers

17 During his reelection campaign in 1916, President Woodrow Wilson used the slogan, "He kept us out of war." In April of 1917, Wilson asked Congress to declare war on Germany. What helped bring about this change?
 (1) Bolshevik forces increased their strength in Germany and Italy.
 (2) Britain was invaded by nations of the Central Powers.
 (3) Russia signed a treaty of alliance with the Central Powers.
 (4) Germany resumed unrestricted submarine warfare.

18 In the 1930s, shantytowns, often called "Hoovervilles," sprang up across the United States because of President Herbert Hoover's
 (1) support for federal programs to provide jobs for the unemployed
 (2) refusal to provide direct federal aid to the homeless
 (3) efforts to help the residents return to their farms
 (4) emergency relief program to provide food to the poor

19 Supporters of a graduated national income tax argued that it was the fairest type of tax because the
 (1) rate of taxation was the same for all persons
 (2) rate of taxation increased as incomes rose
 (3) income tax provided the most revenue for the government
 (4) income tax replaced state and local government taxes

20 Henry Ford produced a more affordable car primarily because his company
 (1) paid lower wages than its competitors paid
 (2) used foreign-made parts
 (3) developed a less expensive method of production
 (4) offered a variety of options to buyers

21 Which pair of events illustrates an accurate cause-and-effect relationship?
 (1) Sacco and Vanzetti trial → ratification of the woman suffrage amendment
 (2) rebirth of the KKK → formation of the Populist Party
 (3) Red Scare → demand for limits on immigration
 (4) high food prices → start of the Great Depression

22 Which situation helped cause the stock market crash of 1929?
 (1) excessive speculation and buying on margin
 (2) unwillingness of people to invest in new industries
 (3) increased government spending
 (4) too much government regulation of business

23 The Neutrality Acts passed by Congress in the mid-1930s were efforts to
 (1) avoid mistakes that had led the country into World War I
 (2) create jobs for the unemployed in the military defense industry
 (3) support the League of Nations efforts to stop wars in Africa and Asia
 (4) help the democratic nations of Europe against Hitler and Mussolini

Base your answer to question 24 on the cartoon below and on your knowledge of social studies.

A Wise Economist Asks a Question

Source: *Chicago Tribune*, August 19, 1931
(adapted)

24 Which factor contributed most to the situation shown in the cartoon?
 (1) low tariff rates
 (2) shortages of consumer goods
 (3) non-regulation of banks
 (4) creation of a national bank

25 The decision of the Supreme Court in *Korematsu* v. *United States* (1944) upheld the power of the president during wartime to
(1) ban terrorists from entering the country
(2) limit a group's civil liberties
(3) stop mistreatment of resident legal aliens
(4) deport persons who work for enemy nations

26 Why was the United States called the "arsenal of democracy" in 1940?
(1) The leaders in the democratic nations of Europe were educated in the United States.
(2) Most of the battles to defend worldwide democracy took place on American soil.
(3) The United States supervised elections in European nations before the war.
(4) The United States provided much of the weaponry needed to fight the Axis powers.

27 Shortly after entering World War II, the United States began the Manhattan Project to
(1) work on the development of an atomic bomb
(2) increase economic production to meet wartime demands
(3) defend New York City against a nuclear attack
(4) recruit men for the military services

28 The experiences of African Americans serving in the military forces during World War II influenced their postwar decision to
(1) renew support for the principle of separate but equal
(2) join the armed forces in record numbers
(3) increase efforts to end racial discrimination
(4) move back to the rural south

29 The main foreign policy objective of the Marshall Plan (1948–1952) was to
(1) stop communist aggression in Korea
(2) fight poverty in Latin America
(3) rebuild the economies of European nations
(4) provide jobs for unemployed Americans

30 During the Korean War, President Harry Truman removed General Douglas MacArthur from command because MacArthur
(1) called for an immediate end to the war
(2) refused to serve under the United Nations
(3) lacked the experience to provide wartime leadership
(4) threatened the constitutional principle of civilian control of the military

Base your answer to question 31 on the cartoon below and on your knowledge of social studies.

Source: Fred O. Seibel, *Richmond Times-Dispatch*

31 The United States carried out the idea expressed in this late 1940s cartoon by
(1) forming a military alliance with Russia
(2) airlifting supplies to West Berlin
(3) accepting Russian authority over West Berlin
(4) agreeing to turn over control of Berlin to the United Nations

32 What was a result of the takeover of Cuba by Fidel Castro?
(1) Relations between the Soviet Union and Cuba worsened.
(2) Many Cuban Americans returned to their homeland.
(3) Trade between the United States and Cuba increased.
(4) Many people fled from Cuba to the United States.

Base your answer to question 33 on the passage below.

"... I was disappointed not to see what is inside Central High School. I don't understand why the governor [of Arkansas] sent grown-up soldiers to keep us out. I don't know if I should go back. But Grandma is right, if I don't go back, they will think they have won. They will think they can use soldiers to frighten us, and we'll always have to obey them. They'll always be in charge if I don't go back to Central and make the integration happen. ..."

— Melba Beals, *Warriors Don't Cry*,
an African American student, 1957

33 President Dwight D. Eisenhower reacted to the situation described in this passage by
(1) forcing the governor of Arkansas to resign
(2) allowing the people of Arkansas to resolve the problem
(3) asking the Supreme Court to speed up racial integration
(4) sending federal troops to enforce integration

34 In 1965, Congress established Medicare to
(1) provide health care to the elderly
(2) assist foreign nations with their health problems
(3) grant scholarships to medical students
(4) establish universal health care

35 The Supreme Court decisions in *Mapp* v. *Ohio*, *Gideon* v. *Wainright*, and *Miranda* v. *Arizona* all expanded
(1) integration of public facilities
(2) rights of the accused
(3) presidential powers
(4) equality in the workplace

36 The main purpose of the War Powers Act of 1973 was to
(1) expand the power of Congress to declare war
(2) limit the president's ability to send troops into combat abroad
(3) allow people to vote on the issue of United States commitments overseas
(4) end the Vietnam War on favorable terms

37 In the *New Jersey* v. *T.L.O.* and *Tinker* v. *Des Moines School District*, the U.S. Supreme Court ruled that
(1) individual student rights are more important than a safe school environment
(2) students can be expelled from school without a hearing
(3) civil liberties can be both protected and limited in schools
(4) the Bill of Rights does not apply to minors

38 In the United States, regional differences in economic development are primarily due to
(1) settlement patterns of immigrant groups
(2) pressure from various religious groups
(3) state and federal election laws
(4) geographic factors in various parts of the nation

Base your answer to question 39 on the chart below and your knowledge of social studies.

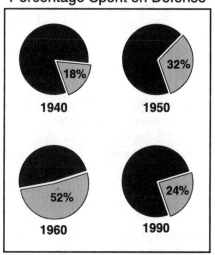

United States Budget, 1940–1990
Percentage Spent on Defense

Source: *Historical Tables*, Budget of the United States Government, Fiscal Year 1997 (adapted)

39 The changes shown on the chart most clearly reflect the
(1) effects of the Cold War
(2) influence of the business cycle
(3) failure of United States military policy
(4) reverses in political party control of Congress

40 In the United States, support for the passage and expansion of the North American Free Trade Agreement (NAFTA) has been strongest among
(1) labor unions
(2) environmentalists
(3) big business
(4) farmers

41 A major goal of the Republican Party since the 1980s has been to
(1) increase welfare benefits
(2) increase the size of the federal workforce
(3) reduce defense spending
(4) cut federal taxes

Base your answer to question 42 on the cartoon that follows and on your knowledge of social studies.

Source: Steve Kelley, San Diego *Union-Tribune*

42 What Native American Indian viewpoint does the cartoonist support?
(1) Illegal immigrants should not be allowed to settle on Native American Indian reservations.
(2) European settlers took Native American Indian land.
(3) Government efforts to restrict immigration should be supported.
(4) Native American Indians support government efforts to stop illegal immigration.

43 During the next 30 years, what will be the most likely impact of the baby boom that followed World War II?
(1) More money will be spent on national defense.
(2) The cost of health care will decrease.
(3) Social Security will have to provide for increasing numbers of retired people.
(4) The elderly will be the smallest segment of the population.

44 Which pair of circumstances represents an accurate cause-and-effect relationship?
(1) more jobs in factories → migration of African Americans from the South to northern cities
(2) establishment of Jim Crow laws → beginning of Reconstruction
(3) Dred Scott decision → passage of the Fugitive Slave Law
(4) closing of the frontier → completion of the transcontinental railroad

45 In a United States history textbook, the terms *bread and butter unionism*, *Gospel of Wealth*, and *mechanization* would most likely be found in a chapter entitled
(1) Reconstruction (1865–1877)
(2) Industrialization (1870–1900)
(3) Imperialism (1898–1905)
(4) The Roaring Twenties (1920–1929)

46 **"Soviets Create Iron Curtain in Eastern Europe"**
"Mao Zedong Leads Successful Revolution in China"
"North Korean Invasion of South Korea Leads to War"

Which development is reflected in these headlines?

(1) the post-World War II expansion of communism
(2) the beginning of détente between the Soviet Union and the United States
(3) the return to an isolationist foreign policy
(4) the beginning of pro-democracy movements during the Cold War

47 Presidents Franklin D. Roosevelt and Lyndon B. Johnson supported domestic policies that
(1) favored only one region of the nation
(2) attempted to increase the wealth of the rich
(3) led to tax cuts for all Americans
(4) provided direct help to those in need

48 The change in the nation's attitude toward membership in the League of Nations and membership in the United Nations shows the contrast between
(1) neutrality and containment
(2) appeasement and internationalism
(3) isolationism and involvement
(4) interventionism and détente

49 The Articles of Confederation and the theory of nullification were both attempts to
(1) strengthen the national government
(2) form new political parties
(3) protect states' rights
(4) strengthen the presidency

50 Which topic has been the focus of four different amendments to the United States Constitution?
(1) voting rights
(2) term limits on federal officeholders
(3) the electoral college
(4) prohibition of alcoholic beverages

PART II: THEMATIC ESSAY QUESTION

Directions: Write a well-organized essay that includes an introduction, several paragraphs addressing the task below, and a conclusion.

Theme: Reform Movements

> *Reform movements have been an important part of United States history.*

Task:

Identify *two* reform movements in the United States since 1800 and for *each* reform movement

- Describe the historical circumstances that led to the need for reform
- State *one* goal of the movement and discuss *two* actions taken by the government, a group, or an individual in support of this goal
- Evaluate the extent to which the reform movement has made an impact on the United States

You may use reform movement in the United States from 1800 to the present. Some suggestions you might wish to consider include the abolitionist movement, Populist movement, Progressive movement, women's rights movement, civil rights movement, and the labor movement.

You are *not* limited to these suggestions.

In your essay, be sure to:

- Address all aspects of the *Task*
- Introduce the theme by establishing a framework that is beyond a simple restatement of the *Task*, and conclude with a summation of the theme.
- Support the theme with relevant facts, examples, and details

PART III: DOCUMENT-BASED QUESTION

Historical Context:
During the 1800s, the federal government promoted westward expansion in a variety of ways. This expansion changed the shape and character of the country.

Task:
Using information from the documents and your knowledge of United States history, answer the questions that follow each document in Part A. Your answers to the questions will help write the Part B essay in which you will be asked to

- Describe the actions taken by the federal government that led to westward expansion during the1800s
- Discuss the impact of westward expansion on the United States

In developing your answers, keep these definitions in mind:

(1) **describe** means "to illustrate something in words or tell about it"
(2) **discuss** means "to make observations about something using facts, reasoning and arguments; to present in some detail."

Part A
Short Answer Questions

Directions: Analyze the documents and answer the short-answer questions that follow each document in the space provided.

Document 1

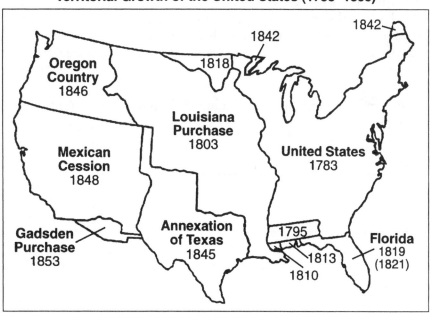

Territorial Growth of the United States (1783–1853)

Source: *Historical Maps On File*, Revised Edition, Facts On File, Inc., 2003 (adapted)

1. Based on the map, state *two* methods used by the United States government to acquire new territory. [2]

(1) _____

_____

Score ☐

(2) _____

_____

Score ☐

Document 2

> *An act to provide for an exchange of lands with the Indians residing in any of the states or territories, and for their removal west of the river Mississippi.*
>
> *Be it enacted by the Senate and House of Representatives of the United States of America, in Congress assembled,* That it shall and may be lawful for the President of the United States to cause so much of any territory belonging to the United States, west of the river Mississippi, not included in any state or organized territory, and to which the Indian title has been extinguished [revoked], as he [the president] may judge necessary, to be divided into a suitable number of districts, for the reception of such tribes or nations of Indians as may choose to exchange the lands where they now reside, and remove there; and to cause each of said districts to be so described by natural or artificial marks, as to be easily distinguished from every other . . .

— Indian Removal Act of 1830

2   Based on this document, state *one* way that the Indian Removal Act of 1830 would affect many Native American Indians. [1]

Score

Document 3

> . . . Instead of this, however, we have been exerting [putting forth] our best efforts to propitiate [gain] her [Mexico's] good will. Upon the pretext that Texas, a nation as independent as herself, thought proper to unite its destinies with our own, she has affected to believe that we have severed [removed] her rightful territory, and in official proclamations and manifestoes has repeatedly threatened to make war upon us for the purpose of reconquering Texas. In the meantime we have tried every effort at reconciliation [restoring harmony]. The cup of forbearance [tolerance] had been exhausted even before the recent information from the frontier of the Del Norte [Mexican-American border]. But now, after reiterated [repeated] menaces, Mexico has passed the boundary of the United States, has invaded our territory and shed American blood upon the American soil. She has proclaimed that hostilities have commenced [begun], and that the two nations are now at war. . .

— President James K. Polk, Message to Congress, May 11, 1846

3   Based on this passage, state *one* reason President Polk asked Congress to declare war on Mexico. [1]

Score

Document 4

> ...Regarding it as a war [Mexican War] to strengthen the "Slave Power," we are conducted to a natural conclusion, that it is virtually, and in its consequences, a war against the free States of the Union. Conquest and robbery are attempted in order to obtain a political control at home; and distant battles are fought, less with a special view of subjugating [conquering] Mexico, than withthe design of overcoming the power of the free States, under the constitution. The lives of Mexicans are sacrificed in this cause; and a domestic question, which should be reserved forbloodless debate in our own country, is transferred to fields of battle in a foreign land...

— Resolution passed by the Massachusetts Legislature opposing the Mexican War;
Massachusetts House Documents, 1847

4 According to this resolution, what was *one* reason the Massachusetts legislature opposed the Mexican War? [1]

Score [ ]

Document 5

Stephen Douglas replied to Abraham Lincoln's question about the Kansas-Nebraska Act in a speech given at Freeport, Illinois. This reply occurred during the second debate in the political contest for the United States Senate seat from Illinois in 1858.

> ... The next question propounded [put forward] to me by Mr. Lincoln is, can the people of a Territory in any lawful way, against the wishes of any citizen of the United States, exclude slavery from their limits prior to the formation of a State Constitution? I answer emphatically, as Mr. Lincoln has heard me answer a hundred times from every stump [platform] in Illinois, that in my opinion the people of a Territory can, by lawful means, exclude slavery from their limits prior to the formation of a State Constitution. Mr. Lincoln knew that I had answered that question over and over again. He heard me argue the Nebraska bill [Kansas-Nebraska Act] on that principle all over the State in 1854, in 1855, and in 1856, and he has no excuse for pretending to be in doubt as to my position on that question. It matters not what way the Supreme Court may hereafter decide as to the abstract question whether slavery may or may not go into a Territory under the Constitution, the people have the lawful means to introduce it or exclude it as they please, for the reason that slavery cannot exist a day or an hour anywhere, unless it is supportedby local police regulations. Those police regulations can only be established by the local legislature, and if the people are opposed to slavery they will elect representatives to that body who will by unfriendly legislation effectually prevent the introduction of it into their midst. If, on the contrary, they are for it, their legislation will favor its extension. Hence, no matter what the decision of the Supreme Court may be on that abstract question, still the right of the people to make a slave Territory or a free Territory is perfect and complete under the Nebraska bill. I hope Mr. Lincoln deems my answer satisfactory on that point. ...

Source: Stephen Douglas, Freeport Doctrine, 1858

5 According to this document, how did the Kansas-Nebraska Act attempt to resolve the issue of slavery in the territories? [1]

Score [ ]

Document 6

... With the secession of Southern states from the Union and therefore removal of the slavery issue, finally, in 1862, the Homestead Act was passed and signed into law. The new law established a three-fold homestead acquisition process: filing an application, improving the land, and filing for deed of title. Any U.S. citizen, or intended citizen, who had never borne arms against the U.S. Government could file an application, improving the land and lay claim to 160 acres of surveyed Government land. For the next 5 years, the homesteader had to live on the land and improve it by building a 12-by-14 dwelling and growing crops. After 5 years, the homesteader could file for his patent (or deed of title) by submitting proof of residency and the required improvements to a local land office.

Local land offices forwarded the paperwork to the General Land Office in Washington, DC, along with a final certificate of eligibility. The case file was examined, and valid claims were granted patent to the land free and clear, except for a small registration fee. Title could also be acquired after a 6-month residency and trivial improvements, provided the claimant paid the government $1.25 per acre. After the Civil War, Union soldiers could deduct the time they served from the residency requirements. . .

— National Archives, *Teaching with Documents: The Homestead Act of 1862*

6   According to this document, how did the Homestead Act encourage the settlement of the West? [1]

_____

_____

Score ☐

Document 7

... Sec.2. *And be it further enacted,* That the right of way through the public lands be, and the same is hereby, granted to said company [The Union Pacific Railroad Company] for the construction of said railroad and telegraph line; and the right, power, and authority is hereby given to said company to take from the public lands adjacent to the line of said road, earth, stone, timber, and other materials for the construction thereof; said right of way is granted to said railroad to the extent of two hundred feet in width on each side of said railroad where it may pass over the public lands, including all necessary grounds for stations, buildings, workshops, and depots, machine shops, switches, side tracks, turn-tables, and water stations. The United States shall extinguish as rapidly as may be, the Indian titles to all lands falling under the operation of this act and required for the said right of way and grants hereinafter made.

Sec.3. *And be it further enacted,* That there be, and is hereby, granted to the said company, for the purpose of aiding in the construction of said railroad and telegraph line, and to secure the safe and speedy transportation of the mails, troops, munitions of war, and public stores thereon, every alternate section of public land, designated by odd numbers, to the amount of five alternate sections per mile on each side of said railroad, on the line thereof, and within the limits of ten miles on each side of said road, not sold, reserved, or otherwise disposed of by the United States, and to which a preëmption or homestead claim may not have attached, at the time the line of said road is definitely fixed: *Provided,* That all mineral lands shall be excepted from the operation of this act; but where the same shall contain timber, the timber thereon is hereby granted to said company. And all such lands, so granted by this section, which shall not be sold or disposed of by said company within three years after the entire road shall have been completed, shall be subject to settlement and preëmption, like other lands, at a price not exceeding one dollar and twenty-five cents per acre, to be paid to said company. . .

— The Pacific Railroad Act, July 1, 1862

7a According to this document, what did the federal government give the Union Pacific Railroad Company to help them construct the railroad and the telegraph line? [1]

_____

Score ☐

b According to this document, how did the Pacific Railroad Act help the U.S. expand westward? [1]

_____

Score ☐

Document 8

. . . The white man, who possesses this whole vast country from sea to sea, who roams over it at pleasure, and lives where he likes, cannot know the cramp we feel in this little spot, with the underlying remembrance of the fact, which you know as well as we, that every foot of what you proudly call America, not very long ago belonged to the red man. The Great Spirit gave it to us. There was room enough for all his many tribes, and all were happy in their freedom. But the white man had, in ways we know not of, learned some things we had not learned; among them, how to make superior tools and terrible weapons, better for war than bows and arrows; and there seemed no end to the hordes [huge numbers] of men that followed them from other lands beyond the sea.

"And so, at last, our fathers were steadily driven out, or killed, and we, their sons, but sorry remnants of tribes once mighty, are cornered in little spots of the earth all ours of right—cornered like guilty prisoners, and watched by men with guns, who are more than anxious to kill us off.

"Nor is this all. The white man's government promised that if we, the Shoshones, would be content with the little patch allowed us, it would keep us well supplied with everything necessary to comfortable living, and would see that no white man should cross our borders for our game, or for anything that is ours. _But it has not kept its word!_ The white man kills our game, captures our furs, and sometimes feeds his herds upon our meadows. And your great and mighty government—Oh sir, I hesitate, for I cannot tell the half! It does not protect us in our rights. It leaves us without the promised seed, without tools for cultivating the land, without implements [tools] for harvesting our crops, without breeding animals better than ours, without the food we still lack, after all we can do, without the many comforts we cannot produce, without the schools we so much need for our children. . . "

— Chief Washakie of the Shoshone tribe from a speech to Governor John W. Hoyt of Wyoming Territory, 1878

8 According to this document, what were **two** criticisms that Chief Washakie had against the white man and/ or the federal government? [2]

(1) _____

_____

Score ☐

(2) _____

_____

Score ☐

Part B
Essay

Directions:

Write a well-organized essay that includes an introduction, several paragraphs, and a conclusion. Use evidence from at least *five* documents in your essay. Support your response with relevant facts, examples, and details. Include additional outside information.

Historical Context:

During the 1800s, the federal government promoted westward expansion in a variety of ways. This expansion changed the shape and character of the country.

Task: Using information from the documents and your knowledge of United States history, write an essay in which you:

- Describe the actions taken by the federal government that led to westward expansion during the 1800s
- Discuss the impact of westward expansion on the United States.

Guidelines:

In your essay, be sure to

- Address all aspects of the task by accurately analyzing and interpreting at least *five* documents
- Incorporate information from the documents in the body of the essay
- Incorporate relevant outside information
- Support the theme with relevant facts, examples, and details
- Use a logical and clear plan of organization
- Introduce the theme by establishing a framework that is beyond a simple restatement of the *Task* or *Historical Context* and conclude with a summation of the theme

INDEX

ILLUSTRATION CREDITS

Chapter 2: Pg. 7: Jarrett Archives; Pg. 8: (t) Texas Department of Transportation, (b) National Archives; Pg. 9: Jarrett Archives.

Chapter 3: Pg. 10: (t) National Gallery of Art, (m) Library of Congress, (b) National Archives; Pg.11: Library of Congress; Pg. 18: Library of Congress; Pg. 27: U.S. Capitol Historical Society; Pg. 33: (l) Library of Congress, (r) Library of Congress, (b) Schomberg Center for Black Culture.

Chapter 4: Pg. 41: (t) Library of Congress, (m) U.S. Capitol Historical Society, (b) U.S. Supreme Court Collection; Pg. 42: U.S. Capitol Historical Society; Pg. 47: National Archives; Pg. 49: U.S. Supreme Court Collection.

Chapter 5: Pg. 71: (t, m, b) Library of Congress; Pg. 72: Library of Congress; Pg. 73: National Archives; Pg. 75: National Archives; Pg. 76: National Archives; Pg. 78: National Archives; Pg. 79: (t & b) Library of Congress; Pg. 84: Library of Congress; Pg. 89: National Archives; Pg. 90: Library of Congress; Pg. 91: Library of Congress; Pg. 92: (t) National Archives, (b) Associated Publishers, Inc.; Pg. 95: (t) National Portrait Gallery, (b) Library of Congress; Pg. 98: Library of Congress; Pg. 99: State Archives of Michigan.

Chapter 6: Pg. 106: (t & m) National Archives, (b) Ford Motor Company; Pg. 107: National Archives; Pg. 110: Library of Congress; Pg. 112: (t & b) Library of Congress; Pg. 113: Library of Congress; Pg. 117: Library of Congress; Pg. 118: (t) National Archives, (b) Louis Hines Collection of New York City; Pg. 119: Ford Motor Company; Pg. 121: National Archives; Pg. 123: Library of Congress; Pg. 124: Library of Congress; Pg. 125: National Portrait Gallery; Pg. 127: (t, l) Library of Congress, (t,r) National Archives, (b, r & l) Library of Congress.

Chapter 7: Pg. 137: (t, m,l & m,r) Library of Congress, (b) Theodore Roosevelt Association; Pg. 138: Library of Congress; Pg. 140: Library of Congress; Pg. 141: Library of Congress; Pg. 145: National Archives; Pg. 147: National Archives; Pg. 151: Library of Congress; Pg. 152: Library of Congress; Pg. 157: Library of Congress; Pg. 158: Bureau of Engraving and Printing; Pg. 161: (l) Library of Congress, (r) U.S. Postal Service; Pg. 165: Schomberg Center for Black Culture.

Chapter 8: Pg. 171 (t) Theodore Roosevelt Association, (m & b) Library of Congress; Pg. 172: National Archives; Pg. 174: Bureau of Engraving & Printing; Pg. 177: (l) Library of Congress, (r) National Archives; Pg. 180: (t & b) Library of Congress; Pg. 181: (t & b) Library of Congress; Pg. 183: National Archives; Pg. 187: War Department; Pg. 188: Library of Congress; Pg. 189: Library of Congress; Pg. 192: Library of Congress; Pg. 199: Library of Congress, Pg. 202: National Archives.

Chapter 9: Pg. 203: (t, & m,l) Library of Congress, (m,r) Franklin D. Roosevelt Presidential Library, (b) National Archives; Pg. 204: Library of Congress; Pg. 206: Ford Motor Company; Pg. 207: National Archives; Pg. 208: (t) Louis Hines Collection, City of New York, (b) National Archives; Pg. 209: National Archives; Pg. 214: National Archives; Pg. 217: (t) Institute for Texan Cultures, (b) Franklin D. Roosevelt Presidential Library; Pg. 218: Franklin D. Roosevelt Library; Pg. 221: National Archives, Pg. 224: (t) Franklin D. Roosevelt Presidential Library, (b) National Archives; Pg. 225: (l & r) National Archives; Pg. 226: National Archives; Pg. 227: National Archives; Pg. 229: Library of Congress; Pg. 230: United Nations; Pg. 232: Library of Congress; Pg. 238: Louis Hines Collection, City of New York; Pg. 244: Library of Congress.

Chapter 10: Pg. 247: (t,) National Archives, (m,r) Library of Congress, (b, l) NASA, (b,r) Library of Congress; Pg. 248: Library of Congress; Pg. 252: Library of Congress; Pg. 254: Library of Congress; Pg. 255: National Archives; Pg. 258: Nicholas Murray, photographer; Pg. 259: (t,b) Schomberg Collection of Black Culture; Pg. 260: U.S. Supreme Court Collection; Pg. 261: National Archives; Pg. 263: Michigan State Archives; Pg. 264: Schomberg Collection of Black Culture; Pg. 267: John F. Kennedy Presidential Library; Pg. 268: Lyndon Johnson Presidential Library; Pg. 275: Library of Congress; Pg. 276: (t) Lyndon Johnson Presidential Library, (b) Library of Congress; Pg. 279: Jarrett Archives; Pg. 281: U.S. Postal Service; Pg. 282: Library of Congress; Pg. 292: Library of Congress.

Chapter 11: Pg. 294: (t) The White House, (m) United Nations; (b) Stewart Milstein, photographer; Pg. 295: Library of Congress; Pg. 296: Bureau of Engraving & Printing; Pg. 299: (t) Bureau of Engraving and Printing, (b) Library of Congress; Pg. 305: (t & b) The White House; Pg. 306: The White House, Pg. 308: The White House; Pg. 309: Ford Motor Company; Pg. 310: United Nations; Pg. 313: United Nations; Pg. 317: (t) Pentagon, (m) NASA. (b) U.S. Supreme Court Collection.

Chapter 13: Pg. 345: Library of Congress; Pg. 346: Library of Congress; Pg. 351: Library of Congress.